LAST STAND AT KHE SANH

LAST STAND AT KHE SANH

The US Marines' Finest Hour in Vietnam

GREGG JONES

DA CAPO PRESS
A Member of the Perseus Books Group

Set in 11.25 point Adobe Caslon Pro by The Perseus Books Group

Library of Congress Cataloging-in-Publication Data
Jones, Gregg, 1959–
    Last stand at Khe Sanh : the U.S. Marines' finest hour in Vietnam /
Gregg Jones. — First Da Capo Press edition.
      pages cm
   Includes bibliographical references and index.
    ISBN 978-0-306-82139-4 (hardcover) — ISBN 978-0-306-82140-0
(e-book)
    1. Khe Sanh, Battle of, Vietnam, 1968. 2. United States. Marine
Corps—History—Vietnam War, 1961–1975. I. Title.
    DS557.8.K5J66 2014
    959.704'3450973—dc23

                                                    2013045206

First Da Capo Press edition 2014

Published by Da Capo Press
A Member of the Perseus Books Group
www.dacapopress.com

Da Capo Press books are available at special discounts for bulk purchases in the U.S. by corporations, institutions, and other organizations. For more information, please contact the Special Markets Department at the Perseus Books Group, 2300 Chestnut Street, Suite 200, Philadelphia, PA 19103, or call (800) 810-4145, ext. 5000, or e-mail special.markets@perseusbooks.com.

10 9 8 7 6 5 4 3 2 1

To those who fought at Khe Sanh, living and dead.

CONTENTS

MAPS

ACKNOWLEDGMENTS

One of the great joys at the end of a long journey such as this is having the opportunity to publicly thank the people who inspired, assisted, and sustained me along the way.

Dennis Mannion and Michael O'Hara introduced me to the brotherhood of Khe Sanh veterans, and over three years entrusted me with their personal stories, introduced me to comrades, read chapter drafts, and offered friendship, counsel, and encouragement. Tom Quigley was the third Khe Sanh veteran to enter my life, and he further enriched this book by sharing his story and persuading reticent comrades to do the same. I can only hope that Dennis, Michael, and Tom consider this book worthy of their generous efforts on my behalf.

Among the larger community of Khe Sanh veterans and family members is a core group of wonderful people who graced my life along the way: Ken Rodgers and his wife, Betty; Ray Stubbe; Paul Knight; Tom Esslinger; James Feasel; Michael Coonan; Bill Martin; William Smith; Edward Feldman; Dan Fisher; Ken Pipes; Ken Warner; Michael Archer; Earle Breeding; Larry McCartney; Dave Norton; Don Shanley; John Roberts; Charles (Toby) Rushforth; Greg and Constance Gibbons; Jim Kaylor; Michael Barry; Maurice Casey; Chuck Chamberlin; Bruce Geiger; Paul Longgrear; and the late James Finnegan. Mike Fishbaugh is an exceptionally kind soul and unsung hero of the Khe Sanh Veterans Association, and on several occasions he shared documents from the National Personnel Records Center in St. Louis, Missouri.

David Powell covered Khe Sanh as a young freelance news photographer in early 1968, and we became friends during many interviews, phone conversations, and emails. I am deeply appreciative that Dave has allowed me to share with readers of this book several of his extraordinary images from Khe Sanh Combat Base and Hill 881 South.

I would like to thank and acknowledge all those who shared their memories in interviews, conversations, emails, and written submissions: Arnold Alderete; Adam Alexander; Richard Allen; Charles Almy; David Althoff; Joe Amodeo; Michael Archer; James Armbrust; Michael Barry; Clifford Braisted; Earle G. Breeding; Calvin E. Bright; Jim Caccavo; Maurice Casey; Charles Chamberlin; George Chapman; John Cicala; Bruce Clarke; Michael Coonan; John Corbett; David Doehrman; Rich Donaghy; Richard Dworsky; George Einhorn; Nick Elardo; Tom Esslinger; James Feasel; Edward Feldman; Lynn Fifer; James O. Finnegan; William Gay; Bruce Geiger; Robert Genty; Lionel Guerra; Jack Haigwood; Joe Harrigan; Billy Joe Hill; Richard Hillmann; Norman Jasper; Keith Kapple; James Kaylor; Neil Kenny; Paul Knight; Lacey Lahren; Larry LeClaire; Guy Leonard; Paul Longgrear; Kevin Macaulay; Dennis Mannion; Bill Martin; Dave McCall; Larry McCartney; Howard McKinnis; Lewis S. Messer II; Ted Mickelson; Ray Milligan; David Norton; Michael O'Hara; Raul Orozco; Steve Orr; Robert Pagano; John Pessoni; Michael Pike; Kenneth W. Pipes; David Powell; Glenn Prentice; Tom Quigley; Henry (Mac) Radcliffe; John Rauch; Mike Reath; Jose Reyes; John Roberts; Ken Rodgers; George (Greg) Rudell; Charles Rushforth; John Sabol; Miguel Salinas; Lawrence Seavy-Cioffi; Don Shanley; James Sigman; William Smith; Ron Smith; David Steinberg; Ray Stubbe; Daniel Sullivan; Mark Swearengen; F. J. Taylor; Jim Thomas; Robert Tipton; Craig Tourte; Matthew Walsh; Ken Warner; Ed Welchel; Steve Wiese; and Michael Worth.

Foreign correspondent Seth Mydans was a friend and mentor during my formative years as a journalist in Southeast Asia, and we shared many adventures in Vietnam, Cambodia, Thailand, Indonesia, and the Philippines over three decades. Seth's careful and enthusiastic reading of the completed manuscript of *Last Stand at Khe Sanh* made this a better book, and reminded me of the joy and passion he always brought to his work as a foreign correspondent. The readers of the *New York Times* were fortunate to have had Seth as their window into the war-scarred nations of Indochina for three decades, and I was fortunate that our paths crossed.

Dr. Charles P. Neimeyer and the staff of the United States Marine

Corps History Division provided kind assistance during my research forays into the various collections housed in Quantico, Virginia. A special thanks to Quantico archivist Greg Cina for his efforts on my behalf on this book and the one before, spanning an epic century of Marine Corps history. At the National Archives and Records Administration in College Park, Maryland, archivist Nathaniel Patch provided valuable insights, as did NARA archivist Paul Brown. A chance meeting at the National Archives brought me into contact with Navy veteran Ralph J. Fries of Escondido, California, who imparted his knowledge on Navy corpsmen in Vietnam.

I would like to thank Dr. Steve Maxner and his staff at the Vietnam Center and Archive at Texas Tech University in Lubbock, Texas, for their magnificent contributions to the work of Vietnam War research over the past quarter-century. Their vast online collection enabled me to continuously backstop and expand on the work I did in my interviews and my research at the National Archives and Marine Corps archives, and I am grateful to have had access to this wonderful resource.

Marine Corps reference historian and blogger Beth Crumley shared her expertise on Marine helicopter operations in I Corps and other facets of Khe Sanh history, and she also introduced me to legendary CH-46 pilot David Althoff. Donna Elliott shared contacts acquired during her impassioned search for her missing brother, Staff Sergeant Jerry W. Elliott, who went missing outside Khe Sanh village on the afternoon of January 21, 1968. My thanks as well to geriatric psychiatrist Kevin Gray, for his encouragement and observations about the impact of post-traumatic stress disorder on Vietnam veterans.

I owe a great debt to Robert Pisor, Eric Hammel, John Prados, and Ray Stubbe, whose trail-blazing books on Khe Sanh served as faithful companions throughout this journey. Ray's attraction to Khe Sanh began in the summer of 1967, when he was assigned to the Marine combat base as a Navy chaplain. Between the time of his arrival and his departure in February 1968, Ray explored much of the Khe Sanh area and immersed himself in the local culture and history. He would eventually transform his diary into a 1,500-page manuscript, which became the core of *Valley of Decision*, co-authored with John Prados, as well as other books, articles, speeches, and sermons. Ray became my friend and ad hoc archivist during this project, imparting his encyclopedic knowledge in letters and frequent phone conversations. He not only illuminated various aspects of Khe Sanh history, but also shared obscure documents and interview transcripts as I wrestled with sundry research and writing challenges. I am grateful beyond words.

A number of Khe Sanh veterans have filled gaps in the historical record by writing compelling memoirs. Particularly useful to me were the Khe Sanh books written by Michael Archer, Bruce B. G. Clarke, John Corbett, William Craig, James Finnegan, Barry Fixler, and Ernest Spencer. Vietnam veteran Jack Wells generously sent me a copy of *Class of '67*, his moving tribute to his classmates from Marine Corps Basic School Class 6–67, including Khe Sanh veteran Terence (Terry) Roach.

I'm grateful to Tom Turner for aiding my research in the genealogy collection housed at the Haggard Library in Plano, Texas. My thanks as well to the following institutions where I found quiet corners to write: Southern Methodist University's Fondren Library Center in Dallas, Texas; Brookhaven College Library in Dallas, Texas; McLennan Community College Library in Waco, Texas; and Collin College Library in Frisco, Texas.

My friend Jon Eig was an early sounding board as I contemplated a book on Khe Sanh in the fall of 2010, and his advice was impeccable. Brent Howard at Penguin's New American Library imprint encouraged my ruminations about a Khe Sanh book and continued to urge me on, even after a rival publishing house acquired the project. Gary Jacobson offered valuable feedback on several early chapters. Doug Swanson took time from his own projects to offer encouragement, read parts of the manuscript, and commune about books, family life, and other topics. Writing sage George Getschow has been a friend and supporter, inspiring me and countless others through the Mayborn Literary Nonfiction Conference in Grapevine, Texas.

Friends and colleagues from various chapters in my life have sustained me with their words and deeds, and I offer special thanks to the following: Steve LeVine and his wife, Nurilda Nurlybayeva; Pat Benic; Alan Berlow; Chris Billing; Jay Branegan; William Branigin; John Carroll; Rick Hornik; David Lamb; Tom Lansner; John Schidlovsky; and Mike Theiler. Many thanks as well to my agent, Jim Donovan, for his work in finding a good home for this book, and for his friendship and counsel in the years since.

The home that Jim found was Da Capo Press, and I am grateful to the professionals at Da Capo and Perseus Books who have shepherded *Last Stand at Khe Sanh* from proposal to publication. My editor, Robert Pigeon, has been a wonderful pillar of support throughout. My heartfelt thanks as well to project editor Cisca Schreefel, copyeditor Michele Wynn, designer Brent Wilcox, and publicist Kate Burke.

Finally, and most important of all, I wish to thank and acknowledge the three people at the center of my universe: my wife of nearly three decades, Ali Nucum Jones; our teenage son, Chris; and my brother, Steve. Without your love and support, none of this would be possible.

INTRODUCTION

During the first months of 1968, Americans were transfixed by the confrontation between US and North Vietnamese Army (NVA) forces at a remote Marine combat base in South Vietnam called Khe Sanh. President Lyndon Johnson feared a disastrous defeat, like the one that had driven the French from Vietnam in 1954. "I don't want any damn Dien Bien Phu," he groused, recalling the French debacle. General William Westmoreland, the supreme American commander in Vietnam, assured his commander in chief: Khe Sanh will not become another Dien Bien Phu. Privately, the general harbored doubts. He ordered his staff to study how the French had lost at Dien Bien Phu, and whether he might now be forced to use tactical nuclear weapons to stave off a crushing defeat.

Over time, Khe Sanh would become perhaps the most emblematic confrontation of the Vietnam War—the centerpiece of Michael Herr's classic book, *Dispatches*, a focal point of Bruce Springsteen's haunting post-Vietnam anthem, "Born in the USA," and the subject of countless other books, articles, paintings, songs, and exhibits.

For war critics and news correspondents, Khe Sanh was a metaphor for the Vietnam War's strategic folly and tactical deceptions: 6,000 US Marines forced to defend an isolated base that General Westmoreland had deemed indispensable, only to abandon it after hundreds of Americans were sacrificed in its defense.

So what really happened at Khe Sanh? What was it like for the young Americans who were there? How has Khe Sanh shaped and scarred their lives? How accurate is the history that has been written about this epic confrontation of the Vietnam War? These were the questions that guided me as I set out on this journey.

• • •

I celebrated my ninth birthday in April 1968, and though I don't have any specific memories of reading about the battle of Khe Sanh or the Tet Offensive, I was certainly aware of the rising death toll in Vietnam and the antiwar protests that were spreading across America. That August, after the local summer baseball league games had ended, I squeezed into the backseat of our 1964 Chevy Impala with my older brother and sister and we set off to the east on a family vacation. Our ultimate destination was Washington, DC, but I persuaded my parents to stop at several Civil War battlefields in our path, and so we hopscotched from Appomattox Court House in southern Virginia, to Richmond (with a side trip to Colonial Williamsburg), and then on to Fredericksburg before finally reaching the nation's capital.

Each day, our journey into America's past was jolted back to the present by newscasts and headlines about the widening war in Vietnam. In Washington, we visited the monuments and toured the White House, where President Johnson was in his final months of office, having announced in late March, amid the mounting antiwar protests, that he wouldn't run for reelection.

We made our way to Arlington National Cemetery and climbed the hallowed slopes, stopping at President John F. Kennedy's grave site before reaching the breathtaking vantage point of the Custis-Lee Mansion.

We couldn't help but notice all the fresh graves around us. And then, as my father captured the scene with his Brownie eight-millimeter camera, we watched in solemn silence as a flag-draped coffin passed on a horse-drawn caisson and, some minutes later, listened reverently as the mournful sound of "Taps" echoed over the hills.

• • •

Back home in Missouri, my family followed events in Vietnam on the *CBS Evening News* and in our local newspaper. Every so often, the paper wrote about some hometown boy who had died in America's service in Indochina. Eventually, fourteen young men from my hometown of about 15,000 people would die in Vietnam.

I read everything I could about the Vietnam War as the years passed. As a twenty-five-year-old journalist in 1984, just nine years after the war ended, I was drawn to Southeast Asia. Eventually, I would spend ten years there, spread over three decades.

At every opportunity, I visited Vietnam—Saigon, Hanoi, Hue, Quang Tri City, Bien Hoa, Cu Chi, Tay Ninh, My Lai, Street Without Joy, all the places I'd read about in my personal quest to understand the war that had claimed the lives of 58,000 Americans. I traveled along much of Route 1 as it followed the coast of the former South Vietnam, and, with Vietnam veteran Chuck Searcy, I ventured up Route 9, to the Khe Sanh area, just south of the old demilitarized zone (DMZ) that had divided Vietnam into the Communist north and American-supported south from 1954 until 1975. In my travels, I interviewed former North Vietnamese Army soldiers, Viet Cong guerrillas, and veterans of the Army of the Republic of South Vietnam (ARVN). I spoke with refugees who had fled Vietnam and returned, and those who had tried to escape Communist rule but never made it out. I visited a vast ARVN cemetery north of Saigon that the war's victors had allowed to fall into shameful disrepair, and I spoke with villagers along the northern fringe of the former DMZ who continued to die and suffer hideous injuries from unexploded ordnance left behind by the battle of Khe Sanh and the American bombing campaign known as Rolling Thunder.

Ultimately, I wanted to write something about the Vietnam War that would rise above the rancorous politics that had poisoned America during the conflict and in the decades since. I wanted to write a book that would capture the experience of ordinary young Americans thrown into these extraordinary events in Vietnam, a tragic sideshow of the Cold War between the United States and the Soviet Union. I decided to tell the story of the legendary confrontation at Khe Sanh in early 1968—the human story of the young Americans who were thrust into this pivotal moment in the Vietnam War.

• • •

Americans began dying at Khe Sanh in 1964, and they would continue dying there long after the siege was declared broken in April 1968. The Hill Fights at Khe Sanh in the spring of 1967 cost the lives of more than 150 US Marines and introduced Americans to the infamous terrain features known as 881 North, 881 South, and 861. To fully develop the storytelling, I limited my scope in this book, focusing on the four-month period from January through April 1968. The men who served at Khe Sanh before and after the siege months have my deepest respect, and my apologies for not being able to tell their stories.

I also focused largely on the American experience at Khe Sanh. It became clear to me early on that there were so many interesting characters and dramatic events involving US forces during these four months at Khe Sanh that it would be impossible to write a book of reasonable length and do justice to the stories of the North Vietnamese and South Vietnamese soldiers who fought at Khe Sanh. I look forward to reading about their experiences at Khe Sanh in future books.

For so long, it was unfashionable to speak favorably about the service of Americans in Vietnam or to acknowledge their sacrifices. Our recent wars in Iraq and Afghanistan have made it clear that it is possible to debate the wisdom of a war, or even actively oppose it, without denigrating the men and women who answer the nation's call. For those who served at Khe Sanh, and elsewhere in Vietnam, this courtesy is long overdue.

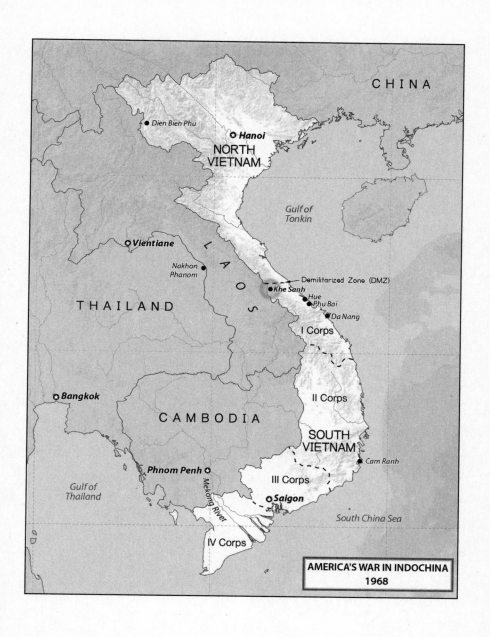

CHINA

Dien Bien Phu ●

● **Hanoi**

**NORTH
VIETNAM**

*Gulf of
Tonkin*

L A O S

○ Vientiane

*Nakhon
Phanom*

THAILAND

Demilitarized Zone (DMZ)
●Khe Sanh
● Hue
●Phu Bai
● Da Nang

I Corps

II Corps

○ Bangkok

C A M B O D I A

**SOUTH
VIETNAM**

● Cam Ranh

Mekong River

Phnom Penh ○

*Gulf of
Thailand*

III Corps

○ Saigon

South China Sea

IV Corps

**AMERICA'S WAR IN INDOCHINA
1968**

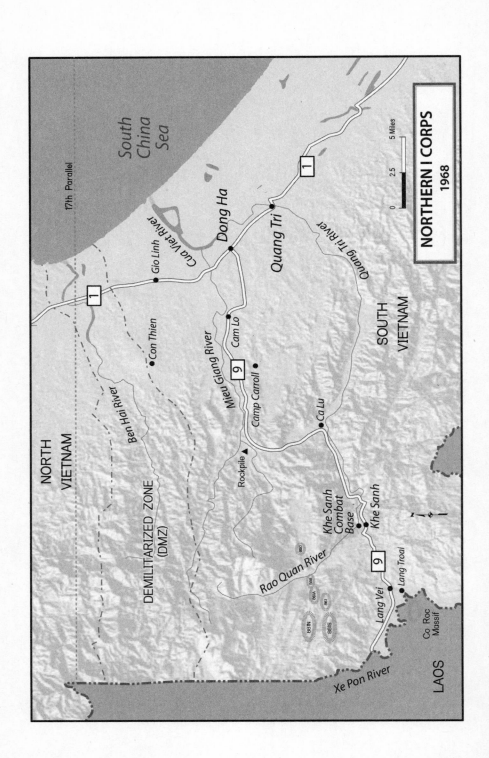

NORTHERN I CORPS
1968

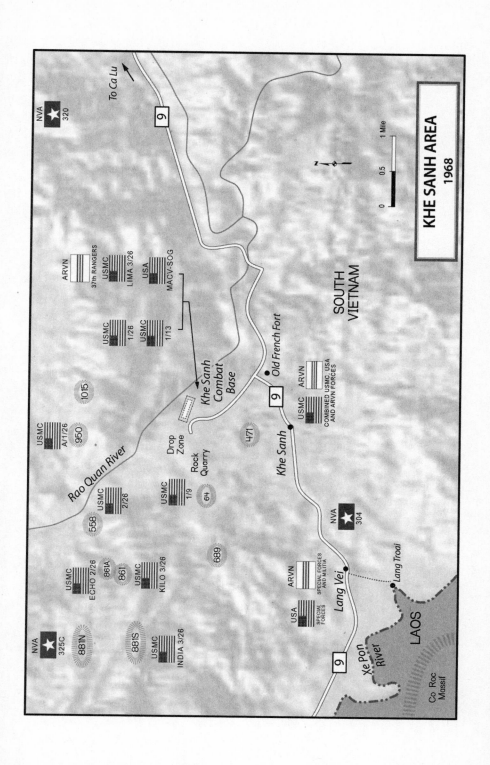

KHE SANH AREA
1968

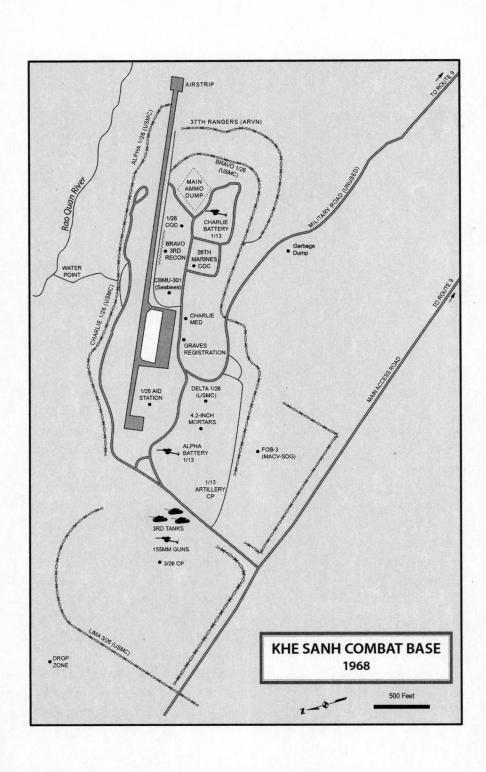

AIRSTRIP

37TH RANGERS (ARVN)

ALPHA 1/26 (USMC)

BRAVO 1/26 (USMC)

Rao Quan River

MAIN AMMO DUMP

1/26 COC

CHARLIE BATTERY 1/13

BRAVO 3RD RECON

26TH MARINES COC

Garbage Dump

WATER POINT

CHARLIE 1/26 (USMC)

CBMU-301 (Seabees)

CHARLIE MED

GRAVES REGISTRATION

1/26 AID STATION

DELTA 1/26 (USMC)

4.2-INCH MORTARS

ALPHA BATTERY 1/13

FOB-3 (MACV-SOG)

1/13 ARTILLERY CP

3RD TANKS

155MM GUNS

3/26 CP

LIMA 3/26 (USMC)

DROP ZONE

MILITARY ROAD (UNUSED)

TO ROUTE 9

TO ROUTE 9

MAIN ACCESS ROAD

KHE SANH COMBAT BASE
1968

500 Feet

January 17, 1968

The Marines splashed across the shallow stream in single file, wide eyes scanning the steamy jungle for soldiers of the North Vietnamese Army. They were only nine in number, American teenagers and young men in their early twenties, formed into a squad assigned to India Company of the 3rd Battalion, 26th Marine Regiment.

Roaming up and down the column was the smoothly athletic squad leader, Corporal Ken Warner, nineteen years old, an avid surfer, baseball player, and Dodgers fan from Long Beach, California. A few hours earlier, he had led his men down from the Marine garrison atop the hill that rose steeply at their backs. The terrain feature was designated 881 South on Marine topographic maps, and it was the first line of defense for Khe Sanh Combat Base, a remote outpost from which US Marines and Special Forces sparred with enemy troops as they funneled into South Vietnam from the nearby Ho Chi Minh Trail in Laos.

The Americans had been trying for weeks to get a fix on two North Vietnamese Army divisions that had slipped into the area, but they had found only tantalizing hints of the nearly 20,000 enemy soldiers. Warner's patrol was part of the daily effort to find the elusive NVA, or at least make sure they didn't sneak up on the Marines atop 881 South or at the combat base at Khe Sanh, five miles to the southeast.

There were 540,000 American military personnel in Vietnam in January 1968, and Ken Warner's journey from the beaches of Southern

California to the jungles of South Vietnam could have been the story of just about any of them. He was the son of a housewife and a World War II Navy veteran who worked on the docks of Los Angeles harbor as a long-shoreman, and life was good. At Robert A. Millikan High School in Long Beach, Ken had played center field on the baseball team and spent most weekends and holidays surfing with his buddies off Baja California. After studying Indochina in a high school history class, he had concluded that the American war was a noble crusade to save the people of South Vietnam from godless communism. He joined the Marines shortly after graduation, and after six months of training as a rifleman, flew to Vietnam with a planeload of replacement Marines.

In April 1967, within a month of his arrival, Warner saw his first action. During a firefight, a corpsman had asked him to look after a wounded Marine from another platoon while he tended to other casualties. Warner knelt over the Marine and tried to stanch the bleeding from a gut wound, but there wasn't much that could be done, so he ended up holding the guy in his lap, telling him over and over, "You're going to be okay." The Marine kept looking into Warner's blue eyes, then glancing away, never uttering a word, and then he died. Unsure of the proper protocol, Warner laid the dead Marine in the tall grass and crawled toward the gunfire.

Like most low-level Marines, Warner wasn't privy to the strategic deliberations underway at the headquarters of America's supreme commander in Vietnam, General William Westmoreland, or the captured intelligence that pointed to an escalating war. Grunts like Warner knew nothing of the June meeting of North Vietnam's ruling Lao Dong Party politburo and its conclusion that the time had come to deliver "a decisive blow" to "force the U.S. to accept military defeat" in Vietnam.[1] All Warner and his buddies knew was that the fighting was getting heavier, and life in the northern border provinces—I Corps, it was called—was getting more dangerous.

Unknown to Warner and his comrades, the ambitious North Vietnamese "1967–68 Winter-Spring Campaign" was underway.

For one terrible week in September, Warner and other Marines had hunkered down in their trenches and fighting holes at the small Marine combat base at Con Thien while the North Vietnamese pounded them.

When the artillery stopped, the Marines had fought off human-wave ground attacks that were broken only after some of the NVA troops had reached the American trench line. Warner lost his squad leader in the fighting, a veteran sergeant who had helped him survive his early months in Vietnam. The laid-back Southern California teenager grew a little bit older, a little wiser, a little harder.

India Company had suffered heavy losses at Con Thien, so the outfit was pulled out of combat for a few weeks to replenish its ranks with newly arrived replacements—FNGs ("fucking new guys") in the Marine patois that Warner had learned from the old-timers. Warner was given command of a squad, and in early December, India was dispatched to the Marine combat base at Khe Sanh, in the far northwestern corner of South Vietnam. On December 26, Warner and his comrades took over the Marine outpost on 881 South, where they could look out into Laos, seven miles to the west, and take up the search for the North Vietnamese troops pouring into the area.

Now, as his men pushed through the tall grass that clotted the stream at the base of 881 South, Warner dropped to the back of the column to make sure no one slipped up behind them.

His point man had broken through the wall of vegetation into a small clearing, which the other Marines were now approaching. Warner was the last to step from the water onto dry ground, and as he did, he heard something behind him.

Splash, splash, splash. And then silence.

Somebody was following them.

Warner sounded a wordless warning to his squad. Hand signals flashed, and the Marines began circling around the edge of the clearing. Within a few steps, they found warm cooking fires. They had walked into an NVA campsite.

The jungle around them was now unnaturally silent. The Marines exchanged worried glances.

Warner got his company commander, Captain William Dabney, on the radio. The squad leader whispered a situation report, even as he braced for the ear-splitting sound of gunfire and explosions.

"I'm going to send guys down the hill," Dabney said in a low voice. "Can you start back up?"[2]

Everyone looked at Warner, wondering how they were going to get out of this mess alive. The Californian pointed to the Marine at the head of his squad, motioning for him to move back across the stream and up the slope of 881 South.

Warner and his men moved as stealthily as they could through the elephant grass and water, but it was too late for that. Warner felt eyes watching them as they moved. He could almost see the NVA around him in the bush, fingers on triggers, poised to fire.

The Marines reached dry ground, and still the North Vietnamese had not attacked. The Americans started up the slope, and as each step carried them farther away from danger, relief swept the column.[3] Why had the enemy soldiers let them live? Warner and his men were baffled, but giddy at their escape.

Ken Warner and his men had been lucky. The NVA soldiers were almost ready to strike the Americans at Khe Sanh, but not quite, and their ambitious plan envisioned far greater victories than the slaughter of nine Marines on patrol.[4]

PART I

CHAPTER 1

Death in the Tall Grass

In the minutes before the operation began, the Marines made small talk. They spoke of food and home, girlfriends and wives, and the time left in their thirteen-month combat tours with the Marines in Vietnam.

The sun broke above the misty green peaks of South Vietnam's most distant corner, revealing a scene of deceptive tranquillity. A thick blanket of fog engulfed all but the highest hill masses, and in the soft early light they appeared like islands awash in cottony white waves. Somewhere beneath that spectral sea, less than a mile north of the Marines as they geared up on Hill 881 South, soldiers of the North Vietnamese Army's 325C Division waited in bunkers and fighting holes hidden in the tall grass.

It was Saturday morning, January 20, 1968.

Hill 881 South (designated by its height in meters) was the farthest outpost of the Marine combat base at Khe Sanh, nearly four miles to the southeast.[1] The hilltop stronghold stood like a sentinel overlooking the border with Laos, and the vital supply lines that the North Vietnamese used to funnel men and materiel into South Vietnam. Over the past week, the Marines of India Company, 3rd Battalion, 26th Marine Regiment, had made contact with the enemy nearly every time they left the hill and started up the slope to their north. Intelligence reports placed two NVA divisions around Khe Sanh, roughly 20,000 men—more than three times the total number of Marines around Khe Sanh.

India's commander, Captain William Dabney, wanted to see what was out there, and he was taking no chances. He ordered his entire company, about 175 men, to gear up. Their destination: a multi-fingered ridgeline a mile to the north—Hill 881 North on Marine topographic maps.

The pre-mission banter by short-timers made Navy corpsman Mike Ray homesick. He had been in Vietnam barely sixty days, which meant he wouldn't get home for another eleven months—unless he was killed or wounded. He was twenty years old, an Iowa farm boy assigned to India's 3rd Platoon, and he missed his wife and young son. He finished a breakfast of canned C-rations and headed to his bunker to check his aid bag one final time. He wanted to make sure he had enough battle dressings, tourniquets, and morphine, in case they ran into trouble. When his bag was ready, Ray scribbled a farewell note to his family, folded the paper, and slipped it into his personal gear.[2]

The platoons formed around 8:00 a.m., and a half hour later, on Bill Dabney's command, the men of India Company made their way through the perimeter wire and headed down the steep north face of 881 South, in search of the North Vietnamese Army.

• • •

For an ambitious officer like Captain William Howard Dabney, a thirty-three-year-old Virginian hungry for combat and glory, Khe Sanh Combat Base had seemed like the perfect posting. It was only fifteen miles south of the demilitarized zone that divided Vietnam into Communist and non-Communist nations, and seven miles from Laos, where the Ho Chi Minh Trail was bustling with North Vietnamese troops headed south to fight the Americans. The enemy was close, and the colonels and generals who might cramp Dabney's aggressive style weren't.

In Marine parlance, Dabney was a "mustang," a former enlisted man who had clawed his way up to the officer corps. He had joined the Marines in 1953, after flunking out of Yale University, and made sergeant before completing his enlistment. He entered Virginia Military Institute, graduated with a degree in English in the spring of 1960, and a few weeks later reentered the Marines as a second lieutenant.

Even in the macho world of the United States Marine Corps, Dabney turned heads. He was six feet four inches, handsome, square-jawed. He was a charming storyteller, with a born leader's grace and confidence. He had burnished his mystique by marrying Virginia Puller, the daughter of America's most famous Marine, retired general Lewis "Chesty" Puller.

When he arrived in Vietnam in September 1967, Dabney was a senior captain, but still waiting to command a Marine rifle company before moving up to major. He got his company within days of arriving in Vietnam but promptly lost it after clashing with his battalion commanding officer (CO).[3] Dabney got a second crack at it before the month was out and took the reins of India Company, 3rd Battalion, 26th Marines.

After several weeks of operations, Dabney and his men, in mid-December, flew to Khe Sanh, where he led the company on a weeklong 3/26 battalion sweep toward the border with Laos and back. The Marines made no contact with the North Vietnamese, but Dabney sensed the presence of the enemy all around. The day after Christmas, he led his men out to the battle-scarred stronghold of 881 South.

The hill that Dabney and his men now called home—along with two neighboring hill masses, 881 North and 861—had been the scene of a fierce two-week battle the previous spring in which 155 Marines had perished and another 425 had been wounded, engagements that became known as the Hill Fights of Khe Sanh. The Marines had attacked the hills with World War II–style frontal assaults, but they were thrown back by enemy troops firing from bunkers and camouflaged holes. American artillery and air strikes pounded the enemy positions, and the Marines awoke one morning to find that the North Vietnamese had slipped away.[4]

Dabney's Marines took over the former enemy redoubt on 881 South and commenced daily patrols in search of enemy troops. They made no contact for the first three weeks, but the signs of a major enemy presence had become unmistakable over the past week.

The previous day, a Marine recon patrol had made heavy contact with the NVA on 881 North and needed help breaking off the fight and getting its wounded out. Dabney's 3rd Platoon had rushed to the scene of the firefight and gotten their comrades to safety, but the recon boys had lost a radio and code sheets, a worrisome turn of events for the Americans.

Dabney's 1st Platoon had gone back in search of the lost radio and code sheets the previous day, January 19, with Corporal Ken Warner's squad in the lead. Warner was pushing his men forward through tall ele-phant grass about 1:30 p.m. when he and the Marine immediately to his front, Gary Joliet, heard the sound of rustling grass to their right. Joliet turned to his left and flashed Warner a quizzical look, as if to say: *What was that?* Before Warner could react, they heard more movement in the grass. Joliet had started to turn back toward the unseen danger when the grass exploded with automatic-weapons fire from the improvised North Vietnamese ambush.

Joliet dropped to the ground with three bullets in his back, and the Marine behind Warner fell wounded, but the big Southern Californian somehow survived the opening barrage without a scratch. After a hard ninety-minute fight, the Marines were able to break contact and with-draw under the cover of air strikes and artillery fire. It was something of a miracle that only one Marine was killed: Warner's M-60 machine gunner, Private First Class Leonard Lee Newton, a nineteen-year-old from Stockton, California, had waged a courageous duel with an NVA machine gunner on the slope above him until he fell dead with a bullet through the eye.

Now, Captain Dabney led his men off his hill and headed north, to-ward the rugged slopes stained with the fresh blood of US Marines.[5]

• • •

It was 1,500 feet from the American perimeter on 881 South to the base of the hill, and on the morning of January 20, the 30° slope was so slippery from fog and winter rains that the Marines had to grab at brush and small trees to avoid tumbling to the bottom. Grunts and curses sounded along the line, along with the clank of equipment, as men lost their footing.

India Company's slow and noisy progress worried Private Michael Pike, an eighteen-year-old Marine from Southern California. He had ar-rived in Vietnam only eight days earlier, and this was his first patrol.[6] He had stuffed the pockets of his jungle utilities with cans of C-rations, filled three or four canteens of water, and draped himself with bandoliers of M-16 magazines and a few hand grenades. As the new guy, Pike got the honor of carrying two white phosphorus rounds for the platoon's 3.5-inch rocket launcher. He was handed a hard-plastic backpack with the two rounds inside and told: strap it on.[7]

As they made their way down the hill, the Marines entered the fog cover that had appeared as a cottony sea from far above. They finally reached the bottom, then waded into a rushing stream that wound around the hill. Second Platoon rifleman Robert Tipton, a nineteen-year-old from Florida, knelt to fill his canteen before rejoining the column as it splashed ahead through soggy ground. The Marines moved cautiously through the thick fog.[8]

•   •   •

After crossing the stream, India Company split into two columns and began to move up parallel fingers of the hill, about 500 yards apart, climbing toward the crest of 881 North. Leading the left column was India's 1st Platoon, commanded by Second Lieutenant Harry F. "Rick" Fromme Jr., a twenty-four-year-old from Jacksonville, Florida; he was followed by Bill Dabney and his small command group and India's 2nd Platoon, led by Second Lieutenant Michael H. Thomas, a twenty-five-year-old from Pawnee, Oklahoma.[9] On the right, angling toward an almost identical grass-cloaked finger, was India's 1st Platoon, led by Second Lieutenant Thomas D. Brindley of St. Paul, Minnesota, a twenty-four-year-old who had played college hockey in Colorado before quitting to enlist in the Marines.

The 1st Platoon moved hard uphill through the thick elephant grass. At the head of the column was Brindley's veteran point man, Private First Class James Collins. A muscular, bull-necked farm boy from the cornfields of central Illinois, Collins was only five days shy of his twenty-third birthday. He was at the end of his thirteen months in Vietnam and was packed and ready to leave 881 South. As a short-timer, Collins could have skipped the patrol. But when his buddies shoved off, there he was, leading the column.

At the rear of Brindley's column were seven reconnaissance Marines. Code-named Team Barkwood, they had been dispatched from Khe Sanh late the previous afternoon, with orders to slip away from the column and recover the radio and code sheets left at the scene of the ambush two days earlier. The team was led by Lance Corporal Charles William Bryan, a high school football player and Boy Scout back home in McKinney, Texas. After basic training, Bryan had volunteered to become a reconnaissance Marine, trained to prowl the jungles in small teams of a dozen men or less in search of enemy troops. He had married his high school sweetheart before heading to Vietnam at the end of September 1967. Assigned to Bravo Company, 3rd Reconnaissance Battalion, Bryan joined the outfit at Khe Sanh. He was popular with his recon buddies because he was a nice guy, he did his job well, and he shared the chocolate-chip cookies his young wife, Deidra, regularly sent.[10] And now, he and his team were impatiently plodding up the hillside at the rear of Tom Brindley's platoon.

Progress was agonizingly slow as the Marines carefully measured each step in the thick fog. Finally, Brindley and his men emerged into sunlight. Near the rear of the column, Team Barkwood's radioman, Robert "PJ" Pagano, a nineteen-year-old from White Plains, New York, gazed up ahead and suppressed a laugh. Only the helmets of the 3rd Platoon grunts were visible above the tall grass, and they looked like turtles bobbing along in a sea of green.

Pagano's reverie was shattered by a familiar sound.

Pop-pop-pop-pop. Pop-pop-pop-pop.

The helmets disappeared.

• • •

By the time Jim Collins spotted the well-camouflaged enemy fighting holes, it was too late. The Vietnamese fired first, and the point man from Illinois fell in the opening volley.[11]

Lieutenant Brindley advanced with his 2nd Squad and directed fire toward the suspected NVA positions that had pinned down his lead elements. The roar of machine guns mixed with the crack of assault rifles and the *whoosh-boom* of Communist rocket-propelled grenades. Bullets snapped and whined through the elephant grass. Enemy soldiers were on both sides of the Americans, firing their weapons and tossing grenades.

"Doc, up!"

Corpsman Mike Ray heard the cry above the noise and felt sick. He was paralyzed by fear, and then his training kicked in. He crawled forward, still terrified, but focused on finding and treating fallen Marines. The first man he found was his squad leader, a sergeant from the hills of Kentucky who loved to sing and strum his guitar on quiet nights. His chin had been ripped from his face. Ray handed the sergeant a large battle dressing to stanch the flow of blood, telling him to get back down the hill.[12]

Ray moved ahead and found a young Marine sprawled in the grass. A piece of grenade shrapnel had struck the man below his left eye and ripped through the roof of his mouth, exiting through his chin. Ray dressed the wounds as best he could and pointed the Marine down the trail.

The corpsman was still snaking his way up the trail when the order to fall back swept through the grass. Panicked Marines popped up and scuttled past in a low crouch, dropping and kicking rifle magazines and grenades as they ran. Ray joined the rush.[13] The spooked Marines ran until they reached a small plateau, a safe distance from the murderous enemy fire.

Ray was still catching his breath from the frantic retreat when a gravely injured Marine was laid at his feet. It was the fallen point man. Ray and another corpsman tried cardiopulmonary resuscitation (CPR), but there was no response. Jim Collins would be making the trip back to Illinois in a military-issue coffin.[14]

• • •

Bill Dabney had watched through field glasses as the fight began, and he quickly saw that Brindley's platoon was pinned down by North Vietnamese fire from a knoll about six hundred feet up the hill. Dabney radioed his young lieutenant: break contact and pull back with your wounded. He also ordered his executive officer, First Lieutenant Richard Foley Jr., attached to Brindley's platoon, to set up an emergency landing zone (LZ) for medevac choppers.

Within minutes, the LZ was secured, and a helicopter settled into the tiny clearing. Several seriously wounded Marines were carried aboard, along with the body of Jim Collins. As the medevac bird thundered off to the east, Lieutenant Foley and his artillery forward observer (FO) radioed coordinates that were quickly forwarded to waiting artillery batteries at Khe Sanh and mortar teams back on 881 South. The North Vietnamese positions above them erupted with explosions.[15]

• • •

On Bill Dabney's command, two squads of Lieutenant Rick Fromme's 1st Platoon on the western finger were maneuvering into position to enfilade the North Vietnamese that had pinned down Brindley's platoon. Fromme's men were thirty yards from the top of a knoll, charging ahead in a skirmish line, when the grass around them exploded with the roar of automatic weapons and rocket-propelled grenades (RPGs). Crisscrossing rounds from NVA .51-caliber machine guns and AK-47 rifles ripped into the legs and torsos of the charging Marines, dropping twenty young Americans in seconds.

Among those falling in the first volley was squad leader Ken Warner. Hot metal from an exploding RPG round had sliced his face and hip and gouged a gaping hole in his right shoulder. Bleeding heavily, Warner couldn't pinpoint the enemy soldiers hidden in the tall grass. He couldn't even see the Marines who had fallen around him, but he could hear their screams and cries of pain.[16]

Fromme's platoon was now completely focused on escaping the enemy killing zone. Murderous NVA machine-gun fire raked the Americans from the left flank. Fromme and several of his men laid down covering fire so corpsmen and other Marines could get their wounded down the hill.

Nearby, the men of Corporal Michael Elrod's 3rd Squad ran for their lives, one at a time, while comrades fired in the direction of the concealed North Vietnamese. Elrod was the only one left when three NVA soldiers charged him. He fired a final round, then sprinted after his men. A bullet smashed into Elrod's heel and ankle, and he collapsed to the ground. He started crawling and didn't stop until he reached the perimeter of Dabney's reserve force down the hill.[17]

For wounded squad leader Ken Warner, there was no easy way out. He ordered two men to help ambulatory casualties crawl away from the fire while he took responsibility for his most seriously wounded Marine, rifleman Bob Coniff, bleeding heavily from both legs. Grabbing Coniff under his armpits, Warner hugged the ground and began dragging the Marine through the tall grass. North Vietnamese machine-gun fire scythed the slope around them, drawn by the swaying grass as Warner forced his way through the thick vegetation.[18]

Their progress was agonizingly slow, measured in inches, and Warner was growing weak from blood loss and exhaustion. He could no longer hear any Marines nearby. He spotted a tree and dragged himself and his comrade beneath it and leaned against the trunk. Cradling Coniff in his lap, Warner said good-bye to his parents and waited to die. As he accepted his fate, he felt a strange calmness come over him, and his brain flashed a simple command: *Just keep going.*[19]

The wounded Marine resumed the torturous retreat through the heavy grass, pulling his even more seriously injured comrade along with him. After an agonizing forty-five minutes, the sound of gunfire and explosions had faded.[20] Warner willed himself on—*just a little more, just a little more.* Finally, a beautiful sight came into view: the cordon formed by the Marines of Mike Thomas's 2nd Platoon.

Ken Warner was among the last Marines from the left column to reach safety. As a corpsman began treating Bob Coniff, Warner did a quick head count. He and his men were a bloody mess, but the entire squad had made it back down the slope.[21] There was more to the miracle: in Fromme's assault, twenty-one Marines had been wounded, some critically, but they would all make it off the hill alive.

●   ●   ●

Mike Thomas had been moving his 2nd Platoon Marines through a small clearing down the slope when the left column came under attack. Private Michael Pike had just walked into the opening when an NVA machine gun fired from about 300 yards off to the left. Pike hit the deck as machine-gun rounds kicked dirt into his face.[22] A sergeant screamed at Pike. "Marine, get your ass up!" Pike scrambled for cover at the edge of the clearing.

In seconds, the platoon's 3.5-inch rocketman screwed together the two halves of his weapon, and another Marine grabbed one of the white phosphorus rounds from Pike's plastic backpack and shoved it in the launcher tube. The rocketman took aim, and a round roared westward and exploded in the distance. As white smoke boiled from the point of impact, a North Vietnamese soldier staggered from a camouflaged bunker. A Marine sniper stepped up and laid his rifle across the rocketman's shoulder. Peering through his scope, he dropped the enemy fighter with one shot.[23]

Within a few minutes, blood-soaked Marines from Fromme's platoon had clawed their way through the elephant grass and into the 2nd Platoon perimeter. A corpsman began pulling wounded men into a bomb crater. He dressed their wounds and tried to calm them.

A Marine CH-46 helicopter—*Frosty Gold* of Marine Medium Helicopter Squadron 262 (HMM-262)—whomped in from the east, banked and turned toward a makeshift LZ alongside the casualty collection point. Under heavy enemy fire, pilot Bob Ropelewski, a twenty-five-year-old captain from Erie, Pennsylvania, slowly backed into the hill. As the ramp of his Sea Knight touched the steep slope, rifleman James Schemelia put his arm around a wounded Marine and walked him inside the helicopter. They were moving toward the front when NVA machine-gun rounds ripped through the fuselage and severed the fuel line. The helicopter burst into flames.[24]

Fighting to control the crippled aircraft, Ropelewski careened toward the streambed below. Schemelia grabbed the wounded Marine he had just helped aboard, pushed him out the back, and jumped after him.[25] Ropelewski, his co-pilot, crew chief, and gunner all managed to bail out in the seconds before the helicopter crashed into the draw about fifty yards below.[26]

Within minutes, Fromme's Marines found Ropelewski and his co-pilot, Steve Stegich. They were waiting with .45 pistols drawn, poised to shoot it out if the North Vietnamese got there first. The Marines also recovered the crew chief and door gunner, injured but alive. James Schemelia had survived serious injury, and he dragged himself out of the heavy brush, found his wounded comrade, and helped him back to the bomb crater to await another medevac aircraft.[27]

● ● ●

About 2:00 p.m., as Bill Dabney's men fought for their lives, an extraordinary drama was unfolding at Khe Sanh Combat Base. A North Vietnamese lieutenant armed with an AK-47 rifle stepped from the jungle beyond the eastern perimeter, dropped his weapon, and surrendered.[28]

Marines hustled the uniformed Vietnamese back inside the base for interrogation, where he quickly confirmed American intelligence reports that two NVA divisions were drawn up around Khe Sanh. The prisoner was fed up with army life, and offered an even more chilling revelation: North Vietnamese troops were poised to strike the American outpost on Hill 861 that night. Once that objective had been seized, he said, they would move against Khe Sanh Combat Base.[29]

• • •

As friendly artillery pounded the North Vietnamese positions on 881 North, Tom Brindley's shaken Marines—the right hand of Dabney's thrust—had regrouped down the slope from the scene of their encounter. They had lost ten men, nine of them wounded and one dead. But Bill Dabney had no intention of walking away from this fight. When the friendly artillery fire tapered off, the order was passed: prepare to take the enemy strongpoint.[30]

The men of 3rd Platoon formed a skirmish line. Bill Bryan and his recon team anchored Brindley's right flank.

"Fix bayonets," Brindley ordered.

Almost as one, the heads of the recon Marines snapped toward the platoon commander. *Fix what?* PJ Pagano thought to himself.[31] Most recon Marines didn't even carry bayonets.

Brindley walked up and down the line, encouraging each man with a knock on the back.[32] On Brindley's shouted command, the Marines started up the hill.

Within seconds, enemy fire ripped through the grass and over the heads of the Americans. The Marines fired their rifles from the hip, like John Wayne in movies they had watched as kids. With Brindley in the lead, waving his .45 pistol, the Marines hit the first row of North Vietnamese fighting holes and broke the enemy line with a flurry of grenade explosions, automatic rifle fire, and bayonet thrusts. The Marines surged ahead and were able to seize the crest of the knoll in close combat with the remaining NVA.

Spilling over the crest, the Marines came under heavy fire from North Vietnamese troops down the reverse slope and to their east. Brindley ran back and forth along the line, pausing long enough to inform Dabney by radio that his men had taken their objective but had lost most of their noncoms and were running low on ammunition.

Seconds later, a rifle round slammed into Tom Brindley's chest. Mortally wounded, he gave one final command: "Keep low, keep going, and stay on line."[33]

. . .

On Brindley's right, Bill Bryan's recon team had tried to flank the NVA position but had run headlong into a small enemy force. The Americans scattered the opposing soldiers and were charging up the hill when they were caught in a murderous crossfire: friendly mortar fire and small arms rounds from the rear, and enemy machine guns and small arms from the front. Pagano had just called off the mortar fire when an M-16 round slammed into the back of his leg, and he fell to the ground.[34]

Lying on his back, Pagano felt an AK-47 round whizz by his head. It ripped through the left arm and shoulder of the team's deputy commander, Lionel Guerra. A new Barkwood team member took one look at the two wounded veterans, dropped his gear, and bolted down the hill.

Bill Bryan appeared in the grass to Pagano's right. "Stay there," the team leader yelled. "I'll come over."[35]

As bullets and grenades ripped the grass from all directions, Pagano lay on his back and worked the radio. He asked friendly units down the hill to hold their fire. He called in artillery support and requested medevac choppers. His hands became numb from the loss of blood, and it became increasingly difficult to key his radio handset. The numbness spread to his chest and face. He was bleeding to death.

Bill Bryan charged through the grass and dived to the ground next to Pagano. "Don't worry, PJ, you're not going to die," Bryan said. The team leader propped himself up on his elbows and was tearing open a battle dressing with his teeth when the crack of an AK-47 sounded nearby. Bryan slumped to the dirt, face first. A bullet had ripped through his armpit and into his chest.

"Bryan, are you okay?" Pagano asked.

"Hit bad," the Texan gasped. "Going to die."[36]

Bill Bryan's head slowly sagged onto Pagano's legs.

. . .

With Brindley and his noncoms down, Dabney ordered Lieutenant Richard Foley up the hill to take command of the 3rd Platoon. The

Marines had formed a tight circle in anticipation of a North Vietnamese counterattack, which aerial observers reported was about to hit them. Only seconds before the NVA surged over the crest, friendly jets screamed to the rescue, dumping high explosives and napalm on the charging enemy force. The Marines bounced like rag dolls as bombs exploded and napalm fireballs boiled into the sky, but the enemy charge was shattered.[37]

• • •

PJ Pagano was lying in the grass several yards east of Brindley's perimeter when the jets made their run. He could hear voices on the radio trying to reach his team, but he was too weak to respond. The lifeless body of Bill Bryan lay across his legs. Pagano stared up at the beautiful blue sky and waited to die.

A Marine F-4 Phantom jet suddenly roared directly overhead, so low that Pagano could see the rivets on its fuselage and feel the heat from its engine. On its second pass, Pagano watched two napalm canisters drop from the jet's wings and tumble toward him. He closed his eyes, covered his face, and waited for the jellied gasoline to incinerate him. But the canisters whooshed past and exploded just over the crest.

Pagano next heard two helicopter pilots talking over his frequency. "Have you been monitoring Barkwood?" one pilot asked.

"Yes, that was a sad situation," the other replied.

Pagano suddenly realized: *They think we're dead.*[38]

• • •

Tom Brindley's shattered platoon had been saved by the air strikes, at least for a few minutes, but the Marines remained pinned down by heavy NVA fire. Bill Dabney now ordered Mike Thomas to take half his platoon and maneuver from the left flank over to Brindley's trapped survivors. Thomas quickly covered the 500 yards that separated the two columns and found Brindley's men. He reinforced the perimeter and began organizing the evacuation of the wounded down the hill.

When it became clear that the team of recon Marines was missing, Thomas led the search through the tall grass to the east. One by one, he and his men found the lost Marines and carried them to safety, until only two remained missing: team leader Bill Bryan and radio operator PJ Pagano.

As Thomas lay in the grass with his men, he received a radio report with the location of the two missing Marines. Blood streamed from a painful facial wound Thomas had suffered, but he insisted on leading the final rescue. The young lieutenant was rising from the grass when he was hit again: one bullet struck him in the head; another tore through his midsection, sliced through corpsman Mike Ray's shoulder, and struck a third Marine in the ankle. Mike Thomas collapsed to the ground, mortally wounded.[39]

• • •

In the tall grass nearby, PJ Pagano had mustered his last bit of strength to let his comrades know that he was alive. He positioned the handset near his ear and pressed his head down on the talk button. "All stations this net, this is Barkwood," Pagano said. "Be advised this station is up."

A few minutes passed before Pagano got a response.

"Barkwood, this is Rainbelt Six Actual." It was Bill Dabney. "I've got six Marines here who have volunteered to come up and get you. You up for it?"[40]

Signals were arranged: the rescue party would stay on Pagano's frequency and ask him to fire two quick shots from his M-16 rifle every so often to guide them. Pagano's hands were so numb that it took all his strength to pull the trigger, but he managed to fire two sets of shots on command. On his third attempt, the rifle bolt locked open. He was out of rounds.

Dark clouds had moved in, and it was beginning to rain. If night fell, Pagano knew he would bleed to death or be killed by NVA soldiers. He heard a rustling in the grass nearby and tensed. The grass parted, revealing the grimy face of a Marine.

"Are you Barkwood?" Sergeant Daniel Jessup casually asked.[41]

Yes, Pagano confirmed.

"What about him?" the Marine asked. He nodded at the Barkwood team leader, still draped over Pagano's legs.

"He's dead," Pagano replied. As he finally allowed himself to accept the terrible truth, Pagano fought to suppress a scream. Bill Bryan, the finest of men and Marines, was dead.

Three Marines, including one of Pagano's wounded teammates, had found the Barkwood radio operator. They cut off Pagano's pack and began dragging him down the hill, a few inches at a time, as the NVA blasted the moving grass. The LZ finally came into sight. Pagano was loaded aboard a medevac helicopter with other casualties, and the bird made its escape under heavy NVA fire.[42]

• • •

Around 3:00 p.m., Bill Dabney had received a radio transmission from the battalion commander: break contact and get your men back to 881 South. There was no explanation—it was always assumed that the NVA was monitoring transmissions, so the less said, the better. Only later that night would Dabney learn about the North Vietnamese defector and his revelations about an imminent attack.

Dabney argued that he could take 881 North if he got reinforcements. His request was denied.[43] By late afternoon, Dabney had accounted for all his men and gotten the most seriously wounded off the hill. He had lost forty-two men in the day's fighting, one-fourth of his force, including seven dead or mortally wounded. The big Virginian gave the order to withdraw.

As the exhausted Marines retraced their steps down the parallel fingers, helicopter gunships and attack jets pinned the North Vietnamese in place. Night was approaching when the last Marine of India Company filed back inside the wire of the outpost on 881 South.[44]

• • •

During the course of the long day, the mood on 881 South had darkened as India's losses had mounted.[45] Lieutenant Tom Esslinger, a twenty-four-year-old Yale University graduate from Ephrata, Pennsylvania, had choppered up to the hill with 3rd Battalion's Mike Company, which was assigned to hold the outpost while Dabney confronted the NVA.[46] Esslinger had joined a group of senior officers as they watched the operation from atop Dabney's bunker.

As the fight raged, the officers sat on the bunker roof in lawn chairs and puffed cigars. Esslinger had watched admiringly through binoculars as Lieutenant Mike Thomas, a close friend, dashed around the lower slopes of 881 North, oblivious to the enemy fire. But as the hours passed, Esslinger's awe had turned to horror after he witnessed the death of Tom Brindley, another good friend and former classmate, and then Mike Thomas.

Esslinger had ducked inside Dabney's bunker, where he broke down and wept.[47]

Now, with the North Vietnamese all around, the mourning of fallen friends and comrades would have to wait. Tom Esslinger helped ready Mike Company for battle, while the men of India Company made similar preparations on their half of the hill. The long day drew to a close on Hill 881 South with the familiar figure of Captain Bill Dabney moving through the darkness, checking his lines, bucking up his men. The great confrontation at Khe Sanh was underway.

CHAPTER 2

The Battle of Hill 861

As the Marines on 881 South awaited the enemy, North Vietnamese sappers moved through the darkness and fog about one and one-half miles to the east. With practiced stealth, they closed on the American outpost on Hill 861—the advance elements of a four-hundred-man NVA assault force poised to strike the Marines of Kilo Company, 3/26.

Approximately twenty paces beyond the northern perimeter of the American stronghold, two Marines were the first to hear the enemy approach. They had drawn listening post (LP) duty on this night and were hiding in a clump of grass, waiting to sound the alarm if the enemy attacked. Periodically, the platoon radio operator called for a situation report, a heart-stopping request on nights when the enemy was about. It would suffice for the LP leader to key his mike a specified number of times, if everything was okay. "If there ain't no jive, give me five," the platoon radioman might instruct. Or: "If you're home free, give me three."[1]

The North Vietnamese troops closing on the hill—the 6th Battalion of the 325C Division's 2nd Regiment—had orders to overrun the American outpost. The 150 Marines and Navy corpsmen assigned to Kilo Company, 3rd Battalion of the 26th Marine Regiment, had orders to stop them.

Back home, the country might be coming apart at the seams over the war in Vietnam and civil rights, but the American melting pot was alive and well in Kilo Company. The Corps had taken young men from every conceivable background—Northerners and Southerners, blacks and whites, jocks and scholars, high school dropouts and college boys—and had broken them down and rebuilt them as peerless warriors, bound by a sense of brotherhood and purpose that transcended race and class and regional pride. It was fashionable in the Army to look down on the Marines and mock their *oorah* bravado, their claims of being stronger and tougher and faster than anyone else defending Old Glory. But for those who had been through boot camp at Parris Island or San Diego or Officer Candidates School at Quantico, the transformation was as real as air or sunlight. They were, and would forever be, United States Marines, guided by an uncomplicated creed: *Semper Fidelis*—Always Faithful, with an emphasis on Always.

The Marine Corps had taken disparate souls like Lance Corporal Dennis Mannion, a garrulous twenty-two-year-old Notre Dame dropout and son of a Connecticut FBI agent, and Sergeant Miguel Salinas, a thirty-eight-year-old Korean War veteran and worldly merchant seaman of humble Mexican migrant stock, and transformed them into highly skilled components of the killing machine that was Kilo Company. The Corps had taken a pair of mismatched twenty-year-olds named Ted Mickelson and Dave Rozelle—the former a short (and short-tempered) Mormon cowboy from Wyoming and the latter a tall, sweet-natured agnostic from Scranton, Pennsylvania—and forged them into a fine M-60 machine-gun team anchoring Kilo's eastern perimeter. The Corps had elevated college-educated men like twenty-four-year-old Norman Jasper from the cornfields of Illinois to company command and more recent graduates, like Benjamin Steve Fordham, the son of an American business executive in Mexico, to platoon leadership.

Holding it all together were career Marines like Melvin Rimel, Kilo's revered gunnery sergeant. At six foot three and 240 pounds, the native of Dawson, Pennsylvania, had earned the nickname Bull as a fledgling Marine recruit at Parris Island in 1953. To members of his family, he was a beloved son, brother, husband, and father of four. Now thirty-three, with fifteen years in the Marine Corps, Rimel was a "lifer," but he was larger than life. For young Marines, Rimel was a surrogate father, tough but fair, and he taught them how to be a Marine.[2]

The two Kilo Marines out on LP duty off the north end of 861 were another unlikely pair, a Louisiana Cajun named Bondurant and a wise-cracking Northern black named Diehl, but the finely honed process of Marine Corps acculturation wasn't foremost in their minds as they listened to the enemy sappers creeping toward their hiding place.

Their radio crackled to life with a reprieve: Captain Jasper wanted all LPs back inside the wire. Bondurant and Diehl ran for their lives. The shaken Marines sprinted back inside the Kilo perimeter, spewing a torrent of oaths. "Motherfucker!" one exclaimed. "There's all kinds of gooks out there!"[3]

• • •

The two Marines weren't exaggerating. The night came alive with the sounds of NVA sappers as they low-crawled up the slope toward the northern perimeter of the American outpost. The approach was gentler there, almost flat in places, whereas the hill dropped off steeply to the east and west.

The American stronghold on Hill 861 measured nearly four hundred yards north to south and about 150 yards east to west. The hill sloped upward toward the north and crested a little over fifty yards above the trench line as it snaked around the northern perimeter. Captain Jasper's command bunker—several layers of sandbags piled around dirt-filled barrels—sat near the crest. The helicopter landing zone was down the hill to the south.

Several sandbagged machine-gun bunkers had been carved into the outer wall of the trench line, spaced every twenty-five yards or so. In between were the fighting positions of Kilo's riflemen. Sergeant Miguel Salinas was positioned with his M-60 machine gun at a crucial point on the northern trench line, overlooking the main entrance to the outpost.

To slow an enemy assault force, the Americans had built an outer barrier anchored by three rows of triple concertina wire, a regular barbed wire fence and swaths of "tangle foot"—tautly stretched barbed wire laid out in a checkerboard pattern a few inches off the ground. Scattered among the tangle foot and concertina were pressure-detonated mines and trip flares that would burn brightly when triggered. Beyond the wire were command-detonated Claymore mines, positioned to spray ball bearings in a deadly fan-shaped pattern toward an assault force, and homemade anti-personnel weapons fashioned from twenty-five pound rolls of barbed wire packed with C4 plastic explosives and a blasting cap.[4]

Now, Miguel Salinas and his 1st Platoon comrades listened to the enemy sappers as they went about their work sizing up the outer American defenses—probing, digging up mines, and snipping wire. The Marines could hear the *tap-tap-tap* of bamboo signal sticks and see pinholes of light flickering on and off like fireflies as the sappers communicated with each other and with the assault forces moving into place behind them. The Marines occasionally tossed grenades toward the sounds and flashes of light. As the tension built, they yelled taunts and insults at their adversaries.[5]

Sometime after 9:00 p.m., Captain Jasper ordered Kilo's artillery forward observer, Dennis Mannion, down to the northern perimeter to see if he could put artillery on the NVA sappers. Mannion and his radio operator, Dave Kron, found the mood tense among the Marines.[6] The enemy sappers were now only thirty or forty yards away, so close that the Americans could hear the high-pitched, singsong tones of spoken Vietnamese. The sappers seemed nonchalant, chatting, even laughing. Other sounds carried through the fog: the slap of a rifle sling hitting the weapon's wooden stock; the *"Shhhhhhhhhh"* of an enemy soldier trying to quiet his comrades; and, strangest of all, a Donald Duck–like noise followed by laughter.[7] The concertina wire hummed as the North Vietnamese shook it, perhaps testing whether it was electrified or rigged with explosives.[8] There were metallic pings as taut coils of concertina were snipped and sprang back into place. The Americans threw more grenades, and the occasional screams or moans of injured North Vietnamese soldiers carried through the night.[9]

It was quickly clear to Mannion that the NVA had crept too close for an artillery strike. He returned to his fighting hole above the 1st Platoon positions and reported his assessment to Captain Jasper.[10] Twice more, Mannion and his radioman made their way down to the front wire to check the situation. They had just returned to their fighting hole after their final trip down to the front line when a figure took shape in the mist. They tensed, and Mannion barked a challenge.

A voice like that of a radio disc jockey sang out, announcing the call letters of a Florida radio station and a balmy weather report. It was corpsman Malcolm Mole, an aspiring DJ from DeLand, Florida. The cheery Mole had crept up the hill to use the latrine the Marines had carved into the slope near Mannion's bunker.

Laughing at Mole's comic relief, Mannion called out in mock anger. "Oh, Doc, come on! Give me a break!"[11]

• • •

Sometime around 12:30 a.m. on January 21, 1968, an RPG round streaked over Miguel Salinas and his 1st Platoon comrades on the northern perimeter of 861 and exploded on the crest of the hill behind them.[12] A green flare lit the night as RPG rounds whooshed in from North Vietnamese positions to the west, smashing into Captain Jasper's command post, machine-gun bunkers, and other key points. Rockets slammed into the hill, one after another, and enemy mortars bisected the hill with rounds that marched along a north-south axis, spraying deadly shrapnel in all directions. Machine-gun rounds and green tracers stitched the darkness.

In the eerie half-light of illumination flares and exploding shells, the Marines of the 1st Platoon could see dozens of NVA soldiers charging toward them, blowing gaps in the wire with Bangalore torpedoes and throwing bamboo mats and ladders over the tangle foot and concertina coils.[13] Miguel Salinas opened fire with his M-60, and other Marines up and down the northern line tossed grenades and emptied M-16 magazines into the enemy charge. Some of the attackers got tangled in the wire and thrashed about as they tried to break free.[14] The screams of wounded NVA troops and Marines mingled with exclamations and warnings of new threats. Salinas screamed in Spanish and bounced around the trench line like a fighting cock.[15]

Several enemy soldiers reached the trench line around Salinas's machine gun, and the fight became a desperate hand-to-hand struggle. A black Marine took up an exposed position atop the machine-gun bunker, pointed his M-16 at the charging NVA soldiers, and pulled the trigger. A Marine from Denver, Colorado, emptied his magazine into the mob, then slashed and stabbed the attackers with a switchblade. Salinas clubbed three or four with his rifle and shot one in the midsection at close range.[16]

Just as suddenly as it began, the attack rolled past Salinas and his comrades. Dead and dying NVA soldiers lay all around them—in the trench line, in the wire, and on the torn ground beyond. Several North Vietnamese soldiers had jumped the trench line and headed up the hill toward Captain Jasper's command post. A few others had made it into the trench on either side of the 1st Platoon line, and they now headed deeper into the American outpost.

• • •

Around midnight, Captain Jasper had dispatched Dennis Mannion to the southern end of the hill to check out reports from the 2nd Platoon that NVA troops were in the elephant grass beyond the western perimeter wire. Jasper instructed the artillery forward observer to confirm the sighting and call in artillery on the enemy soldiers if possible.[17]

Arriving at the 2nd Platoon command post, Mannion peered into the darkness with binoculars, but he couldn't see or hear anything. As he was standing there, scanning the grass-cloaked draw beneath the hill's western perimeter, a green flare spangled the sky. On cue, the entire northwest corner of the hill came under fire from RPGs, rockets, mortars, machine guns, and small arms positioned on ridgelines to the west and north. Mannion and his radioman, Dave Kron, headed toward their fighting position overlooking the northern perimeter, working their way up the road that ran from the LZ to Captain Jasper's command post in the middle of the hill. The entire northern end of the hill was getting hammered by mortars and RPGs, so they veered to their right, moving in a low crouch toward the northeast. Ahead, they could see the silhouette of the command post, backlit by the flash of explosions and the intermittent light of flares that floated slowly to the ground on tiny parachutes.

As they got closer, Mannion could see a body sprawled on the ground outside the command post (CP): it was Kilo's beloved gunnery sergeant, Melvin Rimel. He was lying on his back, eyes open, his massive body pierced and broken by an enemy shell.[18] Mannion knelt at the side of the great Marine and, with his thumbs, gently closed Rimel's eyes.

Tears of shock and disbelief ran down Mannion's cheeks as he stifled a wave of panic: *Oh my God, if they could kill Gunny Rimel, we're all going to die.*[19] From his vantage point, Mannion could see that an RPG or a mortar had demolished the command post. There was no sign of Captain Jasper or anyone else in the command group.

Mannion collected himself and began to formulate a plan. He *had* to get back to the northern end of the hill to call in artillery and see with his own eyes where the rounds were landing or else the NVA could move up reinforcements at will and overrun the outpost. But the hail of bullets, RPGs, and shells had turned the area around his fighting position into a death zone. Even now, as he hunkered with his radioman in the open, they could hear shrapnel whiz by and clang off the steel engineering stakes that anchored bunker walls and perimeter wire. They would have to find another route.

Crouching low to the ground, Mannion and Kron retraced their steps to the LZ and found their way to a small bunker along the western trench line. "Get Charlie 1/13," Mannion ordered, one of the batteries at Khe Sanh Combat Base. "We're going to start calling in artillery."

Kron dialed in the frequency and was stunned by what he heard. "Listen to this," he said, putting the handset to his comrade's ear. Mannion could hear the voices of North Vietnamese soldiers. They were jamming the frequency to block communications between the Americans on 861 and their artillery support.

With their efforts to call in artillery temporarily thwarted, Mannion and Kron started up the western trench line. Every ten or twelve feet, they passed a Marine standing at his post, rifle pointed outward. There were no enemy troops visible to the west, but the Marines occasionally tossed grenades into the shadows to make sure NVA assault forces weren't creeping up on their positions. Mannion asked each Marine they encountered: Is there a man to your right? Each time the answer was yes, and so they kept moving up the trench.

Periodically, when they could get a clear frequency, the two Americans paused to call in coordinates for artillery. When they were unable to get through, alert officers down at the base were firing missions on Mannion's preregistered targets to the west and northwest of the hill.

About an hour had passed since the opening salvo launching the attack, and the intensity of the enemy barrage had ebbed at times. Suddenly, a thunderous explosion rocked the hill, and a greenish-yellow fireball boiled into the sky above the north end. The 106-millimeter recoilless rifle bunker to the left of Mannion's fighting hole had taken a direct hit, and it was now gone.

Mannion and Kron finally worked their way up to the northwest corner of the perimeter. The acrid smell of gunpowder from NVA grenades and shells hung heavily in the air. A Marine bunker came into view, and they could hear and see that a machine gunner was firing short bursts, with every sixth or seventh round a red tracer that streaked toward the northwest. As the two Marines crept close to the bunker, Mannion yelled the gunner's name. "It's Dennis," Mannion called out.

The machine gunner fired a burst, then called back, "Okay."

Mannion and Kron ducked into the bunker, stepping on hundreds of shell casings that littered the floor. "Where's your crew?" Mannion asked.

"I don't know," the gunner replied. "They took off."

"Are there gooks out there?"

The M-60 gunner wasn't sure what was lurking in the fog, but he had a more immediate concern. "They're all up and down this trench line," he warned.

Mannion was stunned. "They're in here?"

"Fuck, yeah," the gunner said. "There's one guy right outside in the trench line. I think he got hit by his own grenade."

Mannion turned the subdued beam of his red-lens flashlight toward the bunker entrance and spotted the small crater from a grenade blast just outside. He stole a quick glance up the trench line and could see a North Vietnamese soldier, sprawled on his stomach, no more than two feet away.

Mannion turned back to the gunner. "Is the guy dead?"

"I think he's wounded, but I don't think he's dead."

"Well, we've got to get up around the corner," Mannion said firmly. He turned to his radioman. "Give me your .45."

Kron handed him the pistol. Squatting down in the bunker's entrance, Mannion slowly stretched his body out into the trench. Lying half on his side, he reached to his left. He touched the enemy soldier's shoulder, then his head. The injured man jerked away. Mannion thrust the pistol forward and fired four times.[20]

Bidding good luck to the machine gunner, Mannion and Kron cautiously continued up the trench line. They came to an abandoned bunker that overlooked the flat area where the North Vietnamese assault had first hit the Marines. Heavy enemy fire from outside the wire prevented them from going any further.

The two Americans eased back out of the line of fire and slipped into a cut in the trench wall. From there, Dennis Mannion and Dave Kron began calling in more artillery and adjusting the fire onto the NVA positions to their west and northwest.[21]

• • •

When the North Vietnamese attack got underway, Captain Norman Jasper, the Kilo commander, was standing in the fighting hole alongside his command bunker near the crest of 861. Ringed by a chest-high wall of sandbags, the hole was near one of the hill's two 106-millimeter recoilless rifle bunkers, carved into the rim of a bomb crater above the northwest trench line. As the NVA barrage pounded the hill, Jasper kept in touch with his platoon commanders and the battalion staff by radio, popping his head above the sandbags periodically to see for himself what was going on or to yell instructions to the Marines in his area.[22]

The cry of "Corpsman!" soon sounded around him. Five Navy corpsmen had been assigned to Kilo Company. One of the two corpsmen with Jasper's command group, aspiring disc jockey Malcolm Mole, scampered down the hill in response to a shout for aid. An RPG round streaked across the slope and exploded, killing the twenty-year-old from Florida.[23]

In the quavering half-light of exploding shells and flares, Jasper and his command group worked the radios and directed fire. When word of a breach in the northern line filtered back up the hill, Jasper radioed 2nd Platoon along the southern and western perimeter: get some men up the hill to plug the breach. Four riflemen and two men from a 4.2-inch mortar team hustled up the slope to join the desperate fight being waged by Miguel Salinas and his comrades.

• • •

M-60 gunner Ted Mickelson and Lance Corporal Dave Rozelle, a twenty-year-old from Scranton, Pennsylvania, heard and saw the assault unfold from their machine-gun bunker on the northeast trench line. It was a nonstop light show of exploding shells and flares, RPGs and tracers. It all vaguely reminded Mickelson of a fierce lightning storm out on his family's Wyoming ranch—except it was louder and more terrifying than any storm he had experienced.

While Mickelson peered out through the bunker's front firing port, watching for an enemy assault on the wire below him, Rozelle stood at the rear entrance, facing westward, to make sure that NVA troops didn't surprise them from behind. A 120-millimeter rocket screamed in from the west and slammed into the slope behind them, and a blinding flash filled the bunker. Mickelson turned back toward the sound and saw Rozelle silhouetted in the bunker entrance. The big Pennsylvanian slowly sank onto a bench along the bunker's back wall. Mickelson heard a sound like water gushing from a faucet. It was blood pouring from Rozelle's femoral arteries, severed by shrapnel or debris.

Mickelson rushed to Rozelle and held him.

"I'm sorry, Ted," Rozelle said. "I'm sorry I didn't kill a gook."[24] And then he died.

• • •

Over on the western trench line, Private First Class Paul Robert Bellamy, a big, easygoing nineteen-year-old from Portland, Oregon, lay dying with a terrible wound. A piece of shrapnel had blown out the right side of his head, but it hadn't killed him. He sat with his back against the trench wall, conversing cogently with his friends as his last minutes slipped away.[25]

• • •

After breaching the northern wire, the NVA assault troops who made it past the 1st Platoon trench line fanned out down the hill. Some, like the one Dennis Mannion encountered, had headed down the western trench line in an attempt to take out the American machine guns. A few took off for the Kilo command post and the interior of the outpost, where they were killed or captured by Marines. One of these enemy soldiers may have fired the shot that found nineteen-year-old Curtis B. Bugger of Kearns, Utah, an assistant machine gunner, killing him in the western trench line with a bullet to the head.

The leader of Bugger's gun team was a Marine from Oklahoma named Billy Ray Moffett, and he continued to blast away at the North Vietnamese off the northwest corner of the hill. Even after his assistant gunner had been killed and his bunker had come under assault from NVA machine guns, mortars, and RPGs, Moffett remained at his post, pouring fire into the main enemy avenue of attack.[26]

• • •

Well-placed enemy mortar fire had taken a heavy toll on the Kilo command group. Gunnery Sergeant Melvin Rimel had been killed, and First Sergeant Bernard Goddard seriously wounded when a piece of shrapnel had sliced his carotid artery. (Goddard fought on with a finger pressed against the torn artery so he wouldn't bleed to death.)[27] Captain Jasper was next.

About ninety minutes into the fight, Jasper was standing outside his command bunker when a flurry of NVA mortar rounds slammed into the hill. Thrown into the air by the force of the blast, Jasper landed in a heap about ten feet away. A piece of shrapnel had struck his cheek below his left eye, which began to swell shut. Another mortar round exploded close to him, and once again he was hurled through the air. Hot shrapnel tore into his right arm and shoulder, and other metal fragments burrowed under his sleeveless flak jacket and lodged in his chest.

Not long afterward, a third mortar round knocked Jasper flying. A piece of shrapnel penetrated his right knee and smaller fragments peppered his buttocks. He landed on a corpsman wounded by the same blast. "Treat your wounds," the Kilo commander told the corpsman. "Then you can treat mine."[28]

• • •

Twenty-five hundred yards to the west, the Marines of India and Mike Companies waited in their trenches for the expected NVA assault to roll up the slopes of Hill 881 South.

Most of the 3/26 battalion staff had remained on the hill after India's daylong fight on 881 North. Clustered in Captain Bill Dabney's command bunker, they followed Kilo's increasingly desperate situation over the battalion radio net. From their vantage point, they could see and hear the deadly NVA barrage that pounded 861—flashes of light in the eastern sky, followed a second or two later by muffled explosions.

Around 2:00 a.m., the radio in Dabney's bunker that had been tuned to the 3/26 battalion net crackled to life. A frantic voice transmitting from 861 cut through the static. "We're being overrun! Command group is all down!"[29]

Major Matthew Caulfield, the battalion operations officer, took the handset. "A Marine unit doesn't get overrun," Caulfield coolly replied. "Now calm down and tell me what is really happening."

The frantic voice belonged to Jasper's executive officer, First Lieutenant Jerry N. Saulsberry. The fear in Saulsberry's voice was palpable as he laid out the grim situation.

"Get your gunny," Caulfield said. "Make sure you rely on him."[30]

"The gunny is dead," Saulsberry replied.

"Get your first sergeant," Caulfield said, mindful of Ben Goddard's stellar reputation.

"He's dying," came the response. (Goddard, in fact, would live.)

Caulfield, a charming Irishman, summoned all his powers of inspiration to steel the overwhelmed lieutenant. "Now Jerry, I know you can do this," Caulfield exhorted. "I want you to take that ball and run with it!"[31]

There was silence on the other end. Finally, Saulsberry responded in a weak voice.

"Run? Did you say *run*, sir?"

"No, no, Jerry!" Caulfield shouted back into the handset. "You gotta stay right there!"

• • •

Jerry Saulsberry held his ground, and so did the rest of Kilo Company as the 3/26 battalion staff mobilized the formidable American firepower in support of Hill 861. With the assistance of Kilo artillery forward observer Dennis Mannion, still huddled along the northwest trench line of 861, a fierce counterbarrage began to saturate the areas where North Vietnamese reinforcements were massing and heavy weapons had been positioned.[32] The tide of battle began to turn.

Under Dabney's direction, the 81-millimeter mortars on 881 South maintained a furious pace. Dabney pulled riflemen from his trenches to keep a steady supply of rounds flowing to the gunners. When the 81 tubes began to glow red-hot and ignite propellant bags before the rounds could be fired, Dabney organized his men to cool one tube with water while the other was being fired.[33] The Marines soon emptied all the hill's canteens and jerry cans, so Dabney ordered his men to pour their stores of fruit juice on the overheated mortars. When the fruit juice ran out, Dabney lined up his men by platoon and the Marines took turns urinating on the tube. By dawn, the Marines on 881 South had fired nearly 1,000 81-millimeter mortar rounds and several hundred 105-millimeter howitzer rounds in support of 861.[34]

The first hint of dawn found the men of Kilo Company shaken and bloodied, but still in control of the hill. During the night, the North Vietnamese assault commander had been overheard in a radio transmission, screaming for his reserves to join the attack.[35] But the American response had been swift and decisive, from the riflemen and machine gunners on 861 to the artillery crews at 881 South, Khe Sanh, and Camp Carroll, further east along Route 9. Dead and dying North Vietnamese soldiers now littered the slopes of 861 and nearby terrain. The NVA attack had been broken.

• • •

After surviving the initial NVA assault, Miguel Salinas and the men of Kilo's 1st Platoon counted their losses and regrouped. Several had been wounded and two killed. The firing tapered off, and the haggard Marines began to move about the trench line.

Salinas knelt down to examine the NVA soldier he had shot at close range during the first minutes of the battle. The man looked neater than the other dead NVA troops he could see caught in the wire and outside the trench line. Salinas found a Catholic rosary in one of the dead man's pockets. In another, he found a cheap plastic wallet with a photograph of the soldier with his wife and young daughter, and a letter the soldier had written.

Salinas couldn't speak or read Vietnamese, but he later had the letter translated by a Communist defector. In it, the North Vietnamese soldier was asking his commanding officer for a leave so he might return home to visit his sick wife. For Salinas, it was a rare glimpse of the humanity on the other side of the savage conflict in Vietnam—a poignant reminder that the NVA soldiers, for all their fearsome reputation, were just like the young Americans on Hill 861 in at least one respect: they were sons and husbands and fathers, and they were frightened and homesick as they joined the battle at Khe Sanh.[36]

• • •

On the hill's northwest corner, Dennis Mannion and Dave Kron emerged from the hole where they had spent the night calling in artillery missions and retraced their steps down the western trench line. They came upon the NVA soldier that Mannion had shot outside the machine-gun bunker. Mannion made a mental note of the enemy soldier's attire: sneakers, greenish-tan shirt and pants, cartridge belt, and pith helmet.

Further down the trench line, Mannion and Kron cautiously made their way to the middle of the hill, and then, in a low crouch, started up the slope toward the Kilo command post. They saw Gunny Rimel's body lying in the dirt off to the right. Near their fighting hole on the hill's northern rim they saw four or five badly mangled NVA dead in an old bomb crater. Below them, a dozen or more NVA soldiers lay sprawled in and under the perimeter wire.[37]

Over on the northeast side of the hill, after hours of incessant noise—explosions, gunfire, and the rattle of his machine gun as he sprayed the darkness with nearly 10,000 rounds—Ted Mickelson was struck by the silence that engulfed the outpost. The calm was abruptly broken by the moaning of a wounded Marine, a recoilless rifleman, lying in the fighting hole a few feet behind Mickelson, his bloody body bristling with flechette rounds that had blown up when the 106 bunker had taken a direct hit. A corpsman arrived and went to work on the wounded Marine.[38]

• • •

The final drama of the attack on Hill 861 occurred as dawn broke. One of the NVA soldiers who had breached the 1st Platoon lines had taken refuge in a phone booth–size latrine on the northern end of the hill. He had neatly laid out his ammunition and food—rice and dried fish—and waited for his final showdown with the Americans. Marines closed in on the lone enemy holdout from three sides, pouring rounds into the wooden structure. The soldier died in a flurry of gunfire, the last casualty of the battle for Hill 861.[39]

• • •

On Hill 881 South, Captain Bill Dabney and the men of India and Mike Companies welcomed the news that their comrades on 861 had survived the night. India Company had burned through most of its M-16 ammo and 81-millimeter mortar rounds over the previous twenty-four hours. Several casualties from the fighting on 881 North still needed to be evacuated down to Khe Sanh.[40] Dabney radioed for helicopter support at first light, and a bird soon swooped low over the hill and settled onto one of the hill's two LZs. Two or three Marines on stretchers were loaded aboard the chopper, along with a couple of walking wounded.

Several hundred yards away, North Vietnamese artillery spotters had watched the helicopter land and had seen the throng of Marines spilling onto the LZ to offload cargo and load the wounded. An NVA 120-millimeter mortar team took aim and dropped a round down the tube.

The roar of the departing chopper's engine and thrashing rotors hid the sound of the enemy rounds leaving their tubes. Just off the LZ, Captain Dabney was standing with his company supply clerk, Private First Class Terry Melvin Johnson, when the first one hit. Dabney jumped into one hole, and Johnson into another. A round landed in Johnson's hole, killing him instantly.[41]

• • •

About 5:30 a.m., as the North Vietnamese assault on Hill 861 sputtered to a close, the Marines on the battered hill were startled by an ominous sound to the southwest, toward the border with Laos, about seven miles away.

BOOM-BOOM-BOOM.

BOOM-BOOM-BOOM.

BOOM-BOOM-BOOM.

A few seconds later, they heard the sound of explosions southeast of their position. Forward observer Dennis Mannion looked at his radio operator. He recognized the sounds of big artillery guns firing, and he knew what it meant.

Khe Sanh Combat Base was under attack.[42]

CHAPTER 3

"Get Up and Man Your Position!"

The final hours of January 20, 1968, found Lance Corporal Michael O'Hara cradling a shotgun as he walked point for a column of Marines that slipped out the east end of Khe Sanh Combat Base and headed into the nearby jungle to set a night ambush. The nineteen-year-old rifleman had been vaguely aware of the heightened activity at the combat base during the day, but like most of the nearly 6,000 Americans at Khe Sanh, he knew nothing of the worried deliberations underway in the regimental command bunker in the heart of the sprawling stronghold.

At the center of those deliberations was Colonel David Lownds, commander of the 26th Marines and Khe Sanh Combat Base. The World War II veteran had spent the first hours of his day preoccupied by India Company's operation to 881 North, and then two important guests had arrived by air. Lownds had devoted the late morning and early afternoon to his visitors, Brigadier General Phillip B. Davidson, military intelligence chief for America's supreme commander in Vietnam, General William Westmoreland, and Colonel Kenneth J. Houghton, chief of intelligence for the III Marine Amphibious Force. He had briefed them on the local situation and showed them Khe Sanh's defenses, but both had come away convinced that Lownds had badly underestimated the enemy threat and had failed to prepare his men sufficiently for the looming confrontation.[1] Before leaving, the intelligence chiefs learned about the surrender of the

North Vietnamese lieutenant and his revelations about Communist plans to attack the Americans that night.[2]

Late afternoon at the combat base had seen a flurry of activity as medevac choppers had arrived, bearing wounded and dead Marines from Bill Dabney's desperate fight on 881 North. As night fell, Marines on watch duty peered into the darkness from Khe Sanh's trench line. Others prepared for listening-post and night-ambush assignments outside the wire. Among them was the contingent from Bravo Company, 1st Battalion, 26th Marines, that included Michael O'Hara. They had slipped into the jungle south of Bravo Company's lines and laid out Claymore mines and fields of fire, then settled into the underbrush to await their prey.

• • •

Back in rural southern Indiana, Michael O'Hara had loved horses and hunting, but becoming a Marine had been his lifelong dream. He was still in elementary school when his older brother by seven years, Wayne, had joined the Corps. Young Michael had spent many a Saturday at the local movie house, watching John Wayne war movies and World War II newsreels about real-life Marine heroes.[3] In a pouring rain in late April 1967, O'Hara had hitchhiked to Bloomington, Indiana, where he enlisted in the Marine Corps. He was eighteen years old.

In early October 1967, O'Hara found himself in Okinawa, Japan, filling out a will and life-insurance forms before boarding a Vietnam-bound Continental Airlines chartered jet packed with replacement Marines. As the aircraft descended through the clouds over Da Nang, jungle-cloaked mountains loomed black and ominous. The raucous Marines fell silent.

A few days later, with his newly issued M-16 rifle in hand, O'Hara boarded a big transport helicopter in Phu Bai. It was a sunny day and a brilliant landscape unfolded below—green mountains, silver waterfalls, lush tropical forests. It was the most beautiful place he had ever seen. About thirty minutes later, the chopper settled onto the runway at Khe Sanh Combat Base in a cloud of red dust, and O'Hara and other wide-eyed Marines grabbed their gear and scuttled away from the thrashing rotors. It was October 11, 1967.

Assigned to the 2nd Platoon of Bravo Company, 1st Battalion, 26th

Marines, O'Hara found the reception less than warm. The Marines had all lost friends, and they weren't eager to make new ones. A few days later, O'Hara and the rest of Bravo Company walked up to Hill 881 South.

O'Hara and a buddy named Don Quinn shared a cramped bunker carved into the side of the hill. The day after they arrived, it rained harder than anything O'Hara had ever witnessed. One wet, miserable day followed another. O'Hara and his buddy fashioned beds out of artillery ammunition boxes, but sleep was hard to come by. All night long, thirty feet from O'Hara's bunker, a 105-millimeter howitzer fired occasional "harassment and interdiction" rounds at suspected enemy infiltration routes.

Hill duty around Khe Sanh was uncomfortable but seldom fatal in the fall of 1967. One day, O'Hara was out on a company-size patrol hacking its way through a wall of the razor-sharp grass when the column abruptly halted. He heard the captain issue a terse command.

"Sniper up."

O'Hara stiffened. *Oh, shit. This is it.*

In a low voice, the captain admonished the sniper. "If you miss him, corporal, you'll be a private when you go to bed tonight."

A shot exploded over O'Hara's head. He braced for the enemy's answer, but it never came. Instead of shooting an NVA soldier, the sniper had bagged a five-point deer. The weary Marines slogged back up Hill 881 South with their prize, and the deer was butchered and chunks of fresh meat tossed into a simmering caldron. That night the men of Bravo Company feasted on the first hot chow they had eaten since arriving on the hill a month earlier.

When they weren't patrolling, the Marines kept busy with mind-numbing work details. They filled sandbags, shored up their crude bunkers, and burned off the contents of half-barrel latrines casually referred to as "shitters." Most afternoons they got an hour to change clothes, dry socks, wash up, and write letters home.

At night they took turns standing watch, or they slipped outside the wire-enclosed perimeter to set ambushes. Worst of all was listening-post duty. A fire team of four Marines would creep into the bush a hundred yards or so outside the wire and hunker down for the night, waiting to sound the alarm should the NVA attack.

One night, O'Hara led a fire team off the east side of 881 South for

LP duty. They had set their Claymore mines in a driving rain and were huddled under a poncho awaiting daylight. The Marines suddenly heard noises between their position and the perimeter wire. O'Hara radioed the command post. "Any friendly troops in our area?" he asked in a low voice.

"Negative," came the response.

The voices came closer. O'Hara's heart pounded. Should he shoot the men? At the last possible second, he whispered an order to hold fire, and the strangers passed by a few feet away.

Some minutes later, the strangers approached once more. Again O'Hara radioed his platoon commander. "Are you *sure* there are no other friendlies outside the wire?"

The reply was emphatic: "No friendlies."

Once again, O'Hara hesitated, and he allowed the shadowy figures to pass.

Back inside the outpost after daylight, O'Hara reported the strange events. A chill ran down his spine when he was informed that another Bravo platoon had sent men out on a night ambush. O'Hara had come within an eyelash of killing his comrades.

The day after Christmas, Bravo Company had rotated off 881 South and returned to the combat base. They took over the portion of the Khe Sanh perimeter designated as Gray Sector, which wrapped around the eastern end of the runway and continued around the southeastern perimeter of the base. By mid-January, the word was out that they were going to get hit by the North Vietnamese, and it was going to be big.

Now, O'Hara and about a dozen men from Bravo Company crouched in the darkness south of the base perimeter wire, waiting for enemy soldiers to walk into their trap. Squad leader Quiles Ray Jacobs, from Compton, California, scanned the low hills ahead through an AN/PVS-2 Starlight scope. A large group of enemy soldiers came into focus in the scope's greenish light: they were hard at work, digging mortar pits. Jacobs radioed the information back to base, and a terse response hissed over the radio: get back ASAP.[4]

They made it back safely, and O'Hara returned to the tent he shared with several other Marines. He stretched out on his cot, worn out by the months of hill duty and a recent bout of dysentery he had contracted after drinking untreated water during a patrol. But he was still keyed up by the ambush duty, and sleep did not come easily.

O'Hara had finally drifted off when he awoke abruptly to the sound of explosions.[5] Groggy and confused, he heard what sounded like bedsheets being ripped. A surge of adrenalin cleared his head, and he realized he was hearing artillery shrapnel tearing through his tent. Grabbing his shotgun, O'Hara bolted outside. At the tent entrance, he collided head-on with another Marine, and they fell to the ground—O'Hara unhurt, the other Marine torn into pieces by an enemy shell. O'Hara dived headlong into the nearest trench.

Every Marine at Khe Sanh had been instructed to find his fighting position and be ready to repel an enemy ground assault in the event of an enemy bombardment. Now, O'Hara and other Marines up and down the line huddled in the trench, paralyzed by fear. Shells and rockets shook the earth, tossing the terrified Americans off the ground and slamming them into the trench walls. Nothing in the John Wayne movies had prepared them for this.[6]

• • •

At 5:30 a.m., Tom Quigley was in the Bravo Company command bunker, nearing the end of his overnight radio watch. The nineteen-year-old corporal was signing his name to a letter he had written a friend when two booms sounded in the distance.

Captain Ken Pipes, the Bravo commander, sat up on his cot. "Was that incoming?" he asked.[7]

"Hell no, captain," drawled an old sergeant from Georgia.

The words had barely left the sergeant's mouth when two explosions crashed outside the bunker.

Rounds fired from North Vietnamese rocket batteries and artillery positioned as far away as Co Roc massif in Laos, eight miles to the west, quickly took out key installations across the base. One NVA round scored a direct hit on the main ammunition dump, detonating shells, grenades, small-arms rounds, and tear gas in spectacular fashion and unleashing secondary explosions that would continue for two days.[8]

Not far from Quigley, Michael O'Hara lay in the trench line as artillery shells and rockets rained down. He felt a sharp pain in his buttocks and looked up to see Corporal Ron Ryan, a big redhead with a handlebar mustache, poised to give him another kick. "Get up and man your position!" Ryan yelled.[9] The M-60 machine gunner in O'Hara's area, Ryan seemed oblivious to the shells as he coolly walked the trench, delivering well-placed kicks to get other frightened Marines on their feet and ready to resist the expected enemy ground assault.

After pulling first watch on the Bravo lines the night before, Lance Corporal Ken Rodgers, a twenty-one-year-old from Casa Grande, Arizona, had slept soundly until the opening rounds jolted him awake. He heard somebody yelling "incoming!" and scrambled into the trench. He was lying on his stomach when something thumped into his back. "I'm hit!" Rodgers yelled.

A Marine who ran to his aid burst into laughter. "They're just dirt clods," he said. "Get up!"[10]

Twenty-two-year-old Navy corpsman John Cicala of Detroit, Michigan, had been running through the trench toward the screams of wounded Marines when everything went black. He awoke on his back and heard someone shout, "Where the fuck is that corpsman?"[11] Cicala felt around in the dark and found his steel-pot helmet. Embedded in it were the fins of a mortar round. Cicala slapped the helmet on his head and hurried toward the screams.

He would forever remember the first man he treated that morning, a young Marine named Jimmy Kirk, whose name and face were etched into his memory because it was the most horrific injury that Cicala had yet encountered in Vietnam. The explosion of the ammo dump had nearly sheared off one of Kirk's legs below the knee. Cicala stanched the bleeding as best he could and swathed the torn limb in a battle dressing before moving on to the next wounded Marine.

Tear gas from the burning ammunition dump soon enveloped the Bravo command bunker, and radioman Tom Quigley now paid the price for having left his gas mask in his tent. Amid his tears, he could hear the terrifying sound of shrapnel shredding the air. Rounds hit closer and closer to the command post. Captain Pipes finally ordered everyone in the bunker to head for the trenches. In the frantic scramble, Quigley got his cartridge belt tangled in a communications wire, and when he finally freed himself, he slithered into a mortar pit.[12]

For the next hour, a handful of frightened Marines crouched in the pit, surrounded by artillery shells. Convinced they were dead men regardless, the men carelessly lit cigarettes and puffed away, flicking their ashes into a shell case. When the enemy fire briefly eased, Quigley and his companions piled into their trench line and waited for the enemy to hit the wire.[13]

• • •

Along the southern edge of the Khe Sanh runway, Navy doctor Edward Feldman was fast asleep in his tent when the attack began. He knew he needed to get to the aid station of the 1st Battalion, 26th Marines, to treat casualties, but his hands shook so badly that he couldn't tie his boots.[14]

Feldman had grown up in midtown Manhattan in New York City, where his father was a manager at a local textile mill and his mother taught school. His comfortable childhood was made even happier by the fact that Manhattan's frequent military parades rolled right past his doorstep. His young imagination was fired by the sight of soldiers and sailors strutting past to pounding drums and the stirring strains of Sousa marches. When he wasn't cheering parades, he loved to watch war movies over and over again at a neighborhood theater.

When he was fourteen, Feldman moved with his family out to the leafy Forest Hills neighborhood in Queens. He graduated from high school in 1958 and earned a pharmacy degree from Columbia University four years later. He thought about seeking a Marine Corps commission but instead married his high school sweetheart and entered medical school in Kansas City, Missouri. In 1966, he graduated as a doctor of osteopathy and began a yearlong internship in Detroit, Michigan.

Feldman found it difficult to focus on his medical career with the United States at war in Southeast Asia, so he entered the Navy as a lieutenant in August 1967 and began hounding a Pentagon contact for an assignment to Vietnam. Feldman's orders came through in November, and eight days before Christmas, he arrived in Da Nang. Before the day was out, he was patching up wounded Marines at a field hospital in Phu Bai. On January 3, 1968, he flew to Khe Sanh to take up a temporary assignment as surgeon for the 1st Battalion of the 26th Marines.

Now, as the barrage of enemy shells merged into an ear-splitting roar,

Feldman finally got his boots tied, grabbed his M-16 and gas mask, and pulled aside the Army blanket that served as the blackout curtain for his tent. Two steps outside was a smoking shell hole the size of a small car. Fifty feet away, the battalion aid station was a pile of fire and rubble.

Feldman sprinted toward the casualty holding bunker, which had been hit but was still usable. The eight Navy corpsmen and three Marine runners on his team were already inside. While some of the corpsmen salvaged supplies from the burning tents, Feldman and the others tended to Marines with shrapnel wounds and cuts from flying debris.

A few minutes later, several Marines arrived with a wounded comrade. Feldman examined the injured Marine and found what looked like a metal pipe protruding from his abdomen. It was the fuse assembly of a mortar round, and it had plunged into the side of Private First Class Robert Mussari without exploding.

Feldman and the Marines carried Mussari to a far corner of the bunker and erected a small blast wall of sandbags around him. Feldman started an intravenous drip and struck up a conversation with Mussari, a nineteen-year-old from Scranton, Pennsylvania, to keep him calm and still. "You're going to be fine," the surgeon assured the injured Marine, far from certain whether he could make good on that promise.[15]

Feldman removed his flak jacket to free his movements and took off his helmet so it wouldn't fall on the wounded Marine or the mortar round. Electric power had been knocked out by the enemy barrage, so Navy corpsman Roger Tillotson taped together four flashlights and held them over the patient as Feldman prepared to begin the operation. There was no time to find surgical gloves in all the rubble, and Feldman couldn't use a scalpel or other surgical instruments—metal-on-metal contact might detonate the round. He would have to do the operation with his bare fingers.

Slowly stretching his body over the blast wall until he could touch Mussari, Feldman placed his fingers around the cylindrical fuse assembly and gently worked his way deeper into the Marine's torn abdomen, carefully freeing cauterized tissue and blood vessels. After fifteen minutes of work, Feldman felt the projectile's rounded nose. He made sure he had separated all the surrounding tissue, then gently held Mussari's intestines in place while a Marine staff sergeant, thirty-year-old Ronald

Sniegowski, slowly lifted the fuse assembly from the patient's body. As Sniegowski gingerly carried the explosive projectile outside for disposal, Feldman packed the wound with gauze.

Dawn was breaking as Bobby Mussari was loaded onto an all-terrain vehicle and driven to the base hospital, Charlie Med, to join the growing queue of wounded Marines awaiting evacuation. Edward Feldman returned to the work of patching up injured Marines, caring for another sixty men before the day was out.[16]

• • •

On the eastern perimeter, Lance Corporal Ken Rodgers had pulled himself together after his brush with the dirt clods and was dispatched down the trench line to check on Bravo's 1st Platoon by the ammo dump that had exploded. He was shocked by the almost surreal scene that appeared through the distorted lens of his gas mask. Unexploded artillery shells, bullets, and other debris littered the trench line and covered the Marines who had sought shelter there. Some of the men had suffered deep cuts, abrasions, and broken bones from big 155-millimeter rounds that had been hurled from the dump and dropped onto them where they lay.[17]

Over at Charlie Med, wounded India Company squad leader Ken Warner had reacted to the opening salvo by grabbing the badly injured comrade he had saved on 881 North the previous day and pulling him into the closest trench.[18]

Ambulance driver Dan Sullivan was searching for casualties around the burning ammunition dump when a howitzer round flung through the air by a secondary explosion smashed into his ambulance and blew up. The explosion shredded all four tires, shattered the windshield, and spattered Sullivan's flak jacket with shrapnel, but the twenty-year-old from Roxbury, Massachusetts, was unhurt. Sullivan, who was already on his second tour in Vietnam, spent the rest of the morning picking up wounded and dead Marines.[19]

On the south side of the runway, the men of Bravo Company, 3rd Recon, were on standby to plug any breach in the Khe Sanh perimeter.[20] Ray Milligan had been in many tight spots on recon missions, but he had never felt such penetrating fear as he did during the opening NVA barrage. He huddled in a bunker with his comrades, head between his legs, waiting to get blown to pieces.[21]

Over in the southwest corner of the base, 4.2-inch mortar crewman Billy Joe Hill awoke to the shriek of incoming rocket and artillery rounds. He and the other men assigned to artillery and mortar units took their positions in gun pits around the base and began to fire at suspected enemy positions.[22]

Second Lieutenant William Smith Jr., twenty-four years old, had just gone into his sleeping bunker for a nap when the North Vietnamese artillery and rockets hit the base. As the fire support coordinator for the 1st Battalion, 26th Marines, Smith worked at the side of the battalion commander, Lieutenant Colonel James B. Wilkinson, coordinating artillery and air strikes. His world at Khe Sanh revolved around the 1st Battalion command bunker and his nearby sleeping bunker, a rough affair built from sandbags and scrap wood, christened the Womb.

The sound of the incoming rounds sent Smith and his comrades in the Womb diving to the bunker floor. They grabbed their packs and ran out the door two at a time, crab-sprinting in a low crouch to the 1st Battalion command bunker, about forty yards away. When it was his turn, Smith bolted down the dirt street for the battalion command post. He was looking to the east, toward Ammo Dump No. 1, when he saw what looked like a greenish-yellow tsunami rushing toward him. It was the shock wave from the dump as it exploded. The force hurled Smith through the air, and he came to rest against a tent stake. Shaken but unhurt, he jumped up and sprinted the final yards to the command bunker.

The atmosphere inside was one of controlled chaos as the battalion staff tried to gather situation reports and preliminary casualty figures. Radios crackled and hissed with reports from platoon leaders and company commanders. Everyone assumed that the enemy barrage was prep fire for a ground attack.[23]

When the NVA assault got rolling, it would be Smith's job to coordinate with the frontline forward observers to call in air strikes and artillery missions on the enemy forces. Smith and his team had preregistered artillery and mortar coordinates so that every platoon and company commander could instantaneously summon precise fire. If Khe

Sanh did get overrun, Smith was poised to make the North Vietnamese pay dearly for the prize.[24]

●　●　●

Near the runway, twenty-one-year-old Navy Seabee Lewis "Sam" Messer of Gardner, Kansas, had spent most of January 20 partying with his buddies. The occasion had been the birthday of one of their fellow Seabees, and they had kept the drunken celebration going through most of the day and well into the night before retiring into their fortified bunker. (The Seabees had two fortified sleeping bunkers; the larger one, known as the Alamo Hilton, was favored by visiting news correspondents.)

Messer was supposed to go on kitchen duty at 5:00 a.m. on the morning of January 21, but the Seabee on watch had awakened him late. He took off down the road to the east toward the chow hall, pulling on his clothes as he ran, knowing he was going to catch hell from the duty sergeant. He was bent low to the ground, tying his boots, when the first rockets screamed from the sky and the air erupted with flying shrapnel, splinters, and debris.[25] Messer dived into the nearest hole.

When he had calmed his nerves, he started working his way back to his fighting hole to get his rifle and await the NVA attack. He would crawl or dart to a hole or section of trench, smoke a cigarette to steel his nerves, and then continue on. It took four hours, but he finally made it back to his comrades.[26]

●　●　●

Over in the Bravo Company, 1/26, sector Corporal Steve Wiese, nineteen, a speedy track and football athlete back home in Redlands, California, had been through enough firefights and artillery barrages to know what was coming next: the NVA would break from cover and charge the wire. Waiting for that moment was worse than enduring the incoming artillery. When the enemy barrage finally tapered off after a couple of hours, Wiese yelled at his buddies to get ready.[27]

The Marines peered out through the smoke and dust and last traces of fog, searching for the first wave of North Vietnamese assault troops. Thirty minutes passed, then an hour, still without any sign of an NVA attack.

The Americans began to cautiously emerge from their trenches and bunkers. Remarkably, the 1st Battalion, 26th Marines, reported only one man killed and thirty-eight wounded in the barrage. While officers prepared casualty reports and damage assessments, teams of Marines armed with garden rakes removed a three-inch layer of shrapnel from the area near the ammunition dump.[28] Others filled sandbags, deepened trenches and fighting holes, and shored up bunkers with sandbags and runway matting. Sam Messer and other Seabees went to work patching holes in the aluminum runway to allow transports to land with badly needed ammunition and supplies. As the men worked, ordnance from the burning ammo dump whined and exploded, fraying already raw nerves.

Sporadic NVA shelling resumed, and the Marines again piled into their trenches and bunkers. The pattern would be repeated throughout the day, and the days that followed.

Over in the Bravo Company, 1/26, lines, Steve Wiese remained vigilant for the North Vietnamese assault. He felt the nervous anticipation each time the latest round of enemy shelling stopped, and he kept scanning the edge of the jungle for any sign of the enemy charge. They were out there, and they were going to strike. Wiese and his comrades at Khe Sanh were now certain of that.[29]

CHAPTER 4

Khe Sanh Village

After weeks of stealth and subterfuge aimed at avoiding contact with the Americans, several thousand North Vietnamese soldiers in the vicinity of Khe Sanh Combat Base burst from their concealed bivouacs during the long night of January 20–21. Among the NVA troops on the move were the six hundred soldiers of the 66th Regiment of the 304th Division, a storied unit that had fought the North Vietnamese Army's first full-blown battle against the Americans at the Ia Drang Valley in November 1965. Now, moving through the fog and darkness around Khe Sanh in the early hours of January 21, they prepared to attack the Saigon government's Huong Hoa district headquarters, three miles south of the combat base, in the village of Khe Sanh.

The North Vietnamese troops assigned to attack Khe Sanh village—members of the 66th Regiment's 7th Battalion—were running late. It was a portentous development, for every minute of delay increased the likelihood that daylight would arrive before they could overrun the 175 Americans, South Vietnamese, and Bru tribesmen defending the fortified district compound. Hard experience had taught the North Vietnamese the inherent risks in a daylight challenge to the Americans, when their adversary's formidable artillery and aircraft could be fully marshaled. Every man and woman wearing the uniform of the North Vietnamese Army had learned to fear US airpower, especially the B-52 bombers that stalked the skies miles above them—unseen and unheard until the jungles erupted in apocalyptic fire and explosions. For those directly beneath the Arc Lights, as the Americans called their B-52 strikes, it would be as though they never existed. Those fortunate enough to find themselves at the edge of the blast radius would emerge from the cataclysm with blood pouring from ears and noses.[1]

The men of the 7th Battalion had narrowly avoided such a fate only the previous day. Just before the North Vietnamese soldiers began the final leg of their march to Khe Sanh village at midday of January 20, US B-52 bombers had carried out an Arc Light strike in their path. Entering the target box soon afterward, the 7th Battalion troops found a landscape of shattered trees and scorched earth, devoid of landmarks and trails. It was hard slogging through the jumbled earth and debris, and "many elements became lost."[2] Nightfall found the troops miles from their staging points, slowed even further by the thickening fog.

At 4:00 a.m., forty-five minutes before the attack on the district headquarters at Khe Sanh was to get underway, blocking forces were still getting into position. Precious minutes were lost while an NVA platoon slipped through the jungle north of Route 9, past a Bru hamlet of straw-thatched huts, and took up positions on Hill 471, about a mile south of the American base. Other NVA forces had been moving into position to ambush any attempt to reinforce the district headquarters once the attack began: one platoon was lying in wait at the junction of Route 9 and the access road to the base, near an old French fort that the US Special Forces had occupied until a few months earlier; another NVA platoon had prepared an ambush along Route 9 west of the village.[3]

A few minutes past 5:00 a.m., the morning calm was shattered by the sound of artillery rounds and rockets leaving their tubes, followed by muffled explosions from the direction of the main American stronghold. The bombardment of Khe Sanh Combat Base was underway, yet the soldiers of the NVA 7th Battalion were still not quite ready.

Around 5:30 a.m., the lead elements of the North Vietnamese assault force triggered trip flares along the western edge of the district headquarters complex. The darkness erupted with the ear-splitting explosions of mortars and rocket-propelled grenades, and the rattle of machine guns and automatic rifles.[4] The men of the NVA 7th Battalion surged toward the perimeter wire of the Khe Sanh village compound.

• • •

Captain Bruce B. G. Clarke of the US Army reacted instinctively when the trip flares erupted a few paces west of his command bunker inside the district compound: he grabbed a radio, got Khe Sanh Combat Base on the line, and began calling out preregistered artillery coordinates.[5] Before long, "variable timed" rounds fired by Marine artillery batteries at the base began detonating about twenty feet above the North Vietnamese troops who now swarmed the district compound's western perimeter.

A 1965 West Point graduate from Kansas, five days shy of his twenty-fifth birthday, Clarke led a four-man US Army advisory team assigned to Huong Hoa district headquarters. He and his team shared the compound with about twenty-five US Marines, seventy-five Bru tribal militiamen, and about seventy Vietnamese officers and soldiers—all nominally under the command of Clarke's counterpart, the Huong Hoa district chief, South Vietnamese Army captain Tinh A-Nhi.[6]

Near the front of the compound, Clarke's team members quickly determined that they were under heavy fire from a Buddhist pagoda just outside the western perimeter wire. Sergeant First Class Jim Perry, an Army medic who had worked at Walter Reed Army Hospital in Washington, DC, before deploying to Vietnam, blasted away at the pagoda with an Al Capone–era Thompson submachine gun.[7]

From trenches and bunkers around the compound's northern end, Marines and Bru fighters fired at muzzle blasts and silhouettes briefly illuminated by shell bursts.[8] The Marines were members of Combined Action Company (CAC) Oscar, the creation of a special counterinsurgency program in which Marine squads functioned like Army Special Forces A-teams. The Khe Sanh village contingent was commanded by a Marine mustang, First Lieutenant Thomas G. Stamper, and its forces were spread thin among three locations: the Oscar-1 platoon and headquarters detachment was based inside the district compound; Oscar-2 was dug in roughly 200 yards to the west along Route 9; and Oscar-3 was located in a Bru hamlet between the village and the combat base.

While the American and Bru forces battled the main North Vietnamese assault along the western perimeter, Captain Nhi's militiamen turned back a threat from the east mounted by NVA soldiers who slipped through a coffee plantation and took cover behind a US Agency for International Development food warehouse. From a concealed bunker atop the warehouse, Nhi's men broke the attack by dropping grenades onto the unsuspecting North Vietnamese soldiers.[9]

Other NVA soldiers fired on the compound from across Route 9, from a restaurant the Americans had wryly nicknamed Howard Johnson's. Small groups of enemy troops charged across the highway toward the northern perimeter, only to be killed by an M-60 machine gun manned by Corporal Verner R. Russell, a Marine from Poplar Bluff, Missouri.[10]

For ninety minutes, the North Vietnamese pounded and probed, but the compound's defenders held firm as night gave way to a gray dawn.

• • •

Along the western perimeter, Corporal Howard McKinnis, a twenty-year-old Oklahoman who had dropped out of college to join the Marine Corps, was peering into the swirling fog, searching for targets, when an explosion knocked him to the bottom of his trench. A high-explosive artillery round had nearly taken him out.[11]

McKinnis jumped to his feet, ready to fight off a wave of North Vietnamese attackers, but all he could see was swirling fog. A quick check revealed that his limbs were intact and he had suffered nothing worse than a "damn good headache."[12] His two Bru comrades weren't as lucky: one was dead, the other bleeding from shrapnel in his knee.

Sergeant John Balanco, a twenty-two-year-old Marine from Oakland, California, dropped into the fighting hole and announced that enemy troops were pressuring Captain Nhi's forces in an old earthen fort that anchored the compound's southern defenses. Could McKinnis lend a hand? McKinnis fell in behind Balanco, and they darted off through the maze of bunkers and trenches. Another Marine, Lance Corporal C. E. "Butch" Still, joined them, and the trio of Americans dashed into the triangle-shaped fort held by sixty frightened soldiers of the South Vietnamese 915th Regional Force.

McKinnis had barely settled into the western trench when at least a hundred North Vietnamese soldiers burst from a tree line about eighty yards away. McKinnis fired in short bursts, sometimes flipping to full automatic when he spotted several enemy soldiers bunched together. The NVA fighters fired from the hip as they ran, not pausing to aim. They closed on the fort as the defenders emptied their magazines, reloaded, and emptied them again. At thirty feet out, only a few enemy soldiers remained on their feet. And then, just shy of the fort, the last one fell.[13]

• • •

On the western fringe of Khe Sanh village, the men of Oscar-2—a Marine sergeant, eleven Marine riflemen, ten Bru Popular Force militiamen, and a Navy corpsman—were engaged in their own desperate fight for survival.

Among the unlikely warriors was an aspiring Southern Baptist preacher from the Texas Panhandle, twenty-four-year-old Navy corpsman John Roberts. On his first full day in Vietnam in July 1967, Roberts was nearly blown up during an enemy artillery barrage. On his second day, the truck driver who was taking Roberts and some Marines up Route 9 to Khe Sanh fell asleep and ran off the road. Roberts broke some ribs but continued on to the Marine combat base, where another truck shuttled him to the outskirts of Khe Sanh village. There Roberts found the Marines of CAC Oscar-2 saddling up for a patrol. Grab your medical bag, doc, he was told, and so he did. By the time he straggled back into camp later that afternoon, Roberts had discovered that Vietnam's emerald jungles weren't nearly as enchanting as they appeared from the air.[14]

Roberts did not adapt easily to his new life as a combat corpsman. He lost weight, lived in fear of being maimed, captured, or killed, and pined for his wife and unborn child back in Texas. During a supply run to Khe Sanh Combat Base, he sought out Protestant chaplain Ray Stubbe, and they talked and prayed. The Communists can kill your body, Stubbe counseled, but they can't kill your spirit. Roberts returned to Khe Sanh village at peace with himself and his situation, and threw himself into his perilous work.

Now, as gunfire and explosions shattered the darkness around him, Roberts heard the cry "Corpsman up!" and rushed to the Oscar-2 command bunker. Sergeant Roy Harper had been peering into the darkness through his firing port when a Communist RPG round had exploded and a piece of shrapnel had sliced into his face. Roberts found the Oscar-2 commander bathed in blood, with his eyeball dangling on his cheek. The corpsman carefully put the eyeball back in its socket and applied a pressure bandage, and Harper rejoined the fight.

Another Oscar-2 Marine, Corporal Dan Sullivan, shook off the concussion of an exploding enemy round and began returning fire with his M-16 rifle. He emptied one magazine, then another and another. When the rifle jammed, he switched to a Browning Automatic Rifle.[15]

Communist assault troops closed on the outpost, elusive shapes in the half-light of explosions and muzzle flashes. A Marine private first class exposed himself to enemy fire to hurl grenades and curses at the charging North Vietnamese. At one point, Roberts came almost face-to-face with an enemy fighter charging the wire. Squeezing a long burst from his M-16, Roberts nearly cut the man in two.[16]

After two hours of fighting, the men of Oscar-2 were running low on ammunition, and most had suffered at least superficial shrapnel wounds from grenades and RPGs. But the arrival of daylight seemed to spook the enemy troops. They fell back, leaving behind the bodies of dozens of comrades, torn and bloodied forms, tangled in the perimeter wire and scattered across the ground beyond.[17]

•   •   •

The initial North Vietnamese attacks on the district compound and the Oscar-2 outpost had failed. The remnants of the 7th Battalion had faded back into clumps of trees and jungle to tend to their wounded and await reinforcements.

Inside the district compound, Jim Perry, the advisory team medic, had transformed his bunker at the front of the headquarters building into a medical station. He had braved enemy fire to treat the wounded, carrying the most seriously injured back to his bunker.[18] Captain Bruce Clarke chain-smoked unfiltered Camel cigarettes while continuing to call in artillery strikes. Sergeant John Balanco had shrugged off multiple shrapnel wounds to continue with his rounds, surviving several near misses with the incoming RPG and mortar fire as he delivered ammunition and encouragement to the compound's defenders.

Late in the morning, Clarke made his way to the compound's southern sector to check the defenses in the area where Howard McKinnis had helped fight off an enemy charge. Clarke slipped inside an unmanned bunker and peered out just in time to see a North Vietnamese sapper crawling toward the perimeter wire in front of him. The sapper had a long pole with a block of explosives attached to the end. The Army captain pointed his sawed-off M-79 grenade launcher at the man and squeezed the trigger. A flechette round packed with steel darts ripped the enemy soldier in two.[19]

Around midday, the skies over Khe Sanh village had cleared just enough for a Marine forward air controller (FAC) to make his way to the battlefield in a small spotter plane. Two flights of jets followed, unleashing bombs and napalm on a tree line sheltering NVA soldiers.[20] But just as suddenly as he had appeared, the Marine FAC flew off. "Sorry," he radioed Clarke. "That's all I can do for you."[21]

Clarke relayed an urgent appeal to his boss, Robert Brewer, the senior Military Assistance Command, Vietnam (MACV) provincial adviser in Quang Tri City, thirty miles to the east. (Brewer's position was a cover for his activities as a CIA operative.) About half an hour later, a tiny Cessna O-1E "Bird Dog" spotter plane appeared over Khe Sanh village. In the cockpit was Captain Ward Britt, a US Air Force forward air controller who had picked his way through a maze of peaks and valleys to reach the battlefield.

For the remainder of the afternoon, Britt diverted aircraft from missions along the Ho Chi Minh Trail to attack targets around the embattled outpost.[22] Flying below the minimum ceiling—a risk the fighter pilots were not required to take—a succession of jets dropped bombs and napalm on targets that Britt had marked with white phosphorus rockets or smoke grenades he tossed out of his cockpit window.[23]

In the district compound's command bunker, Captain Nhi relayed radio intercepts about Communist reinforcements on the way, which Clarke promptly forwarded to Britt. One such North Vietnamese radio transmission included an urgent plea for a full company of medics and stretcher bearers.[24] With each new report, Britt would bank to the southwest and circle the area, braving nearly constant ground fire, until he found the enemy troops advancing toward the village. In minutes, a new flight of American aircraft would arrive and eliminate the threat, buying a little more time for the defenders of Khe Sanh village.[25]

• • •

By late afternoon, the situation inside the district compound was grim. Ammunition and medical supplies were running low, and some eleven South Vietnamese and Bru fighters were dead and twenty-nine wounded. Even worse, NVA reinforcements were on the way to deliver the coup de grâce.

Captain Clarke and Lieutenant Stamper had begun asking the Marine combat base for reinforcements and ammunition around midday, but heavy enemy fire had prevented helicopters from landing. One had managed to pass over the compound and push out a couple of boxes of ammunition for the M-1 and M-2 rifles carried by the indigenous forces, but that was it.

Under a standing contingency plan, Colonel David Lownds had dispatched reinforcements from Khe Sanh Combat base, but the Marines had been recalled before reaching the village because of fears of an NVA ambush. Intent on conserving forces to defend the base, the Marines had made a cold-blooded decision: the defenders of Khe Sanh village were on their own.

Bruce Clarke's boss, Quang Tri Province senior adviser Robert Brewer, began working his considerable contacts to resupply the embattled district compound, with mixed results. One chopper managed to offload ammunition and supplies while braving heavy NVA fire coming and going, but four other attempts were driven away. Brewer's deputy, Lieutenant Colonel Joseph Seymoe, a forty-one-year-old West Pointer from Waco, Texas, volunteered to lead a combat assault that would deliver supplies and fifty South Vietnamese soldiers. Late in the afternoon, ten helicopters of the 282nd Assault Helicopter Company—the Black Cats—headed west from Quang Tri: five loaded with troops; two bearing ammunition, medical supplies, and water; and three Huey gunships acting as heavily armed escorts.

In the fading light, twenty-year-old pilot Gerald "Mac" McKinsey eased the lead helicopter inside an old French fort at the junction of Route 9 and the access road to Khe Sanh Combat Base, about three-fourths of a mile east of the village. As the skids touched the ground, a platoon of North Vietnamese troops burst from camouflaged holes and opened fire.

McKinsey had gotten his aircraft about ten feet off the ground and was nosing forward when an NVA squad leader, Tran Dinh Ky, rose to his feet and fired an RPG. The rocket slammed into the chopper's midsection, and the aircraft plunged to the ground and came to a rest upside down at the base of the hill. McKinsey and the flight commander, Captain Tommy Stiner, escaped through the shattered windshield, but the mission commander, Lieutenant Colonel Seymoe, was pinned in the chopper's twisted carcass. There was no sign of the crew chief or gunner.[26]

As NVA troops headed down the slope toward the crash site, two trailing Hueys landed near the burning wreckage and three men jumped off to aid their comrades. The first Huey took off after recovering Stiner's crew chief. The second aircraft quickly abandoned the rescue and lifted off, leaving behind gunner Jerry Elliott. He was never seen again.[27]

Enemy troops closed on the downed helicopter, and McKinsey fell mortally wounded with a bullet to the head. After concluding that Seymoe was dead, Stiner and a crewman from one of the Hueys, Danny Williams, made a run for it. The two Americans made it to the Oscar-3 outpost near the combat base after a harrowing all-night trek.[28]

Back at the Khe Sanh village compound, Captain Bruce Clarke received a terse update on the relief expedition. "We didn't get the troops on the ground," one of the pilots of the aborted mission radioed, with no elaboration on the disaster that had just unfolded. "We're gone."[29]

• • •

In the command bunker of the 26th Marines, radio operator Steve Orr, from Sacramento, California, had followed the unfolding drama in Khe Sanh village with growing horror. Orr's best friend, Michael Archer, from Oakland, California, was in the Huong Hoa district compound as one of the temporary radio operators who rotated from the combat base every few days to help out Lieutenant Stamper at CAC Oscar. Orr and another comrade had been next in line to replace Archer and radioman Steve Tidwell, and now he feared he would never see his friends again. He had spoken on the radio with Archer several times during the day, and Archer had kept asking whether relief was on the way. "Yeah, yeah, we're going to come get you," Orr had assured his friend. Now, after overhearing Colonel Lownds and Lieutenant Colonel James Wilkinson, commander of the 1/26, make their fateful decision to recall the relief force, Orr didn't have the heart to tell his friends that help wasn't coming.[30]

• • •

As the battle for Khe Sanh village continued throughout the day, the Marines on Hill 861 braced for another NVA attack. The mangled bodies of North Vietnamese soldiers lay scattered around the hill. Others lay tangled in the perimeter wire or crumpled in the cleared areas beyond. A patrol that ventured outside the wire found more dead soldiers, piles of bloody bandages, and blood trails into the jungle.[31]

Around midday, the fog had finally cleared and helicopters arrived with crates of ammunition, medical supplies, and reinforcements. Dead and wounded Americans were loaded aboard for the return flight to the combat base. Among the living were Captain Norman Jasper and Sergeant Major Tom Goddard, still holding his perforated carotid artery to keep from bleeding to death, as well as six or seven North Vietnamese prisoners, all wounded and so small that two had been strapped to each stretcher.[32]

Among the new arrivals was a pair of young Navy corpsmen, both in-country barely a month. Larry LeClaire, twenty-one, hailed from New Orleans, Louisiana; his friend Christian Feit, twenty, was from the tiny borough of Smethport in the rugged hills of northern Pennsylvania. As LeClaire and Feit ran down the ramp of a CH-34 helicopter, Marines yelled, "Get in the trench! Get in the trench!" The corpsmen dashed into a slit in the ground flanked by crates of mortar shells.[33]

A group of Marines arrived at the LZ with a dead comrade wrapped in a poncho liner. As the somber procession passed, Gunnery Sergeant Melvin Rimel's arm slipped out from beneath the liner. LeClaire's eyes were drawn to the big Marine's left hand, and the wedding band that glistened on his finger.[34]

• • •

Throughout the day, Americans at the combat base and the hill outposts had spotted NVA troops moving about with impunity, setting up mortars, sniping, shelling. Every arriving aircraft at the base drew enemy fire, as did the mere sight of two or more Marines.[35]

Darkness brought fears of an enemy human-wave assault. The defenders of 881 South reported heavy movement north of the hill. At the base, jittery Marines of Lima Company, 3/26, opened fire on an enemy unit moving near their position west of the runway.[36]

Around 11:00 p.m., Bill Dabney's Marines on 881 South were hit by automatic weapons and mortar fire, and an enemy ground assault seemed at hand. At 11:30 p.m., an illumination round burst over the hill, another harbinger of a North Vietnamese attack, or so it seemed. But midnight came and went without an assault, and the weary Marines could only wait.

• • •

At the Marine Oscar-2 outpost on the western outskirts of Khe Sanh village, hopes of holding off another assault had faded. The small band of Marines and corpsman John Roberts had resolved to kill as many North Vietnamese as they could before dying.[37]

But fortune smiled on the Americans when the nightly fog failed to arrive. In the starlit skies, a Douglas AC-47 gunship—the vaunted Spooky—arrived to keep watch over the embattled defenders of Khe Sanh village. The aircraft crew dropped illumination flares that exposed North Vietnamese forces as they massed for an attack and then proceeded to slaughter the enemy soldiers with their moaning miniguns.

On the ground, the defenders watched the awesome spectacle and awaited the North Vietnamese. A sparring match ensued, with Captain Clarke calling in an artillery mission for each sniper round fired in their direction. At one point, the ground shook and the southern sky flashed as a flight of B-52 bombers unleashed an Arc Light strike on NVA forces moving north to join the battle.[38]

• • •

Dawn broke clear and crisp over Khe Sanh village on Monday, January 22. The weary defenders had remained in their fighting holes, bunkers, and trenches throughout the night, guns and grenades at the ready, but the North Vietnamese attack never came.

Sunrise had raised spirits, but uncertainty still hung over the compound. Nothing had been heard from the Oscar-2 outpost for hours. As the bleary-eyed soldiers at the district headquarters maintained their vigil, a commotion swept the lines. A formation of armed men came into sight, approaching the compound from the west, along Route 9.

There were shouts, unintelligible at first before the words could be made out. "Don't fire! We're coming in!"[39] It was the Marines of Oscar-2.

The front gate was flung open, and the defenders of the district compound welcomed the bloodied Marines and Bru fighters.

The uncontested movement of the Oscar-2 force raised the question: Where were the North Vietnamese? Patrols slipped out of the compound and found shocking scenes of carnage: there were a hundred or more dead enemy soldiers, blood trails, and scores of abandoned weapons. While patrols searched for the North Vietnamese, a UH-34 chopper from Marine Medium Helicopter Squadron 362 (HMM-362), the "Ugly Angels," evacuated thirty-eight wounded men in seven shuttle flights to the combat base.[40]

The safe passage of the Oscar-2 Marines and the discovery of the North Vietnamese pullback had unleashed jubilation among the defenders of Khe Sanh village.[41] But a pair of radio transmissions quickly shattered the mood. Colonel Lownds informed Captain Clarke that the compound had been deemed indefensible, so the Marines would no longer provide artillery support—a death sentence for Clarke and his men if they stayed.[42] Around the same time, Sergeant Balanco was ordered to prepare the CAC Oscar Marines for evacuation—without their Bru fighters. Later that morning, the Marines boarded helicopters that ferried them back to the base.[43]

After much agonized discussion between the senior provincial adviser, Robert Brewer, and his South Vietnamese counterpart, Quang Tri Province chief General Ngo Quang Truong, Clarke was ordered to evacuate the district headquarters.[44]

Refusing a seat on an evacuation helicopter, Clarke organized an orderly withdrawal to Khe Sanh Combat Base with Captain Nhi and his South Vietnamese and Bru fighters. The column passed through an area teeming with North Vietnamese troops and marched into the Special Forces compound without the loss of a single man.

In the fight for Khe Sanh village, the vaunted NVA 66th Regiment had suffered 154 killed and 486 wounded, among them the commander of the 7th Battalion.[45] Twelve South Vietnamese soldiers and seven Bru had been killed and twenty-five wounded. Miraculously, not a single American died in the battle.

As night fell on January 22, NVA troops claimed the district headquarters compound that they had failed to take in battle. It was a bitter turn of events for Bruce Clarke and his Army comrades at Forward Operating Base 3 (FOB-3) along the southwestern perimeter of Khe Sanh Combat Base. The fall of the first district government in South Vietnam had damaged the prestige of the Saigon government and its American backers, and it put the Special Forces camp at Lang Vei, along Route 9 west of Khe Sanh, in an untenable position. But the American lines of defense at Khe Sanh had been tightened, and for a badly outnumbered force, the consolidation made tactical sense.

General William Westmoreland had placed a high-risk bet that American artillery and air power would save the Marines at Khe Sanh, even in a confrontation with a much larger enemy force. Now, with the opening engagements concluded, General Vo Nguyen Giap and the formidable North Vietnamese force that had converged on Khe Sanh were poised to put Westmoreland's gamble to the test.[*]

---

[*] Scholarship over the past decade has revealed General Giap's objections to key elements of the North Vietnamese plan to win the war in 1968. In particular, Giap opposed widespread attacks on South Vietnamese cities—the so-called Tet Offensive—but was overruled by Communist Party leader Le Duan and other comrades. It is likely no coincidence that Giap sought medical treatment in Hungary in the fall of 1967, and didn't return to Hanoi until early February 1968—after the move against Khe Sanh and the Tet Offensive had begun. See Merle L. Pribbenow II, "General Vo Nguyen Giap and the Mysterious Evolution of the Plan for the 1968 Tet Offensive," *Journal of Vietnamese Studies*, Vol. 3, No. 2 (Summer 2008), pp. 1–33. I have written this account as events were viewed by the American military command and President Johnson: as a showdown with the mastermind of Dien Bien Phu, General Giap. I am grateful to Dr. George C. Herring, Alumni Professor of History Emeritus at the University of Kentucky, for bringing to my attention these revelations.

CHAPTER 5

Muscle Shoals

I n the blue skies over Khe Sanh Combat Base on Monday, January 22, an unfamiliar craft had joined the usual assortment of military transports, spotter planes, and helicopters that plied the crowded air space of Quang Tri Province. An astute observer would have noted that the new arrival was a twin-engine P-2 Neptune, developed for the Navy by Lockheed in World War II, and it was far removed from its usual maritime duty of anti-submarine patrols.

The precise nature of the Neptune's business over Khe Sanh and the reason that its familiar gray-and-white color scheme had been painted jungle-green was a closely guarded military secret. Only a select few in the American chain of command knew that this particular plane was one of a dozen Neptunes that had been plucked from an Arizona boneyard, fitted with old Norden bombsights and given the innocuous designation of Observation Group 67 (VO-67).[1] Fewer still knew that for the past two months, the squadron had been flying out of a remote base in Nakhon Phanom, Thailand, part of a top-secret effort to stem the flow of North Vietnamese troops and supplies to southern battlefields, and that only three days earlier the VO-67 crews had been ordered by America's supreme commander in Vietnam to turn their full attention to the defense of Khe Sanh.[2]

With 20,000 North Vietnamese soldiers now surrounding the 6,000 Americans at Khe Sanh, and another 20,000 enemy troops nearby, General William Westmoreland was marshaling every conceivable weapon for a decisive confrontation. The centerpiece of his plan to deal the North Vietnamese a crippling blow was a coordinated campaign of massive air strikes and artillery missions, a veritable waterfall of destructive power bearing an evocative code name: Operation Niagara.[3]

A myriad of intelligence sources had been tapped to build an exhaustive target list for the campaign. And now, with the help of the low-flying Neptunes of VO-67 and a squadron of CH-3 "Jolly Green Giant" helicopters flying out of the same remote base, Westmoreland aimed to bolster Niagara with a secret weapon nearly two years in the making.

• • •

From the beginning of America's escalation of the war, US commanders had sought to stop North Vietnam from arming and supplying Communist forces in the South. In March 1965, US commanders had launched a systematic bombing campaign—Rolling Thunder—to force an end to North Vietnamese intervention. But even as the bombing expanded to a lengthening list of strategic targets, doubts about the campaign's ultimate success persisted in Washington.[4]

One of Rolling Thunder's early skeptics was US Secretary of Defense Robert McNamara. In early 1966, the former Ford Motor Company president read a deputy's memo that underscored the bombing campaign's mixed results. The memo also noted a proposal by Harvard Law School professor Roger Fisher to build a "border barrier" that would quarantine South Vietnam from Communist infiltration. Despite the misgivings of his military chiefs, McNamara ordered the Army to begin work on a system of "route and trail interdiction devices."[5]

McNamara also asked a group of civilian weapons experts to study the feasibility of a high-tech fence that could block the influx of North Vietnamese troops and supplies. The forty-seven scientists assigned to the project were collectively known as the Jason Division, named for the leader of the Argonauts in Greek mythology. In August, they submitted four reports that highlighted the disappointing bombing results and endorsed construction of an anti-infiltration barrier across northern Laos and South Vietnam. McNamara ordered work on a barrier fence to proceed.

By the fall of 1967, McNamara's "Strong Point Obstacle System" was fast becoming a reality. US Marines in the northern I Corps sector of South Vietnam had occupied a line of outposts that stretched along Route 9, from the coast westward to Khe Sanh. The final piece awaiting deployment was a network of electronic sensors that would allow the Americans to track and destroy North Vietnamese trucks and troops entering South Vietnam.[6] As part of that effort, the United States also embarked on a more sophisticated effort to cut the taproot of the Communist resupply network, the Truong Son Strategic Supply Route in eastern Laos, the series of jungle roads and tracks better known to Americans as the Ho Chi Minh Trail.

In November, twelve Navy crews flying modified P-2 Neptunes arrived at the Royal Thai Air Force base that would serve as nerve center for the clandestine Operation Muscle Shoals (later changed to Igloo White). Known to American covert operators as "the end of the line at the edge of the world," Nakhon Phanom lay in far northeastern Thailand, nine miles from the Mekong River, which formed the border with Laos.[7] The newly arrived crews of VO-67 had been trained to use World War II Norden bombsights to drop camouflaged electronic sensors along infiltration routes.

McNamara's scientists had drawn on naval anti-submarine warfare and oil-industry technology to devise the sensors for Muscle Shoals. Most were cylinder shaped, three to four feet in length, and weighed less than twenty pounds. Radio transmitters would relay sounds and seismic data to an EC-121B aircraft orbiting overhead, which would pass the data to a secret facility in Nakhon Phanom packed with the latest IBM mainframe computers. If everything worked as planned, data analysts in Thailand would be passing real-time information from activated sensors to US operational commanders in South Vietnam—all within thirty to forty-five minutes.[8]

In their first days at Nakhon Phanom, VO-67 pilots familiarized themselves with North Vietnamese infiltration routes and anti-aircraft batteries by flying combat missions with Air Force forward air controllers along the Ho Chi Minh Trail in Laos. Most of the VO-67 pilots had backgrounds similar to that of Commander Adam Alexander, an Ohio native who had joined the Navy after graduating from high school in spring 1948. He had earned his pilot's wings in 1950 and saw six months of combat in Korea as navigator on a PB4Y2, the Navy version of the B-24 bomber. Now thirty-seven years old, with nearly two decades of Navy service, Alexander had never undertaken an assignment so shrouded in mystery as VO-67.[9]

On November 25, the first VO-67 Neptunes took off from Nakhon Phanom to field test the Muscle Shoals program. They began by seeding the jungle with small anti-personnel "gravel" and "button" mines, cracker-size pieces of fabric that exploded on contact and activated acoustic sensors. They also dropped sensors of two varieties: seismic detectors modeled on oil-industry geophones and acoustic devices developed from US Navy anti-submarine sonobuoys.

The microphone-equipped acoustic sensors, known as Acoubuoys, had been designed to drift into the treetops on camouflaged parachutes. The seismic devices—ADSIDs (Air Delivered Seismic Intrusion Detectors)—had a weighted spike on one end and were designed to stick in the ground like a lawn dart. To effectively transmit vibrations from passing trucks or troops, the seismic sensors had to be dropped in carefully plotted strings within thirty feet of the targeted trail or track.

With North Vietnamese truck traffic through eastern Laos soaring by a factor of five in the closing months of 1967, Muscle Shoals had been rushed into the field. It was hardly surprising that "a nightmare of fault[y] detections, analysis, and correction" plagued its early weeks of operation.[10] But the sensors worked—sometimes too well, the analysts discovered, as the devices picked up the sounds of tigers, rock apes, and American air strikes. The glitches were resolved, and by December 7, Muscle Shoals was fully operational in eastern Laos and providing real-time reports for US units.

The successful deployment of the Muscle Shoals sensors could not have come at a better time for General Westmoreland and his plan to engage North Vietnamese forces in a decisive confrontation. On January 19, Westmoreland ordered VO-67 to shift its focus from the Ho Chi Minh Trail to Khe Sanh. The following day, in treetop-level missions, fixed-wing Neptunes and CH-3 helicopters began laying strings of sensors on the approaches to Khe Sanh.[11]

Defense Secretary McNamara and his scientists had envisioned

Muscle Shoals as an anti-infiltration device rather than a tactical weapon in a fluid combat setting. Sensor analysts in Nakhom Phanom were still fine-tuning the best methods for deploying and interpreting the devices as the North Vietnamese forces closed around Khe Sanh.

Now, as the battle got underway, the sensors emerged as a wild card with enormous potential. General Giap had committed three divisions of his finest troops to the move against Khe Sanh in the belief that they could mass and maneuver undetected under the cover of fog and darkness. What if the sensors stripped away that cover and denied North Vietnamese forces their critical advantages in mobility and stealth? General Westmoreland and the small group of Americans privy to the Muscle Shoals program aimed to find out.

CHAPTER 6

The Walking Dead

Khe Sanh's days as a sleepy backwater had ended abruptly with the battles of January 20–21. Now, from Hill 881 South and Lang Vei in the west, to Hill 558 northeast of the combat base, the North Vietnamese went about the work of wearing down and bleeding the Americans. During daylight hours, the North Vietnamese pounded the base and its outposts with artillery, rockets, and mortars and harassed them with snipers. At night, NVA soldiers crept up on listening posts and probed the perimeter wire of the base and outposts, setting off trip flares, cutting wire barriers, tossing grenades, and staging hit-and-run attacks.[1]

In a surreal development for the frazzled Americans atop Hill 861, a Marine Corps field historian armed with a reel-to-reel tape recorder stepped off a resupply chopper the day after the North Vietnamese attack and spent nearly forty minutes conducting interviews with eight men. As fighter jets roared overhead and dropped bombs on the nearby ridgelines, the Marines recalled their experiences in the battle.

Among those telling their stories was the modest machine gunner from Oklahoma, Corporal Billy Ray Moffett, who had risen to the challenge in his first fight, pouring machine-gun rounds into the NVA attackers even as his gun attracted heavy enemy fire. "I was scared shitless," Moffett said softly. "There's no way getting around that. I don't think anybody was as cool as they should have been. It was hell, really."[2]

• • •

At Khe Sanh Combat Base, January 22 had begun with a predawn probe by the North Vietnamese at the western end of the base. Marines of Lima Company, 3/26, had spotted twenty-five to thirty-five North Vietnamese soldiers crawling toward their wire and opened up with M-79 grenade launchers and light anti-tank weapons. When the firing stopped after a few minutes, the NVA force was seen dragging the bodies of comrades off to the southwest.

Groups of North Vietnamese troops, some as large as seventy to ninety men and some carrying large packs, were occasionally spotted moving through clearings and along ridgelines.[3] Along the eastern and southeast perimeter of the American base, the Marines of Bravo Company, 1/26, found themselves in a war of nerves with NVA snipers firing from the surrounding jungle. At one point, a sniper unleashed half a dozen rounds and the Marines responded with automatic weapons and M-79 grenades. When the sniper resumed firing about twenty minutes later, the Marines called in an artillery strike on his suspected position, and the firing stopped.[4]

NVA artillery fire continued to pound away at the command bunker occupied by Colonel David Lownds and his 26th Marines staff. Nearby, a row of plywood-reinforced tents that had housed the base commissary, the post office, and other facilities lay in ruins. The area looked like a ghost town, deserted "except for an occasional man nervously running from one place to another."[5] Around 10:00 a.m., a North Vietnamese artillery round screamed from the sky and exploded outside a regimental communications workshop. When the smoke and dust settled, a pair of twenty-year-old Marines lay dead.[6]

The attack on Khe Sanh village the previous day had triggered a terrified exodus, and Vietnamese and Bru civilians had fled to the combat base with what few belongings they could carry. Lownds had refused entry to the refugees, fearing that enemy soldiers or spies might be among them.

On the morning of January 22, a frightened crowd of about 1,500 Vietnamese and ethnic Bru—young and old; men, women, and children—still huddled at the main gate. Hurried discussions between American and South Vietnamese officials produced an agreement to evacuate the Vietnamese, but not the Bru. The South Vietnamese I Corps commander, General Hoang Xuan Lam, insisted there was no place for the minority refugees, so they were told to return to their homes, now a no-man's-land between the combat base and the converging North Vietnamese troops.[7] The virtual abandonment of the Bru people at Khe Sanh stands as a sordid chapter for the Americans and South Vietnamese, ultimately leading to the deaths of as many as several thousand men, women, and children caught in the escalating battle.

Throughout January 22, transport planes and helicopters landed at the combat base to offload medical supplies and ammunition, flying out with loads of Vietnamese civilians. More than 1,100 noncombatants would be safely evacuated from Khe Sanh in this fashion over the next twenty-four hours. Late in the afternoon, shuttle flights of transport helicopters began to arrive and disgorge ranks of Marines—the men of the 1st Battalion, 9th Marines, rushed to Khe Sanh to bolster its defenses.

Darkness arrived, and the defenders of Khe Sanh once again braced for a ground attack. Shortly after 7:00 p.m., the first nighttime listening-post teams filed outside the perimeter wire, and over the next forty-five minutes, eight other teams of three to five Marines slipped into the bush. Inside the wire, two twenty-five-man reaction forces were briefed and readied for action.[8]

Soon enough the night came alive with the sounds of enemy movements. Around 10:00 p.m., Bravo Company, 1/26, reported seeing lights and hearing "heavy noise" and the "sounds of heavy digging" in front of their lines. Just after 11:00 p.m., a Charlie Company, 1/26, Marine peering through a Starlight scope spotted four North Vietnamese soldiers on his perimeter wire. A friendly artillery illumination round was fired, exposing a small group of NVA soldiers but no larger attack. The Marines opened up with M-16 rifles and an M-79 grenade launcher, and the North Vietnamese soldiers scrambled for cover, leaving behind a dead comrade in the wire.[9] The firing ended, and the tense wait resumed.

• • •

Shortly after 5:00 a.m. on Tuesday, January 23, the weary listening-post teams made their way back inside the base. Daylight patrols were readied to begin the work of checking perimeter wires for cuts or explosives laid by enemy sappers and to locate enemy trenches or signs of an impending attack. Later in the morning, the day's first fixed-wing transports and helicopters began to arrive with pallets of ammunition, medical supplies, and boxes of C-rations. Four large crates addressed to "Fifth Graves Registration Team, Khe Sanh," were also unloaded. Inside were 4,000 pounds of body bags.[10]

As supplies and reinforcements arrived, Colonel Lownds and his superiors pored over maps and prepared to reposition troops in anticipation of the next North Vietnamese move. A top priority was finding a place for the newly arrived men of the 1st Battalion, 9th Marines.

The battalion had been in nearly constant combat in Vietnam since December 1966, and its hard-luck reputation had earned it a grim moniker: the "Walking Dead." In February 1967, the battalion had been accompanied by the acclaimed French war correspondent Bernard Fall, whose two classic books on Vietnam had included *Hell in a Very Small Place*, on the French defeat at Dien Bien Phu. Fall had been with Alpha Company, 1/9, on February 21, 1967, as it patrolled the Communist enclave north of Hue known as the "Street Without Joy" (the title of Fall's other book about the French war in Vietnam). In the deepening afternoon shadows that day, Fall stepped on a land mine that killed him, along with two Marines.[11]

A far bloodier day in the summer of 1967 had etched the battalion's name in Marine Corps history. On July 2, Alpha and Bravo companies of the 1/9 had kicked off Operation Buffalo by pushing up Highway 561 along the DMZ near Con Thien, about thirty miles northeast of Khe Sanh. The Marines had been ambushed by a large North Vietnamese force, and Bravo Company was decimated, its company commander, two platoon leaders, and artillery forward observer among the dead. The survivors hung on until the arrival of reinforcements, among them a courageous young Virginian by the name of Captain Henry "Mac" Radcliffe. By nightfall, Alpha and Bravo Companies had sustained the heaviest single-day losses incurred by the Marines in Vietnam: 84 men killed (including eight Navy corpsmen), 190 wounded, and nine missing. Mac Radcliffe earned a Silver Star and command of Alpha Company.

In the aftermath of the July bloodletting, the ranks of the 1/9 had been replenished with scores of young replacements. Command of the battalion had been given to Colonel John F. Mitchell, who had earned a Silver

Star as a young platoon commander at the Chosin Reservoir in Korea. Seventeen years later, arriving at Khe Sanh with a coveted general's star in his sights, Mitchell's youthful pluck and self-confidence had taken on the hues of arrogance.

Now, in the rising morning light on January 23, Mitchell and the Marines of the Walking Dead marched away from the Khe Sanh perimeter and took up positions on high ground about a mile to the southwest, around a rock quarry dug by Seabees during runway work at the combat base the previous summer.

• • •

Colonel Lownds had welcomed his temporarily detached 2nd Battalion back to Khe Sanh one week earlier, and now the outfit's Echo Company was also on the move. Its assignment was to shore up the northern approach to the base by fortifying a spur about 200 yards northeast of Hill 861.

For Captain Earle Breeding, Echo's up-from-the-ranks commanding officer, the move was a welcome opportunity to prove his mettle as a combat commander. A native of Washington, DC, and the neighboring Maryland suburbs, the thirty-four-year-old Breeding had first joined the Marine Corps in 1952, when tight finances and his father's illness had forced him to drop out of college.[12] After serving out his enlistment, Breeding had enrolled at the University of New Mexico in 1956 with an eye on returning to the Corps as an officer.

Breeding reentered the Marines as a second lieutenant in the spring of 1961, and he had risen to captain by the summer of 1967, when he finally got his long-sought orders for Vietnam. He arrived at 3rd Marine Division headquarters in Phu Bai to discover that he was destined for anti-tank duty but wangled a coveted infantry command by plying personnel officers with bottles of prized whiskey. He was assigned to the 2nd Battalion, 26th Marines, and soon landed command of Echo Company.[13]

After arriving at Khe Sanh in mid-January, Breeding had led Echo Company up to the high ground north of the combat base, to Hill 558, where he began running patrols along the Rao Quan River. Breeding and his boys were still operating around 558 when the North Vietnamese struck on January 21. Now, Breeding prepared to lead his men to their new digs on a strategically valuable piece of land just east of Kilo Company's outpost on Hill 861.

On a straight line, Echo Company's destination lay only about a mile southwest of Hill 558, but the terrain was steep and broken, with sharp elephant grass and vegetation. The Marines set out around 8:00 a.m. on the morning of January 22, but the march quickly bogged down. The grass was so thick that the men on point became exhausted after hacking away at the wall of vegetation for only five or ten minutes.[14] It was the coolest time of the year around Khe Sanh, but daytime temperatures still ranged into the high seventies, and the oppressive tropical humidity made it feel much hotter.

Among the suffering, sweat-soaked Marines pushing through the hills was a raw-boned nineteen-year-old rifleman named David Norton. A former high school football halfback and defensive back, Norton had grown up in a good family in Charlotte, North Carolina. As a teenager, he had closely followed the news about America's deepening role in Vietnam. In his final weeks of high school, he and some friends decided to enlist in the Marine Corps.[15]

In the spring of 1967, Norton was undergoing advanced combat infantry training at Camp Pendleton in Southern California when the bloody Hill Fights unfolded on the slopes of Hill 861 and 881 North and South around Khe Sanh. A premonition came over him one day as he read a news article about the fighting on Hill 861. Norton announced to his fellow Marines, "I'm going to be right there."[16] Now, five months into his Vietnam tour, Norton and his comrades were struggling to scale the slopes of this infamous hill mass.

Late afternoon of January 22 found the men of Echo Company still clawing their way up the steep eastern slope of the spur soon to be known as Hill 861 Alpha. It was a grueling slog even for the fittest and toughest men in the company, like the 1st Platoon's rocketman, David McCall.

Nineteen years old, a wiry five feet eight inches and 145 pounds, "Big Dave" McCall had been a star athlete back home in Minneapolis, Kansas, lettering in four sports.[17] He enlisted in the Marines and arrived in Vietnam on November 10, 1967, the 192nd birthday of the Marine Corps. In his two months in Vietnam, McCall had experienced the usual mix of firefights, night ambushes, and boring guard duty. Early in his tour, he had dozed off on night watch and suddenly felt someone beside him. He opened his eyes to find a lieutenant in his face. "If I was a gook, you'd be dead," the lieutenant said quietly, and then walked away. From that moment on, asleep or on watch, McCall never let anyone get close without his knowing about it.

Night was falling when the exhausted Marines finally reached their destination. Much to their dismay, 861 Alpha was overgrown with high elephant grass and lacked fields of fire and natural defensive positions. If the enemy decided to attack, they would be in trouble, but the boys of Echo Company were too tired and angry to care. They made a perimeter, then "basically just sat down."[18]

In the darkness and gathering fog, Earle Breeding checked his ragged lines, such as they were, and returned to his makeshift command post to wait out the night. His radio operators had suffered more than most after lugging their PRC-25 field units as well as their personal gear, an extra 23.5 pounds weighing on every step, and they were out almost as soon as they hit the ground. Taking pity on the exhausted men, Breeding let them sleep, and he slipped the radio piece in his ear. If they made it through the night, they could worry about clearing and fortifying 861 Alpha tomorrow.[19]

CHAPTER 7

"Should We Withdraw from Khe Sanh?"

The legendary North Vietnamese general Vo Nguyen Giap would spend the final decades of his life assuring foreign interviewers that his campaign against Khe Sanh in 1968 was never intended to duplicate his victory over the French at Dien Bien Phu. It was a declaration of transparent self-interest, especially given how events played out, but critics of General William Westmoreland would seize on Giap's pronouncements as confirmation that the North Vietnamese at Khe Sanh merely sought to divert American attention away from urban centers in advance of Tet holiday attacks. The truth about North Vietnamese objectives will probably never be known with certainty, but Giap's commitment of three reinforced divisions to the opening stage of the Khe Sanh campaign was certainly more than was necessary for an effective ruse.

The Khe Sanh campaign was all part of an elaborate master plan, TCK-TKN, which laid out the end game against the Americans as a three-act drama. NVA forces had executed Phase I in the late summer and fall of 1967, launching attacks against remote targets like Con Thien, the Marine combat base along the DMZ. The strikes were aimed at drawing US forces out of the population centers and inducing Westmoreland to "launch operations along South Vietnam's borders," according to Phillip Davidson, Westmoreland's intelligence chief at the time.

By the final days of January 1968, Communist forces were nearly ready to launch Phase II of Giap's plan, coordinated attacks on South Vietnamese cities, which were supposed to inspire a sympathetic population to rise up against the American-backed government.

At Khe Sanh, the ground was already being laid for the climactic Phase III, "a large-unit conventional battle," with Khe Sanh the logical target.[1]

• • •

Whether Giap planned the campaign against Khe Sanh as a ruse or a decisive blow, his opening moves certainly evoked his signature triumph against the French.

After the French had reclaimed the valley of Dien Bien Phu in the far northwestern corner of Vietnam in November 1953, Giap's Communist Viet Minh forces had methodically encircled the enemy stronghold and bombarded it from the commanding heights. On March 13, 1954, the Viet Minh began reducing French strong points at Dien Bien Phu in human wave attacks. Simultaneously, Giap's anti-aircraft batteries began choking off French aerial resupply efforts. On May 7, after fifty-five days of fighting, the doomed outpost surrendered.

At Khe Sanh, Giap had initiated a stealth encirclement of the Americans in early January 1968, and the opening attacks of January 20–21 began the process of driving in American defenses from the north and the south. He had wholly committed two divisions—about 20,000 troops—to the effort: elements of the 304th Division had moved against Khe Sanh village from the south, while units of the 325C had hit Hill 861 from the north. A regiment of the 324th Division had been positioned within fifteen miles of Khe Sanh to perform supply duties, and the 320th Division, another 10,000 men, was less than a day's march northeast of Khe Sanh.[2]

The North Vietnamese struck again on the evening of January 23 by overrunning a Laotian Army outpost at Ban Houei Sane, fourteen miles west of Khe Sanh. The Americans quickly learned from survivors that Communist forces had used Soviet-made PT-76 light tanks in the attack, the NVA's first armor-backed assault of the war. With the district headquarters at Khe Sanh village and Ban Houei Sane in their hands, the

North Vietnamese now set their sights on the US Special Forces camp at Lang Vei, only four miles southwest of Khe Sanh.

As internal Communist accounts have since made clear, quick victory wasn't the objective of the North Vietnamese at Khe Sanh. Instead, they were content to goad the Americans into rushing reinforcements to the embattled base and bleeding US forces as time passed.[3] If Khe Sanh fell at some point in the future, it would be the coup de grâce that would force the United States from the war. For now, General Giap and his troops would gradually turn up the pressure, playing on US fears of Khe Sanh becoming America's Dien Bien Phu. And while Westmoreland focused on Khe Sanh, Giap would spring his next surprise.

• • •

As at Dien Bien Phu, the North Vietnamese forces set about weakening Khe Sanh and its outposts with artillery, mortar, and sniper fire. The bulk of the damage was inflicted by two NVA artillery regiments, the 45th and 675th, now scattered through the rugged countryside west of Khe Sanh. The North Vietnamese had targeted Khe Sanh with 212 heavy weapons, including eight 152-millimeter guns, sixteen 130-millimeter guns, thirty-six 122-millimeter guns, more than one hundred 122-millimeter rocket launchers, and a supporting cast of assorted smaller guns and howitzers. To protect the artillery from American air strikes, the North Vietnamese had forty-two 37-millimeter anti-aircraft guns, twelve 57-millimeter guns, and 130 anti-aircraft machine guns.[4] Highly mobile mortar teams had completely surrounded the American outposts, and they unleashed deadly fire that was targeted and adjusted by artillery forward observers, who had established camouflaged positions around the combat base and forward posts.

On Hill 861, Dennis Mannion, the Kilo Company artillery forward observer, was engaged in the same deadly pursuit. In the aftermath of the January 21 attack, two large containers addressed to Mannion had arrived on the hill. One contained a pair of powerful naval binoculars capable of spotting NVA soldiers and other potential targets up to ten miles away. The other held a Night Observation Device (NOD). The evening of its arrival, Mannion had powered up the device and scanned the ridgeline about 500 yards to his west. In the scope's gauzy green light, he spotted about twenty North Vietnamese soldiers hard at work, digging new positions and moving supplies and equipment.[5] He arranged for one of the hill's 106-millimeter recoilless rifles to unleash a round on the NVA, the opening salvo of Mannion's relentless test of wits with the North Vietnamese forces that surrounded 861.

Sleeping in snatches, Mannion settled into a routine that began at first light and continued late into the evening. During daylight hours he would scan the nearby hills and draws with his naval binoculars in search of targets. When he found something, he would call in the coordinates to the Fire Direction Center at the combat base, then adjust the rounds as they landed. At night, Mannion would scour the area with the NOD, a more powerful version of the Starlight scope.

At the combat base and the hill outposts, an urgent effort was underway to deepen trenches and move bunkers and command posts underground. Every arriving helicopter was greeted by enemy mortars and sniper fire, and, in between, mortar rounds sporadically pounded the hill as enemy spotters called in targets of opportunity. The North Vietnamese lacked night vision devices, so the Marines moved about the hill outposts more confidently in the darkness. But night also brought fears of being overrun by the NVA.[6]

The cumulative stress of the random enemy fire and mounting casualties weighed on the young Americans.

Early in the afternoon of January 24, corpsman Larry LeClaire heard an explosion near his position on 861, followed by frantic shouts of "Corpsman up!" He hurried up the trench with his medical bag, which was packed with the usual assortment of battle dressings, tourniquets, bags of blood expander, and other items. An enemy mortar round had landed in the trench line, apparently right on top of a Marine, and all that remained for LeClaire was a bloody pile of flesh around a pair of Marine combat boots. Human brains pulsated on the trench wall. Fighting the urge to throw up, LeClaire ran back to the platoon command post. He had just informed the lieutenant about his grisly discovery when the cry sounded again: "Corpsman up!"[7]

LeClaire retraced his steps up the trench and carefully made his way past the remains he found moments earlier. His nostrils were filled with the rusty-iron scent of blood mixed with the acrid smell of the enemy round. LeClaire found another Marine lying in the red clay at the bottom of the trench. The man was in shock, bulging eyes locked in a death gaze.

As LeClaire tended to the man, it occurred to him that this was the duty area of his friend, corpsman Christian Feit. *Where is Feit? He should be here.* LeClaire soon learned the terrible truth: his fellow corpsman had been standing about thirty feet from the enemy round when it hit, and a piece of shrapnel had struck him in the right temple. LeClaire found Feit and did what little he could.

A medevac chopper arrived and the dying Marine and gravely wounded corpsman were loaded aboard, along with the scant remains of their dead comrade. The Marine was pronounced dead by doctors at the combat base. Twenty-year-old Christian Feit died on a Navy hospital ship the following day.[8]

• • •

Around 5:30 p.m. that afternoon, January 24, the North Vietnamese unleashed the heaviest bombardment since the opening barrage three days earlier. Artillery and rockets pounded the combat base and the American outposts on 881 South and 861.

Just south of the Khe Sanh runway, the men of Bravo Company, 3rd Recon, huddled in bunkers jerry-rigged from pieces of timber, railroad ties, runway matting, and sandbags. Nineteen-year-old Dave Doehrman had worked in an International Harvester farm machinery plant back home in Fort Wayne, Indiana, before joining the Marines the previous summer. Ray Milligan, the shy son of a welder from Deptford, New Jersey, had dreamed of becoming an FBI agent or a policeman, but his grades weren't good enough for college, so he had joined the Marines. Only the day before, the wiry Milligan had celebrated his twentieth birthday.

Now, without warning, the recon bunkers were plunged into dusty blackness. Doehrman and the men around him coughed and gasped for air as blood oozed from their noses and ruptured eardrums. A few seconds passed before the Marines realized that a rocket had slammed into the trench.

Nearby, recon Marine Ray Milligan sat in the swirling dust and darkness of his shattered bunker as a friend who went by the nickname Elvis screamed and cried in fear. Milligan silently rocked back and forth. *Don't go nuts*, he told himself. *Don't go nuts.*[9]

Outside, Kevin Macaulay, a young recon radio operator from New York, and other Marines clawed at the shattered recon bunker that had taken a direct hit. Four dead and sixteen wounded were pulled from the debris.[10]

Before the day was out, NVA artillery and mortar fire had killed seven Americans and seriously wounded twenty-four at Khe Sanh.[11]

• • •

Most of Khe Sanh's defenders had been in combat prior to January 21. They had experienced night ambushes, LPs, blind patrols through elephant grass, and other assorted terrors. But the enemy artillery, rocket, and mortar barrages tested these young men like never before. Offensive skills learned in boot camp and advanced infantry training were useless in this kind of warfare. A man could dig deeper, wear his helmet, zip his flak jacket, keep one ear cocked for the sound of an enemy mortar round leaving the tube or the distant boom of a big gun—and still be killed by a lucky shot or a pea-size piece of shrapnel. This hard reality had existed since the men had set foot in Vietnam, but random terror had been woven into the fabric of daily life at Khe Sanh.

A few men broke. A distraught corpsman went to Protestant chaplain Ray Stubbe after the first day or two of shelling and said he couldn't take it. The corpsman returned on January 26 and pleaded for Stubbe's help in getting out of Khe Sanh. At Charlie Med, the main base hospital, the corpsman was diagnosed as suffering an "acute anxiety reaction" and was administered the anti-psychotic drug Thorazine. He was evacuated from Khe Sanh later that day.[12]

Most of the defenders of Khe Sanh suffered in silence.

For years afterward, Bravo Company, 1/26, rifleman Michael O'Hara would be too embarrassed to talk to his Khe Sanh brothers about the terror he had felt during the artillery bombardments, particularly in those moments when Soviet-made 152-millimeter guns hurled eighty-eight-pound shells into the base with the fearsome roar of a runaway locomotive. When he finally revealed his feelings at a Khe Sanh Veterans

Association reunion in 1993, O'Hara was astonished—and relieved—to learn that all his comrades had shared his fears.

"You just had to find a hole, get in, and hope to God it wasn't your number," O'Hara recalled. "When the shells landed, it was just like the whole earth shook. The mortars and the RPGs could damn sure kill you, but they weren't nearly as terrifying. That Russian artillery will eat your brain cells out."[13]

• • •

Amid the terror, selfless acts of courage became commonplace at Khe Sanh. On January 25, a CH-46 helicopter from HMM-262 landed on Hill 881 South for an emergency medevac mission. A wounded Marine whose head and eyes were heavily bandaged was being led to the chopper by two comrades when NVA mortar rounds dropped from the sky. The two escorts and the wounded Marine hit the ground. Aboard the waiting bird, Corporal Ernesto Gomez of Pasadena, California, looked out to see the wounded Marine blindly trying to find the chopper. Gomez dashed across the LZ, pulled the man to the ground, and shielded him with his body. When the explosions stopped, Gomez and the wounded Marine scrambled to a nearby rocket crater for cover. Another crew member ran out to help them, and together they got the wounded Marine aboard the helicopter and safely delivered him to Charlie Med.[14]

Some acts of courage demanded the ultimate price.

On Hill 861 on January 26, a two-squad patrol from the recently arrived 2nd Platoon of Alpha Company, 1/26, filed through the wire on the northern slope and headed into the draw northwest of the hill. Passing over the area in a chopper five days earlier, 2nd Platoon radio operator John Rauch had been struck by the lushness of the green jungle that cloaked its slopes. Now, the draw was a shattered moonscape of water-filled craters, splintered and scorched trees, burned grass, torn earth, and the stench of smoke and decaying bodies.[15]

The Marines of the lead squad reached the bottom of the draw and started up the western slope. From his fighting position on 861, Dennis Mannion tracked the patrol's progress through his binoculars. He had walked that route many times in the previous month, and he had called in countless artillery strikes on the area in the days since the January 21 attack.

The forest cover had been blown away, and the Marines were clearly visible through the shattered trees more than three hundred yards away.

The Marines were advancing up the western slope when Mannion's radio operator, Dave Kron, suddenly shouted, "Movement! Gooks!"[16] Mannion swung his binoculars to the right. About fifty yards from the Marines, two groups of NVA soldiers emerged from hiding and formed a line parallel to the Marines.

The Alpha Marines never saw the North Vietnamese machine-gun bunker dug into the hillside and camouflaged with toppled trees, logs, and limbs. The gun opened up, and shouts and screams filled the draw. Marines dived for cover and began to return fire. The patrol's two machine gunners moved forward as the column spread out into battle positions. Heavy NVA fire quickly pinned the Marines in place.

As he hugged the ground, John Rauch tersely briefed an officer back on 861. His lieutenant took the radio handset and read off map coordinates for mortar support, and within seconds about eight 81-millimeter rounds slammed into the NVA positions. The lieutenant shouted an order, and the Marines began to move forward again.

Still tracking the action through binoculars, Mannion watched as one Marine stood up and fired his M-79 grenade launcher at the North Vietnamese. Instead of dropping to the ground while he reloaded, the grenadier kept striding ahead toward the danger. He pumped another round into the uprooted tree trunks where the machine gun was hidden, then another, "oblivious to the bullets that were stitching the dirt around him as he progressed,"[17] as Mannion later recalled.

The grenadier was a handsome and athletic nineteen-year-old from Raleigh, North Carolina, Private First Class Dwight "Tommy" Denning. He had been in Vietnam less than two months, but Denning didn't show it. He had drawn a bead on the enemy machine gun hidden in the tangle of brush, and he continued firing and reloading as he walked directly into the teeth of the enemy fire. Denning was dropping another round into the open breech of his M-79 when an NVA bullet pierced his left eye and ripped through the back of his head. The weapon dropped from his hands, and Denning collapsed to the ground.

Minutes after the firefight began, the Marines were ordered to break contact. Covered by their comrades on 861, they pulled back across the draw and retraced their steps to the American stronghold above them. Four Marines carried Tommy Denning up the hill and laid his body on the ground near the perimeter wire.

Among the Marines trudging back inside the outpost was radioman John Rauch, and he paused over the lifeless body. He had never seen a dead Marine before. The handsome face that had been so full of life a few minutes before was now empty and gray. Rauch found his place in the trench line and sank to the red earth. His body shook. The adrenalin of combat ebbed away, leaving in its place an aching black hole. Rauch and his comrades sat quietly in the trench line, stunned by the death of their friend.[18]

• • •

Less than a week into the North Vietnamese campaign, Khe Sanh Combat Base and its outposts faced a growing challenge to meet daily needs for food, medical supplies, ammunition, and other critical items such as water purification chemicals and bunker construction materials.[19] Helicopters and transport planes braved inclement weather and enemy fire to carry out resupply sorties. Crates of C-rations and other supplies were dropped by parachute into a cleared zone beyond the western perimeter.

Most vulnerable of all were the four hilltop outposts guarding the northern approach to Khe Sanh—881 South, 861, 861 Alpha, and 558. They were entirely dependent on helicopter resupply, even for their water needs, and each arriving flight had become a magnet for North Vietnamese mortar fire. A chopper pilot had no more than thirty seconds to land, offload, take on medevac cases, and get off the LZ before the first rounds hit.

For the combat base itself, the issue of potable water loomed as a potentially crippling weakness. The base pumped its water from a stream along the Rao Quan River some 500 yards outside the northern perimeter wire. The commander of the 3rd Marine Division, Major General Rathvon Tompkins, had been aware of this Achilles heel in Khe Sanh's defenses for at least a month, but he hadn't passed the information up the chain of command.[20]

Now, in late January, General Westmoreland was appalled to learn about Khe Sanh's vulnerability. If the North Vietnamese cut the line or contaminated the source, the base would run out of water within a week.[21] As a last resort, Khe Sanh's water needs would have to be supplied by air.

Mindful that the French defeat at Dien Bien Phu had stemmed in part from a failed effort to resupply the garrison by air, Westmoreland had mobilized an impressive collection of aircraft to sustain his forces at Khe Sanh. His aerial resupply capabilities far eclipsed anything the French could muster in their losing effort at Dien Bien Phu. But Westmoreland had not counted on having to shuttle thousands of gallons of water each day to Khe Sanh. His well-laid plans were suddenly in jeopardy.

• • •

In the early morning of January 29, the expected enemy ground attack finally seemed underway when General William Westmoreland's MACV headquarters in Saigon received an urgent message from the sensor analysts in Nakhon Phanom, Thailand. "Many troop movements of large and small units from Laotian border as far S[outh] as 10 miles below Khe Sanh. All movements toward Khe Sanh. Seems to be Big Push." By dawn, two North Vietnamese troop concentrations had been identified. One of them had closed within six miles of the combat base.[22]

The commander of Forward Operating Base 3, the Special Forces compound at Khe Sanh, readied a patrol to scout enemy activity in that direction. Around 8:30 a.m., Specialist Fifth Class William Wood led a Special Forces team and a contingent of Bru fighters toward Hill 471, between the combat base and Khe Sanh village. Moving through heavy elephant grass on the hill's lower slopes, the patrol was ambushed at almost point-blank range. Sergeant Gary Lee Crone fell in the first volley with multiple wounds. Shot through both knees, Wood limped away from the kill zone and was rescued by helicopter along with one other American. Left behind were Crone, who was presumed dead, and another Special Forces operator, Michael Thomas Mahoney.[23]

Back at FOB-3, Captain Harlan "Rip" Van Winkle organized twenty-four men for a mission to rescue the two missing Americans. Their numbers included a seven-member Special Forces assault team designated as Hatchet Force Denver, and a lone Marine, Private First Class F. J. (Jim) Taylor, who knew the terrain from his time with Combined Action

Company Oscar-2 in Khe Sanh village. Rounding out the force were sixteen Bru fighters.[24]

Just minutes after four choppers inserted the men on the lower slope of Hill 471, the North Vietnamese attacked. Almost immediately, Van Winkle's second in command, First Lieutenant Grenville Sutcliffe, was hit in the throat by grenade shrapnel as he tried to direct gunships to an NVA machine-gun position.[25] Grenades rained down on Van Winkle and his outnumbered men, wounding most of the Americans with shrapnel. Sergeant First Class Charles Tredinnick fell with a mortal chest wound.[26]

In the critical minutes that followed, helicopter gunships kept the recovery force alive on Hill 471. The North Vietnamese had drawn so close to Van Winkle and his men that the choppers fired almost on top of them. On one pass, the gunships missed Taylor and Van Winkle by inches and accidentally shot a Bru fighter in both legs. The support finally allowed the embattled men to break free and maneuver to the hill's northern slope. They hunkered down while a Marine forward air controller called in air strikes from his position overhead. As helicopter gunships and fighter jets pounded the North Vietnamese with cannon, bombs, and napalm, the bloodied Van Winkle and his men walked back to FOB-3.[27]

• • •

The enemy is attempting to "dig his way into Khe Sanh [to avoid] our tremendous firepower (as he did at Dien Bien Phu)," General William Westmoreland wrote in a January 29 cable to Admiral Ulysses Simpson Grant Sharp, the American commander in the Pacific.[28] Westmoreland had just returned from I Corps, where he had conferred with senior commanders about the threat against Khe Sanh. He had ordered his staff historian to prepare a study on the lessons of Dien Bien Phu.

There were hints that General Giap had something else up his sleeve—reports from recent arrests and interrogations suggested the Communists were poised to attack South Vietnam's urban centers—but Westmoreland dismissed these as attempts to divert attention from I Corps.[29] He remained convinced that Khe Sanh was the main event.

The American commander was hardly alone in his preoccupation with Khe Sanh. Over the past month, President Lyndon Johnson had become obsessed with the subject.

For Johnson, and indeed for all Americans, the war in Vietnam had reached a critical juncture. Throughout 1967, Johnson had watched antiwar sentiment rise and his approval ratings fall. In November, he had brought General Westmoreland back home to talk up the outlook in Vietnam. Westmoreland had sounded all the optimistic notes that Johnson wanted the American people to hear. On November 19, during a National Press Club speech, Westmoreland described how the war had reached a point "when the end begins to come into view."[30]

While Westmoreland publicly hinted at victory, Johnson privately confronted the growing pessimism of one of his closest advisers. Defense Secretary Robert McNamara's doubts about the war had reached a breaking point, and on November 1, he had presented Johnson with a memo urging a cap on US troop levels and suspension of the bombing campaign.[31] Weary of McNamara's increasingly dissonant views, Johnson cut him loose. On November 29, he announced that McNamara would be leaving the Pentagon after seven years to head the World Bank.[32]

In December, Johnson had been informed that the North Vietnamese were stockpiling supplies and massing tens of thousands of troops around the DMZ. A Communist offensive was expected, with Khe Sanh the likely target. Westmoreland had assured the president that the enemy offensive was born of desperation rather than strength, but Johnson was concerned. He had been in Congress fourteen years earlier when President Dwight D. Eisenhower had briefly considered using nuclear weapons to save the French garrison at Dien Bien Phu. Now Johnson faced the haunting specter of a remote American base being besieged by Communist forces commanded by the mastermind of Dien Bien Phu.

Johnson's uneasiness over Khe Sanh escalated to alarm after he received an unsolicited warning from the capital's most influential pundit. On January 10, hawkish syndicated columnist Joseph Alsop had suggested in a lunch with Johnson's national security adviser, Walt Rostow, that US forces at Khe Sanh were poised to follow in the disastrous footsteps of the feckless French. Khe Sanh presented the North Vietnamese with their "best opportunity for a Dien Bien Phu," Alsop warned. "And the enemy is looking for a Dien Bien Phu."[33]

Johnson and Rostow now pressed General Earle Wheeler, chairman of the Joint Chiefs of Staff, to make sure that Westmoreland could handle the threat. The opening Communist attacks against Khe Sanh on January 21 had triggered more phone calls and cables, all infused with the ghosts of Dien Bien Phu.

In a January 29 phone conversation with Wheeler, General Westmoreland laid out all the preparations he had made to defend Khe Sanh: two extra Marine battalions had been moved to the stronghold in the previous week; other troops had been shifted to I Corps for use in an emergency; massive artillery support was in place; and the North Vietnamese were being hammered with about forty B-52 sorties and five hundred tactical air sorties each day.[34]

Drawing on his conversation with Westmoreland and a subsequent meeting with the Joint Chiefs, Wheeler wrote a 460-word memorandum for the president. "General Westmoreland stated to me that, in his judgment, we can hold Khe Sanh and we should hold Khe Sanh," Wheeler wrote. "He believes that this is an opportunity to inflict a severe defeat upon the enemy."[35] Furthermore, the Joint Chiefs were satisfied with Westmoreland's preparations and his rationale for standing his ground at the vulnerable American outpost. Thus, Wheeler concluded, the Joint Chiefs "recommend that we maintain our position at Khe Sanh."

Shortly after 1:00 p.m. on January 29, President Johnson convened a meeting in the White House Cabinet Room to poll his military commanders in person and make a final decision about Khe Sanh. In attendance were General Wheeler and the four service chiefs, national security adviser Walt Rostow, and Secretary of Defense Robert McNamara.

Johnson went around the table and questioned each member of the Joint Chiefs. "Have we done all we should do?"[36] he asked. "Are we convinced our forces are adequate?"

The nation's top military commanders once again reassured the president.

"Should we withdraw from Khe Sanh?" Johnson pressed.

"No," he was told. Militarily and psychologically, Khe Sanh was too important.

For the moment, Lyndon Johnson had heard enough. America would stand and fight at Khe Sanh.

PART II

CHAPTER 8

"Hell in a Very Small Place"

A s President Johnson's pivotal meeting with the Joint Chiefs of Staff was breaking up in Washington, North Vietnamese and Viet Cong forces on the other side of the world were launching the first attacks of General Giap's Tet Offensive, a series of coordinated strikes aimed at the heart of South Vietnam's urban centers. Over the next few hours, Communist troops attacked the provincial capitals of Pleiku, Khanh Hoa, Darlac, and Quang Tri, as well as the I Corps headquarters at Quang Tri and the huge US bases at Da Nang and Cam Ranh Bay.

Daylight of January 30 in Vietnam brought even worse news. More attacks were planned throughout South Vietnam that evening, reported General Phillip Davidson, chief of intelligence for Westmoreland's Military Assistance Command, Vietnam (MACV). At 9:45 a.m., the South Vietnamese government canceled the annual Tet holiday truce.[1]

At Khe Sanh on January 30, the North Vietnamese continued to punish the Americans with artillery, rockets, mortars, and sniper fire. Incoming rounds at the combat base ignited a fire in an ammunition supply point, and Sergeant Jesus Roberto Vasquez, a twenty-year-old Marine explosive ordnance disposal technician from El Paso, Texas, was among those who joined the frantic effort to put out the flames. Spotting a burning 81-millimeter mortar round, Vasquez grabbed it. Before he could hurl the shell into a bomb crater, it blew up in his arms, and Vasquez became the latest American to die at Khe Sanh.[2]

True to General Davidson's belated warning, the Communist Tet Offensive erupted in full fury in the early hours of January 31 with urban attacks launched by an estimated 84,000 Viet Cong cadre and North Vietnamese Army regulars. The fighting engulfed thirty-six of forty-four provincial capitals and South Vietnam's six largest cities, including the ancient imperial city of Hue, which was seized by Communist forces in a fierce assault. In Saigon, Viet Cong commandos breached the US Embassy compound, the presidential palace, and Tan Son Nhut Airbase.

General Giap had planned the offensive as a means of triggering an uprising against the US-backed government in Saigon, the next phase in his quest to end the war in 1968. A short-term objective was an improved position in anticipated peace talks with the Americans, part of the overall Communist strategy of fight-and-talk.

For his part, General Westmoreland remained convinced that Khe Sanh was the prize coveted by Giap. In Westmoreland's analysis, the urban attacks were a ploy aimed at drawing American forces away from Khe Sanh.

The defenders of Khe Sanh had been spared the ferocious ground attacks of the Tet Offensive, but the calibrated violence continued to kill and maim a few more Americans each day: four dead on January 31; one on February 1; another four on February 2; two on February 3. The rising death toll paled in comparison to the carnage at Hue and elsewhere, but that was little consolation to the Americans at Khe Sanh as they watched a rising number of comrades flown away in body bags.

• • •

The mounting casualties and ever-present threat of an overwhelming enemy assault had cast a pall over Hill 861 in those early days of February. Mortar and sniper fire raked the hill every day. The draw where Tommy Denning had been killed had become such a popular staging ground for enemy mortar teams that the Marines had nicknamed it "Times Square."

The sound of each mortar blast was the starting gun in a race for life. It would take about twelve to fifteen seconds for the first round to hit, so the cry of "Incoming!" would set off a desperate scramble for cover. The first impact would usually be followed in quick succession by another three or four, any one of which could be deadly in the close quarters of Hill 861.

As the hill's artillery forward observer, Dennis Mannion's job was to remain in place when the cry of "Incoming!" went up. He would spend those anxious seconds trying to fix the location of the enemy mortar team, and even as the rounds were falling, he would begin calling in artillery missions on the suspected coordinates.

Mannion had his work routine down by the second week of the enemy offensive. He would begin each day by scanning the ridgelines west of the hill to see if anything looked different—freshly turned dirt or any other sign of movement or massing of enemy troops. He would touch base with his air counterpart on the hill, Corporal Paul Knight, who returned from "R&R" (rest and recreation) in Hawaii in early February. They would compare notes with the forward air controller circling overhead in his small Cessna spotter and work up a series of strikes on the NVA-held ridgelines to the west, typically capped off with a couple of artillery fire missions, "just to shake up anybody who might be over there."[3] Afterward, Mannion would eat breakfast and write letters for a while before renewing his search for targets.

Bad weather and NVA fire had disrupted helicopter resupply missions to the hill outposts, resulting in chronic (and sometimes critical) food and water shortages by early February. Daily allotments were cut to two C-ration meals and one canteen of water. Sometimes men went without food for a day or two until supply choppers could get through.

Before the siege, Mannion had maintained an active social life on the hill. Now he spent any spare time in elaborate efforts to improve his chances of surviving an enemy assault. He and three other colleagues began work on a deep bunker that would eventually extend ten feet down into the hill and include an escape tunnel leading to a foxhole about twelve feet away. Once the bunker was completed, the men worked each night on the underground passageway, which they christened "Tom," after one of the tunnels in *The Great Escape*. It gave them a sense that they were doing *something* to even the odds.[4]

Still, spirits flagged on the hill. Most men had already experienced a few close calls, and another North Vietnamese ground attack was expected any day. The grim prospects led Mannion on January 31 to write a pair of farewell letters to his parents and his best friend back in Connecticut.

"I want to say that I'm not afraid of dying," Mannion wrote his friend. "I'll just feel sorry for my folks, brothers, and sister. And you. There's no way I can describe what good friends we two are and how much your ugly presence means to me."[5] Mannion slipped a farewell letter to his parents into the envelope and asked his friend to pass it on if he didn't make it back.

Four days later, on Sunday, February 4, Mannion turned twenty-three. Late that afternoon, he settled into the sandbag enclosure along the northern end of the hill that he and Dave Kron had used as their bomb shelter before the siege. There Mannion began to prepare his birthday meal of C-ration beans and franks.[6] He cooked off the grease with a c-rat heat tab and stirred in some melted cheese and bread he had saved from other meals. He leaned back against the northern wall of the uncovered shelter and was about to start eating when he heard a familiar sound.

Whump. Whump. Whump. Whump.

The report of the first mortar round leaving its tube had stirred an instinctive reaction in Mannion's brain. *Get to the bunker.* He had always done everything he could to improve his odds of surviving Vietnam. In recent days he had inserted extra fiberglass panels in his flak jacket and buttressed his steel-pot helmet with protective plates. Now, a flash of defiance overruled his better judgment. *My food is ready, and it IS my birthday. Fuck it.*[7]

Mannion heard the first round explode close to the LZ near the southern end of the hill. The second impacted halfway up the slope. The third landed closer still, on the crest. He waited for the last round to hit.

Mannion was airborne by the time his brain registered the deafening *Boom*. The projectile had exploded just outside the double layer of sandbags at his back and the force knocked him flying, but the sacks of red Khe Sanh soil had absorbed the brunt of the blast and shrapnel. He lay on his back, gasping for breath but otherwise unhurt.

When his head cleared, Mannion saw that his carefully prepared meal was splattered all over his filthy utilities and flak jacket. Dusting himself off, he set to work picking the chunks of red clay out of his cheesy beans and franks. Mannion wished himself Happy Birthday, then began spooning the mess off his pants and into his mouth.

• • •

In Washington, an air of crisis now gripped the White House. The onset of the Communist attack on Khe Sanh had been followed by the seizure of the US spy ship *Pueblo* and its crew by North Korea on January 23. And then came the stunning Communist attacks that engulfed South Vietnam's largest cities in combat.

The Tet Offensive had sharpened Johnson's fears of a disaster at Khe Sanh. Key members of Congress nervously questioned whether Westmoreland knew what he was doing. "Are we prepared for this attack?" Senator Robert Byrd of West Virginia had pointedly asked the president in a January 30 White House briefing for congressional Democrats.

Johnson began to ponder his nightmare scenario: a situation so dire that only the use of tactical nuclear weapons could prevent Khe Sanh from falling to the North Vietnamese. On February 1, General Earle Wheeler, Johnson's chairman of the Joint Chiefs, sent an "eyes only" cable to General Westmoreland and Admiral Sharp, America's Hawaii-based commander in chief in the Pacific theater, in which he raised the issue of using tactical nuclear weapons at Khe Sanh.[8] Wheeler asked his commanders to let him know "whether there are targets in the area which lend themselves to nuclear strikes, whether some contingency nuclear planning would be in order, and what you would consider to be some of the more significant pros and cons of using tactical nukes in such a contingency."

While General Westmoreland discreetly formulated his response, Johnson continued to fret about Khe Sanh's fragile supply line and the prospect of the American base being isolated like the French at Dien Bien Phu. He phoned General Wheeler on the evening of February 2 to ask again about Westmoreland's abilities to reinforce and resupply Khe Sanh if bad weather and North Vietnamese anti-aircraft fire shut down the airstrip. Once again, Johnson raised the prospect of being forced to use nuclear weapons to save Khe Sanh.[9]

Wheeler had spoken to Westmoreland a few hours earlier, and the Joint Chiefs chairman relayed to the president the current thinking of the MACV commander. Westmoreland believed a major ground attack on Khe Sanh could come as early as that evening and predicted "a bloody fight." But he remained "confident that the position can be held."[10]

On February 4, Wheeler formally briefed the president on General

Westmoreland's latest response to Johnson's concerns about Khe Sanh. Once again, Westmoreland had emphasized the superior US fire support and airlift capabilities in place for Khe Sanh's defense.

As for tactical nuclear weapons, Westmoreland didn't foresee the need to use them "in the present situation." However, Westmoreland allowed, a significant deterioration in the state of affairs along the DMZ could require drastic action to stave off a catastrophic defeat. "Under such circumstances," Westmoreland wrote, "I visualize that either tactical nuclear weapons or chemical agents would be active candidates for employment."[11]

• • •

By early February, Lyndon Johnson was not the only American consumed with the ominous turn of events in Asia. America's newspaper front pages and nightly newscasts were dominated by coverage of the *Pueblo* crisis, the Tet Offensive, and the siege at Khe Sanh. A steady parade of journalists and photojournalists was making the trek to Khe Sanh, and their reports painted a grim picture.

The new arrivals were stunned by the appearance of the American stronghold. The Marine combat base had become a scarred and debris-littered moonscape, its shredded tents and shattered buildings replaced by a subterranean world of sandbagged bunkers and trenches. Arriving journalists quickly learned that death lurked around the airstrip. The savvy hustled for cover with an urgency of movement that the defenders had wryly christened the "Khe Sanh shuffle."

It was perhaps inevitable, given the distrust that existed between the correspondents and General Westmoreland, that the tone of news coverage out of Khe Sanh implied doom and official miscalculation. The Dien Bien Phu analogy didn't originate with the correspondents, but it became a pervasive theme in articles bearing the Khe Sanh dateline.

In fairness to the correspondents, it was difficult to grasp Westmoreland's strategic vision at Khe Sanh. They could see and experience firsthand the jerry-rigged defenses, the dank, rat-infested bunkers and trenches, the random death and terror of enemy barrages. On the other hand, they could not see the death and terror experienced by the North Vietnamese troops surrounding Khe Sanh as Westmoreland's Operation Niagara of artillery and air strikes exacted a rising toll.

In Washington and Saigon, a debate was underway as to whether America's stand at Khe Sanh was destined to end badly. By the first week of February, President Lyndon Johnson was so engrossed by this question that he had installed a terrain model of Khe Sanh in the White House Situation Room. No assurances by General Westmoreland could allay his concerns.

Just weeks before his death while on patrol with the Marines of the "Walking Dead" in February 1967, Bernard Fall had published his much-anticipated book on the French defeat at Dien Bien Phu. Fall's critically acclaimed account was a devastating reconstruction of the debacle that ended French colonial rule in Vietnam, and its title had evoked the suffering endured by French and Viet Minh troops during the fifty-five-day siege: *Hell in a Very Small Place.*

Now, informing an American audience about the great showdown in the distant hills of South Vietnam, *Newsweek* conjured the ghosts of Dien Bien Phu. "Khe Sanh," the magazine declared, "was shaping up into another version of hell in a very small place."[12]

• • •

In the heart of the combat base, several feet beneath the ragged trench lines and scarred red earth, life proceeded at a high-octane pace in the underground bunker that housed the Command Operations Center (COC) of the 26th Marines. The COC bunker was the nerve center for the combat base and its outposts, "a labyrinth of whitewashed rooms lit by bare bulbs and bustling with staff officers and enlisted aides," as one visitor described it, a tomb-like world of squawking radios, jangling telephones, stale cigarette smoke, and unwashed bodies.

Westmoreland had anchored his quest for victory at Khe Sanh on Operation Niagara, the waterfall of artillery and air strikes that was supposed to negate the North Vietnamese advantage in numbers and decimate their ranks. But the NVA troops were masters of camouflage and concealment, and even in such large numbers as the two divisions arrayed around Khe Sanh, the enemy soldiers were hard to find.

The search for targets was endless. Reports flooded the COC each day, shards of information pouring in from patrols, artillery forward observers, aerial observers, forward air controllers, other human sources, radio intercepts, signals intelligence, and sensor readings. But the piece-meal reporting made it difficult to discern patterns of enemy movements, concentrations, and current locations. The challenge was how to shape such disjointed intelligence into a coordinated campaign of air strikes and artillery fire.

Westmoreland's subordinates had begun assembling a first-rate team to handle target intelligence and execution at Khe Sanh on the eve of the North Vietnamese attack. An energetic Army captain from Missouri named Mark Swearengen reported to the base on January 18 to co-ordinate fire from sixteen long-range 175-millimeter guns at two fire bases along Route 9 northeast of Khe Sanh: Camp Carroll and a seven-hundred-foot karst outcropping known as the Rockpile. A new regimen-tal intelligence (S-2) officer, Jerry Hudson, arrived to manage the torrent of tactical information flowing in and out of Khe Sanh. Their vital role in Khe Sanh's defense reached new heights when they were joined by a dark-skinned stranger who strode into the regimental COC on January 23 with the pretentious air of a British aristocrat.

Swearengen reacted as so many did when first confronted by Captain Munir Mirza Baig, United States Marine Corps. Baig burst into the bunker with a native kukri knife at his waist, "and spoke as though he were there to single-handedly save Khe Sanh." Swearengen wondered: *Is this guy crazy?*[13]

Now thirty-six, Baig was smart and well read in eighteenth-century siege warfare doctrine, World War I artillery tactics and techniques, even the writings of General Vo Nguyen Giap. His brilliance was rivaled by his eccentricities. Born in 1932 into a prominent Muslim family in British India, Baig was the son of a Sandhurst-trained cavalry officer who later served in the British colonial administration and foreign service. When British India was granted independence and partitioned along religious lines in 1947, Baig's father became a diplomat for the new government of Pakistan.[14]

After splitting his childhood among India, Britain, and France, Baig returned to Britain to complete secondary school and attend Cambridge University. In his early twenties, he had earned a master's degree in busi-ness in Canada, where his father had been posted as a Pakistani diplo-mat. He had briefly worked for retailing giant Sears Roebuck before being allowed to enlist in the Marine Corps as a fledgling private. Three years later, after gaining US citizenship, Sergeant Baig was discharged so he could enter Marine Corps Officer Candidates School. He emerged with the gold bars of a second lieutenant.

Harry Baig, as he was now known, logged two years in Marine artillery before expanding his expertise to include counterintelligence. In the late summer and early fall of 1964, he embarked on a daring personal reconnaissance of South Vietnam's I Corps sector, traveling by jeep up to the DMZ with only a driver. Baig spent the next three years shuttling between Vietnam and the United States in various artillery and intelligence capacities. He returned to I Corps in September 1967 to serve with the 3rd Marine Division's intelligence section. When the North Vietnamese moved against Khe Sanh, Baig was dispatched to the base to coordinate target intelligence.

Baig quickly won over his comrades in Khe Sanh's Fire Support Coordination Center. He was physically unremarkable—he wore horn-rimmed glasses and stood five feet seven inches and weighed only 125 pounds—but he possessed an iron constitution that enabled him to work eighteen-hour days. He didn't suffer fools, but his infectious energy and humor endeared him to his colleagues in the COC.[15] He bantered easily about being a Muslim in a sea of Christians, and routinely announced that he was ready to kill some North Vietnamese "infidels."

Baig's official designation was 26th Marines target information officer. Working with regimental intelligence chief Jerry Hudson, he plotted every known enemy position on note cards, one card for each 1,000-meter map grid. Baig had soon identified 3,000 targets within a 15,000-meter radius (about nine miles) from Khe Sanh.[16] He coordinated B-52 strikes and special air support missions with 3rd Marine Division headquarters, and more discreetly, he became Khe Sanh's resident expert on the electronic sensors that now blanketed the approaches to the base. Baig elevated his work to an art form, taking sensor data and other intelligence and meshing it with his knowledge of local terrain and North Vietnamese tactics to identify imminent attacks and inflict heavy blows on the enemy.

Like a mad scientist, Baig did his work at night, preferring to sleep during the day while frontline artillery and air observers called in strikes on an ad hoc basis. Baig disdained this approach as chaotic and "vulgar." As darkness fell, Baig seized the stage, and with the instincts of a maestro, he would craft a symphony of artillery and air strikes that began to take a rising toll on the North Vietnamese.[17]

• • •

Robert McNamara's electronic sensors had been derided by senior generals during the early discussions about the Muscle Shoals program, but the devices quickly proved their worth at Khe Sanh. Sensor readings not only revealed enemy troop concentrations of one hundred or more but also the speed and direction in which the troops were moving. The raw data were shared with Harry Baig in the COC bunker even as the EC-121 aircraft overhead relayed the information to the top-secret facility in Thailand known as Dutch Mill, where IBM 360-40 mainframe computers churned out spreadsheets from which analysts fashioned reports for Baig.

By early February, Baig was devouring the sensor data. He had mastered the layout of the sensor strings, which allowed him to match activation patterns with his knowledge of NVA operational doctrine. It was still an imprecise science, but the sensors pulled back the shroud of fog and darkness that the North Vietnamese used to conceal attacks and improve positions, allowing Baig to almost "see" the enemy soldiers as they moved about.

On the night of February 3, the sensors northwest of Hill 881 South erupted with activity and continued to indicate the movement of large numbers of enemy troops until the early morning hours of February 4. The enemy soldiers had appeared on the sensor grid about two and one-half miles northwest of the American outpost, then turned south and continued moving past the western flank of 881 South. When they were clear of the hill, they turned east, toward Khe Sanh. And then, they disappeared. A sensor string southeast of 881 South was never activated, suggesting the troops had sought cover nearby.

As he tracked the enemy, Baig had concluded that the column was a Vietnamese resupply convoy. He had called in artillery fire on the unseen enemy force as the sensors registered the movement, but there was no way to know whether any damage had been done.

That evening, Sunday, February 4, Baig and his comrades watched as the sensors once again crackled with activity along the same route. Midnight arrived, and the movement stretched into the early morning hours of February 5. Baig reached a chilling conclusion: rather than a resupply convoy, they were tracking an NVA regiment, and the estimated 1,500 to 2,000 troops were moving into position for an attack.[18] The sensors southeast of 881 South once again had not activated, which seemed to rule out the combat base as the objective. Baig concluded the target was 881 South. His colleagues concurred.

It was a race against time now to see whether the enemy force could be destroyed by artillery before it was able to strike. Baig projected the likely location of the enemy column. Assuming a pace of about 1.25 miles per hour—"NVA rate of march in darkness and mist"—he drew a line eastward from the last sensor triggered. It ended at a point south of the American outpost atop 881 South. Baig framed the point with a target block measuring 1,000 meters by 300 meters (roughly 1,100 yards by 330 yards), bounded on each end by 1,000-meter lines that arced across the hill's southeastern and southwestern slopes.

At 3:00 a.m., American artillery opened up on the target box Baig had drawn. For half an hour the guns blanketed the area with high explosive shells and walked rounds across the southern flanks of 881 South. Sensors south and southwest of the hill erupted with activity suggestive of urgent enemy movements. The acoustic devices captured a scene of terror unfolding inside the target box, relaying to the American analysts "the voices of hundreds of men running in panic through the darkness and heavy fog."[19]

The Vietnamese had suffered a heavy blow, and a likely attack on 881 South had been broken. But in his scramble to preempt the assault, Harry Baig had committed a rare oversight. Two NVA battalions had avoided the American trap, and they were now poised to hit the Marines on Hill 861 Alpha.

CHAPTER 9

The Battle of Hill 861 Alpha

Around 3:00 a.m. on Monday morning, February 5, Second Lieutenant Don Shanley moved in a low crouch along the northern perimeter trench of the Marine outpost on Hill 861 Alpha. After two months in Vietnam, the twenty-three-year-old platoon commander had found that his periodic line checks served two useful purposes: they kept his men on their toes, and they gave him an opportunity to get to know the forty Marines and two corpsmen under his command.

Most of the time, Shanley's men—collectively the 1st Platoon of Echo Company, 2nd Battalion, 26th Marines—were glad to see their "LT." But on nights when the enemy was about, the lieutenant could sense the agitation when he would suddenly appear in the darkness. "What the fuck are you doing this for, lieutenant?" the Marine might say. "I nearly blew you away!"[1] Now, Shanley moved cautiously to the next Marine along his line, whispering his identification well in advance so he didn't spook one of his boys and get blown away.

As he made his rounds, Shanley passed on the latest warning that battalion headquarters had relayed to his company commander, Captain Earle Breeding: there was "major movement" around their hill, or so battalion honchos claimed. Shanley was skeptical. He and his boys had heard similar warnings for days, and the false alarms were wearing them out.

Thirteen days had passed since their exhausting march to the hill, and the 150-odd Marines and eight or so Navy corpsmen of Echo Company had transformed the thickly vegetated knoll into a crude fortress. They had not been attacked in those anxious first days on the hill, but they had suffered from shortages of food and water. In desperation, the Marines tried to lick the dew off ponchos and cut open bamboo and banana trees to collect whatever water they could.

On the first day, Captain Breeding had walked Don Shanley out on a promontory overlooking the hill's gently sloping northern approach. "If they hit us, this is where they're coming through," Breeding had said. And then he had opened his arms and instructed Shanley: "This is your area, from here to here. Start setting in."[2]

Shanley and his men went to work with their Marine-issue "entrenching tools." Rocketman Dave McCall used captured Chinese dynamite to knock down three-foot-diameter trees and towering stands of elephant grass and to clear fields of fire to the west and northwest—the likeliest avenue of a North Vietnamese attack. McCall had packed a roll of concertina wire with C4 explosives and set it off, scything the grass on the southeastern corner of the hill to create a landing zone for helicopter resupply and medevac missions.[3]

The centerpiece of 1st Platoon's critical stretch of perimeter was a salient constructed around a large bomb crater left over from the Hill Fights the previous spring and christened "Crater City" by Shanley's Marines. Shanley dug his hole on the south side of the crater, and that became the platoon command post. To his left and right, the men of 1st Platoon used their "e-tools" to scoop out fighting holes and gun pits along a four-foot-deep trench that soon looped around the hilltop. The nerve center of the garrison was Captain Breeding's company command post, carved into the crest of the hill, about sixty-five yards behind Shanley's men.

Shanley cut an impressive figure: handsome, blond hair, blue eyes, a lanky five feet eleven inches, with the easy grace of a gifted athlete. He had been a backstroke champion on the nation's top-ranked high school team in Winnetka, Illinois, and his achievements in swimming and academics earned him admission to Stanford University in 1962. He swam for Stanford while majoring in history and earned his degree in 1966. He began graduate studies at the University of California–Berkeley business school but quit to enter Marine Corps Officer Candidates School the following spring—a decision that stunned his friends, many of whom were vehemently against the war. But Shanley had a keen sense of history, and his inherent curiosity fueled within him a desire to "check out this great defining social struggle" that America had embraced in Vietnam.

Upon arriving in Vietnam, Shanley was assigned to Echo Company of the 2nd Battalion, 26th Marines. He was smart enough to know that he needed to keep his war-hero fantasies in check until he learned the ropes. "What do I need to know to stay alive?" he asked his men.[4] When he got ready to take his platoon out on a patrol or ambush in those first weeks, he would press his squad leaders, "Do you think this is a dumb way to do it? I'm open to a better way, so sound off now."

The Marines in Shanley's care were a diverse lot: black, white, and brown; Northerners and Southerners; hometowns that ranged from farming villages to big cities. Private First Class Jack Bogard, twenty-one, of Sycamore, Ohio, kept things loose around Crater City by shouting out, "Good morning, Vietnam!" (appropriated from Armed Forces Radio DJ Adrian Cronauer, as Shanley would later learn); Private First Class Martin Luther Rimson, eighteen years old, sang in nightclubs back home in Detroit, Michigan, and his comrades around Crater City were treated to silky-smooth strains of "Moon River" and other tunes; and then there was Lance Corporal Joseph Molettiere, also eighteen, who couldn't stop talking about the baby his young wife was expecting back in South Philadelphia.[5]

Now, in the predawn chill of February 5, Shanley finished his rounds about 4:00 a.m. and returned to his hole just in time to hear the three Marines in his listening post frantically keying their radio handset to sound a silent alarm. Whatever they had seen or heard, Shanley couldn't do anything without more information. He decided to grab a few minutes of shut-eye while his radioman monitored their PRC-25 unit for alarms or updates. Shanley hadn't known many pleasures in his two months in the bush, and now he decided to air out his feet for the first time since arriving on 861 Alpha. He had started unlacing one boot when Crater City erupted with explosions and gunfire.[6]

• • •

As mortar rounds, rocket-propelled grenades, machine guns, and assault rifles pounded the 1st Platoon perimeter, Shanley hurriedly tied his boot lace and sprinted the twenty yards to the northern edge of his line. He slid into one of the front holes and found himself beside a wounded Marine he didn't immediately recognize.[7] Shanley had barely processed what was happening when he was stunned and temporarily blinded by an explosion. Seconds passed, perhaps longer. When his vision returned and his head began to clear, he discovered that his M-16 rifle had been shattered beyond use, leaving him with two grenades with which to defend himself.

Peering from the hole, Shanley saw North Vietnamese soldiers all around him, dashing through the wire in twos and threes, jumping over his trench line as they headed deeper into the American outpost. One enemy soldier stopped over Shanley's hole and looked down at Shanley and the wounded Marine before continuing on his way.[8]

Shanley was frozen in place, still stunned by the shell burst and sheer terror, when a familiar voice shook him from his stupor. "One! One!" It was the call sign for a platoon commander. "One, get your ass back here!"[9] It was Shanley's tough platoon sergeant, McChurty G. Allen.

Shanley jumped up and dashed back up the hill toward the voice, diving head-first into the first hole he found. As the platoon commander popped his head out of the hole, Sergeant Allen fired several shots toward him. Three NVA soldiers fell dead around Shanley.

● ● ●

First Platoon rocketman Dave McCall was fast asleep behind the front positions around Crater City when the North Vietnamese mortar rounds shattered the night. He bolted to his fighting hole but found no sign of the two Marines who were supposed to be there. In front of the hole, McCall found a fresh mortar crater where he had left his M-16 rifle on a bipod.

Peering ahead, McCall couldn't see any NVA soldiers yet, but he figured they were just beyond the wire, waiting to force their way through the perimeter as soon as the mortars fell silent. McCall began throwing grenades as fast as he could along the perimeter wire. He realized the M-60 machine gun to his right wasn't firing, so he dashed into the pit.

The gun was on its stand, but it was twisted like a pretzel. The gunner and his assistant were lying at the bottom of the hole, moaning in agony.

McCall heard the sickening thud of a heavy object as it smacked into the dirt floor and bounced twice. He dived toward the trench line but only managed to get his head and upper body out of the pit before the enemy hand grenade exploded. Metal shards ripped into McCall's right leg, and the blast wave slammed him against the dirt wall and dropped him onto his back. He grabbed the remnants of his right leg. It felt like a wet sponge. Back home in rural Kansas, McCall had been faster than just about anyone in his high school. A thought flashed through his brain: *Well, my running days are over.*[10]

Another grenade dropped into the gun pit, a little farther away than the first. McCall pulled his helmet over his face and waited. He heard the deafening roar and felt the hot metal shred the tissue, muscles, and nerves of his left leg.

Seconds passed, maybe minutes, before a Navy corpsman he knew only by his nickname—Wild Man—darted into the hole. The corpsman checked the wounded machine gunner and his assistant first and was examining McCall's injured legs when another grenade plopped into the pit. The corpsman stepped into the blast path, and when he turned around, McCall could see Wild Man's face had become a bloody mask.

"We gotta get out of here, *now!*" McCall yelled. He dragged himself onto his left leg and hopped into the trench. The blinded corpsman felt his way out of the hole, and the two badly injured Americans helped each other through Crater City. They climbed out of the trench and slowly made their way up the grassy slope toward the center of the outpost.

The corpsman cleared enough blood and debris off his face to see out of one eye, then headed off to get help. McCall crawled deeper into the grass and dragged himself into a shallow depression. As the battle raged, the wounded rocketman lay on his back, staring up at the flare-lit sky.

• • •

First Platoon rifleman Dave Norton was asleep in a clump of grass along the northwest trench line, about thirty feet from Crater City, when the attack began. He slid into his fighting hole and ducked for cover as mortar rounds pounded the 1st Platoon positions. The barrage subsided, and one of the three Marines in Shanley's listening post outside the wire came running up the hill, shouting, "The gooks are coming! The gooks are coming!"[11]

Norton and his best friend, rifleman Joe Molettiere, peered into the darkness but couldn't see anything. The panicked voice of a Marine suddenly sounded from a 60-millimeter mortar pit about ten feet behind them. "Who's there? *Who's there?*" Norton heard the sound of boots hitting the ground, and the Marine opened fire. Two NVA soldiers fell dead between the trench line and the mortar pit.

The sounds of battle swept the hill—shouts and screams mingling with the roar of explosions and gunfire. Norton was reassured by the sound of his squad's M-60 as gunner John Ingram, a big, brawny Tennessean, sprayed the fog and darkness beyond the Crater City lines.[12]

A voice called out to Norton and Molettiere from the direction of Crater City. "Wounded man here! Wounded man here!" Norton and Molettiere reacted to the call for help and found their friend, Martin Luther Rimson, the silky-voiced singer from Detroit. A mortar had nearly severed one of his legs, but he was still conscious and alert. The two Marines dragged Rimson back to their position. Norton yelled for a corpsman, and one quickly appeared.

The corpsman had started to work on Rimson's leg when suddenly a cry carried across the hill. "Gas! Gas! Gas!" On Captain Breeding's orders, the Marines had tossed tear-gas grenades to slow the NVA onslaught, and the choking fumes had begun to settle into the trenches.

Molettiere had gotten his gas mask on and was kneeling over Rimson when the blinding red flash of a mortar round engulfed the Marines. Molettiere took the brunt of the blast and was torn apart. Rimson had been shielded from instant death by Molettiere, but he was in bad shape. The fate of the corpsman was unknown.

In the wavering light of overhead flares, Norton initially thought his right arm had been blown off at the elbow. In fact, it was still attached, but the bones had been ripped from his forearm, resulting in the grotesque extension of his hand and lower arm. A corpsman bandaged Norton's mangled limb, dressed a shrapnel gash in his knee, and gave him a shot of morphine to dull the pain.

As the soothing drug took effect, Norton stretched out along the trench line. In his good hand he clutched a knife. He was ready to die fighting.

• • •

From his command post about fifty yards behind Crater City, Echo commander Earle Breeding tried to make sense of the chaos. "The gooks are coming!" had quickly become "Gooks in the wire!" and then "Gooks in the trench line!" The frantic shouts had swept the lines of Echo's 2nd and 3rd platoons and circled the hill. Reports from the perimeter suggested a general attack on all sides, so Breeding ordered his troops to throw teargas grenades to slow the enemy onslaught.[13] To his superiors, he broadcast an appeal for all available artillery support.

Word of the attack rocketed up the chain of command, crossed the Pacific, and landed on desks at the Pentagon and the White House Situation Room, twelve time zones behind Vietnam. The question that quickly worked its way back down to Khe Sanh: was the attack the opening move in the anticipated North Vietnamese attempt to overwhelm the American stronghold?

The attack had unfolded in textbook North Vietnamese Army style, and the initial barrage had reflected the careful reconnaissance work that was a Communist hallmark in Vietnam. As soon as the initial barrage had ceased, sappers wielding Bangalore torpedoes had blasted gaps in the few strands of barbed wire the Marines had strung around the perimeter of 861 Alpha.

Lieutenant Don Shanley had reached a frontline hole in time to witness the first NVA assault teams as they dashed through the breach in his lines and spread into the interior of the American outpost. Some of the NVA soldiers went to work widening the breach by attacking 1st Platoon positions from inside the American lines, tossing grenades and firing RPGs and AK-47 rifles at fighting holes and bunkers where Marines had sought shelter. Others, like the pair of NVA soldiers Dave Norton had heard creeping up on the 60-millimeter mortar pit behind his position, had pushed up the hill to sow chaos and confusion. Still others had swept over the crest and opened fire on the 2nd and 3rd platoon lines from behind.

The enemy had gotten the drop on the Echo Marines with a ferocious first strike, but illumination rounds fired by the company's mortars quickly allowed Breeding to determine that his lines were intact along the southern perimeter and eastern and western flanks, and there was no sign of attack in those areas. Just as Breeding had anticipated, the northern perimeter was the focal point of the enemy thrust. Don Shanley had confirmed the breach in his lines and reported that small groups of NVA troops were continuing to sprint into the American outpost.[14]

As injured Marines trickled back from the 1st Platoon lines, Breeding began to reclaim the initiative. To contain the NVA soldiers inside his perimeter, Breeding had Echo's acting executive officer, Second Lieutenant Alec J. Bodenweiser, redeploy fire teams from the secure southern end of the hill to a new defensive line taking shape behind the 1st Platoon's shattered perimeter. Breeding personally took on the larger problem of shutting down the flow of enemy troops to the fight. Nine minutes after the attack began, rounds from the 105-millimeter howitzers at Khe Sanh Combat Base began screaming over the hill to pound the northwest approach to 861 Alpha and suspected NVA assembly areas nearby.

•   •   •

Along the northern perimeter, the remnants of Don Shanley's 1st Platoon fought for their lives. Shanley had lost more than half of his forty men in the first minutes of the fight. His trenches, fighting holes, and gun pits were soaked with the blood of his dead and wounded Marines.

Light-hearted PFC Jack Bogard, one of Shanley's favorites, had been part of the listening post outside the northern perimeter when the attack began, and he made it back to his fighting hole. He had dragged a wounded comrade back up the trench line and was trying to save another buddy when he was struck by enemy fire and killed.[15]

Some of the NVA soldiers who had dashed through the breach now stood over the trench line and fired down at trapped Marines.[16] In the fast-moving battle, Shanley and other survivors were pinned in their positions behind Crater City. Shanley managed to maintain radio contact with Captain Breeding as enemy soldiers blasted away at him with an AK-50 machine gun on the far side of the crater. The enemy gunfire and shrapnel gouged a deep groove in the back of Shanley's hole, about three inches above his head. Corporal William Johnson crouched beside the platoon leader and kept the NVA attackers from advancing with a flurry of well-placed grenades.[17]

Ignoring the heavy fire, a fearless weapons platoon corporal, Tom Eichler, headed down the trench line toward the northern perimeter to check on comrades and spread the word to fall back to a new line behind Crater City. Near the perimeter's northernmost point, he came upon three severely wounded Marines lying in the bottom of their M-60 machine-gun hole. Eichler hoisted one of the injured men on his back and headed up the trench line, but he ran headlong into an NVA soldier in the narrow passageway. Whirling around, Eichler began running back down the trench as the enemy soldier opened fire. Eichler felt the bullets smack into the flak jacket of the wounded Marine draped over his shoulder.[18]

Eichler found his way blocked by another NVA soldier who was firing a rocket at Americans farther down the trench. With the wounded Marine still on his back, Eichler grabbed the enemy soldier and strangled him with the strap of his rocket pouch.

Over the next few minutes, Eichler managed to avoid the marauding enemy soldiers while carrying three injured Marines to safety. He had returned to the front line one last time to warn any survivors to fall back when he came upon a chilling sight. Three young Marines had been blown apart in a hole, and visible in the intermittent light were "ten long, bloody marks from the top of the hole to the bottom, made by the bloody hands of one of those Marines who had attempted to crawl out before he died."[19]

• • •

On Breeding's request, supporting fire from nearly every American position in the Khe Sanh area was now blanketing the northwest approach to his hill and likely NVA assembly areas nearby. As the shells rained down, Lieutenant Don Shanley kept bringing the fire closer and closer to his line. "Drop 5–0 [fifty meters]," he would yell into his radio handset, and the 105-millimeter howitzer gunners would place more rounds that much closer to the American perimeter.

Down at Khe Sanh Combat Base, targeting officer extraordinaire Harry Baig recovered from his initial shock and embarrassment at having missed the threat to 861 Alpha and swung into action. One of the NVA battalions he had overlooked had launched the attack on Earle Breeding's Marines, so now Baig drew on his knowledge of enemy doctrine and tendencies to destroy the reserve battalion moving into position to finish off the American outpost.

In an extraordinary hourlong effort, the Americans pounded the North Vietnamese with artillery and radar-directed air strikes. Three batteries of the 1st Battalion, 13th Marines, artillery regiment at Khe Sanh laid protective fire on the slopes of 861 Alpha while a fourth battery hammered the area below the breach in Echo's perimeter "and then rolled down the slope to prevent the enemy from retiring or being reinforced."[20]

At the suggestion of Captain Mark Swearengen, the 175-millimeter artillery liaison officer assigned to Khe Sanh, the big Army guns at Camp Carroll and the Rockpile along Route 9 laid a wall of steel across the base of the hill to destroy the reserve battalion as it moved into position. The guns marched a deadly barrier of 174-pound high-explosive shells to within 200 meters (220 yards) of Echo's northern perimeter. Inside that buffer, the smaller Khe Sanh guns dropped a rolling barrage on the North Vietnamese troops that were poised to enter the American perimeter or had just been thrown back by Breeding's defense.

Radar-directed air strikes pounded the area beyond the "wall of steel," dropping bombs on enemy mortar clusters and possible assembly areas for NVA reinforcements. Marines on Hill 558 pounded away with 106-millimeter recoilless rifles while Bill Dabney's three 105-millimeter howitzers and two 81-millimeter mortars delivered crucial fire from 881 South.[21] While bracing for the NVA to hit their outpost, the Kilo 3/26 Marines on Hill 861, only about 200 yards southwest of 861 Alpha, bled the NVA assault force with 106-millimeter recoilless rifles and machine-gun fire.

While their comrades on the ground and in the skies kept North Vietnamese reinforcements at bay, Earle Breeding's Marines carried the fight to the Communist forces inside the wire and those still coming through the breach. Echo's 60-millimeter mortar section leader, Corporal Billy E. Drexel Jr., led a squad down the hill and set up a tube behind Shanley's position. While fending off NVA assault troops with grenades, Drexel and his squad dropped over three hundred rounds just beyond the 1st Platoon's perimeter.

• • •

The Marines assigned to positions away from the northern perimeter were spared the brunt of the opening NVA barrage, but the terror and uncertainty of the North Vietnamese attack quickly spread through their lines. Among those listening anxiously to the sounds of battle along the northern line was one of the youngest and greenest of Echo's grunts, Private Larry McCartney, just eighteen years old. Assigned to Echo's 3rd Platoon, McCartney's fighting position on the western trench line marked the point where 3rd Platoon lines tied in with those of the 1st Platoon.

In those uncertain first minutes, the Marines along the western line braced for the NVA to come charging up out of the steep draw that separated their outpost from the American outpost on 861. Soon there were gunshots to their rear, and the Marines realized that enemy soldiers were loose in the interior of the hill. Some of the Marines turned inboard to meet that threat while others continued to watch the darkness to their front. In the pulsating light of illumination flares, the Marines along the western perimeter caught glimpses of NVA soldiers making their way northward through the draw to join the attack on the shattered 1st Platoon lines.

Further down the western trench line, near the hill's southwest corner, 3rd Platoon rifleman Jim Kaylor, a nineteen-year-old from Costa Mesa, California, was removing his boots after completing a two-hour watch when the attack hit. Kaylor and his squad mates got the news by radio that NVA troops had breached the perimeter. They soon were exchanging small arms fire with enemy troops as they moved northward through the draw.

Kaylor was focused on that area when he heard the distinctive pop of an enemy AK-47 rifle behind him, and a burst of bullets streaked by his head and ripped into his front parapet. Kaylor and other Marines swung around in astonishment and saw a lone NVA soldier, about ten feet away. By the time Kaylor fired, the enemy soldier had disappeared into the fog.

Friendly artillery rounds streaked over Kaylor's position, followed by one "short" round that exploded directly overhead. Kaylor heard the shrapnel as it whizzed by him and spattered the ground and sandbags around him. A dagger-shaped shard of metal missed Kaylor's left shoulder by a couple of inches as it speared a sandbag.[22]

• • •

After awakening to the roar of exploding mortars, Matt Walsh, a 3rd Platoon fire team leader from North Yonkers, New York, got his men in position and ready to repel the enemy attackers. When the word flashed down the western trench line that the enemy was inside the perimeter, Walsh turned two of his men inboard to make sure they didn't get hit from behind.

Almost immediately, Walsh got word to ready his fire team to help plug a breach in 1st Platoon's perimeter on the northern end of the hill. Walsh and the three men who rounded out his team set off along the western trench line toward the sound of the heavy gunfire and explosions. As they made their way forward, a flurry of mortar rounds hit the line around them. They dived to the bottom of the trench and waited for the barrage to taper off, then started moving forward again.

Walsh and his men finally reached the area that had been pounded by the North Vietnamese mortars and RPGs at the onset of the attack, and they began to carefully work their way closer to the breach. The trench was clogged with bodies and pieces of bodies. As he crawled through the carnage, Walsh spotted a foot with a North Vietnamese Army boot on it. "We got NVA bodies in the trench!" he yelled back to his men. "Watch yourself!"[23]

As Walsh and rifleman Michael Worth picked their way through the mass of bodies, Private Joe Roble, twenty, from Latrobe, Pennsylvania, accidentally bumped a dark form lying at the bottom of the trench. It was a human body, and it suddenly moved. Roble dropped down to see whether it was an American or Vietnamese and how badly the man was hurt. As he knelt, an NVA soldier raised an AK-47 rifle and pressed it against Roble's forehead. Before the enemy soldier could pull the trigger, the last wisp of life left his body, and the weapon fell to the ground. "Did you see that?" Roble gasped to his comrades.[24]

The four Marines moved even more warily now. The breach came into view, and they tossed a few grenades toward the torn wire to finish off any enemy soldiers still around. An hour or so earlier, North Vietnamese had overrun this area in a vicious close-quarters battle. Now, Matt Walsh and his fire team saw no sign of life.[25]

• • •

The sounds and smells of the battle washed over Dave McCall as he lay in the tall grass up the slope from Crater City. Although he was now losing blood from his mangled leg, his practice of tying his jungle utilities to the top of his boot "to keep critters out" had probably saved his life. When McCall had hopped away from Crater City, the movement of his body had set his boot spinning, which had tightened his pants against the stump of his leg like a pressure bandage.

McCall stared up at a sky lit by illumination rounds, exploding enemy shells, and outgoing friendly artillery. The air was heavy with the pungent smell of gunpowder and artillery propellant. Above the roar of battle, he heard the dying screams of one of his closest friends, Lance Corporal Louis Franklin Staples, twenty-one, from Chesapeake, Virginia, whose legs had been blown off by the mortar fire that hit Crater City.

There was movement in the grass, and two NVA soldiers crept up beside him, whispering to each other. One held a rocket launcher and the other an AK-47 rifle. McCall lay as still as he could, feigning death. An American grenade plopped into the grass and exploded, killing the North Vietnamese and spraying McCall with shrapnel. The unseen Marine tossed another grenade, and McCall heard it smack the ground close by. He had lost his helmet somewhere, and now he had just enough time to yank his flak jacket over his head as shrapnel shredded his back and shoulder.

The grass parted and McCall looked up to see the familiar face of his weapons platoon sergeant and another Marine he didn't recognize. McCall raised his hand and called out to the Americans. The barrels of two M-16 rifles snapped in his direction.

"Who is it?" the sergeant demanded.

"It's McCall."

"How bad are you hurt?"

"Pretty bad."

The weapons sergeant and the other Marine laid McCall in a poncho and began dragging him toward the eastern trench line. Every few seconds, they would stop and fire a few rounds, then continue on. Slipping in and out of consciousness, McCall periodically awakened and called out, "Be careful with my leg!"

They finally reached the company aid station, in a bomb crater on the south side of the hill. A corpsman kept McCall alert and talking as he tied off the wounded Marine's useless leg and started to work on his assorted shrapnel wounds.

● ● ●

Don Shanley and the 1st Platoon survivors scattered above Crater City stayed alive long enough for help to arrive. With a nose for action, Corporal Tom Eichler arrived with a box of grenades and started pelting the NVA attackers.

While Shanley continued to work the radio, Corporal Bill Johnson maintained effective fire on the nearby NVA. When there was a lull in the enemy fire, Johnson hopped out of the hole and crawled across the twenty-five-foot crater. A flare burst, and Shanley was shocked to see his corporal standing up on the southern lip of Crater City, blasting away with his M-16. "Get your ass down!" Shanley screamed.[26] Johnson made it back to the hole unscathed.

At 5:20 a.m., about one hour and twenty minutes after the battle began, the North Vietnamese fire tapered off. For the moment, at least, Breeding's Marines had beaten back the enemy attack.

● ● ●

In the gray dawn, Don Shanley surveyed the carnage and destruction around him. The full extent of his losses had yet to be revealed: seven of his young Marines were dead, most of them still lying in a bloody stretch along the northern perimeter that was clogged with the bodies of Americans and North Vietnamese, and had yet to be reclaimed. "Okay," Shanley announced to his motley force of 1st Platoon survivors and reinforcements from other Echo units, "We're going to counterattack."[27]

Clutching a .45-caliber pistol, Shanley got as many as a dozen men on line above Crater City. With Shanley at the center, the line surged toward the northern perimeter.[28] At the front lip of the bomb crater, Shanley saw a couple of dead NVA soldiers. He also found a dead Marine whom he didn't recognize. In another fighting hole, he discovered the body of one of the newest men to join his platoon, Alan Ray Smith, a nineteen-year-old private first class from the central Ohio village of Sunbury, dead on his forty-eighth day in Vietnam.

On the right flank, smoke from hot shrapnel rose around 3rd Platoon rifleman Jim Kaylor and his buddy Michael Lucas as they moved northeast toward the perimeter trench, firing their M-16 rifles. Kaylor reached the trench and jumped in. He was relieved to have some cover from the enemy fire. He spotted the body of a Marine sprawled over the parapet nearby and pulled the dead American back into the trench.

At the northernmost point, Shanley directed men into fighting holes and organized the removal of wounded Marines.

Kaylor heard a shout.

"There's one right in front of your hole!"

The Marines swung their rifles over the parapet and blasted an NVA soldier crawling in front of the trench line. Kaylor stared at the dead man for a long time, until his friend yanked him below the parapet. "You want to get your head blown off?"[29]

• • •

At almost the precise moment the attack on 861 Alpha got underway, the North Vietnamese launched two hours of rocket and mortar fire on the combat base. Hill 881 South also came under fire. It was a common tactic for the North Vietnamese, an attempt to prevent the American artillery from coming to the aid of the embattled outpost.

The question of whether the combat base or other outposts were about to face a ground attack remained open for the next two hours. At 4:14 a.m., when the seriousness of the attack on 861 Alpha had become apparent, Colonel Lownds issued a "red alert" for all forces at the combat base. At 5:01 a.m., the Marines of Lima Company, 3/26, at the western end of the base, reported seeing a green star cluster in the sky about 550 yards in front of their position—a common NVA signal launching a ground attack. But the minutes passed at the base without any sign of North Vietnamese assault troops.

• • •

At 6:16 a.m., NVA troops burst from cover and once again charged the northern perimeter of 861 Alpha. The attack lacked the ferocity of the earlier strike, and it was quickly broken. The elusive battalion of NVA reserves that Harry Baig had feared might doom 861 Alpha had never appeared. In all likelihood, it had been decimated by the American artillery fire and air strikes.

In the growing light, Captain Earle Breeding left his command post atop 861 Alpha and made his way down to the northern perimeter. He found Don Shanley and congratulated the young lieutenant on a job well done. Breeding noticed that Shanley had blood on his head and asked, "Are you hit?"

Shanley wasn't even aware that he had been struck by a small piece of shrapnel at some point in the fight. "I'm okay," Shanley said. "No big deal."[30]

Breeding and Shanley made the rounds of the 1st Platoon perimeter. Dave Norton was still lying in the trench line, waiting to be carried back over the hill to await medevac choppers. "Good job, Marine," Breeding said. "We kicked their ass."[31]

• • •

Around 9:30 a.m., the first medevac choppers threaded their way through the wispy fog down to the hill. Marines were standing by with stretchers laden with their wounded comrades when NVA mortar rounds began to hit nearby. Earle Breeding quickly nixed any thoughts of ditching the wounded and taking cover. "No one moves!" the Echo commander ordered.

The first CH-34 helicopter settled onto the grassy LZ, and the casualties were loaded inside. In less than five minutes, Echo's wounded arrived at Khe Sanh Combat Base. There, Navy surgeons and corpsmen checked vital signs and packed and bandaged assorted wounds.

Even with his badly mangled arm, Dave Norton was alert enough to recognize the corpsman cutting off his clothes and boots: they both had been patients at a Phu Bai hospital a few weeks earlier. Norton's wounds were rechecked and bandaged to control the bleeding, and then he was moved to a holding area to await a medevac flight out of Khe Sanh.

As he lay on a stretcher at Charlie Med, Norton suddenly realized that the wounded Marine next to him was Martin Rimson, the friend he had helped carry back up the trench line in the fight's opening minutes. The aspiring singer from Detroit had lived through the night, but he was no longer lucid. He was talking softly and fast, but Norton couldn't understand what he was saying.[32]

A big C-130 transport plane arrived and stretchers loaded with the Echo wounded were carried inside for the short hop back to the coast. During the flight, Dave McCall, the wounded Echo rocketman, spotted Martin Rimson on a nearby stretcher. "How's my buddy, the black kid over there?" McCall asked an attendant.

The crewman checked, then turned back to McCall. "Man, he's gone. He didn't make it."[33]

●　●　●

Navy surgeons in Da Nang were able to save rifleman Dave Norton's arm. There was nothing that could be done for rocketman Dave McCall's leg. During the five days McCall spent in a Phu Bai hospital, a Marine colonel visited, accompanied by a captain with a box of Purple Hearts. "Congratulations, Marine," the colonel said as he laid a Purple Heart on McCall's covers.

McCall was transferred to a hospital in Japan, where he underwent more surgery. The American grenade that may have saved his life by killing the two NVA soldiers standing over him cost him part of his stomach. His various wounds had left him in bad shape.

One day in mid-February, an orderly arrived with trays of food for McCall and the patient next to him. "Huh!" the orderly exclaimed. "Dave McCall and Dave Norton—two Daves in a row!"

McCall leaned over and took a long look at the bruised and swollen face of the Marine in the bed next to him. "Norton, is that you?"

The rifleman from North Carolina raised himself with great effort before slowly turning toward the familiar voice. A faint smile lit his face. "Hey, you made it!" Norton said.

"Hey," McCall said, "you made it, too!"

McCall soon drifted off to sleep, happier than he had been in days. When he awoke, Dave Norton was gone, headed back to the States for another year and a half of medical treatment. McCall would soon follow. Decades would pass before the two wounded Echo comrades would meet again at a Khe Sanh veterans reunion in the 1990s.[34]

• • •

Back on Hill 861 Alpha, the last of Echo's wounded were flown out on helicopters that had offloaded ammunition, medical supplies, seven replacement Marines, and a tall, graying man in clean jungle utilities with two cameras hanging around his neck.

David Douglas Duncan, a former Marine and famous war photographer, had just arrived in Khe Sanh the day before, and had talked his way onto a chopper headed to the scene of the latest action. He made his way to the northern end of the Echo outpost to bear witness to 1st Platoon's savage fight. Among the enduring images he captured during his few hours on the hill was one of Tom Eichler and mortarman Billy Drexel as they surveyed the torn bodies of North Vietnamese soldiers beyond the northern wire. Another photo captured a nineteen-year-old Echo sniper, Lance Corporal Albert Miranda, squeezing off a shot at an enemy soldier; alongside Miranda in the photograph were a fellow sniper, Lance Corporal David Burdwell, twenty, of Wichita Falls, Texas, and Lieutenant Alec Bodenweiser of Portland, Oregon.

Among the wide-eyed replacement Marines who scrambled out of the back of a CH-46 helicopter and into the hellish tableau was Mexican-born Jose Luis Reyes Jr., an eighteen-year-old from the Los Angeles suburb of San Fernando.[35] Making his way through the blood-stained trenches and fighting holes of Crater City, Reyes felt the fear rising in his throat. *What in the hell have I gotten myself into?* he thought.

Reyes made his way past blood-spattered, hollow-eyed survivors of the night's battle, desperate to find someone who would teach him "how to stay alive." He looked around and saw a Marine with the name "Pancho" scrawled across the back of his flak jacket. Back home, Reyes had grown up watching *The Cisco Kid,* a television series about the cowboy-era exploits of two good-hearted desperadoes, the Cisco Kid and his sidekick, Pancho. Reading that name on the back of a Marine momentarily broke the tension for Reyes, and he yelled, "Hey, Pancho!" The Marine turned around, took one look at the scrawny Hispanic kid in the fresh jungle utilities, and replied, "Hey, Cisco!" From that moment on, Reyes was Echo's "Cisco Kid."

• • •

In the battle for 861 Alpha, Earle Breeding had lost thirty-three men, killed and wounded about 20 percent of Echo's total strength. The 1st Platoon sustained a 75-percent casualty rate. Eight young Americans were dead: former Boy Scouts and altar boys, a husband and father-to-be. The oldest among them was twenty-one, the youngest, eighteen. On the forms they had filled out before arriving in Vietnam, six had identified themselves as "Caucasian," one as "Negro," and one "American Indian." There were two Buckeyes from Ohio, a pair of Texans, one each from New York, Pennsylvania, Michigan, and Virginia. And now, they were loaded aboard choppers to begin their final journey home.

• • •

For the defeated North Vietnamese, there were no medevac choppers or transport planes to whisk them to warm beds and well-staffed hospitals out of harm's way. The survivors melted back into the jungle to regroup; the wounded were laid on stretchers and carried back to underground field hospitals across the border in Laos, where they would face the constant threat of obliteration by American B-52 strikes.

The American victory at 861 Alpha was a setback for the North Vietnamese in their ambitious Khe Sanh campaign. But patience and persistence were prized virtues in the North Vietnamese Army. As Earle Breeding and the bloodied Marines of Echo Company braced for another round, NVA forces a few miles to the south were poised to strike America's most vulnerable outpost at Khe Sanh.

CHAPTER 10

"Tanks in the Wire"

For the US Special Forces at Lang Vei, four miles southwest of Khe Sanh Combat Base along Route 9, Tuesday, February 6, unfolded in what had become familiar fashion since the North Vietnamese campaign had gotten underway in late January. There had been a North Vietnamese mortar attack at midmorning, followed by a dusk artillery barrage that had hammered the camp with fifty rounds of 152-millimeter shells. Now, an hour before midnight, the sounds of unusual enemy movements suggested another long night ahead for the twenty-four American Green Berets and nearly five hundred indigenous troops dug in at the hilltop outpost.

The Green Berets had been America's pioneers in the area, driving up narrow Route 9 to hoist the Stars and Stripes over an old French bunker at Khe Sanh in 1962. The arrival of the Marines four years later had cramped the style of the freewheeling Army irregulars, so the Special Forces boys had built a new camp further west along Route 9, less than two miles from the Laotian border.

From their new base at the Bru village of Lang Vei, the Green Berets had organized the local tribesmen into armed Civilian Irregular Defense Group (CIDG) units and patrolled the surrounding hills and North Vietnamese infiltration routes. Their work dovetailed with the cross-border activities of the clandestine MACV "Studies and Observations Group" (MACV–SOG), which operated out of Forward Operating Base 3 at Khe Sanh.

Over the past year, the war had engulfed Lang Vei with a vengeance. On March 2, 1967, two US Air Force planes had mistaken the village for an enemy enclave and dropped napalm that killed 135 Bru men, women, and children and injured 213.[1] On May 4, during the Hill Fights around Khe Sanh, the Special Forces camp had been partially destroyed in a ground attack by the North Vietnamese.[2]

Captain Frank Willoughby had arrived in the late summer to oversee construction of a new Special Forces outpost several hundred yards west of Lang Vei village, even closer to the Laotian frontier. Under Willoughby's supervision, Navy Seabees had studded the dog-bone-shaped camp with concrete bunkers and a steel-reinforced underground Tactical Operations Center (TOC).

The North Vietnamese campaign against the Marine base at Khe Sanh had put Lang Vei in the path of the massing enemy forces, and the Green Berets had braced for an attack after the Laotian border outpost at Ban Houei Sane fell on the night of January 23–24. More than five hundred soldiers of the Royal Laotian Army's 33rd Elephant Battalion fled eastward along Route 9 to Lang Vei, bringing with them 2,200 dependents. The civilians moved into the village and the Laotian soldiers took over the old Special Forces camp.

The Laotian battalion commander and his throngs of refugees had proved to be a distraction for the Special Forces at Lang Vei, and after the morning mortar attack of February 6, a helicopter had dropped off a lanky Green Beret officer with a graying flattop haircut to lend a hand. As commander of Company C of the 5th Special Forces Group (Airborne), Lieutenant Colonel Daniel F. Schungel was Captain Willoughby's direct boss, and he had arrived to manage the high-maintenance Laotian battalion commander and the tense refugee situation.

Later in the day, when the twilight NVA artillery attack had ended around 7:00 p.m., the camp bustled with night defensive preparations by Lang Vei's welter of American and indigenous forces. At the top of the pyramid was Captain Willoughby's twelve-man unit, Special Forces Detachment A-101, which worked with fourteen Vietnamese Special Forces to oversee nearly three hundred indigenous troops broken into four CIDG militia companies. Additionally, Lang Vei's capabilities had been strengthened by a mobile strike force company—a

Mike force, in Special Forces parlance—comprising six Green Berets and about 160 Hre tribesmen.

As night fell over Lang Vei, a platoon of Hre fighters from Lieutenant Paul Longgrear's Mike force company exited the main gate along Route 9 and headed west toward a fortified observation post several hundred yards away. In command was Sergeant First Class Charles Lindewald Jr., a heavy-weapons specialist from La Porte, Indiana. The thirty-five-year-old Lindewald had arrived in Vietnam with one of the first Green Beret A-teams six years earlier, and as a symbol of his veteran status, he wore around his neck the tooth of a tiger he had killed in one of his early missions.

The Mike force column was nearing the forward outpost when Lindewald's indigenous troops sensed an ambush. They blasted away at the brush before bolting back to camp, warning of "beaucoup VC."[3] After Longgrear convinced the Hre to head back out, Lindewald had barely gotten the platoon settled in their forward post when once again they began hearing unusual noises in the darkness.

As the night wore on, strange sounds kept the forces in the main camp on edge as well. In the southeastern sector, the CIDG troops of the Vietnamese 104 Company reported vehicle engines in the direction of Lang Troai, an abandoned Bru border village to their southwest. Around 9:00 p.m., three trip flares erupted along the perimeter of the Mike force post, prompting Lindewald's soldiers to take potshots at suspicious shapes and shadows. The noise panicked the main camp's four CIDG companies, and they, too, fired into the darkness for several minutes before order was restored.

About 10:00 p.m., Sergeant Nickolas Fragos, a twenty-three-year-old Greek immigrant, had started his three-hour watch in the observation tower that jutted from the subterranean command bunker.[4] The first hour proved eventful when a trip flare erupted outside the 104 Company area, and Lang Vei's defenders once again stitched the darkness with gunfire before order was restored. Midnight arrived, and a few minutes into the new day, Wednesday, February 7, one of the Green Berets at the Mike force outpost west of camp radioed the command bunker: "I think I have VC below me."[5]

Another trip flare burst into brilliant light outside the 104 Company lines, and this time Nick Fragos could see it was no false alarm. Two

North Vietnamese soldiers were clearly visible as they snipped away at the perimeter wire, but not for long. The alert 104 troops dropped the pair with a flurry of gunfire.

A vehicle behind the fallen NVA soldiers switched on its spotlight and scanned the camp's defenses for a few seconds, then smashed through the wire. Fragos yelled into his radio handset, "They've got tanks!"[6]

• • •

In the minutes that followed, North Vietnamese infantry backed by eleven Soviet-made PT-76 light tanks hit the Special Forces camp from the south, east, and west. Simultaneously, the Mike force observation post west of Lang Vei came under heavy mortar and automatic-weapons fire, followed by tanks and infantry.

Inside the command bunker, Captain Willoughby radioed the Marines at Khe Sanh and requested artillery fire on preregistered targets along the camp's southern approach. He also called the Special Forces in Da Nang to get a forward air controller overhead and arrange for air strikes, gunships, and illumination. The Marines reacted skeptically to the report of tanks, and seventeen precious minutes ticked by before the Khe Sanh batteries began firing.[7]

Meanwhile, Lieutenant Colonel Schungel took charge of ground defenses around the command bunker. Working with Fragos and another Green Beret, Schungel began firing M-72 light anti-tank weapon (LAW) rounds at two NVA tanks that were wreaking havoc along the camp's southeastern perimeter. As Schungel sent LAW rounds down the slope, a boom reverberated from a nearby 106-millimeter recoilless rifle position. On his own, Sergeant First Class James William Holt of Hot Springs, Arkansas, the thirty-two-year-old chief medic of A-101, began pumping out deadly fire. A thirty-seven-pound armor-piercing shell smashed into a tank with a burst of flames. Holt was joined by Staff Sergeant Peter Tiroch, and he found his mark with another round. Fire and smoke boiled from the crippled tank.

A third tank churned up the dirt track from Lang Troai, wheeled around the two burning carcasses, and blasted away at the bunkers defended by 104 Company fighters. Holt disabled this adversary as well, then finished it off with his final armor-piercing round. The Green Beret medic headed off to the ammo bunker to retrieve more armor-piercing shells and was never seen again.

Two more NVA tanks pulled up and began pounding the 104 Company bunkers and trenches. Forty-five minutes into the fight, North Vietnamese tanks and infantry overran the camp's southeastern sector.[8]

• • •

When the attack began, Lieutenant Paul Longgrear, twenty-four, was asleep in his bunker near the Tactical Operations Center. The young Mike force commander roused Sergeant John Early, then pumped out four or five illumination rounds from an 81-millimeter mortar before switching to high-explosive projectiles, which he blindly fired toward the likely enemy staging points to the south and west.[9]

Longgrear cut a Hollywood casting director's image of a Green Beret: six foot one, square-jawed, athletic, cocky. Less obvious was the rootless, restless rebel that lay within. He had lived much of his pre-Army life along America's impoverished back roads, from his birth in the struggling southern Illinois river town of Cairo in 1943, to his hardscrabble childhood in southeast Missouri and northeast Arkansas. His father had abandoned his mother the day Paul was born, and the boy grew up rudderless, "trying to figure out who I was and how to become a man."[10]

By high school, Longgrear had embraced hell raising as his life's calling. He got his first fake ID when he was fifteen, and while other teenagers in Jonesboro, Arkansas, were attending church socials and school dances, Longgrear was sneaking into juke joints, dancing and drinking. From his sophomore year of high school on, he lived by himself. He was a star football player, until he clashed with the coach and got kicked off the team.

Longgrear spent the next five years drifting from Arkansas to Oregon to California, working as hard as he played—making glass, building roads, bending iron, harvesting potatoes. He dabbled at college, but his rebellious ways would always get him into trouble and he'd hit the road again. He was working construction in West Sacramento, California, hanging out with his friends at the local Hell's Angels motorcycle club, when his draft notice arrived.

From his first day in the Army in June 1965, Longgrear felt at home. He rose to sergeant, then earned a coveted slot in Officer Candidate School. He taught infantry tactics at Fort Benning, Georgia, and got married at the end of 1966. But his restless streak won out, and he completed Special Forces training and left for Vietnam in October 1967.

Now, as Longgrear pumped mortar rounds skyward to slow the North Vietnamese attack, a familiar figure darted into the pit. "Uh, what's up, doc?"[11] Staff Sergeant Dennis Thompson, a twenty-five-year-old from Portland, Oregon, said in his best Bugs Bunny voice.

"In case you haven't noticed, we're under attack," Longgrear nonchalantly replied.

"Oh, I wondered what all the noise was!" Thompson joked, as he joined Sergeant Early in preparing mortar rounds for the jaunty Mike force lieutenant.

They were still cranking out rounds a few minutes later when an NVA tank clanked over the crest of the hill, no more than one hundred feet away. Longgrear hoisted an anti-tank weapon and squeezed the trigger, but nothing happened. He tried another LAW, and it, too, misfired. He fired a third. The round deflected off the tank's armored hull and disappeared into the night sky; the tank had been too close for the round to arm and explode.

Longgrear hadn't destroyed the enemy tank, but he had gotten its attention. With a chilling mechanical whine, the gun turned toward the Green Berets. "Hey guys," Longgrear shouted, "I think it's time we got out of here."[12] The three Americans scrambled out of the mortar pit before the tank could fire. They would carry on the fight elsewhere.

• • •

NVA tanks backed by infantry now pressured Lang Vei's defenses from all sides. Small-arms fire rose in a roar, punctuated by the explosions of tank rounds, LAWs, mortars, satchel charges, and grenades. In the east, the Bru fighters of the 101 Company battled enemy tanks and infantry to their front and rear. In the west, the 102 and 103 Companies were in the process of being overrun by tanks and ground troops.

The Mike force observation point, along Route 9 west of the camp, had been quickly surrounded in the battle's opening minutes. Sergeant

First Class Kenneth Hanna provided a grim situation report by radio: Charles Lindewald had been gravely wounded in the chest by automatic-weapons fire, and the encircled outpost was "under heavy attack." And then, as the outpost was overrun, the radio line went dead.[13] Inside the Lang Vei command bunker, Captain Frank Willoughby's radios crackled with tank sightings: one coming up Route 9 from the east, three from the west, two in the drop zone between the old and new camps.

As the attack entered its second hour, friendly artillery and air strikes had barely slowed the attack. Casualties were mounting, and the perimeters collapsing. By 2:00 a.m., only the inner compound around the Tactical Operations Center bunker was still holding out.

• • •

After his brush with the enemy PT-76 gunner, Paul Longgrear had headed to the command bunker to join several tank-killing teams organized by Lieutenant Colonel Schungel. The Americans concentrated fire on a tank grinding up the hill from the southeastern sector, and LAW rounds exploded against the welded-steel hull with a "great shower of orange [sparks]."[14] The tank finally lurched to a halt, and three crew members armed with AK-47s crawled out. Schungel and a South Vietnamese lieutenant killed them with grenades and small-arms fire.

When they had exhausted their supply of anti-tank weapons, Schungel and his handful of Green Berets prepared to make a last stand around the command bunker. Longgrear was watching the eastern approach when four NVA sappers draped with satchel charges came into view about thirty yards to his front. Longgrear dropped the NVA soldiers with a burst of seven or eight rounds from his CAR-15 rifle. The Mike force medic, Specialist Fourth Class James L. Moreland, tossed a grenade into the bodies to make sure they were dead.

The grenade flash caught the attention of a nearby tank, and it began moving toward the Green Berets. As the tank approached the TOC, its main gun slowly turned toward the Americans. Longgrear ducked into the bunker entrance and was on his way down the stairs when a tank round knocked him to the floor.

At point-blank range, the North Vietnamese tank had fired a shell from its 76-millimeter gun at Schungel and a handful of other men crouched behind a barrier of weighted barrels. The barrier had saved their lives, but the men had sustained assorted injuries. First Lieutenant Miles Wilkins had been crushed by the barrels; Schungel had been concussed by the blast and tossed several feet; and Specialist Fourth Class William McMurray had been temporarily blinded by the explosion, and his hands were mangled.

As the injured Americans huddled outside the TOC entrance, the tank destroyed the bunker's steel observation tower with a blast from its main gun. A LAW round fired from up the hill smashed into the tank at almost the same instant that Schungel tossed two hand grenades. The tank's hatch popped open and flames billowed out, but no crew members emerged.

Schungel dragged the injured McMurray behind some sandbags, and then he and Wilkins hobbled away from the TOC, toward Route 9. Near the northern perimeter, they slipped inside the wooden structure that served as the main living quarters for the A-101 team—and waited for daylight.[15]

• • •

On the north side of the camp, four Green Berets led by Sergeant First Class William Craig had formed one of the final pockets of resistance. A savvy, forty-one-year-old Korean War veteran and the senior enlisted man in Detachment A-101, Pappy Craig had become the vital eyes-on-the-ground for an air controller circling overhead, helping direct air strikes on hotspots and relay Lang Vei's requests for artillery missions and illumination.

As the minutes passed, Craig's transmissions grew more desperate. In his final broadcast at 2:45 a.m., he called in an air strike on a tank sitting on top of the TOC. Craig signed off and prepared to exit the camp with four Green Berets and forty Bru fighters.

The breakout was underway when machine-gun fire from the east blocked Craig and Sergeant Peter Tiroch in their tracks. They waited for the overhead illumination to fade, then sprinted across Route 9 and settled into a bamboo thicket about one hundred yards beyond the perimeter. When a friendly air strike hit close enough to spray them with shrapnel, the two Americans put another hundred yards between them and the camp. Satisfied they were out of the line of fire, they hid in a dry creek bed to wait out the night.[16]

• • •

At 1:50 a.m., as dire reports from Lang Vei worked their way up the various chains of command within the Marines, Special Forces, and MACV headquarters in Saigon, Major General Rathvon Tompkins, commander of the 3rd Marine Division at Dong Ha, ordered his men at Khe Sanh to break out new anti-personnel "controlled fragmentation munitions" (COFRAM) that had been rushed to the base for use against an NVA ground assault. But the word came back from the Special Forces at Lang Vei: hold off on the artillery to allow air strikes to continue.[17]

In the critical hour that followed, Tompkins continued to press for the use of the "firecracker" rounds. Speaking by phone with Captain Harry Baig in the 26th Marines command bunker at Khe Sanh, Tompkins asked that his recommendation be conveyed to the Special Forces commander at Lang Vei: halt the air strikes long enough to allow the anti-personnel "firecracker" rounds to be fired on the embattled camp, and then resume the air coverage.

At 2:45 a.m., a Lang Vei radio transmission was relayed to General Tompkins. "All troops above ground are enemy. Request arty and air. Tanks on hill south and southwest of us."[18]

About fifteen minutes later, the first "firecracker" rounds fired by gunners at Khe Sanh Combat Base exploded over the Lang Vei Special Forces camp. Twenty-eight rounds of the anti-personnel munitions were fired during a five-minute period, followed by five minutes of high-explosive and variable-timed rounds designed to detonate about twenty to thirty feet above the ground. The artillery was halted, and air strikes on the Lang Vei perimeter resumed.

At 3:15 a.m., Khe Sanh informed General Tompkins that communications with Lang Vei had been lost again.

• • •

Only one island of resistance remained inside the Special Forces camp: the underground Tactical Operations Center, a reinforced concrete bunker measuring thirty-nine by twenty-five feet and located in the heart of the outpost. Inside the bunker were eight Americans: Captain Frank Willoughby, Lieutenant Paul Longgrear, Sergeant Nickolas Fragos, radio operators Franklin Dooms and Emanuel Phillips, Sergeant John Early, Sergeant Arthur Brooks, and Mike force medic James Moreland. There were also about fifteen South Vietnamese, including Lieutenant Pham Duy Quan, commander of the CIDG militia forces at Lang Vei.

The tank that had nearly killed the Green Berets outside the TOC had also destroyed the bunker's radio tower and generator. In the initial scramble to secure the bunker, Early and Moreland had been wounded when they had tried to retrieve an M-60 machine gun from the observation tower. Now, as the sounds of battle faded, the silence inside the bunker was broken only by occasional whispers, hissing radios, and the groans of the badly injured John Early.

Sometime after 3:00 a.m., North Vietnamese soldiers attacked the TOC by dropping fragmentation and tear-gas grenades, satchel charges, and incendiaries down the main entrance, observation tower, and air shafts along the bunker's opposing walls. As the bunker occupants wept and gagged from the noxious fumes, they heard shouts from outside. A voice called out in Vietnamese, warning that the bunker was about to be blown up and ordering the occupants to come out.[19] Before the Americans could react, the South Vietnamese had scrambled to the surface and surrendered. Shortly afterward, the Americans heard shots fired outside the TOC but never learned the fate of their South Vietnamese comrades.

As dawn approached, a massive explosion ripped the north wall of the TOC. The North Vietnamese had dug a shaft beside the air vent and detonated explosives, tearing a sizable hole in the bunker wall. The blast battered the Green Berets with chunks of concrete and hurled them around the room. All but Sergeant Fragos were knocked unconscious.

When Paul Longgrear awakened, North Vietnamese soldiers were swarming around the blast hole and other openings, "throwing hand grenades, pouring gasoline down the breathing ports and setting the place on fire."[20] Longgrear and Fragos scrambled around the bunker to revive injured comrades and prepare the room for a last stand.

Already bleeding from cuts to his head and wrist, Longgrear was wounded again by a grenade that drove a metal shard into his ankle. Another grenade exploded about eighteen inches from Captain Willoughby.

Hot metal pierced his torso, but he saved himself by shielding his upper body with a flak jacket.

As the bunker filled with choking smoke and toxic fumes, the Green Berets sought cover behind pillars and debris and shielded themselves with flak jackets, chairs, and tables. Six of the eight Americans were now wounded. Unable to see or breathe, Longgrear crawled into a corner, covered his mouth, and prepared to die. Radio operator Franklin Dooms managed to raise a forward air controller flying overhead. "They're killing us!" he yelled. "Somebody help us!"[21]

• • •

Circling more than 1,000 feet above Lang Vei, Covey 688 sat in the cockpit of his twin-tailed Cessna O-2A aircraft and listened to the dying pleas of the eight Green Berets. The forward air controller had joined the fight to save Lang Vei about two hours earlier, after a short flight across Laos from his base in Ubon, Thailand. Sporadic radio transmissions had revealed that there were several Green Berets in the command bunker and three others at the old camp, but not much else was known.

Around 7:45 a.m., a pair of Navy A-1H Skyraiders had arrived from the carrier USS *Coral Sea* and checked in with Covey 688. The lead A-1 pilot, Lieutenant Commander Rosario "Zip" Rausa, knew the tricky terrain and the bad weather in this area all too well. A native of Utica, in upstate New York, the thirty-two-year-old Rausa had lettered in football, basketball, and baseball at Middlebury College in Vermont while earning an English degree in 1957. He had enlisted in the Navy and earned his wings two years later.[22] He was already on his second combat deployment to Vietnam, well on his way to 150 missions and 498 carrier landings.

Rausa and his wingman, Lieutenant Larry Gardiner, were part of Navy Attack Squadron (VA) 25, the last such unit still flying Douglas A-1 Skyraiders—squat, single-engine, propeller-driven fighters. The Spad, as it was dubbed, after the famed World War I fighter, could fly "low and slow" while carrying up to 8,000 pounds of ordnance, and it could take considerable battle damage and remain airborne. Right now, Zip Rausa, Larry Gardiner, and their lumbering Skyraiders were the last hope of the Green Berets in the TOC—if only the controller could somehow get the A-1 pilots beneath the clouds and into the fight.

As Covey 688 orbited a fishbowl-shaped pocket in the clouds with the A-1s in tow, another forward air controller, Covey 252—twenty-eight-year-old Air Force captain Charles "Toby" Rushforth III—arrived and began circling nearby in his O-2A. Nearly seven years earlier, when he was graduating from the University of Connecticut with a degree in international relations, Rushforth could scarcely have imagined circling a remote South Vietnamese battlefield in a tiny Cessna. But he had emerged from college at a time when President John F. Kennedy was challenging Americans to serve their country, and Rushforth responded by joining the Air Force. He earned his wings in 1963 and started flying big KC-135 tankers. He had finished a stateside tour in 1967 and considered leaving the Air Force to become a civilian airline pilot, as many of his peers were doing. But America was fighting in Vietnam, and Rushforth decided he needed to see "what wars are like."[23]

Rushforth volunteered for Vietnam and was trained as a forward air controller and assigned to the 20th Tactical Air Support Squadron in Da Nang. He had logged several dozen missions north of the DMZ by January, when he was assigned to support a new operation known as Niagara, to help American ground forces thwart a major North Vietnamese move against the Marine combat base at Khe Sanh.

When Rushforth had taken off from Da Nang on this morning at 7:10 a.m., he had been briefed about the trouble at Lang Vei. He knew that tanks and North Vietnamese troops had penetrated the compound and a number of Green Berets were trapped in the TOC, but little else. Now, circling above the camp, Rushforth quickly gathered just how critical the situation was. He listened as a Green Beret radioed from the TOC, "Get these guys off us, or it's over."[24]

As they orbited around their pocket in the clouds, Covey 688 and Rushforth searched for an opening. They both spotted the dark patch that indicated thinning clouds and a glimpse of the jungle below. "I'm going down and check it out," said Covey 688.

Rushforth watched the O-2A disappear into a "sucker hole," knowing full well the pilot could just as easily fly into the side of a hill on the other end as find clear skies. A minute or so later, Covey 688 popped back up into the fishbowl. He had found some navigable sky over Lang Vei, beneath five hundred feet. "I think there's enough room to work in here," he told the A-1 pilots. "Are you willing to give it a try?"

Under existing air wing regulations for such sketchy flight conditions, Rausa was supposed to abort the mission. But there were Americans beneath those clouds, and he knew they were probably going to die if he didn't help them. "Let's do it," Rausa said.[25]

Another desperate appeal from the Lang Vei command bunker crackled from the radio. "If you can't do anything now," said radio operator Franklin Dooms, "we're finished."[26]

Covey 688 headed down into the hole once again, this time with Zip Rausa close behind, followed by Larry Gardiner. Seconds later, Rausa broke free of the clouds above the smoldering ruins of Camp Lang Vei. He made one pass, unleashing 250-and 500-pound bombs on the NVA soldiers swarming the TOC. Gardiner followed suit. Skimming the treetops, the pilots came around for another pass, and then another, dropping their remaining bombs and scouring the camp with automatic cannon fire. Dead and dying enemy soldiers soon littered the ground around the bunker.

Inside the TOC, the Green Berets could hear the sounds of aircraft, muffled explosions, and screams. The North Vietnamese attack ended abruptly.[27]

By the time Rausa and Gardiner exhausted their ordnance, the skies over Lang Vei were clearing. Four more Skyraiders from AV-25 arrived, loaded with anti-personnel cluster bombs and napalm, and controller Toby Rushforth directed them to their targets in the camp below. The four Skyraiders completed their runs, and a pair of A-1s from the 1st Air Commando Squadron based in Nakhon Phanom, Thailand, swooped in to strafe and bomb the hilltop around the TOC and the camp's western half.

Around midmorning, Rushforth handed off to the next forward air controller and headed back to Da Nang. More A-1s were on their way from the *Coral Sea*. In all, twelve AV-25 pilots would fly sorties in support of Lang Vei during the day. For the time being, they had saved the lives of the eight Green Berets trapped inside the TOC.[28]

• • •

Daybreak had heralded the beginning of another effort to save the embattled Green Berets in the TOC, this one launched by three Special Forces medics overseeing the Laotian army troops at the old Lang Vei camp.

Sergeant First Class Eugene Ashley Jr. boasted more military experience than his two young colleagues combined, having spent sixteen of his thirty-six years in the Army. Born in Wilmington, North Carolina, Ashley had grown up in New York City. He enlisted in the Army in 1950 and after seeing action in the Korean War, decided to make military service his career. After a long infantry stint, he qualified for Airborne and entered the Special Forces.

When the attack on Lang Vei began, Ashley had dispatched one of his young comrades, Sergeant Rich Allen, to get the Laotian troops to fire illumination rounds in support of the embattled Special Forces camp to their west. The twenty-one-year-old Allen ran to the quarters of the colonel in command of the Laotian battalion to present the request. The colonel was entertaining a female companion and rebuffed the young Green Beret, so Allen whipped out his .45-caliber pistol and stuck it under the Laotian commander's chin. The colonel ordered his mortars to deliver the illumination for Camp Lang Vei.[29]

As the battle raged to their west, Sergeant Ashley helped coordinate the delivery of illumination, air strikes, and artillery support for friendly forces. When radio contact with the TOC was lost, he took the lead in coordinating air strikes against the swarming NVA soldiers. At first light, Ashley prepared to launch an effort to rescue the men trapped in the command bunker.

Around 7:00 a.m., Sergeant Ashley and Green Berets Rich Allen and Joel Johnson led a column of about sixty Laotian volunteers up Route 9 toward the Special Forces camp. The relief force was nearing the camp's perimeter when A-1 pilots Zip Rausa and Larry Gardiner pulled off their life-saving strikes. When the Skyraiders had finished, Ashley organized his two young Green Berets and their motley force of Laotian and indigenous fighters in a ragged skirmish line.

The assault force pushed westward through the 101 Company sector, past torn bodies and scorched and shattered bunkers. North Vietnamese machine guns near the TOC opened up, and the indigenous fighters broke and ran. The Green Berets fell back to the camp's eastern entrance.

Ashley coordinated more air strikes, then launched a second assault. Green Berets Pappy Craig and Peter Tiroch had emerged from hiding to join the latest attack, and the assault force surged up the hill toward the TOC until fierce NVA fire forced the attackers to the ground.

Rich Allen had sought cover behind a low dirt mound, a few feet below a bunker occupied by an NVA machine-gun team. He rolled from his hiding place and fired a three-round burst at the bunker from a Browning Automatic Rifle he had taken from a dead soldier, then rolled back behind the mound. Twice more Allen performed the maneuver. Machine-gun rounds began to kick up around his hiding place, followed by grenades. Allen clutched the rifle to his chest, then log-rolled down the hill as grenades exploded behind him. He dropped into a trench and was still plotting his next move when a grenade bounced down the hill and stopped an arm's length from his body. Allen braced for the explosion, but the grenade was a dud. He scrambled down the trench and found the remnants of the broken assault force.[30]

After more air strikes, Sergeant Ashley mounted a third assault, this one aided by 60-millimeter mortar fire laid down by Green Berets Peter Tiroch and Joel Johnson. Once again they were driven back. A fourth attempt met with the same result.

Around 10:50 a.m., Ashley radioed the TOC and asked the trapped Green Berets to hit the NVA from behind as the relief force approached. A fifth assault got underway. Ashley and his men had fought their way to within about thirty yards of the TOC when Rich Allen dropped down to change magazines. A burst of automatic rifle fire flashed past him and slammed into Sergeant Ashley's midsection, piercing Ashley's chest and exiting his back. Allen slapped a battle dressing on the entry wound, then hoisted his 220-pound comrade over his shoulder and started down the hill. He ran until his legs gave out, then dragged and carried the wounded Green Beret on a makeshift litter.

When they reached Route 9, Allen and others laid Sergeant Ashley in a Jeep, and they roared down the hill to the old camp. They had just skidded to a halt when an incoming round hit nearby. A piece of shrapnel ended the life of Sergeant First Class Eugene Ashley Jr.—the only recipient of a Medal of Honor during the 1968 fighting at Khe Sanh.

Rich Allen survived the battle unscathed.

• • •

After escaping the NVA tanks outside the command bunker, Lieutenant Colonel Schungel and Lieutenant Wilkins had found sanctuary in the A-101 team house along the camp's northern perimeter. Around 3:30 a.m., Schungel killed five NVA as they approached the house, but an explosion had wounded Schungel in the right leg, so the two Americans crept away and crawled beneath the camp dispensary further to the west.

Around 9:30 a.m., Wilkins was slightly wounded in the leg during a strafing run by friendly aircraft. The two Americans hobbled across Route 9 and headed east. They survived another strafing by US aircraft, and Schungel was wounded again by North Vietnamese fire, but they made it safely to the old camp.

• • •

As the desperate struggle for Lang Vei played out, acrimony between the Marines and Special Forces at Khe Sanh came to a head. Three weeks earlier, General William Westmoreland had asked the Marines to confirm a contingency plan that called for Khe Sanh Combat Base to support the Special Forces at Lang Vei with artillery and ground troops in an attack. In fact, the Marine command at Khe Sanh had concluded weeks earlier that it would be foolhardy—if not suicidal—to attempt an overland relief of Lang Vei.[31] For reasons that have never been explained, the Marines failed to warn Westmoreland of their concerns. Instead, the American commander was assured that the Lang Vei contingency plan would be honored.

In the early morning hours of February 7, facing a widening attack by North Vietnamese tanks and troops, Captain Willoughby had radioed the Marines at Khe Sanh to ask for execution of the relief plan. Separately, the commander of Special Forces in Vietnam, Colonel Jonathan Frederic Ladd, had awakened General Westmoreland in Saigon to request assistance for Lang Vei. When Westmoreland informed Ladd that the decision remained in the hands of the Marine command in I Corps, the Special Forces commander on his own began organizing a force to save Lang Vei.[32]

Around 3:40 a.m., the air center at Khe Sanh Combat base reported that a C-130 was inbound with about one hundred Special Forces personnel aboard. Colonel Lownds alerted the 3rd Marine Division commander, Major General Rathvon Tompkins, who lodged a complaint with his boss. The III Marine Amphibious Force commander, General Leonard Cushman, ordered the plane's diversion from Khe Sanh around 4:00 a.m.[33]

At almost that exact moment, a conference call got underway in I Corps, and one of Ladd's officers formally asked III Marine Amphibious Force headquarters to dispatch a relief force to Lang Vei at first light. General Tompkins rejected the request, declaring that such an attempt by the Marines at this critical moment, when the combat base itself might be facing an imminent attack, "would be a lot of foolishness." General Cushman, and then General Westmoreland, supported the decision.[34]

Shortly after daybreak, having twice deferred Colonel Ladd's request for the relief of Lang Vei, Westmoreland flew to Da Nang for a previously scheduled conference with Marine and Army commanders in I Corps. When Westmoreland once again parried the question of a Lang Vei relief mission, Ladd phoned Westmoreland's deputy. General Creighton Abrams gave Ladd the green light to work with the Marine air commander in I Corps to devise a rescue plan using Special Forces personnel.[35]

At the FOB-3 compound at Khe Sanh Combat Base, word was passed to twenty-seven-year-old Army major George Quamo to find fifty volunteers to rescue their comrades at Lang Vei. "Look, it's a suicide mission," Quamo told his senior noncommissioned officer (NCO), Sergeant Skip Minnicks. "I don't think we're coming back, but I can't leave those fellows over there."[36]

• • •

Through the morning, and into the early afternoon, the trapped Green Berets were in sporadic radio contact with Sergeant Ashley, and they had listened with rising hopes as he mounted successive rescue attempts. After the fifth assault, Colonel Schungel broke the bad news in a radio transmission from the old camp: Sergeant Ashley was dead, the Marines weren't coming, and there would be no further attempts to retake the hill until the following day.

In the TOC, Paul Longgrear "went crazy." He screamed and swore and cursed those responsible for their abandonment. "Look," the Mike force commander announced, "you people can stay down here and die like worms if you want, but I'm going up and die like a man."[37]

Captain Willoughby announced, "If he goes, we all go." He radioed Schungel, "Sir, we're coming out."

A plan was devised: An incoming flight of A-1 aircraft would make three passes, bombing and strafing the bunkers occupied by NVA troops. The Green Berets would then emerge from the TOC and escape to the northeast as the aircraft made simulated passes to freeze the NVA in place.

About 2:30 p.m. the Skyraiders began to pound the camp with bombs, napalm, and 20-millimeter cannon. The Green Berets prepared to make their break. Medic James Moreland, delirious from his head wound, reacted violently when Longgrear tried to get him on his feet. After huddled discussion, the Green Berets made the hard decision to leave Moreland behind.

Longgrear picked his way up the command bunker's ruined staircase as the Skyraiders completed their third pass, emerging into daylight as the aircraft began their decoy runs. The other Green Berets exited the bunker and began hobbling toward the camp's northeastern corner.

Trailing behind his comrades as the rear guard, Longgrear spotted a North Vietnamese machine-gun nest to his right and charged the position, firing a burst from his CAR-15 as he ran. As the NVA gun team crumpled to the ground, Longgrear's rifle jammed and his injured ankle gave way. He flipped through the air and fell on his back. It appeared to his colleagues that he had been gunned down by the North Vietnamese.

As he lay on the ground, Longgrear prepared to shoot himself rather than be captured. His wife's voice played in his head, repeating her parting words when he had left for Vietnam: "I'll be praying for you." An A-1 Skyraider roared overhead, and Longgrear made fleeting eye contact with the pilot. The pilot dipped his wings in encouragement. The gesture energized the wounded Green Beret, and he heard his wife's voice again, "I'll be praying for you," and then another voice—God himself, as

Longgrear tells it. The hell-raising Green Beret resolved that he would not die on this hill.

Longgrear dragged himself to his feet and limped after his comrades. He cleared the crest of the hill, then started down toward the gate along Route 9, where the other Americans were about to roar away in a Jeep. They spotted Longgrear and shouted encouragement. He reached the vehicle and dived inside. The driver, a brave Vietnamese Special Forces comrade, navigated the enemy-infested stretch of road to the old camp and rolled to a stop, safely delivering the seven Green Berets who had made it out of the command bunker.[38]

• • •

North Vietnamese mortars and automatic weapons were pounding the old Lang Vei camp around 5:00 p.m. when the helicopter-borne rescue force took off from the FOB-3 compound at Khe Sanh Combat Base. Major George Quamo had pulled together about a dozen US Special Forces operators and forty indigenous Montagnard fighters for the operation. As A-1 Skyraiders and jet fighters prowled overhead, the armada of Army and Marine gunships and transport helicopters circled the old Lang Vei camp.

An Army UH-1D transport chopper dropped from the formation and settled onto the old camp's shell-torn airstrip, amid a swarm of panicked Laotian soldiers. Big Paul Longgrear—his head bandaged and body rejuvenated by intravenous fluids—waded into the mob and enforced order with menacing glares and the butt of his jammed CAR-15. A path was cleared and the most seriously injured Green Berets were helped aboard the Huey, which thundered away toward Khe Sanh.

Four Marine CH-46 helicopters landed and disgorged Major Quamo's security force, which quickly fanned out to safeguard the landing zone. The remaining Americans boarded one CH-46, while the other helicopters were filled with the camp's ranking Vietnamese officers and NCOs, interpreters, and seriously injured indigenous fighters. The Marine helicopters clattered off into the twilight.

Up the hill at Camp Lang Vei, First Lieutenant Thomas E. Todd, an engineering officer from Da Nang, had spent a harrowing night dodging NVA tanks and troops before hiding in the emergency medical bunker.

In the late afternoon he had made his way to the TOC, hoping to find other Americans, but they were gone. Amid the bomb-shattered ruins, Todd saw the body of one Green Beret: the mortally injured medic, Specialist Fourth Class James Moreland. As Todd turned away from the bunker, he glimpsed a helicopter over the old camp. He sprinted down the hill, arriving just in time to board one of the last choppers that had returned to extract Major Quamo's relief force.[39]

Other live Americans remained on the ground at Lang Vei. Dennis Thompson, the wisecracking Mike force member, had already been captured once by the North Vietnamese and had escaped over the past hours. He made radio contact with a forward air controller as the evacuation was underway and tried to make it to the old camp's airstrip. When the choppers took off, the forward air controller was preparing to land his Cessna on the airstrip to rescue Thompson. But NVA troops arrived and chased the Green Beret back into the brush. Shortly afterward, Thompson was captured a second time.

Two other Green Berets had been taken prisoner by the North Vietnamese: Sergeant First Class Harvey Brande of Long Beach, California; and Specialist Fourth Class William McMurray of Scottsdale, Arizona. Over the coming days, the three captive Green Berets would be marched up the Ho Chi Minh Trail into North Vietnam. They would remain there until their release with other American prisoners of war in 1973.

• • •

The Green Berets and their indigenous troops had fought bravely at Lang Vei, but in the end they could not overcome the North Vietnamese armor. Fourteen of the twenty-four Green Berets at Lang Vei were rescued; all but one—Sergeant Rich Allen—had been wounded. In addition to a Medal of Honor posthumously awarded to Sergeant Eugene Ashley, the Distinguished Service Cross was bestowed on Lieutenant Colonel Daniel Schungel and Major George Quamo, leader of the rescue effort. Nineteen Silver Stars and three Bronze Stars were also awarded to the Green Berets who defended Lang Vei.

America's indigenous allies at Lang Vei also paid dearly: 209 of the nearly 500 South Vietnamese and tribal fighters who began the battle were listed as killed or missing, and another 75 were wounded. Over the next twenty-four hours, some 160 Montagnard soldiers who had been left at the old camp evaded NVA forces as they made their way overland to Khe Sanh Combat Base. The Marines feared there were Viet Cong or NVA infiltrators among them and disarmed the men, refusing to allow them inside the base. The Green Berets at FOB-3 were furious, and they arranged to fly their allies to Da Nang.

The North Vietnamese had attacked Lang Vei with eleven Soviet-made PT-76 tanks, the first Communist use of armor against the Americans in South Vietnam. US ground and air forces destroyed seven of the tanks during the battle and the following day. Estimates of NVA losses at Lang Vei range between 80 and 250 killed and nearly 200 wounded.[40]

• • •

At Lang Vei, the North Vietnamese Army had scored its biggest victory thus far in the Khe Sanh campaign. Its forces now controlled Route 9 from the Ho Chi Minh Trail in Laos to the foothills east of the Marine base.

Much later, there would be Marines such as Captain Bill Dabney, commander of US forces on 881 South, who would claim that the North Vietnamese had blundered by seizing Lang Vei, clearing the way for unrestricted B-52 strikes along the Route 9 corridor west of the combat base.[41] But such tactical nuances mattered little to the Americans on the ground as night fell over Khe Sanh Combat base and its outposts on February 7.

Despite their bravery, American forces had been defeated, and in stunning fashion. In command posts and communication bunkers around the Khe Sanh area, Marines had huddled around radios to follow the battle at Lang Vei—the frantic shouts of "tanks in the wire," the desperate pleas for help, and the chilling sounds of an American outpost being overrun. Now, the Marines at Khe Sanh Combat Base listened intently for the sound of enemy tanks clanking down Route 9, and they anxiously awaited the waves of North Vietnamese ground troops that seemed certain to follow.

CHAPTER 11

The Battle of Hill 64

In the foggy predawn of Thursday, February 8, Second Lieutenant Terence Roach Jr. prowled the tiny hilltop outpost that was home to the sixty-odd men of Alpha Company's reinforced 1st Platoon, a unit of the 1st Battalion, 9th Marine Regiment—the hard-luck Walking Dead. "Stay alert," he exhorted his Marines as they peered into the darkness from their football-shaped perimeter, just over a mile west of Khe Sanh Combat Base. "We've got movement all around."[1]

For a young Marine Corps officer, just starting day sixty-two in his Vietnam tour, Roach was swimming in deep waters. As if commanding a Marine rifle platoon in I Corps at this critical juncture in the war wasn't perilous enough, Roach and his men were stuck on an exposed knob, more than 500 yards from the nearest friendly troops, between the two North Vietnamese Army divisions closing on Khe Sanh Combat Base. Only a day earlier, their neighbors some three miles to the southwest—the US Special Forces at Lang Vei—had been overrun. And now, Terry Roach and his men were hearing movement all around them in the dark.

Colonel John Mitchell had envisioned the Alpha-1 outpost as an early warning system for the rest of his battalion, which was positioned to the southeast of Roach and his men, on high ground where rock had been quarried for the runway improvements at the combat base the previous August. Mitchell had ordered Roach's risky deployment without consulting Alpha Company's commanding officer, Captain Henry "Mac" Radcliffe, who had been delayed in transit to Khe Sanh. When Radcliffe arrived a day or two later, he tried to persuade Mitchell to bring Roach and his men back into the main lines. "It's like dangling bait," the young captain had protested, but the battalion commander would not relent.[2]

Radcliffe did what he could to give the outpost a fighting chance. He added three M-60 machine-gun teams to the pair of guns already on the hill and assigned two 60-millimeter mortar crews, pushing the strength of the outpost to about sixty-four men. For that reason, not its elevation, it would become known as Hill 64.

Terry Roach hadn't asked for the assignment, but it was exactly the sort of challenge he relished. Growing up in a big Irish Catholic family in Birmingham, Michigan, a suburb of Detroit, young Terence had been steeped in American history by his father, and together they donned homemade period costumes and participated in Civil War battle reenactments and black-powder musket competitions.[3] Tall and lanky, with a long, angular face, Roach played baseball in high school and filled a scrapbook with news clippings about his beloved Detroit Tigers. He had enlisted in the Marine Corps reserve while working part-time and studying at Wayne State University. He completed boot camp at Parris Island, and after earning his history degree from Wayne State, entered Marine Officer Candidates School at Quantico, Virginia. In May 1967, just days after the Hill Fights around Khe Sanh, Roach returned home in the uniform of a Marine second lieutenant and married Lynn O'Connor, a dark-haired beauty he met at Wayne State. He completed Basic School training with Class 6–67 that fall and left for Vietnam on November 30.

Stepping off the plane in Da Nang on December 9, Roach was eager for action. At Phu Bai, he slipped away from his Quantico classmates and jumped on a Marine truck headed to Camp Evans, where he was given command of Alpha Company's 1st Platoon.[4] He saw his first action around Christmas along the "Street Without Joy," the scrubby coastal strip near Hue that had bedeviled French forces in Vietnam. On December 27, during a patrol, Roach made a rookie mistake when he aggressively ordered his platoon beyond a creek that was supposed to be the outer boundary of his operations that day. His men were ambushed, and the platoon sergeant and a corpsman were killed.[5]

Roach learned fast, and he impressed Captain Radcliffe with his maturity.[6] He was tough but fair with his men, an optimist by nature. Around Camp Evans, Roach brightened the mood by singing Irish folk songs and rowdy ballads about gunrunning Irish Republican rebels. The death and uncertainty that hung over his daily life was tempered by thrilling news from home: Lynn was six months pregnant.

At Khe Sanh, Roach had embraced his dangerous assignment. He dubbed his tiny forward outpost "Radcliffe's Roost" and pushed his men hard to prepare for the coming battle.[7] The stronghold measured only about sixty by forty yards and was ringed by a trench that the men studded with sandbagged bunkers about every ten or fifteen feet. Concertina wire coiled around the lower slope. The area between the wire and the trench line was seeded with command-activated Claymore mines, each positioned to scythe an attacking force with seven hundred steel balls sprayed in a 60° arc.

After long days spent improving trenches and bunkers, filling and stacking sandbags, and clearing fields of fire from the surrounding brush, Roach's men were worn out. Nightfall brought the demands of watch duties, and so the men were lucky to get three hours of fitful rest.[8]

By the first week of February, the North Vietnamese had become brazen in their movements around the hill. At night, roving enemy soldiers probed the concertina wire, occasionally triggering warning flares. Sometimes the Americans would awaken to find logs laid across their perimeter wire or Claymore mines reversed toward their lines.[9]

On Monday and Tuesday, February 5 and 6, the North Vietnamese pounded the main battalion lines and Hill 64 with mortar and recoilless rifle fire, wounding ten Marines.[10] On Wednesday, as North Vietnamese forces attacked the US Army Special Forces at nearby Lang Vei, Corporal James Feasel led a patrol that found matted grass beneath the northwest perimeter of Hill 64, where enemy soldiers had been watching the outpost.[11]

Now, after an unnerving night of enemy activity around the hill, Lieutenant Roach stopped along the western trench line, outside the bunker of his eighteen-year-old 2nd Squad leader, Corporal George Chapman. "There's a lot of activity out there," Roach said to Chapman, one of thirteen children born to a West Virginia coal miner and his wife, the fifth boy in his family to join the Marine Corps. "Keep an eye on your bunkers."[12]

Chapman checked his four bunkers along the western line of Hill 64 one more time and returned to the sandbagged hooch he shared with a twenty-two-year-old Navy corpsman from Michigan, Mike Coonan. Without warning, recoilless rifle rounds and rocket-propelled grenades slammed into the hill, followed by screams and heavy gunfire. It was 4:15 a.m. on the morning of February 8.

• • •

The initial North Vietnamese barrage shattered the 1st Platoon's western perimeter, destroying bunkers and killing or wounding about twenty Marines in an arc that stretched from Corporal Feasel's 1st Squad in the south to the edge of Sergeant Joseph Sutherland's 3rd Squad in the north. Four of the hill's five machine guns were either knocked out or quickly overrun. Recoilless rifle and RPG rounds destroyed two of Chapman's four bunkers and badly damaged a third. Chapman emerged from his bunker to see North Vietnamese troops charging up the slope toward the hill's northwest corner. He squeezed the clacker to detonate his Claymore mines, then began throwing grenades and firing his M-16 at the advancing enemy.[13]

Private Edward Wayne Welchel had been in Chapman's farthest bunker along the northwest line when the attack began. A grenade stitched Welchel with shrapnel and knocked his helmet and rifle flying. As he grabbed for his M-16 in thick smoke, Welchel heard Vietnamese voices outside. He bolted for the trench line but got tangled up with another comrade.[14] In their panic, the two Marines left their nineteen-year-old fire team leader, Lance Corporal Jeffrey Walsh of Bethel Park, Pennsylvania. He died at his post.

Welchel and his comrade hurled themselves into the next bunker to their east, where three Marines were holding out. Private First Class Gerry Clemson, a twenty-year-old from Geneva, Ohio, had been in Vietnam only fifty-five days, but he took on the role of the cool veteran as he tried to calm Welchel. An explosion rocked the bunker, and Welchel once again scrambled into the trench line. Clemson and twenty-three-year-old PFC William Colegate, from Red Bud, Illinois, died defending the bunker.[15]

While a handful of Marines along the northern trench line fought on, Welchel and others fell back in the face of the advancing North Vietnamese. Chased by enemy gunfire and grenades, the retreating Marines reached the hill's northeast bend, then started down the eastern trench line.

In the M-60 machine-gun bunker anchoring the northern line, eighteen-year-old Arnold Alderete had been awake when explosions erupted to his left. Alderete had grown up in San Antonio, Texas, near the Alamo, and had moved to Southern California with his mother when he was fifteen. He dropped out of high school two years later, joined the Marine Corps, and had been in Vietnam since mid-October. Now, as explosions and gunfire rattled across the hill, Alderete heard the sound of running feet and terrified shouts: "Gooks in the trench line!"[16]

Alderete and his assistant gunner, Private Allen McKinley, an eighteen-year-old from Gary, Indiana, prepared to join the retreat. Alderete grabbed his M-60 and was moving toward the bunker entrance when a thunderous explosion ripped the trench line where McKinley had just disappeared. Alderete crawled out to the trench and spotted the muzzle of an AK-47 just before a Chicom grenade clanked off his helmet. Smothering the grenade with his helmet, Alderete lunged back toward the bunker. The blast wave swept over him, spraying his legs with shards of hot metal.

Fortified by a jolt of adrenalin, Alderete grabbed his M-60 and jumped into the trench. Two North Vietnamese soldiers stood facing him, a few feet away. Alderete fired first, ripping the NVA soldiers apart in a spray of 7.62-millimeter rounds. Still firing on full-automatic, he backed down the trench line to the east. He tripped over something, and a hand grabbed his leg. It was McKinley, his assistant gunner, badly wounded but alive. "Don't leave me!" McKinley pleaded.

"Hang on to me," Alderete said. With the wounded Marine clutching his leg, Alderete awkwardly backed down the trench line, firing bursts toward the west to discourage any pursuing enemy soldiers. They curved around the northeast corner and headed down the eastern line.[17]

• • •

In the minutes before the attack, Lieutenant Roach had stopped along the northeast perimeter to warn the 3rd Squad leader, Sergeant Joseph Sutherland, to keep his men alert because of the movement around the hill. He moved on down the eastern side, toward Feasel's 1st Squad sector along the southern perimeter.[18]

A pair of privates, rifleman Michael Barry and grenadier Ronald Rountree, were on watch duty at the front of the bunker they shared with Sutherland and fire team leader Edward O'Connor when they heard an explosion and a scream from the area of Chapman's squad, to their left. Barry already had his helmet and flak jacket on, and he quickly snapped on his cartridge belt, grabbed some M-16 magazines, and dashed through the trench to his fighting position, a few yards to the west. Clutching his M-79, Rountree found his place about three yards beyond Barry as heavy gunfire and explosions crashed to their left.

As Barry searched for a target, Lieutenant Roach came running up from the south. He spoke briefly with someone behind Barry, then moved past, toward Rountree's position, and began firing his M-16 rifle and throwing grenades in the direction of the NVA attack. "I'm out of grenades," Roach yelled at one point. "Barry, you have any grenades?"[19]

Barry tossed two grenades to Roach, one after the other, and the lieutenant hurled the explosives toward the brunt of the NVA attack rolling in from the west. Seconds later, three or four grenades smacked into the ground around Roach. The platoon commander dived for a bunker as explosions ripped the trench line.

Almost simultaneously, a dark object banged into Barry's helmet with enough force to drop him to his hands and knees. He grabbed the object—a hissing Chicom grenade—and jumped to his feet to hurl it beyond the trench line. The grenade had just left his right hand when it detonated.

Hundreds of metal fragments and splinters ripped into Barry's body, dropping the young Marine to the bottom of the trench in a paroxysm of pain. His head throbbed. Gingerly raising his right arm into the flare light, Barry was relieved to see his hand. It was blackened and smoking, the skin on his little finger flayed to the bone, fingernails and flesh studded with metal splinters, but still more or less in one piece. His flak jacket bristled with metal shards. From Barry's right calf to his armpit, blood seeped from dozens of lacerations.

As Barry lay there, someone jumped into the trench, nearly on top of him. It was Private Lawrence Cioffi, an artillery scout observer assigned to the hill about three days earlier to coordinate fire support. He had a panicked look on his face, and he didn't have a helmet, flak jacket, or weapon. "They overran my bunker," Cioffi blurted. "I've got to find a radio. Have you seen the lieutenant?"[20]

"Yeah," said Barry, "the lieutenant's over there." He gestured to the spot where he had last seen Terry Roach before the flurry of Chicom grenades. Cioffi mumbled something and bolted in the opposite direction, toward the southern end of the hill.[21]

Shortly after his encounter with the forward observer, Barry heard a familiar voice. "Barry, are you okay?" It was his fire team leader, Corporal O'Connor.

"I've been hit," Barry said.

"What about the lieutenant?"

"He's up there," Barry said. "I think he's dead."

"Can you get to him?" O'Connor asked.

Barry crawled forward until he spotted a body. He could see Marine combat boots, but not the man's face. "Is anybody in there?" Barry yelled at the bunker just beyond the body.

There was no answer.

Barry came under fire, and dirt fell on him from enemy bullets gouging the trench wall by his head. Scuttling like a crab, he retreated back down the trench until he could see Corporal O'Connor, standing in the short trench that linked their bunker to the main line. "I didn't see the lieutenant," Barry said. "I don't see anybody else."

The words had just left his mouth when a grenade smacked into the short trench near O'Connor. Barry flattened himself along the main trench wall as the grenade exploded. Seconds later, O'Connor barreled into the main trench, one hand clamped over his bloody face. The wounded fire team leader turned left and disappeared down the hill to the south, away from the surging enemy attack.

Barry turned back toward the north and scanned the no-man's-land he had just escaped. His eyes spotted movement, and then his blood ran cold. Just beyond the bunker where Lieutenant Roach had fallen, Barry saw helmets bobbing up and down. They were the distinctive headgear of the North Vietnamese Army.[22]

• • •

Captain Mac Radcliffe was awakened in his bunker at the rock quarry within seconds of the first shots. "Alpha-1 is under attack," the watch officer said. The Alpha Company commander could hear the rattle of gunfire and boom of mortars, RPGs, and recoilless rifles. He radioed for Lieutenant Roach but got 1st Platoon radioman Jimmy Rizzo instead.

"What the hell is going on out there?" Radcliffe demanded.

"We're under attack," Rizzo said. "They're in the wire."[23]

"Let me speak to your actual," Radcliffe said, using radio code for the unit commander.

"The 1-actual [platoon commander] isn't here," Rizzo replied. "He's checking out what's going on."

"Get the 1 and tell him to give me a sitrep," Radcliffe ordered.

A short time later, Rizzo and Radcliffe spoke again by radio. The enemy was overrunning the hill, the radioman said. "You gotta come get us, Skipper. They're all over the place. Alpha-6, come get us."[24]

• • •

On the south side of the hill, Corporal James Feasel, the eighteen-year-old leader of Roach's 1st Squad, grabbed his M-16 and a bag of magazines, slapped on his steel-pot helmet, and stepped from his bunker into the trench.[25] His first instinct was to find Lieutenant Roach to coordinate their defense, so he headed west, toward the auxiliary trench leading to the platoon command post near the middle of the hill.

A streetwise New York City native, Feasel had taken only a step or two when a bright flash about twenty yards ahead stopped him in his tracks. Two North Vietnamese soldiers had set up a mortar on the roof of a gutted Marine bunker, and they were firing on American positions to the east. Feasel waited until the mortar flashed again to make sure they weren't friendlies, then dropped the NVA team with a burst of rifle fire. He found the cutoff to the command post and hurried up the hill.

By February 1968, Jimmy Feasel had been in Vietnam for seven months, and he knew how to handle himself. He had grown up in the rough Hell's Kitchen neighborhood of Manhattan's West Side, a lanky kid who lived to play hockey. When he was sixteen, his parents divorced, and Feasel decided it was time to find his own way in the world. He finished tenth grade, then enlisted in the Marine Corps.

For a boy who had never been out of New York City, boot camp at Parris Island was like a voyage to another planet. Feasel arrived with seventy-eight recruits from the Northeast, but he wound up being assigned to a newly formed platoon from the Deep South. He had never met a Southerner before, so he got a quick schooling in Dixie language and culture, black and white. After Parris Island and advanced infantry training in North Carolina, he drew a six-month assignment to the US naval base at Guantanamo Bay, Cuba. He turned eighteen in April 1967, and three months later began his tour in South Vietnam.

A rifleman by Military Occupational Specialty (MOS), Feasel arrived in Vietnam a sinewy six feet one and 175 pounds. He was assigned to Alpha Company of the 1st Battalion, 9th Marines and in his first month at Con Thien took a piece of shrapnel in his leg. After three weeks in the hospital, he returned to duty. During his second tour at Con Thien in the fall, Feasel experienced his first firefight and the loss of his platoon leader and company commander in one well-placed shot from an enemy recoilless rifle. Captain Mac Radcliffe took over Alpha Company and impressed Feasel as "a good man, good leader, and good combat officer."[26]

Feasel was still sizing up his new platoon commander, but right now he only wanted to find Terry Roach so they could head off the NVA attack that seemed to be hitting Hill 64 from at least three sides. Feasel reached Roach's L-shaped command bunker, ducked inside, and made a right turn into the main room. It was empty. As he turned to leave, gunfire sounded just outside and radioman Jimmy Rizzo hurled himself through the entrance. Enemy soldiers were in hot pursuit, so the radioman and Feasel scrambled into the bunker's main room.

The attackers began pounding the bunker with AK-47s, Chicom grenades, and RPGs. Bullets smacked into the walls of stacked sandbags, and explosions shook the squat structure, bursting one of Feasel's eardrums. Feasel and Rizzo took turns defending the bunker entrance. When one emptied a magazine, the other jumped into place and started firing. Each grenade or burst of rifle fire from the Marines provoked a fusillade from the North Vietnamese. At one point, a Chicom grenade exploded in the entrance as Feasel craned his head around the corner. He jerked back, but not before three tiny pieces of shrapnel embedded in his eye.

As the minutes passed, the trapped Marines debated their next move. Rizzo suggested they try to shoot their way out. Feasel insisted they fight on until help arrived.[27]

Feasel had just fired another magazine and stepped away to reload when Rizzo bolted outside. Rifle and machine gun fire crackled, and Rizzo staggered back inside the bunker entrance, his chest and abdomen pierced with bullets. Feasel dragged the radioman into the main room, then resumed his fire. Behind him, Rizzo lay on his back, dying.

"Jimmy," the radioman called to Feasel. Then again: "Jimmy."[28] They were Rizzo's last words.

Feasel was on his own now, out of grenades and running through his M-16 magazines. Every few seconds he would peep around the corner, fire a few rounds out the entrance, and yank his head back. He could hear heavy firing and explosions outside, but he had no idea how the battle was going. He was wary when a voice called out in English, "Is there anybody in the bunker?" Fearing a ruse, Feasel said nothing. And then the same voice: "If somebody's in there, you better yell, because I'm going to throw a grenade in."

Feasel hesitated, and then he replied, "Yeah, I'm in here." The New Yorker eased his head around the corner. Standing in the bunker entrance was a big Marine.[29]

• • •

The NVA had punched through the western perimeter, and assault troops were now moving into the interior of the American outpost, gaining ground along the northern and western lines. Chapman's 2nd Squad had been reduced to a pocket of wounded survivors in the care of corpsman Mike Coonan. Along the northern line, one of the few Marines still alive was Corporal Robert Wylie, who played dead as NVA soldiers rifled his pockets.[30]

Private Michael Barry was one of the last Marines near the northeast corner, and after spotting the bobbing NVA helmets, he tried to shoot two enemy soldiers looking in his direction. The rifle exploded, knocking Barry backward. He picked himself up and started backpedaling down the trench line to the south. He was trying to make sense of everything that had happened in the past few minutes when a sharp command snapped him back to the moment: "Get the guys out of that bunker. We're pulling back."[31]

The bunker in question housed an M-60 team led by a gunner known as Scotty—Lance Corporal James Frank Scott of Mobile, Alabama. Over the past few nights, Barry had heard Scotty telling stories about a wild week of R&R he had just enjoyed. Now Barry stood at the back of Scotty's bunker and called out, "Hey, we're pulling back. Can you guys come out?" Barry pulled the poncho back from the entrance and found the barrel of Scotty's machine gun in his face.

Scotty tried to bolt down the hill, but he rammed into Barry, and both men fell to the bottom of the trench. The M-60 gunner was trying to wriggle free when a Chicom grenade bounced off Barry's chest and dropped between Scotty's legs. The brunt of the blast ripped into Scotty's lower body. Hot shrapnel tore into Barry's left forearm, and the blast wave slammed him into the trench wall.

Barry lay on his back, his brain processing this latest shock, when a body lunged onto his chest. "Get away!" Barry shouted, shoving at the form that he feared was an NVA soldier trying to kill him. Then he realized it was Scotty, screaming and clawing in his agony. Staggering to his feet, Barry lurched down the trench. Spotting a cut in the trench wall, he climbed inside.

Just south of Barry, several Marines had piled into bunkers that looked out on the main battalion lines, more than 500 yards away. Some were wounded, others overcome with fear. Whatever their reasons, they had checked out of the fight, leaving about twenty or fewer Marines to battle on.

• • •

While the NVA attack progressed, two Marines were launching an extraordinary effort to deny the enemy control of the interior. Private David Ford, a 2nd Squad rifleman, and machine gunner Arnold Alderete met in the eastern trench line and roughed out a plan. Stuffing their pockets with grenades and clutching automatic weapons, they headed into the hill's interior.[32]

From the area around Roach's command bunker, the two Marines stormed over the crest toward enemy-held positions along the northwest corner. They raked the area with automatic fire and grenades, then sprinted back over the hill amid a flurry of NVA fire and grenades.

The 1st Squad grenadier, George Einhorn, spotted the familiar lope of his close friend Dave Ford and another Marine as they pulled off one John Wayne–style charge after another over the hill. Einhorn joined the pair and tried to drop an M-79 round onto the NVA, but the grenade landed dangerously close to the Marines and the muzzle blast attracted enemy fire. After Einhorn had fired two or three rounds, Ford leaned toward his friend. "George," he yelled, "don't shoot that thing again."[33]

When Alderete and Ford began to run low on ammunition, they threw grenades. When they ran out of those, they scampered down toward the 1st Squad area to rearm.[34]

•   •   •

By the time Jimmy Feasel made his escape from the platoon command post and returned to the southern trench line, the battle for Hill 64 had reached a critical juncture. The attackers were still gaining ground across the hill, and more than half of the sixty-odd American defenders were dead or wounded, including the platoon commander and platoon sergeant.

Command and control inside the outpost had collapsed, a fact that Captain Radcliffe had quickly gathered as he tried to get a situation report from the hill.[35] Unable to reach Lieutenant Roach or even his radio operator after their initial exchanges, Radcliffe had contacted the other commissioned officer on the hill, weapons platoon lieutenant Francis Beirne Lovely. Radcliffe wanted Lovely to get the hill's two 60-millimeter mortars firing and adjust rounds from the battalion's 81-millimeter mortars onto the attackers. Lovely was talking nonstop, but Radcliffe couldn't get answers to his questions. The Alpha Company commander finally cut him off. "Put somebody on the damn radio that can talk to me!"[36] Someone in the bunker took the line—probably Sergeant Joe Miller—but he, too, shed little light on the situation.

In fact, the situation was even worse than Captain Radcliffe imagined: Lieutenant Roach, radio operator Jimmy Rizzo, and platoon sergeant Bernard B. McKinney were dead; and Lovely's 60-millimeter mortar teams were hiding in their bunkers rather than firing on the NVA. A similar state of disarray existed in two of the hill's three rifle squads: Chapman's 2nd Squad had been virtually wiped out in the west; the 3rd Squad had been driven from its northern positions and its leader, Sergeant Joe Sutherland, had joined Lovely and Miller in their bunker.

Feasel found his squad largely unscathed and swelling in size as survivors from the shattered 2nd and 3rd Squads asked what they could do to help. Feasel huddled with grenadier George Einhorn and one of his fire team leaders, Corporal Roy McDaniel, a twenty-year-old from Kansas City, Missouri, and laid out his plan: they would set up a half-circle defensive perimeter—a "180," as their advanced infantry training instructors had called it—that would stretch from the hill's northeast corner to the southwest. Strongpoints would block the NVA advance down the eastern and western lines. Arnold Alderete and Dave Ford would shore up the center of the hill.[37]

As Alderete and Ford headed into the hill's interior once again, Feasel made other assignments. Fire team leader Roy McDaniel headed off with nineteen-year-old PFC Guy Leonard to secure the right flank, near the hill's northeast corner. The outpost didn't seem to be getting mortar or artillery support other than illumination rounds, so Feasel asked his grenadier, George Einhorn, to fire 40-millimeter grenades to slow the flow of NVA troops into the fight from the west.[38]

As Einhorn pumped rounds into the western sky, Alderete and Ford took up positions behind the platoon command bunker and engaged NVA soldiers firing from the western trench line and bunkers they had overrun. When Alderete and Ford ran low on ammo, they threw their last grenades and began hurling rocks. As they braced for another NVA push before dawn, Alderete and Ford made a pact: when the final assault hit, they would fight to the death.[39]

• • •

The 60-millimeter mortars that Captain Radcliffe had placed on Hill 64 were silent, but a young lieutenant in charge of the battalion's 81-millimeter mortars back at the rock quarry had sprung into action. In short order, the mortars were pumping out illumination and high explosive rounds in the hill's defense.[40]

Back home in Illinois, Maurice Casey had been teaching fourth grade at an elementary school in the Chicago suburbs when he enlisted in the Marines in 1966. After dropping out of pilot's training, he had entered the Basic School at Quantico as part of Class 6–67. Among his classmates was Terry Roach. Casey and Roach had arrived in Vietnam on the same flight in December, and they were at Phu Bai drawing their combat gear when Roach had taken off and beat Casey to the temporary 1/9 headquarters at Camp Evans. Roach's zeal earned him the coveted command of a rifle platoon, leaving Casey with a less glamorous billet: 81-millimeter mortars. Now, Roach and his rifle platoon were in trouble, and Casey was doing all he could to keep his classmate and his men alive.

Casey was in constant communications with a Marine radio operator who had been assigned to the artillery forward observer sent to Hill 64 a few days earlier. When the observer had fled their bunker behind the northern trench line, radio operator Richard W. Smith had remained in place as the North Vietnamese attack had smashed through the American line and driven the remnants of Sutherland's 2nd Squad back down the slope in disarray. Smith had radioed the 81-millimeter mortars at the rock quarry and began performing the artillery observer's duties on his own.[41]

Now, as Casey listened over the open radio line, Smith called in missions on targets along the likely enemy avenues of attack to the west and northwest. Smith's bunker had been partially collapsed by enemy fire, but he had threaded his radio antenna through a crack in the jumbled sandbags. As marauding NVA soldiers roamed the American trench line only a few feet away, Smith called in mortar rounds closer and closer to the hill.[42]

As the rounds neared the American perimeter on Hill 64, Casey and the Marine running the plotting board grew increasingly concerned that they were going to kill their comrades. Casey finally ordered a cease-fire. "I need to talk to your Whisky-6," he said to Smith. The radioman explained that his Whisky-6—the forward observer—had left him. Casey radioed battalion headquarters for guidance. "It's your call," he was told.

As precious seconds ticked by, Smith pressed the case for close-in fire. "The bad guys are up and running around killing people, and they're the only ones that are going to get hit," he said. "If you don't [fire], they're going to finish off the guys that are here."[43]

Casey gave the order to his men: fire away.

• • •

Assigned to anchor the right flank of the new defensive line, 1st Squad fire team leader Roy McDaniel had set off up the hill with one of his men, Private First Class Guy Leonard. As they passed the 60-millimeter mortar pit closest to the east side of the hill, McDaniel heard a sound inside the mortar team's bunker. He yelled a challenge: "If you're American, you better answer up or we're going to throw a grenade inside."

A voice called back, "Wait! We're in here! We're Marines!"[44]

A member of the mortar team emerged. "Come on," McDaniel told the frightened mortarman. "We're going to get online and try to push them back."

The mortarman protested, "I don't have a weapon."

"Go on back to the rear there and get a weapon," McDaniel commanded, "There are plenty of them."

McDaniel and Leonard began crawling up the slope. Explosions ripped the night and showered them with shrapnel, dirt, and debris. They passed a few yards to the east of the platoon command bunker and continued on. Moving past the second 60-millimeter mortar pit, they saw no sign of the American weapons team. (The mortarmen had sealed themselves inside their bunker with sandbags and would survive the battle.)

McDaniel and Leonard crawled over the crest of the hill and stopped when they were within easy grenade range of the northern trench line. From their vantage point, lying behind some sandbags near the second mortar bunker, the two Marines could see North Vietnamese soldiers firing from the trench, and from inside and behind abandoned bunkers. Occasionally, an enemy soldier would dash to another position, his uniform and distinctive helmet visible in the light of explosions and flares.

The Americans began countering the enemy fire with their M-16 rifles and grenades. McDaniel had spooked Leonard with his first grenade toss. The fire team leader had rolled onto his back and pulled the grenade pin, then let the spoon fly with his hand cocked in the throwing position, about six inches from Leonard's head. Leonard counted to himself—*one, two*—while stifling an urge to yell: "Throw that thing!" But McDaniel didn't want to give the enemy time to throw the grenade back, so he took his time before chucking the explosive at an enemy soldier he had spotted. Much to Leonard's relief, Corporal McDaniel finally threw the grenade, and an explosion ripped the trench line nearby.

After perhaps an hour in their exposed position, McDaniel and Leonard noticed a flurry of movement to their left, in the western trench that had been held by George Chapman's squad when the battle began. The two Marines unleashed a fusillade of M-16 fire at the fleeting shapes, and the movement stopped.

On McDaniel's signal, Leonard began crawling in that direction. The two Marines slid into the trench, almost on top of the enemy soldiers they had gunned down. One of the NVA fighters was coiled at the bottom. "He's still alive," Leonard said to Corporal McDaniel, grabbing the wounded man's AK-47 rifle.

"Finish him off," McDaniel ordered.

Leonard raised his M-16 and fired a three-round burst into the back of the enemy soldier's head.[45]

Before the two Americans could contemplate their next move, a grenade exploded between them, knocking them to the bottom of the trench in a burst of hot shrapnel. Another explosion blew Leonard's rifle and helmet down the hill, and Leonard collapsed onto the NVA soldier he had just killed.

A Marine emerged from a bunker a few feet away and, with the assistance of another American, dragged Roy McDaniel to safety. The rescuer was George Chapman, the 2nd Squad leader, aided by corpsman Mike Coonan.

Guy Leonard staggered to his feet and wiped enough blood from his eyes to survey his surroundings. His gut told him that he was a dead man if he stayed on this side of the hill. Armed with only a mess-kit knife,

Leonard lurched down the trench toward the south, in search of his comrades in the 1st Squad.[46]

• • •

When Sutherland's 3rd Squad pulled back in disarray, the NVA had missed an opportunity to attack down the eastern trench line. Private Mike Barry took up a position in the trench with two Marines who were part of Feasel's new defensive line. Unlike the disheveled men Barry had seen from the overrun areas, these Marines had helmets, flak jackets, and rifles. One of them handed Barry an M-16 and a couple of sandbags.

After a few minutes, a Marine came into view from the north. His face and movements embodied the fear that Barry had seen so many times during the fight. The man didn't have a weapon, and he was bleeding from a gash in his right jaw. A short time later, another wounded Marine hobbled down the trench and continued past. The Marine with the injured jaw reappeared and joined Barry and the other two men at their makeshift strongpoint.

Barry was sitting with his back against the trench wall, looking north, when an American M-26 grenade arced through the air in their direction and dropped into a supply area just off the line. When the explosion passed, he aimed his rifle to the north, expecting to see charging NVA soldiers. Instead, a Marine sprinted out of the supply area, blood streaming from his face.

The North Vietnamese attack that Barry and his three comrades expected didn't materialize, and it soon became apparent that the grenade had been tossed by a lone enemy soldier. One of the Marines could see the NVA soldier when he popped up from the area where Lieutenant Roach had fallen. The Marine kept up a running commentary as he matched wits with the enemy fighter, squeezing off a round each time the man hurled a grenade.

"Almost got him!"[47] "Damn, almost got him!"

Barry fired a few rounds up the hill in an attempt to distract the NVA soldier long enough for the other Marine to get off a kill shot, but their adversary was too wily. As night gave way to half-light, the deadly cat-and-mouse game on the eastern trench line played out.[48]

• • •

In the battle's opening minutes, Captain Radcliffe had picked up his land-line telephone and informed his battalion commander that the Alpha-1 outpost was under attack. Colonel John Mitchell ordered Radcliffe to sit tight until the situation became clearer.[49] More conversations followed, and Radcliffe's frustration grew with the rising fury of the North Vietnamese attack. When Mitchell ordered the Alpha Company commander to wait until daylight to mount a relief mission, Radcliffe fumed, "That will be too damn late."[50] He hung up the phone, then turned to his executive officer. "Tell Mitchell I'm out checking the lines if he calls," Radcliffe said. He headed outside to round up volunteers for a relief force.

At 7:40 a.m., Radcliffe led a force of about twenty men through the wire of his lines at the rock quarry. He and his men passed through a minefield and started down into the little valley, toward the embattled American outpost.[51]

● ● ●

As day broke, the Alpha-1 survivors were greeted by a surreal sight: Their comrades at the rock quarry were at their positions and ready for battle, but they weren't firing. Some were sitting on top of their bunkers, observing the fight on Hill 64, like spectators "watching a movie."[52]

It wasn't by choice.

Delta Company rifleman George Gregory Rudell, a wiry twenty-year-old from Little Rock, Arkansas, had been awake most of the night. A little after 4:00 a.m., Rudell saw an explosion near the crest of Hill 64, followed by the twinkling of gunfire that gave the appearance of "hundreds of lightning bugs up and down the hill."[53]

As flares burst over the outpost of Alpha Company's 1st Platoon, about 500 yards away, Rudell prepared to open fire on the NVA soldiers he could see scrambling up the slopes. But his platoon commander ordered the Marines to hold fire, for fear of hitting their own men.

The Marines at the rock quarry watched in horror as the battle raged. Rudell and his comrades cursed the nameless bastards somewhere up the chain of command who prevented them from going to the aid of their brother Marines, or even firing in their defense.[54] Even more inexplicable, there didn't seem to be any mortars or artillery firing in support of

Hill 64, or at least none that Rudell could see or hear.[55] Finally, after daylight, Delta Company was given permission to fire. Rudell and his comrades picked out targets among the NVA moving up and down Hill 64 and opened up with their M-16s and M-60s.

Nearby, a pair of M-48 tanks at the rock quarry had also been denied permission to put fire on the slopes of Hill 64 during the predawn hours. The light of day gave tank commander Joseph Harrigan a better appreciation of the close combat on the hill. Following the action through his 40:1 power telescope, Harrigan spotted a pair of Marines up the slope exchanging fire with NVA soldiers inside the perimeter. The Marines scrambled around, throwing grenades and even rocks at the enemy soldiers. Harrigan rolled his tank around, trying to get a clean shot, but the protagonists were too close.[56]

Around 8:30 a.m., Harrigan was finally allowed to fire his main gun at targets outside the Marine perimeter. He spotted about thirty North Vietnamese soldiers at the base of Hill 64, breaking off the fight. Harrigan's tank and its twin each unleashed six 90-millimeter shells at the retreating enemy.[57]

Forward air controller Charles "Toby" Rushforth, flying overhead after his adventure over Lang Vei the previous day, inadvertently stumbled onto the battle underway on Hill 64. Khe Sanh Combat Base hadn't informed him that a firefight was underway in that area, much less that a Marine outpost was fighting for its life. Rushforth arranged for some A-1 Skyraiders from the *Coral Sea* to be diverted from another mission around Khe Sanh. Dropping down through the overcast, they made strafing runs off the west side of the hill and dropped a few bombs on NVA troops they spotted.[58]

• • •

As small groups of enemy troops began to stream away from the hill, Corporal Jimmy Feasel and the Marine who had aided his escape from Lieutenant Roach's bunker retrieved an M-60 from the destroyed machine-gun bunker nearby and set it up in Feasel's bunker. When a group of about thirty retreating NVA appeared in their field of fire, a Marine opened up with the M-60 while Feasel and others along the southern line blasted away with M-16s. Still other Marines exchanged fire with the dwindling numbers of NVA soldiers sniping at the Americans from the western trench line.

Hunkered in the southern line a few minutes later, Feasel heard shouts and turned to see the Marine who had rescued him, inexplicably sitting exposed on top of a bunker. As other Marines yelled for their comrade to take cover, a shot rang out. The Marine tumbled to the ground, one of the last Americans to die on the hill.[59]

Shortly afterward, Feasel was in the entrance to his bunker, talking to one of his men in the trench line, Corporal Henry York, when the crack of another shot carried across the hill. A bullet hit York just below his right eye. Seconds later, another bullet ripped through Feasel's ear. York's wound was fatal, and grenadier George Einhorn feared that Feasel was soon to follow. As blood spurted from Feasel's ear, Einhorn wrapped a large bandage around his squad leader's head.

Stunned, but still very much alive and cranky, Feasel barked, "Georgie, how do you expect me to see? You got my eyes covered."[60]

The red-stained bandage was adjusted and Feasel returned to the fight, looking like a character in Archibald McNeal Willard's iconic painting of bloodied-but-unbowed American patriots in 1776.

• • •

After surviving two grenade blasts with Roy McDaniel, Private First Class Guy Leonard embarked on his perilous journey down the western trench line as he tried to make it back to friendly territory. Working his way down the zigzag line, Leonard surprised two NVA soldiers from behind and killed or incapacitated them with his mess-kit knife. It was a final test of fortitude, and Leonard emerged from the foggy dawn like a bloody apparition and rejoined the Marines along the southern perimeter.

Leonard's fire team leader, Roy McDaniel, wasn't as fortunate: he survived the grenade blasts without serious injury but was killed by enemy fire in the bunker along the western line where George Chapman and corpsman Mike Coonan were holding out.[61]

Small firefights and sniping were still flaring across the hill when a barrage of automatic weapons rounds erupted from the south. Marines along the southern line wheeled toward the sound, bracing for a renewed attack. But the gunmen were Marines at the rock quarry, and their target appeared to be some unseen enemy forces along the hill's southern base.

As he scanned the western trench line for NVA troops, Jimmy Feasel heard a commotion behind him. He turned and saw a Marine jump into his section of the trench, with others close behind. It was Captain Mac Radcliffe's relief column.

Radcliffe's point man, Corporal Robert Genty, a plumber's son from the Chicago suburb of Oak Park, was due to leave Khe Sanh, but he kept finding reasons to remain with the Walking Dead. Now he headed toward a Marine who wore a bloody bandage around his head and seemed to be in charge. "Which way are the gooks?" Genty asked Jimmy Feasel.[62]

Feasel pointed toward the west.

As Genty and other Marines headed across the southern trench line toward the enemy-held area, Captain Radcliffe sent more Marines up the eastern trench to press the counterattack around the north. Radcliffe, meanwhile, pushed into the middle of the hill with a handful of men. Under fire from NVA troops scattered along the western rim, Radcliffe ducked behind the platoon command bunker. An NVA soldier in a southwest bunker took Radcliffe under fire, and bullets smacked into sandbags next to the company commander's head. When a Chicom grenade sailed through the air toward him, the left-handed Radcliffe caught it in his right hand and awkwardly tossed it back toward the thrower.[63]

Radcliffe tried to take his tormentor out with grenades, but the fire continued. He yelled to Feasel, "Got any more grenades?"[64] Feasel tossed one to the captain, and Radcliffe hurled it toward the NVA soldier. The enemy fighter still would not die. Feasel threw another grenade to Radcliffe, and this time the captain threw a perfect strike. An explosion ripped the area around the NVA soldier, and a human leg flew into the air.[65]

Radcliffe and his men turned their attention to other NVA holdouts. Robert Genty moved up from the southwest corner and cleared out a bunker with a grenade and a burst of rifle fire. He reclaimed the next bunker with the same combination. One by one, the Americans took out the remaining NVA positions.

As the American counterattack swept across the hill, the welcome voice of Captain Radcliffe reached the ears of squad leader George Chapman and corpsman Mike Coonan, still trapped in their battered westside bunker. Chapman and Coonan had survived repeated attacks and probes as they kept watch over three wounded comrades who couldn't be moved. At one point Chapman heard the chilling sounds of NVA soldiers beating to death two Marines in an adjacent bunker. Unable to save his men, Chapman tossed a grenade inside to avenge their deaths.

Spurred by the sound of Radcliffe's voice, Chapman and Coonan sneaked out of the bunker to get help. As they ran down the trench line toward the south, a rifle cracked and a bullet slammed into Chapman. Coonan and rifleman Dave Ford pulled the 2nd Squad leader around a bend, and the corpsman went to work. A bullet had penetrated Chapman's flak jacket, punched through his chest, and exited his back. One lung had been punctured, and he was gagging and choking on blood that gurgled up from his chest. Coonan dressed the wounds and leaned Chapman up against the trench wall. The tough West Virginian would live.[66]

● ● ●

Twenty minutes after the American counterattack got underway, and nearly five hours after the battle began, there were no more enemy soldiers left to kill. Bodies and parts of bodies clotted the trenches and shattered bunkers. In places, broken young men, American and Vietnamese, lay atop one another in their final repose.

Twenty-seven Americans had been killed in the fighting: twenty-six men assigned to Hill 64, including platoon commander Terry Roach, and one man who fought with Radcliffe's relief force. The light casualties sustained by the relief force were a testament to the brave work done by the defenders of Hill 64 before help finally arrived.

In defeat, the North Vietnamese had paid dearly. The hill and the surrounding area were littered with the bodies of some 150 of their dead.

Across the hill, bloody and exhausted men began the grim work of carrying their dead and wounded down the southern slope to all-terrain vehicles that had arrived from the combat base. As Corporal Jimmy Feasel and corpsman Mike Coonan carried a stretcher bearing the body of twenty-year-old Roy McDaniel, the weary corpsman tripped on a tree

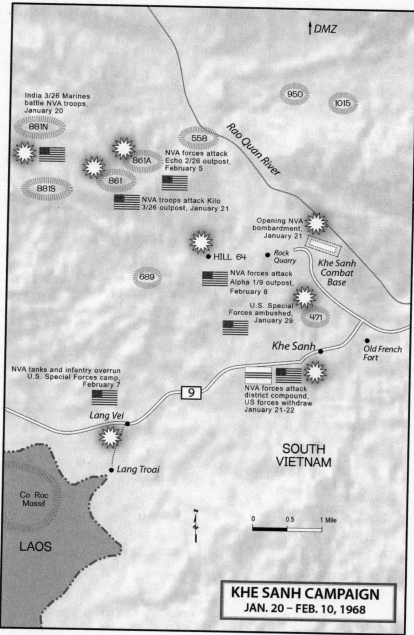

Opening attacks at Khe Sanh, January 20–February 10, 1968.

stump and the body slid to the ground. Feasel gently placed his fire team leader back on the stretcher.

Coonan and Feasel had handed off the stretcher and started back up the hill when an officer's voice stopped them in their tracks. "Where are you guys going?"

"We got more Marines to bring down," Feasel said.

"You men have done enough," the officer declared. "Get yourselves over to Charlie Med."[67]

Wearily, they climbed into a vehicle. The caravan bearing the living and the dead of Alpha Company's 1st Platoon lurched down the dirt track to Khe Sanh Combat Base. The bloody knoll they had held against long odds disappeared behind them.

CHAPTER 12

"Home Is Where You Dig It"

In their twenty days at the gates of Khe Sanh, the North Vietnamese Army forces had fought five battles. They had won two, forcing the Americans from Khe Sanh village and Lang Vei, and they had lost three, failing in their attempts to overrun the Marine outposts at Hills 64, 861, and 861 Alpha. They had suffered heavy casualties and had little to show for their sacrifices.

Undeterred, the North Vietnamese now began the second phase of their Khe Sanh campaign. Bypassing and effectively isolating the American hill outposts, the NVA 325C and 304th Divisions turned their attention to the grand prize: Khe Sanh Combat Base. Under the cover of darkness, the North Vietnamese began encircling the base with a network of trenches, bunkers, and spider holes. From these positions, the NVA would be poised to launch an assault that would breach the American stronghold.

For the Americans dug in at the combat base or on one of the high points to the west or to the north, nothing had changed. NVA artillery, rockets, and mortars continued to pound their positions at random, and enemy snipers still added a personal touch to the mayhem. The chronic winter weather of low-hanging clouds made it more difficult for North Vietnamese spotters to identify targets, but it also allowed Communist gunners to operate with reduced fear of US air strikes.

Of greater concern to Colonel David Lownds and the 6,000 men under his command at Khe Sanh was the deteriorating supply situation. General Westmoreland had made the calculated gamble that enemy anti-aircraft fire and foul weather couldn't prevent his fleet of transport planes and helicopters from keeping the American stronghold equipped and provisioned, but the supply chain was already fraying. Food, water, and other essential items were in short supply on the hill outposts, and the concern was that the problem would only get worse.

The North Vietnamese had moved guns into place to cover the air approaches to Khe Sanh, and arriving American fixed-wing aircraft and helicopters now had to run a deadly gauntlet of fire on their final approach. Pilots, air crews, and ground personnel devised a frenetic routine to elude the NVA gunners, and its fundamental principle was perpetual motion. Transport aircraft never stopped moving, so cargo pallets were shoved off the back ramps of big C-130s and C-123s, and passengers jumped clear, as the aircraft trundled across the base, hounded by enemy mortars and rockets.

Stretcher bearers from Charlie Med loaded wounded aboard moving aircraft, leaving passengers trying to get out of Khe Sanh as the last priority. In a typical departure early in the campaign, Lance Corporal Keith Kapple and several other Marines who had completed their tours or were leaving for R&R sprang from a slit trench off the runway as a C-123 transport rolled past, tossed their seabags into the back, and leaped onto the heaving cargo door as the plane gathered speed and prepared to begin its takeoff sprint amid exploding shells.[1]

The Americans were not privy to the NVA's decision to shift its focus to the combat base, but they had anticipated siege tactics from General Giap. The North Vietnamese commander had claimed one of modern military history's greatest siege victories against the French at Dien Bien Phu in 1954. Oddly enough, given the American preoccupation with Dien Bien Phu, General Westmoreland had waited until the first week of February to commission his staff historian at MACV headquarters, Colonel Reamer W. Argo Jr., to analyze Khe Sanh's similarities with Dien Bien Phu and other classic sieges.

On Saturday, February 11, Colonel Argo presented his findings to Westmoreland and his staff at MACV headquarters at Saigon. Laying out the context of the showdown at Khe Sanh, Argo explained that siege warfare had produced mixed results through history, but modern weaponry had shifted the advantage to besieging forces. In all but two twentieth-century examples he and his team examined, the aggressors had prevailed over the defenders in siege confrontations. And then, narrowing his focus to the crisis at hand, Argo informed his audience, "It appears that Khe Sanh is following the pattern of previous sieges."[2] So how could the Americans avoid a disaster? Ominously, he advised that "urgent consideration be given" to dispatching an outside force to Khe Sanh to break the siege.

Westmoreland's staff was stunned.

The American commander himself rejected his aide's gloomy conclusions. He pointed to US air and artillery superiority and the availability of ground reinforcements as hedges against defeat at Khe Sanh—the same arguments Westmoreland had made in his earlier discussions with General Wheeler and President Johnson. Khe Sanh could be held, and it *would* be held, he insisted. Westmoreland closed the discussion with an emphatic declaration: "We are not, repeat, NOT, going to be defeated at Khe Sanh."[3]

• • •

The growing pessimism over Khe Sanh extended beyond Westmoreland's inner circle.

The American commander had seemingly calmed the Dien Bien Phu questions from Washington when the Communists kicked off their Tet Offensive on January 30–31. As if that hadn't jangled nerves enough in Washington, the spotlight returned to Khe Sanh with the NVA ground attacks of February 5–7. Khe Sanh "can and should be defended," General Wheeler, chairman of the Joint Chiefs, told Johnson in a National Security Council meeting at the White House on Wednesday, February 7. "It is important to us tactically and it is very important to us psychologically. But the fighting will be very heavy, and the losses may be high."[4]

Vietnam dominated the official conversation in Washington, even at social gatherings, and Khe Sanh was the top concern.[5] Johnson was now meeting daily with his military high command and senior advisers to discuss the crisis in Vietnam. Street fighting raged in Hue, and intelligence reports pointed to a new round of Tet Offensive attacks before the week was out. The bigger question hanging over Washington was the timing of the expected NVA ground attack on Khe Sanh Combat Base. General Lew Walt had advised National Security adviser Walt Rostow that "all indications point to an attack on Khe Sanh in force, and soon." But General Wheeler on February 9 suggested the enemy was "going to take his time at Khe Sanh."[6]

Other developments added to the uneasiness over Khe Sanh. The enemy's surprising use of tanks at Lang Vei had been compounded by rare sightings of North Vietnamese aircraft in the Khe Sanh area. North Vietnamese MiG fighters had been observed practicing bombing runs, and Wheeler told the president that General Giap might deploy his aircraft for the first time "in support of ground action or in an effort to shoot down our B-52s."[7]

Hanoi couldn't challenge America's air superiority over Khe Sanh—the North Vietnamese possessed too few Soviet-made MiG fighters and Ilyushin-28 bombers to do that. But Communist air attacks could exacerbate strains in the American resupply effort and, as Secretary McNamara warned, "have spectacular psychological impact." In response, a US Navy guided-missile ship and other vessels armed with Terrier missiles steamed into the Gulf of Tonkin.

Resupplying Khe Sanh remained the overriding concern. "How is the supply problem at Khe Sanh?" President Johnson pressed in his February 9 meeting with the Joint Chiefs of Staff. "Will artillery and rockets knock [the airstrip] out? Can we rely on roads?"

McNamara gently reminded the president, "There is no road available up there." Wheeler tried to be reassuring. "As long as we use B–52s and tactical air," he responded, "we will be able to keep our resupply up."

Johnson tried to pin his military chiefs down on what to expect at Khe Sanh. He wanted to know whether the loss of the airfield would force Khe Sanh's evacuation. Wheeler equivocated, leaving it to General Harold K. Johnson, the Army chief of staff, to lay out the grim possibilities. He gave fifty-fifty odds to holding Khe Sanh and conceded that losing the air link would be a serious blow. "This is one of the hazards you have to accept," the Army chief bluntly told the president.[8]

Saturday, February 10, brought bad news from Khe Sanh. North Vietnamese gunners had hit a Marine KC-130 transport on its approach to the Khe Sanh airstrip, and the plane burst into flames after a crash-landing, killing eight Americans. Within forty-eight hours, the Air Force quietly banned further C-130 landings at Khe Sanh Combat Base, and the Marines curtailed their use. Smaller C-123 transport and helicopters would now have to shoulder more of the burden if Khe Sanh's air link were to be maintained.

Johnson's military high command had maintained a united front in advocating a stand at Khe Sanh, but dissenting voices had begun to urge the president to reconsider. Among the influential skeptics was retired general Maxwell Taylor, the former Joint Chiefs chairman and ambassador to South Vietnam, who expressed "very deep concerns" about Khe Sanh to Johnson in a series of written communications and meetings in early February.[9]

Aware of Taylor's counsel, and perhaps sensing the growing doubts of his commander in chief, General Wheeler advised President Johnson that Westmoreland was prepared "to execute a tactical withdrawal if this becomes desirable and necessary."

Every day, it seemed, the conflicting opinions on Khe Sanh mounted. On February 13, the CIA had a tabletop terrain model of Khe Sanh delivered to the White House to aid the president in his deliberations, and he began holding briefings around the mock-up in the White House Situation Room. The following day, Maxwell Taylor made his final case to Johnson in a blunt letter. "I know that Khe Sanh is very much on your mind as it is on mine," the former general and ambassador wrote. "It may be too late to do anything about the situation; if so, we should put doubts behind us and prepare for the fight." But if there was still time to avoid a showdown at Khe Sanh, "we should move quickly."[10]

Adding to Johnson's burden, news stories speculated that the United States had "stockpiled" nuclear weapons in South Vietnam for possible use at Khe Sanh. The White House and Pentagon vigorously denied the stories and insisted, untruthfully, that the issue hadn't been discussed. Privately, President Johnson ordered General Westmoreland to stop his secret deliberations on the possible use of nuclear weapons at Khe Sanh.[11]

Johnson was torn. "Frankly, I am scared about Khe Sanh," he told his national security team in a White House meeting. A nightmare scenario haunted him: the Khe Sanh runway gets knocked out, blocking the landing of fixed-wing aircraft; helicopters become Khe Sanh's lifeline; and then NVA gunners "pick off the helicopters." Underscoring the obvious, Johnson told his advisers, "I have a mighty big stake in this. I am more unsure every day."[12]

• • •

By the first week of February, the defenders of Khe Sanh Combat Base had settled into a grim routine, each new day a variation of the one before. In between the NVA rockets, shells, and sniper fire, enlisted men filled sandbags, improved or repaired trenches and bunkers, burned excrement, and performed other menial tasks. After two weeks of shelling and rocket barrages, the base had taken on the ambience of a post-apocalyptic shantytown. To dig deeper was to live, or at least improve one's chances of living, and so they dug. The grunts topped their trenches with sandbag parapets and layered bunker roofs with the sturdiest scraps they could scavenge, working on the theory that if their ramshackle shelters didn't collapse under the sheer weight of the protective layers, they could survive all but a direct hit.

Black humor flourished amid the madness. Among the more colorful displays was the pair of Bravo 1/26 grunts, Calvin Bright and Lloyd Scudder, who would run into the open and taunt NVA gunners, then dive for cover just before the mortar rounds started to hit.[13] Wry handwritten signs adorned the jumbled piles of sandbags and rubble that passed for bunkers. "Home Is Where You Dig It," read one sign, and so it was. Private First Class John Corbett, assigned to an 81-millimeter mortar team, found an incongruous metal street sign in a pile of rubble and erected it over his foxhole: "W DICKENS AV."[14]

In defiant acts of provincial pride, Marines flew flags from bunker roofs—city flags, state flags, Confederate flags, even a Scottish coat of arms, salvaged from the abandoned Combined Action Company Oscar-2 outpost at Khe Sanh village, and now fluttering over the FOB-3 bunker of its original owner, Marine F. J. Taylor. Shrapnel-pierced *Playboy* pinups hung from latrine doors and bunker walls. In between explosions, the sounds of Motown and the Beatles blared from battery-powered turntables and reel-to-reel tape recorders.

America's supreme commander in Vietnam, General William Westmoreland (left), confers with President Lyndon B. Johnson at Cam Ranh Bay, South Vietnam, on December 23, 1967. Westmoreland sought a decisive showdown with his Communist adversaries in 1968. *(LBJ Library photo by Yoichi Okamoto)*

North Vietnamese General Vo Nguyen Giap defeated the French by encircling and overrunning a remote outpost at Dien Bien Phu in 1954. Giap's move against Khe Sanh was part of a larger plan to humble US forces in South Vietnam in 1968. *(VA001466, Douglas Pike Photograph Collection, The Vietnam Center and Archive, Texas Tech University)*

By early 1968, 20,000 North Vietnamese Army troops were converging on isolated Khe Sanh Combat Base. The US Marine base is viewed here from the south, looking north toward the Demilitarized Zone.

(source unknown)

With his trademark cigar in hand, Colonel David Lownds (seated, at right) watches from a comfortable folding chair in his smoke-filled command bunker at Khe Sanh as his men plot fire-support missions against enemy forces. Lownds had 6,000 Marines under his command to defend Khe Sanh and its forward hill outposts.

(David Douglas Duncan/The Harry Ransom Center at University of Texas at Austin)

The first line of defense for Khe Sanh was a Marine outpost on Hill 881 South, under the command of Captain William Dabney (below). The Americans kept a wary eye on 881 North (above), a base for North Vietnamese infantry, mortars, and rockets throughout the siege.
(David Powell)

In the weeks prior to the siege, US Marines launched patrols from 881 South and nearby Hill 861 in an attempt to find the elusive North Vietnamese Army forces infiltrating the Khe Sanh area. The patrols honed the skills of young platoon commanders like India Company's Mike Thomas (top), seen with his men during a westward sweep toward the border with Laos. Above, the Marines of Kilo Company 3/26 move through lush elephant grass on the northern slope of 861 on the final day of 1967. At right, an India 3/26 squad leader, Corporal Ken Warner, dries his feet on 881 South.

(Richard Dworsky/Dennis Mannion/
Courtesy of Ken Warner)

North Vietnamese forces attacked the Kilo 3/26 outpost on Hill 861 in the early hours of January 21, 1968. Two days later, the Marines of Echo 2/26 established an outpost on 861 Alpha, seen at the right edge of this photograph.

(Ray W. Stubbe)

Artillery forward observer Dennis Mannion called in critical fire support during the attack on 861 and in the weeks that followed. He located targets during daylight hours with the powerful naval binoculars seen here, and employed a sophisticated Night Observation Device after nightfall.

(Courtesy of Dennis Mannion)

The North Vietnamese struck 861 Alpha on the morning of February 5, 1968, and penetrated the northern perimeter of the Echo Marines. Captain Earle Breeding (above) appears in good spirits as he works his radio in the aftermath of the attack. Daylight revealed enemy dead strewn around 861 Alpha.

(David Douglas Duncan/Harry Ransom Center at University of Texas at Austin)

Marine helicopter pilots and crews helped sustain Khe Sanh's hill outposts at considerable personal risk. The CH-46 Sea Knight shown here is preparing to transport American casualties from 861 Alpha down to Khe Sanh Combat Base after the February 5 battle.
(David Douglas Duncan/The Harry Ransom Center at University of Texas at Austin)

"My Staff on Radcliffe's Roost," Second Lieutenant Terence Roach (fourth from right) wrote on the snapshot he sent his pregnant wife, Lynne, in Michigan. A few days later, on February 8, 1968, Roach and twenty-five of his men were killed in an attack on "Radcliffe's Roost," better known as Hill 64. New York City native James Feasel (far right) was twice wounded as he helped organize the hill's defense. West Virginian George Chapman (third from right) was seriously wounded but survived a harrowing night amid bands of marauding enemy soldiers. Two other Marines shown here were among the dead: Corporal Jerry Burkhead (second from left), a machine gunner, and platoon sergeant Bernard B. McKinney (fifth from left, wearing glasses).
(Courtesy of Lynn Roach Fifer)

North Vietnamese gunners exacted a rising toll on US Air Force and Marine aircraft and crews flying in and out of Khe Sanh. On February 22, Captain James T. Riley and his copilot, Lieutenant Cary C. Smith, were taking on wounded Marines under enemy shellfire at Khe Sanh Combat Base when the main rotor on their CH-53 snapped and smashed through the cockpit, killing Riley and Smith. An injured crew member is being laid on a stretcher in this photograph.

(Cpl. L.F. George, US Marine Corps/National Archives)

A crash crew at Khe Sanh Combat Base sprays fire-retardant chemicals on a burning C-123 damaged by enemy fire.

(David Powell)

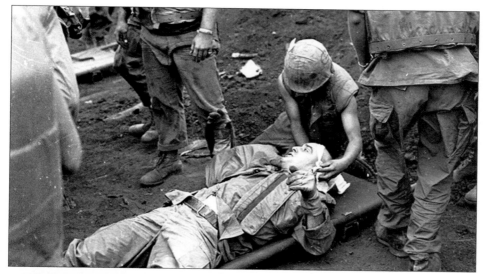

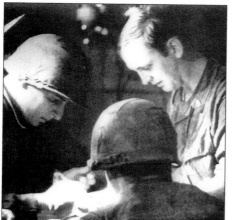

More than 2,500 casualties were treated at the main medical facility at Khe Sanh Combat Base, Charlie Med. The commander of Charlie Med, Dr. James Finnegan (right), is seen here operating on a casualty with the assistance of his close friend and comrade, Dr. Edward Feldman (left). The surgeons, corpsmen, ambulance drivers, and stretcher bearers of Charlie Med (below) performed heroically during the siege.

(David Powell/Courtesy of Dr. James Finnegan/Courtesy of Daniel Sullivan)

The Marines led the defense of Khe Sanh Combat Base, but Army, Navy, and Air Force personnel played crucial roles. The guns of Lieutenant Colonel John Hennelly's 1st Battalion, 13th Marine Regiment provided vital support to the hill outposts during the seventy-seven days of siege.

(David Powell)

Among the heavy weapons anchoring the northern perimeter at Khe Sanh Combat Base were Lieutenant Bruce Geiger's US Army "Duster" light tanks and "Quad Fifty" guns, which were mounted on Army trucks.

(Bruce Geiger)

Lieutenant John Dillon, a platoon commander with Bravo 1/26, looks out over the company's lines along the southeastern perimeter at Khe Sanh Combat Base.
(Michael O'Hara)

Californian Steve Wiese was one of Bravo's most experienced squad leaders at Khe Sanh. His combat skills helped him survive the devastating ambush of a February 25 patrol and the March 30 "payback assault."
(Courtesy of Steve Wiese)

The Marines on the hill outposts sparred constantly with the North Vietnamese, exchanging small arms fire, mortars, and grenades. Photographer David Powell chronicled the work of a Marine sniper team on 881 South.
(David Powell)

The North Vietnamese around 881 South took a pounding from artillery missions and air strikes coordinated by Corporal Robert Arrotta, seen here in his bunker on 881 South.
(David Powell)

The defenders of 881 South defied the North Vietnamese siege forces with their daily flag-raising ceremony (above), timed to the second to avoid incoming mortar rounds. Concealed by the morning fog, the Americans could stretch their legs, shoot the bull, and savor their C-rations. Lieutenant Chuck Schneider serenaded the defenders of 881 South with his guitar and was joined in song by comrades such as Lieutenant Tom Esslinger (at left), commander of Mike Company on the hill. *(David Powell)*

When the Air Force suspended C-130 landings at Khe Sanh in February, supplies were delivered by air drops (above) and parachute-rigged pallets shoved off the rear ramps of transport planes as they skimmed a few feet above the runway.

(David Powell)

In late February, CH-46 helicopter pilot David Althoff and his superiors devised an elaborate operation to improve the success rate of supply missions to the hill outposts. When the Super Gaggle got underway on February 24, support aircraft smothered suspected enemy positions with napalm, high explosives, tear gas, and smoke (above), allowing transport helicopters to drop thousands of pounds of badly needed supplies to the outposts (left).
(David Powell)

The siege was in its final days in late March when India 3/26 squad leader Ken Warner joined the exodus of Marines who had completed their combat tours. By the time he reached this transit barracks in Da Nang, Warner's face radiated joy and relief at having survived Khe Sanh. He left Khe Sanh, and then Vietnam, with his close friend Fulton "Fuzzy" Allen, an India Company machine gunner.
(Courtesy of Ken Warner)

In recent decades, survivors have renewed cherished ties at annual reunions of the Khe Sanh Veterans Association and private gatherings like this one in April 2012, hosted by Echo 2/26 commander Earle Breeding at his home in Ruidoso, New Mexico. Standing, from left to right, are: rifleman Jim Kaylor; artillery forward observer Bill Maves; company commander Earle Breeding; rocketman Dave McCall; rifleman Larry McCartney; and mortarman Jim Carmichael. Kneeling, from left to right, are: rocketman Jose (Cisco) Reyes; platoon commander Don Shanley; and sniper Al Miranda.
(Sue Hutchison/Ruidoso Free Press)

One of the many distinct groups at Khe Sanh Veterans Association reunions is comprised of men who served with Bravo 1/26, steeped in so much heartbreak and heroism at Khe Sanh. From left are: corpsman John "Doc" Cicala; rifleman Michael O'Hara; and company commander Ken Pipes.
(Courtesy of Michael O'Hara)

In his crisp dress-blues, his chest adorned with medals and ribbons, Ken Pipes honors the service of America's fighting men and women at public events.
(Ken Pipes)

While the grunts worked and waited along the perimeter trenches, staff officers went about their duties in the subterranean bunkers that sprawled beneath the scarred red clay. As base commander, Colonel David Lownds found himself besieged from outside by the North Vietnamese, and from inside by a growing troupe of American news reporters and photographers who had converged on I Corps to chronicle the showdown at Khe Sanh. Overnight, the journeyman colonel found himself in the world spotlight. In a *New York Times* "Man in the News" profile, published on February 12, the mustachioed Lownds was seen bustling about his besieged stronghold in flak jacket, steel-pot helmet, and rumpled utilities—resolute and ready. "My mission is to stay," Lownds declared, "and I intend to stay."[15]

Almost overlooked in the kinetic bustle of Lownds's command operations center was the work of Captain Harry Baig and his comrades of the Fire Support Coordination Center. Out of the limelight, they continued to pore over intelligence reports from the hill outposts and scrutinize sensor readings and topographic maps as they planned each day's air and artillery strikes under the rubric of Operation Niagara. In the round-the-clock struggle to deny General Giap his objective, the Americans were giving as good as they were getting. Niagara's rising toll was difficult to quantify, given the elusive nature of the North Vietnamese Army, but American air observers skittering overhead and close-in patrols out of the combat base spotted enough NVA bodies and blood trails to conclude that enemy losses were not insignificant.

But one question continued to haunt the Americans: Could Operation Niagara eliminate the NVA threat before Khe Sanh's fragile supply line snapped?

• • •

Despite worsening supply problems, spirits remained high for most at Khe Sanh Combat Base. But the mood was tense after the events of the past week—the bloody assault on 861 Alpha, the loss of Lang Vei, and the still-closer attack on Hill 64. Recon Marine Dave Doehrman knew Green Berets at Lang Vei from past missions, and he had followed the battle on his team's PRC-25 radio. Bravo Company, 3rd Recon, had been designated the quick-reaction force that would try to plug any breach in the combat base perimeter when the NVA struck. *It shouldn't be long now*, Doehrman concluded. *They're getting ready to overrun the base.*[16]

Along the southwest perimeter, radio operator Ron Smith had listened to the radio chatter during the Lang Vei attack. The twenty-year-old son of a Michigan truck driver had been on guard duty at the southwest gate on the morning of February 7 when a gunnery sergeant came by and gave him and another Marine a satchel charge and showed them how to use it. "If a gook tank shows up, shove this up under the turret, pull the pin, and run like hell," the gunny instructed. Smith thought, *I'm going to run like hell before that.*[17]

Anxieties soared when scores of Vietnamese and Laotians, some of them armed, started showing up at the gate. They were refugees from Lang Vei, and their numbers included soldiers from the sketchy Royal Laotian battalion and their families. But the Marines, Colonel Lownds chief among them, once again feared there were local Viet Cong or NVA mixed in with them, and so hard-and-fast orders were given to Ron Smith and others on guard duty: nobody gets in the gate.

The attack on Hill 64 on the morning of February 8 brought the NVA offensive within earshot of the American combat base, and for Marines along the line, every nocturnal probe and movement now became a harbinger of the big attack. Reports of revving tank engines, the movement of tracked vehicles, sappers at the wire—everything imaginable (and imagined) filtered back from the front lines. Rumors swept the base that the NVA was massing for human-wave attacks, "like Korea and Pork Chop Hill."[18]

The Marines scoffed at the Seabees and their soft Navy ways, but the onset of the siege meant that the once-mundane tasks performed by the Seabees had become life-and-death matters. Sam Messer was reminded of that one February day as he drove a forklift across the airstrip to pick up some cases of C-rations. An enemy mortar round nearly picked him out of his seat, and it knocked him flying. Messer crawled into a bunker, where he came face-to-face with a visiting general. "Marine, are you okay?" the incredulous senior officer asked, staring at the jagged schrapnel bristling from Messer's flak jacket.

The siege had thrust upon the Seabees the challenge of keeping the runway open, which required venturing onto the airstrip as soon as the shells and rockets stopped falling to clear debris and patch any holes. The runway was constructed of interlocking aluminum mats, each about three feet by eight feet and weighing one hundred pounds. The Seabees initially tried to expedite the work by cutting the sharp edges off torn mats and filling the holes with plaster, but the patches were unsatisfactory. Then they began tearing out the sections around a shell crater, filling the hole (sometimes big enough to stand in), and laying new matting—a painstaking process that gave the NVA snipers and mortar teams even more time to find the range.[19]

Charlie Med ambulance driver Danny Sullivan was driving along the airstrip on February 10 when a smoking KC-130 transport dropped from the skies on its approach to Khe Sanh. The plane's cargo hold was filled with huge fuel bladders needed to power generators at critical facilities around the base, and enemy machine-gun fire had pierced the fuselage and ignited the gasoline.

The pilot managed to land the aircraft but careened off the side of the runway. The aircraft exploded into flames. Sullivan jumped out of his ambulance and ran to the burning craft, pulling one man to safety through a rear hatch. A figure engulfed in flames appeared at the hatch, and Sullivan helped him to the ground and put out the fire with his hands. Lance Corporal Jerry W. Ferren had been badly burned over most of his body, and he screamed in agony. "We're going to get you to Charlie Med," Sullivan said. "You're going to be alright."[20]

Sullivan laid the injured man in his ambulance and roared off to Charlie Med. Behind him, other Marines tried to save men still trapped inside the wreckage. Three crew members and five passengers died from burns or other injuries.

The incident profoundly affected the men who had witnessed the crash or helped rescue the men trapped inside. Danny Sullivan resigned himself to a grim fate: he wasn't going to leave Khe Sanh alive.[21]

• • •

Almost to a man, the surviving American wounded (and several North Vietnamese) from the battles in and around Khe Sanh shared one common experience: they had received emergency treatment at Charlie Med, the main medical facility at Khe Sanh Combat Base, before being evacuated by air to military hospitals and hospital ships along the coast. Charlie Med was a collection of tents clustered near the center of the base, about thirty yards south of the helicopter pad alongside the runway. When the fighting began, a waist-high wall of sandbags was hastily erected around the triage and treatment tents, which afforded doctors and corpsmen some protection from flying shrapnel if they worked in a low crouch over wounded men laid on the floor.

The problems at Charlie Med did not end there, and an energetic Navy surgeon named James Finnegan was hastily ordered to Khe Sanh to take charge. A twenty-nine-year-old native of Pittsburgh, Pennsylvania, Finnegan had logged two years of general surgery in the States before spending four months as a combat surgeon in Delta Med at Dong Ha Combat Base. He arrived at Khe Sanh on a Huey helicopter gunship, door gunners banging away at the jungle below them during their approach. As soon as the bird touched the ground, the gunners shouted at Finnegan, "Get the hell out!" He did, and within minutes Jim Finnegan was awash in the blood of the first of more than 2,000 casualties he would treat at Khe Sanh.[22]

At Charlie Med, Finnegan led a team that included twenty-six corpsmen and three Navy surgeons: Joseph W. Wolfe, from Rutledge, Tennessee; Donald John Magilligan Jr., of Brooklyn, New York; and Edward Feldman, the New Yorker who had removed a live mortar round from a Marine's midsection while on temporary duty at the 1/26 aid station. Their facility was bereft of the X-ray machines and other sophisticated equipment found at rear-area hospitals, for Finnegan's team had one mission: resuscitate and stabilize the wounded, then get them on medevac flights as fast as possible.

Ed Feldman's first full day at Charlie Med was Saturday, February 10, a day that took a dire turn after the KC-130 crashed and burned off the Khe Sanh runway. The work of stabilizing the injured continued into the night. Late that evening, Feldman volunteered to oversee the evacuation of casualties on a medevac chopper due to arrive shortly after midnight.

The drill called for stretcher bearers to time their thirty-second dash so they met the chopper as it settled onto the helicopter pad. As Feldman and the others made their way to the pad with their casualties, mortars began to explode nearby. As the rounds came closer, two stretcher bearers panicked and prepared to bolt for cover. Feldman chambered a round in his .45 and announced, "We don't abandon our wounded."[23] The medevac flight arrived, the wounded were carried aboard, and the helicopter thundered off into the night. Only then did Feldman and the others run for cover.

The surgeons at Charlie Med had learned much about combat medicine in their months in Vietnam, namely, that high-explosive shells and flying shrapnel caused much more tissue damage and blood loss than the gunshot wounds they had seen back in America's urban emergency rooms. Head-wound cases were immediately directed into the treatment tent, where a tracheotomy was performed, breathing tube inserted, and intravenous drip placed in the groin area. A close inspection would follow to find any other wounds. Chest wounds were intubated to remove blood or fluid from the thoracic cavity, and then a large-bore IV tube would be inserted to replace the lost blood and fluid in the patient's body as fast as possible.

The doctors walked from station to station, supervising the work of corpsmen, stepping in only to perform intrusive procedures. Surgery was performed as a last resort. Once bleeding was controlled and vital signs were passable, a patient was readied for evacuation.

Finnegan did what he could to ease the strain at Charlie Med. Shortly after arriving at Khe Sanh, he had convinced the 26th Marines brass to approve construction of an underground bunker. The Seabees were working on it, but it wouldn't be ready until the end of the month. In the meantime, they would have to sweat out the NVA incoming while they worked on casualties.

By mid-February, Finnegan had brought order to the chaos at Charlie Med. He and his surgeon-teammates set a calm and collegial tone. The four doctors shared a small bunker, where they slept on cots and sat around in utilities stiffened by mud and blood, cooking C-rations and shooting the bull. Feldman had become Finnegan's indispensable wingman, skilled at his work, cool under fire, wickedly funny, and popular with the Marines.

As the commanding officer at Charlie Med, Finnegan attended the regimental briefing in the Command Operations Center bunker every morning, listening intently as various staff officers reported on the latest developments. After Lang Vei, all the reports from the front lines pointed to an imminent NVA attack. At the morning briefing, a large topographic map was unveiled to show five possible assault paths the North Vietnamese would take—five huge red arrows, punching through the perimeter and into the heart of Khe Sanh Combat Base. One arrow caught Finnegan's attention, as it plunged from the northern perimeter down through Charlie Med.

When the briefing was over, Finnegan pulled aside a staff officer. "What am I supposed to do if that's the arrow they pick?" he asked.

Not to worry, the major said. The reaction force would stop the enemy advance.

But how long would that take? Finnegan pressed.

Hard to say, the major conceded. "I would suggest that you arm all your people with M-16s and bayonets and dig fighting holes."

Finnegan was incredulous.

"Doc," the major said, "you gotta do your best until we get there."

Back at Charlie Med, Finnegan lightened his briefing with gallows humor. "They're talking about the NVA overrunning the base," he said. "If it happens, we could crawl under some parachutes and lie still until the NVA pass."[24]

● ● ●

For the NVA to reach Charlie Med from the north, they would first have to breach the northern perimeter held by Charlie Company of the 1st Battalion, 26th Marines. The 1/26 had been Ed Feldman's outfit during his temporary assignment to Khe Sanh in January, and he had forged friendships with its young company commanders and their beloved battalion CO, Lieutenant Colonel James B. Wilkinson. Feldman had accompanied the battalion on a reconnaissance operation along the Laotian border January 8 through 12, and it had been the greatest adventure of his life.

At the 1/26, Feldman had gotten to know a storied Marine who had recently joined the battalion, Sergeant Major James Thomas Gaynor. A mustachioed forty-seven-year-old from Louisiana, Gaynor had joined the Marines when he was seventeen and had been captured by the Japanese at Corregidor in 1942. He had survived the Bataan Death March and four years in a Japanese prisoner of war (POW) camp, and later fought in Korea. Nearing retirement, he had passed on a cushy rear-area billet to join the 1/26 at Khe Sanh on January 2.

The reconnaissance operation hadn't made contact with the NVA, and in mid-January, with growing signs that the enemy was out there and closing on Khe Sanh, Charlie 1/26 had been given the northern perimeter to defend. Under Captain David L. Ernst, the Blue Sector, as the area was known, was in good hands. A native of upstate New York, Ernst was tough but good humored, "one of those skippers you'd follow anywhere."[25] He had proven himself during the January operation, and once again when the shells started falling on the morning of January 21.

In his bunker along the Charlie Company lines, Ernst grew close to his two young radio operators, Lance Corporal Joseph Bailey, who carried the battalion radio, and Lance Corporal Chuck Chamberlin, who monitored the company net. Like Ernst, Bailey was from upstate New York, but he was the antithesis of the tough Marine—a short, witty, and affable young man of Irish Catholic heritage, with a shock of dark hair that wouldn't have passed muster back in the rear. He knew his stuff when it came to communications and had taught Chamberlin the ropes—how to handle the battalion and company radios, communications between platoons, the landline phone system. When he got a package from home, Bailey was unfailingly generous, and he recently shared his latest bounty with Chamberlin and other buddies: Lipton soup in a bag; chocolate chip cookies, Spam, and Tabasco sauce.

The twenty-year-old Chamberlin had grown up all over the place as an Air Force brat—Alaska, California, Illinois, Washington—but his parents split up when he was a high school junior, and he moved with his mother and younger sister to the Bay Area of Northern California. He quit school in his senior year and went to work for a funeral home that had the contract for deceased Army personnel coming back from Vietnam. He would drive to the Oakland Army Terminal, unload shipping cases bearing dead soldiers, and roll the remains to waiting morticians, who would prepare the bodies for shipment home to their families. It was gruesome work, and it factored in his decision when he received his Army draft notice in the fall of 1966. With memories of all those dead Army boys in his head, Chuck Chamberlin joined the Marines.

Chamberlin had arrived in Vietnam in late 1967. By mid-February, the days at besieged Khe Sanh had begun to run together—the artillery barrages and the sniping, the endless waiting for the NVA attack, the constant shadow of random death. That was how it was, one day blurring into another, until something bad happened to you or someone close to you. For Chamberlin, that day was Thursday, February 15.

A week had passed since the fall of Lang Vei and the attack on Hill 64, and everyone at Khe Sanh was on edge, waiting for the big assault. Just after 3:00 p.m., Joseph Bailey was on radio watch in the Charlie Company command bunker, and Chamberlin was asleep on a cot ten feet away. About ten minutes after the hour, Bailey reminded Chamberlin that it was his turn on the radio. Like everyone at Khe Sanh, Chamberlin was worn out, and it took him another minute or two to drag himself off the cot. He stood up to put on his flak jacket and helmet, and in that instant an NVA rocket slammed into the bunker.[26]

The world around Chamberlin went dark, and there was a terrible buzzing in his head and a ringing in his ears. A thick log column had shielded him from the blast, but not Bailey. Through a curtain of dust and smoke, Chamberlin could see that his friend was face down on the wooden bench he had been straddling, arms dangling at his side. Chamberlin started across the bunker, but tripped on a body. Sergeant Major James Thomas Gaynor, the legendary Marine, had been checking the Blue Sector lines and had just stopped by the Charlie Company CP to check in with Captain Ernst. Now he was lying at Chamberlin's feet.

Chamberlin took Joe Bailey by the shoulders and gently leaned him against a wall of sandbags. The back of Bailey's head was wet. His eyes had rolled into his head, and his skin was cold and clammy. Bailey vomited, and his legs started shaking. Chamberlin didn't know what to do, and so he hugged his friend.

Captain Ernst appeared, and he shoved Chamberlin aside and began wrapping a field bandage around Bailey's head. Ernst was oblivious to his own serious injuries, including a severed artery in his arm that spurted blood. Chamberlin grabbed a bandage and cinched it around the captain's wound.

At Charlie Med, Ed Feldman was dismayed to see Captain Ernst and Sergeant Major Gaynor among the six casualties brought in from the rocket attack. Lieutenant Colonel Wilkinson arrived, and he exhorted the unconscious Gaynor. "Talk to me, Sergeant Major. Talk to me, Sergeant Major."[27] Finally, Feldman gently said, "He can't hear you, Colonel."

Around dusk, a CH-53 set down on the Khe Sanh helicopter pad, and the Charlie Company casualties were loaded aboard. Lieutenant John M. Kaheny, a rising 1/26 staff officer, had lived with Gaynor for the past month and they had grown close. Kaheny had just been granted leave to return home to visit his dying father, and now he helped carry Gaynor's stretcher aboard the helicopter. The CH-53 headed east into the waning daylight, with Kaheny cradling the sergeant major's head in his lap. As the helicopter neared the Delta Med hospital at Dong Ha, Gaynor died.[28]

Captain Dave Ernst would lose his arm, but he would live. His war was over. Lance Corporal Joseph T. Bailey, the sweet-natured radioman, died at a hospital four days later. His friend, Lance Corporal Chuck Chamberlin, escaped serious injury. He remained at Khe Sanh to carry on.

CHAPTER 13

"What the Hell Is Out There?"

Throughout February, a trickle of men came and went from the Khe Sanh hill outposts as helicopter flights braved winter rains, fog, and enemy fire to keep the Marines alive. Among the new arrivals on 881 South was radioman Ron Smith, who got orders transferring him from the combat base and on Friday, February 9, boarded a CH-34 helicopter bound for the western anchor of the Khe Sanh defensive line. "When I give you the sign," the crew chief instructed, "get the hell off." Smith did as he was told and then heard somebody on the ground yelling, "Get down! Get down!" He threw himself into a shallow ditch as NVA mortar shells crashed nearby. When the barraged ended, Smith asked the nearest Marine, "Where can I find Bob Arrotta?"[1]

Mortar fire had wounded the forward air controller on 881 South in the early days of the siege, and Corporal Robert Arrotta, twenty-one, had taken over the job. The diminutive Marine from Bethesda, Maryland, quickly impressed Bill Dabney with a coolness and professionalism far beyond his years. Dodging enemy fire as he prowled the hill with his team, Arrotta worked his radios (call sign India 14), identified targets, verified map coordinates, and deftly synchronized close-air strikes with artillery fire and incoming helicopter flights. As high explosives and napalm summoned by Arrotta rained down on NVA troops and weapons sites around 881 South, the bearded controller was hailed by comrades as the "Mightiest Corporal in the Marine Corps."[2]

Ron Smith found his way to Arrotta's bunker, where he quickly discovered that life on the hill outposts was even worse than what he had experienced at the combat base since January 21. Food and water were harder to come by, and enemy fire was more concentrated. The Marines had limited their exposure to incoming rounds by moving underground, transforming their shallow trenches and slapdash above-ground shelters into deep passageways, underground bunkers, and "bunny holes" carved into the trench walls.[3]

Bob Arrotta was living in a bunker that he and two other Marines had hacked deep into the hillside of 881 South. They had covered the floor with wooden pallets and furnished the bunker with three cots. They rigged a bunk for Smith by hanging a stretcher from the ceiling with communications wire. Illumination was provided by a flashlight bulb wired to a spare radio battery.

By the second week of February, supply problems caused by bad weather and NVA fire had reached critical levels on all the hill outposts. The caloric intake of the men had been reduced to two C-ration meals a day, and hungry scavengers combed the garbage dumps on all the hills with renewed urgency.

Well-intentioned efforts by rear-echelon supply officers to boost morale sometimes went awry. In February, a cargo net packed with supplies was dropped onto 881 South during the afternoon. When the Marines ventured out to retrieve the supplies after dark, they were chagrined to discover hundreds of cups of ice cream among the usual cartons of C-rations and other items. The ice cream had melted, but the Marines were not about to discard the rare treat. Everyone on 881 South slurped down their share, then suffered through the resulting diarrhea.

Beleaguered as they were, the Marines on the hill outposts remained upbeat and defiant. On 881 South, Bill Dabney had added a flourish to his daily flag-raising ceremony by having a lieutenant bugle an up-tempo rendition of "To the Colors" while two Marines raised the Stars and Stripes on an RC-292 radio antenna. It was all over in less than thirty-five seconds, timed precisely so the Marines could dive for cover just before the first NVA mortar rounds hit.[4]

On 881 South, the American outpost farthest from Khe Sanh and closest to the NVA infiltration routes, Dabney tried to preempt an attack with random "mad minutes," in which his Marines on cue would blast away to their front for sixty seconds. It kept the NVA off balance while letting the Americans blow off steam and make sure their weapons were in good working order. Dabney also encouraged his men to act on their hunches if they heard movement or saw something suspicious. His ammo bunkers were full and well protected, so Dabney was generous in his use of mortars, automatic weapons, and grenades to prevent his stealthy adversary from massing around him.[5]

The NVA had positioned their big artillery and rockets on both sides of the Laotian border, so 881 South and 861 took on the added role of early warning system for Khe Sanh Combat Base. At the first sound of fire, Dabney's radiomen would alert the base with a cry of "Rockets! Rockets!" or "Arty! Arty!" Down at the base, a horn would sound, giving men about five seconds to find cover before the first explosions.[6]

Operation Niagara's deadly toll had forced NVA soldiers to revert to stealth in their movements around the hill outposts and the combat base, and sightings of the enemy became rarer as February wore on. The grunts on 881 South were startled one day to see an NVA soldier running along a ridgeline several hundred yards away. Several Marines opened fire with their M-16s, and the enemy soldier fell, then jumped up a second or two later and started running again. He fell a second time, but once again broke into a sprint. His legs churned furiously as M-16 bullets streaked by, until the soldier collapsed into a bomb crater. The Marines were laying odds on whether he was dead or not when a few seconds later a head popped above the rim of the bomb crater. In grudging admiration of their wily adversary, the Marines burst out laughing.[7]

• • •

On 861, the men in Kilo Company, 3/26, were dealing with the same hardships: too little food, too little sleep, too much incoming, and too much anxiety as they waited for the enemy to attack. The Marines were reminded every day of the near miss they had experienced in the predawn North Vietnamese attack of January 21: several of the NVA dead had remained tangled in the concertina wire along the hill's northern perimeter, and the flesh of the fallen enemy troops blackened and decayed, until all that remained were uniformed skeletons.[8] Dennis Mannion, the Kilo company artillery forward observer, found himself wondering as he looked out at the NVA skeletons: *Is that what's going to happen to me?*

The North Vietnamese had occupied a ridgeline about 500 yards west of 861, and from there, as well as from other positions on the slopes and draws north of the American outpost, the enemy had continued to pepper the hilltop with mortar and recoilless rifle rounds. Mannion knew the terrain well from the daily patrols off 861 he had accompanied in the three weeks prior to the siege, and his hunt for targets with his air counterpart was well informed by that knowledge.[9]

Nineteen-year-old Paul Knight was a rail-thin six-footer from Missoula, Montana, and he had undergone forward air controller training with Bob Arrotta before winding up at Khe Sanh. Knight had missed the early days of the siege while he was burning some R&R with his girlfriend in Hawaii, and he had returned to 861 in early February, armed with some new Rolling Stones and Aretha Franklin records for his battery-powered record player. As the music played, Knight and Mannion went to work pounding the NVA around 861 with a powerful one-two punch of artillery and close-air strikes.[10]

By mid-February, daily artillery and air strikes had burned and pulverized everything from the once-lush gulch at the western base of 861 on up and over the NVA-held ridgeline to the west. Yet hardy North Vietnamese soldiers somehow survived the cataclysm. Mannion and Knight watched in amazement one day as a lone NVA soldier stood up and blasted away with his AK-47 rifle at an American jet on its napalm run. The soldier kept firing until he was obliterated in a ball of fire.[11]

At least three times a week until the end of February, American aircraft would bomb the ridgeline west of 861 at some point during the night. Some nights a Spooky gunship appeared overhead with its moaning mini-guns and hosed down suspected NVA positions. If the close-air strikes were spectacular, the B-52 Arc Lights were like a window into the apocalypse. The massive air strikes and artillery lifted spirits on the hills, but they caused Dennis Mannion to contemplate the extreme nature of the enemy threat that demanded such an unprecedented American response. Mannion wondered: *If they're using this much firepower, what the hell is out there?*[12]

• • •

Along the northern line of Hill 861, Sergeant Miguel Salinas—Korean War veteran, merchant seaman, and incumbent M-60 gunner—filled the long stretches of down time by holding court with a cast of young understudies. He organized such crude competitions as farting and smelly-armpit contests and games of "fly poker" (grab the most flies from a crumb-sprinkled table and you win the hand). Food became currency in the raunchy competitions.

Salinas told stories about his stint as a machine gunner in Korea and his travels as a merchant seaman. "Hey, Pop, you ever been to Italy?" a young Marine from the sticks would ask the worldly Salinas. And Salinas would regale the pimply, sex-starved teenagers with wild stories about his carnal escapades in various Italian ports of call.[13] As food and water became even more scarce, the Marines stopped dreaming of sex and beer and became obsessed with food and water. Pop Salinas merged his fantasies in a recurring dream in which he was sitting nude under a waterfall, a cold beer in his hand and a naked woman at his side.[14]

From the *Time* magazines his father sent him, Dennis Mannion knew that Khe Sanh was big news back home, so he started writing American companies to tell them that the Marines on Hill 861 wanted them to know how *great* their product was. As Mannion and his buddies had hoped, packages eventually started arriving on the hill: bottles of premium gun oil, packets of "Funny Face" powdered drink mix, boxes of M&Ms, Tabasco sauce, and Necco wafers.[15]

On the southern perimeter of Hill 861, Jim Thomas performed the dual role of corpsman and sanitation officer. It was a nearly impossible assignment, given the tropical climate and the lack of water for personal hygiene or even washing wounds.[16] One young Marine with a minor shrapnel wound came to Thomas with red streaks running up his arm. Like many on the hill, he was terrified of risking a medevac flight to Khe Sanh. Thomas took one look at the spreading infection and ordered the Marine onto the next chopper that made it in.

Doc Thomas did what he could to ease the burden on his young Marines. He stood watch at night to give the worn-out grunts a break and built them a sheltered outhouse in a demolished bunker so they could perform bodily functions without getting shot. The waste was collected in halved fifty-five-gallon drums, which were regularly burned off along with the rats that Thomas snared in a network of traps.

Practical jokes leavened daily life, and the soft-spoken corpsman was a frequent target. Thomas retaliated one day by shoving a deactivated grenade down the back of a habitual joker. When the shaken Marine finally calmed down, he plotted his revenge. Thomas had carved a two-room "hooch" into the hillside. He had papered the earthen walls with *Playboy* and *Penthouse* centerfolds and had even built a chimney to vent smoke from his kerosene lantern. One day he emerged from his shelter to find a pipe sticking out of his chimney, with a handwritten sign: "Urinal."[17]

• • •

By mid-February, the NVA troops arrayed against the hill outposts had settled into their own routine, which revolved around sniping and mortaring, and firing an occasional recoilless rifle round into the American strongholds. The Americans had dug deep and had learned to live with the incoming, for the most part. But it was a game of chance, and the unlucky died.

On 881 South, Lieutenant Tom Esslinger had aged well beyond his twenty-four years since taking command of Mike Company, 3/26, on February 1. The early days had been especially harrowing as the NVA pounded away at 881 South with their Russian-made 120-millimeter mortars and 130-millimeter artillery pieces. As Esslinger walked his lines, he kept his anxieties to himself but was reassured to find that he wasn't the only one scared out of his mind. Some days the cacophony of rockets, heavy artillery, and mortars was more or less constant, and other days it was just two or three rounds. The only thing the Marines on the hill outposts could predict was the fire that would greet an incoming helicopter.

On 861 Alpha, young Private Jose "Cisco" Reyes had been among the handful of reinforcements rushed to the hill on the morning of February 5. Seasoned hands like rocketman Barry Fixler taught him the ropes in those first days, and Reyes settled into the precarious existence that passed for daily life on the hill. He had never smoked back home in Los Angeles, but he started on the hill. There was so much stress from the incoming, the probes, the long night watches, and the constant threat of death. Most of the men were hollow-eyed and exhausted. Reyes would light a cigarette to keep himself awake on watch duty, cupping his hands around the stick of burning tobacco to avoid giving away his position. When he invariably dozed off, the cigarette would burn his fingers and wake him up.

Reyes also learned hard lessons about the fickleness of fate. Huddling in his fighting hole as mortar rounds crashed around him, he reached for his 3.5-inch rocket launcher and found it shredded with shrapnel. A friend took shrapnel to the head from an incoming round and then thrashed about in agony. "Oh, my God!" the Marine gasped. "What's going to happen to my wife?" And then he died.[18] Another Marine was guarding the chow cache on 861 Alpha when two mortar rounds came in and sheared off both legs and one arm. "They're not good enough to kill me," the gritty Marine told a comrade.[19]

On a typical day on 861, Jim Thomas responded to the cry for a corpsman after mortar rounds hit the hill. He found a distraught Marine standing over a lifeless comrade. "Doc, that's my best friend—can you help me?" Thomas examined the fallen Marine, a handsome kid with blond hair. There was hardly a mark on his body, but he was dead. Thomas put the Marine in a body bag and helped carry him up to the LZ for transport to the combat base. But a winter front moved in, cloaking the hill in mist and fog, and the body lay beside the LZ for five days. By the time the decomposed corpse finally reached Graves Registration down at Khe Sanh, Thomas knew the family would be denied the solace of an open-casket funeral.[20]

The foul weather that rolled across the hills in mid-February made it even more difficult to deliver supplies and evacuate the wounded and the dead, piling more stress on all concerned. The wounded and dying men stuck on the socked-in hill outposts stood to lose the most, of course, but the psychological toll reverberated outward, from distraught comrades who could only watch their brothers-in-arms suffer and sometimes die, to the air officers at Khe Sanh Combat Base coordinating the desperate pleas for emergency medevac flights, to the helicopter crews who made heroic attempts to reach the hills in almost zero-visibility conditions, sometimes with nothing but aching failure to show for their exhausting hours in the air.

Captain Rich Donaghy was the regimental air officer for the 26th Marines, and it was his job to advise Colonel Lownds and his staff and coordinate the use of fixed-wing aircraft and helicopters in support of Khe Sanh Combat Base and its hill outposts. A native of New York City, born in Brooklyn and raised in Queens, Donaghy knew the climatological vagaries of the area all too well, having arrived at Khe Sanh in October, at the height of the rainy season. He had turned twenty-five at Khe Sanh on February 10, and now, operating with the call sign Intrigue 14 Actual, he found himself having to weigh the lives of wounded Marines on the hill outposts against the lives of helicopter pilots and crews trying to evacuate casualties in extremely treacherous flying conditions.[21] Sometimes, as if Donaghy wasn't already painfully aware of the life-and-death nature of his decisions, an air officer or someone else on a hill outpost would come on the line to underscore the stakes: "If you don't get somebody up here soon, this guy's not going to make it."[22]

Such was the case with Corporal Homer Taylor Jr.

At 5:30 a.m. on Friday, February 16, Taylor, a twenty-one-year-old Marine squad leader from Memphis, Tennessee, was walking along the trench line on 881 South when a mortar drove shrapnel into his temple and shoulder. A corpsman prepped the wounded Marine for the short medevac flight down to the combat base, but thick fog enveloped the hill. All day Saturday the fog never lifted, but Taylor was still hanging on.

Later in the day, Taylor's condition worsened. His comrades stood on the LZ into the night, waving handheld flares and strobes as they tried to talk a chopper down through the fog, but the pilot finally had to give up. In the early hours of Sunday morning, February 18, the fog lifted and a helicopter took off for 881 South. Before it could land, a radio operator on the hill informed the pilot that the medevac status had been downgraded from "priority" to "routine." Homer Taylor had died.[23]

Two days later, helicopters were inbound to the hill outposts when Lance Corporal Terry Smith, another radio operator who worked with Bob Arrotta, broke from cover on 881 South to wave an incoming bird away from an LZ that had been registered by NVA mortar teams. As the pilot veered away, a round hit the zone and Smith fell with a severed femoral artery.[24]

While corpsman Ronald V. Bowling tried to stanch the blood flow, crack CH-46 pilot Dave Althoff swooped back to the hill to pick up the wounded Marine. Althoff rushed the casualty down to Charlie Med, but Terry Smith's wounds were too severe. "I grew up a lot today," Bob Arrotta wrote afterward. "My best friend died in my arms."[25]

• • •

The Marines at Khe Sanh Combat Base had spent the two weeks after Lang Vei strengthening their defenses against a human-wave assault supported by tanks. The perimeter was ringed by fields of anti-personnel mines—M14 "toe-poppers" that cracked the bones in a man's foot and leg but usually weren't lethal, and M16 "Bouncing Betties," a nasty German invention that sprang up about waist high before spraying steel balls in all directions. Powerful anti-tank mines were added, along with barrels of *fougasse*, a potent napalm mix that would be detonated as enemy troops closed on the perimeter.

A work party from Lieutenant William Gay's detachment of combat engineers was outside the eastern wire one day in February, laying more anti-personnel mines, when South Vietnamese Army Rangers on the perimeter started screaming. The Americans dived to the ground as the ARVNs opened fire over their heads at North Vietnamese nearby. When the firing eased, one of the team members, John Pessoni, raised his head. A buddy flashed Big John a look of horror, and Pessoni choked back a wave of fear. "Oh shit, did I get hit?"[26] His friend started laughing. "No, you got a turd on your face."

In the middle of a minefield, Big John had managed to find a chunk of human excrement.

The fear and tension dissolved into howls and hoots, and soon the entire team was convulsed with laughter. The shooting died away, and the giddy Americans made their way out of the minefield and back through the Ranger lines. The South Vietnamese didn't know what to make of their crazy allies.[27]

• • •

On Wednesday, February 21, Khe Sanh began its second month under siege. Two weeks had passed since the North Vietnamese Army's stunning assault on Lang Vei. After so many false alarms and sleepless nights, the Marines once again concluded the Communists had completed their careful preparations and were poised to launch the big attack. At 12:45 p.m., as if in confirmation, the North Vietnamese launched a rare daylight probe against the eastern end of the base. As artillery, mortars, and rockets slammed into the stronghold, about a company of NVA troops—perhaps one hundred men in all—advanced to the edge of the treeline and opened fire on the ARVN Rangers.

The fighting reverberated across the Khe Sanh plateau as opposing snipers, mortar teams, and artillery batteries exchanged fire. At 1:00 p.m., a rocket smashed into the airstrip, closing Khe Sanh's lifeline for the remainder of the day.[28] Meanwhile, the formidable forces of Operation Niagara crisscrossed the skies over Khe Sanh, killing the North Vietnamese in their trenches, spider holes, bunkers, and gun emplacements. From 9:00 a.m. on February 20 to 9:00 a.m. the following day, forty-eight US Air Force B-52 bombers hammered the Khe Sanh area with sixteen Arc Light strikes—a staggering 1,200 tons of ordnance. By Thursday morning, another thirty B-52 bombers had dropped an additional 750 tons of high explosives on the North Vietnamese around Khe Sanh.[29] Low-flying Marine, Navy, and Air Force attack jets dumped 256 tons of napalm and high explosives on NVA positions in eighty-two close-air sorties on February 21 alone.

Meanwhile, the battle to maintain Khe Sanh's fragile lifeline hung in the balance.[30] The combat base and its outposts devoured as much as 235 tons of supplies daily, and by February only a fraction of that amount was getting through on most days. Parachute drops off the western end of the base had become the safest means of delivering supplies to Khe Sanh. On February 16, the Americans had introduced a hybrid method known as "low-altitude parachute extraction system," or LAPES, in which parachute-rigged pallets were pushed off the back ramp of a C-130 as it swooped low over the airfield. The pallet would careen down the runway like a runaway sled until slowed by the parachute.

The winter *crachin,* a constant fine mist, had closed in around the hill outposts, and food and water supplies were growing critically short. On 861, rations had been reduced to one canteen, and then half a canteen of water and one C-ration meal per day. On 861 Alpha, Marines sucked on pieces of bamboo they gathered in the draw off the hill's western flank.

The daily rations for some men consisted of a can of C-ration peaches.[31] A platoon of Alpha Company, 1/26, on Hill 950 had run out of water. And on 881 South, food and water supplies were so low that Captain Bill Dabney convened a council to consider whether the Marines should abandon the post and fight their way to the combat base or some other point.[32]

On February 21, 143 tons of supplies reached Khe Sanh by air, but not without the sort of drama that had become an almost daily occurrence. A C-130 flying low over the airstrip came under NVA fire as it was executing a LAPES supply drop, and its tail section clipped a bunker, burying two Marines beneath a heap of sandbags and debris. Marine Reggie Lee Vance died shortly after midnight from his injuries.

• • •

The North Vietnamese pressure increased on Thursday, February 22, with a massive barrage of artillery fire, rockets, and mortars. Captain James T. Riley of Zeigler, Illinois, a thirty-two-year-old pilot with Marine Heavy Helicopter Squadron 463, had already flown two resupply missions to Khe Sanh during the day when he heard a radio request for a medevac mission at the combat base. Riley volunteered to take it. The wounded Marines were readied near the airstrip's freight ramp for a quick evacuation, and around 4:45 p.m., Riley maneuvered his chopper into position to take the casualties aboard.

As heavy mortar and rocket fire crashed around his aircraft, Riley held in place until the wounded were loaded. A shell-burst critically damaged the chopper before he could pull away, and Riley ordered the casualties removed while he tried to save his aircraft and crew. He coaxed the aircraft off the ground, but severe vibrations quickly forced him back down. As the chopper settled onto the tarmac, the main rotor blade broke away and sliced through the cockpit, killing Riley and his co-pilot.[33]

• • •

Among the Americans seeking shelter in a trench line off the western end of the runway during the February 22 barrage were Father Robert Brett, the 2/26 battalion chaplain, and his assistant, Private First Class Alexander Chiu. Brett had spent the previous day on 861 Alpha and

861, administering communion and granting plenary indulgence to Marines. (Kilo Company forward observer Dennis Mannion was among those receiving a plenary indulgence from Father Brett on Hill 861.) Brett and Chiu had flown back down to the combat base at the end of the day and were trying to catch a flight to Hill 558 as the barrage raged. Nearby their companions in the trench was Lance Corporal Julius "Corky" Cartwright Foster, a twenty-nine-year-old Marine reservist who had advertised his desire to be sent to Vietnam by walking 404 miles from his West Virginia home to reenlist at Camp LeJeune, North Carolina.[34]

Just before 5:30 p.m., an NVA rocket screamed in from the west and dropped into the narrow trench line, killing six Americans and wounding nine. Among the dead were Father Brett, Alexander Chiu, and Corky Foster, the inspired West Virginian who had fulfilled his wish to fight in Vietnam.

CHAPTER 14

"Proud to Be a Marine"

Friday, February 23 was the most hellish day of all for the defenders of Khe Sanh. Over seven terrifying hours, beginning in the late morning, more than 1,300 shells, rockets, and mortar rounds pounded the combat base and the hill outposts.[1] Casualties would prove light for such a ferocious bombardment, a testament to the digging and fortifying the men had done in the month since the siege began. Still, twelve Americans were killed—eight at the combat base, three on 881 South, and one on 861—and nineteen wounded seriously enough to require evacuation.

The butcher's bill could have been worse, but that was little consolation for the comrades of the fallen. Charlie Med surgeon Ed Feldman lost his friend Lieutenant Kim Johnson, who had been with him the night he removed the mortar round from the Marine's abdomen. Tall and blond, a gentle twenty-seven-year-old reserve officer from Fresno, California, Johnson was also a devout Mormon, a husband and father. His bunker took a direct hit and his neck was broken, but there wasn't a mark on his body when they dug him from the rubble.[2]

On Hill 881 South, Lieutenant Tom Esslinger had been in command of the Mike Company sector for a little more than three weeks. He had seen his young Marines conquer the "nearly paralyzing fear" of the early days of the siege and transform their piece of the hill into an impregnable fortress. The twenty-four-year-old Esslinger had been greatly aided in his leadership of Mike Company by two savvy gunnery sergeants under his command: Eugene Charles "Gene" Wire, the classic tough-love gunny, a mantle earned after devoting eighteen of his thirty-seven years to the Marine Corps; and thirty-two-year-old Edward Robitaille, a fourteen-year Marine veteran, more soft-spoken in his role as commander of Mike Company's weapons platoon.

Robitaille had begun his Vietnam tour of duty as the siege at Khe Sanh was getting underway, and after arriving on 881 South, he became close friends with Gunny Wire. They had dug a hole beneath the rim of a bomb crater left over from the Hill Fights, and they would meet there to have a smoke, sip coffee, and talk about their lives back in the world.

Around midday on February 23, Esslinger was in his bunker when several large-caliber enemy artillery shells slammed into his area. It wasn't long before his radio crackled with a terse casualty report: "007 has been hit, over," a voice announced.

Esslinger's heart sank: the number seven was a reference to any company gunnery sergeant, and "007" was Mike Company's inside joke for identifying their pair of gunnies. Esslinger steeled himself, then asked, "Which one?"

"Both," came the reply.

"How bad?" Esslinger asked.

"K."

Esslinger felt sick. *K? Killed in action? No way.*

The lieutenant sprinted from his bunker to the crater that had become the refuge of the two gunnies. Just inside the lip, where Robitaille and Wire had dug their hole, Esslinger spotted a new shell crater. There was plowed up dirt and shrapnel, but no sign of either man.

A team was organized to dig out the blast hole while Esslinger radioed all stations on his company net to request a position report on both gunnies. But no one had visual contact with them, and an examination of the blast hole soon confirmed the worst: an incoming round had landed squarely on Paul Robitaille and Gene Wire, and they had left the world together, leaving behind only a blood-soaked patch of earth.

For Tom Esslinger, February 23 would be the worst day of his life.[3]

• • •

The shell fire eased by nightfall, and the defenders of Khe Sanh settled in for another long vigil. On Hill 861 Alpha, Echo Company, 2/26, rifleman Jim Kaylor had drawn straws with a pair of lance corporals and close friends, nineteen-year-old Gerrie George Jefferies and twenty-year-old Carlos Cruz Aguirre, to decide who would sleep inside their bunker along the western side of the hill. Kaylor lost, so he stretched out in the trench line about ten feet away.[4]

Around midnight, friendly "harassment and interdiction" artillery fire from Khe Sanh screamed low over the hill, toward some unknown target to the north. Fifteen minutes into the new day, February 24, two rounds "of unknown origin" slammed into the Echo Company outpost on 861 Alpha. One hit the bunker where the two M-60 gunners, Aguirre and Jefferies, were sleeping, burying the two Marines beneath sandbags, rocks, and dirt.[5]

Jim Kaylor and other Marines rushed to the pile of rubble and began tearing it away to reach their comrades. About fifteen minutes later, the lifeless bodies of Aguirre and Jefferies were finally pulled from the debris.

• • •

As the weeks passed and the Marines analyzed their intelligence and tried to anticipate where the North Vietnamese would attack, the southeastern perimeter had become an area of intense focus. It was the Gray Sector in the Khe Sanh Combat Base defensive scheme, held by the ARVN Rangers and the Marines of Bravo Company, 1/26, and aerial photographs had revealed an expanding network of NVA trenches in the adjacent jungle.

The southeastern sector was a logical avenue of attack for the North Vietnamese. It was close to Khe Sanh village, which the NVA had occupied, and Route 9, which now bustled with Communist truck convoys after dark. The North Vietnamese activity in the area had been closely tracked by Harry Baig and his comrades at the Fire Support Coordination Center, and the Americans had devised "mini Arc Lights" and "micro Arc Lights" for the North Vietnamese siege forces in that area—carefully plotted saturation bombing carried out by low-flying American attack aircraft as close as 500 meters (about 550 yards) to the combat base.

The North Vietnamese took the punishment and continued to extend their siege lines and bunker complexes closer and closer to the American and South Vietnamese lines on the east. As the days passed, aerial photographs revealed wide assault trenches leading toward the southeastern perimeter of Khe Sanh Combat Base.[6]

The men of Bravo Company, 1/26, had waited for weeks to mix it up with the North Vietnamese. During the attack on Lang Vei, the company commander, Captain Ken Pipes, had gotten his men ready for battle, but nothing had happened. Bravo radioman Tom Quigley and his buddies had come across a story in Stars and Stripes that quoted Colonel Lownds as saying, "We will defend Khe Sanh to the last man," and they had laughed about that. "Glad he's confident," Quigley had quipped. Ever so quietly, Quigley had stockpiled grenades and ammo in his hooch "for an Alamo-style last stand."[7]

On February 13, a Bravo platoon had gone outside the wire to provide security for a mine-laying detail while the ARVN Rangers pushed several hundred yards southeast of the base in search of NVA forces. The Bravo Marines had set up in a lush bamboo thicket, beyond the heavily mined swath of cleared terrain that stretched about two hundred yards beyond the perimeter wire. Small-arms fire crackled to their front, and the Bravo boys waited nervously. The wide-eyed Marines had watched the triumphant ARVN Rangers file past them on their return to the base, clutching a recoilless rifle they had captured from the North Vietnamese. It had been a good day for the much-maligned ARVNs, and the boys of Bravo had gotten an increasingly rare glimpse of the world outside the wire.[8]

That night, Lance Corporal Ken Rodgers and another Bravo Marine had been called down to their platoon command post. There were two ARVN Rangers carrying a body—in the darkness it wasn't clear if he was a South Vietnamese or an NVA soldier—but Rodgers and his buddy were ordered to walk their ARVN counterparts over to Graves Registration. It was pitch black and they stumbled around for a while, but they finally reached their destination, near Charlie Med, and the two Americans and the two ARVN Rangers carried the stretcher inside and set it down.

A sergeant came over to handle the transfer of the corpse, and as Rodgers was explaining the situation, he heard somebody running down a hall. A young man popped into view, yelling to someone behind him, "Hit me! Hit me!" A second later he reached up, smoothly caught a severed foot in a boot, and yelled, "Touchdown!" Rodgers laughed, but the eyes of the ARVN Rangers widened with horror and they quickly left. For the Graves Registration personnel who spent their days handling the torn bodies of young Americans at Khe Sanh, black humor helped keep them sane.[9]

• • •

Down on the Bravo Company lines, Corporal Steve Wiese was ready for the North Vietnamese to make their move. In the meantime, the lanky Californian perfected his time-honored Marine Corps skills as a master scavenger. Wiese had overseen the construction of the bunker he shared with three other Marines, a structure made of stacked sandbags that measured six feet by eight feet, and about six feet deep. The floor was covered with sandbags and layers of empty bags to make it more comfortable for sleeping. A poncho hung over the entrance. Wiese's prized possession was a cot he had commandeered.

The four Bravo Marines had spent the past weeks strengthening their bunker to the point where it would survive a rocket strike, and Wiese was confident they had succeeded. He and his buddies had chopped down a tree outside the wire and used a section of the thirty-inch trunk as the roof, then layered it with runway matting. On top of that they stacked a layer of 105-millimeter howitzer ammo canisters packed with dirt, capped with two alternating layers of sandbags and runway matting. In mid-February, Wiese and his comrades had been in their bunker when an NVA mortar exploded outside. It sounded close, but only after the barrage ended did Wiese discover that they had survived a direct hit. It was a proud moment for Wiese and his comrades.

Wiese didn't fear death, but he was terrified by the prospect of being maimed. He had seen too many mangled bodies in Vietnam, and he didn't want to wind up like that. One of his buddies in the bunker, a Mexican American named Miranda, lived in fear of getting blown up by an NVA rocket. He had dug a hole in the bottom of their bunker that he hoped would save him if they took a direct hit. Wiese gave him a hard time about it: "Hey Miranda, I don't know if we would find you down there." Miranda would reply, "I don't care, man. If I get killed I get killed. I just don't want to get blown up."[10]

Around February 23, as the NVA stepped up the pressure on the combat base, Bravo's executive officer, Lieutenant Ben Long, stopped by to let him know that the latest intelligence indicated an imminent attack. Long mentioned that higher-ups wanted prisoners if the line was overrun, so they could interrogate them to learn more about NVA plans.

Wiese began to plot. Once in a while he could hear the NVA digging at night—the *clink* of metal as a pick or shovel hit rock—and so he decided: *I'm going to go out there and capture a gook*. He gathered his squad and shared his idea. They would sneak out of the wire with nothing more than a K-bar knife and a pistol, find the NVA trench line, grab a gook, and drag him back to Bravo's lines. During the course of the day, every Marine in Wiese's squad came to him to volunteer for the mission.

Another Bravo squad leader pulled Wiese aside. Corporal Ken Claire hailed from the Sierra foothills of Northern California, and he was known for his trademark Tarzan yell and other antics, but he was also one of Bravo's finest Marines. "I hear you're going on a suicide mission tonight," Claire said to Wiese. "I want to go."[11]

Before nightfall, Wiese was summoned before a senior officer who knew all about his plan. He threatened Wiese with charges if he led anybody outside the wire. As the chastened squad leader turned to leave, the colonel stopped him short. "Corporal Wiese," the officer barked, "it is men like you that make me proud to be a Marine."[12]

Steve Wiese and his band of would-be raiders stood down, but their opportunity to go head-to-head with the North Vietnamese would come soon enough. Late on the afternoon of February 24, Wiese and the other squad leaders of Bravo's 3rd Platoon were put on notice: Get your men ready. We're going outside the wire in the morning to have a look.[13]

CHAPTER 15

Super Gaggle

B y February 1968, a typical day in I Corps had taken on a well-worn routine for Marine CH-46 helicopter pilots like Dave Althoff: up at 5:00 or 5:30 a.m., swig some coffee, wolf down some dry scrambled eggs, stash some C-rats in the chopper, and then head into the morning briefing before hitting the skies.

Marine Aircraft Group 36 and its three hundred-plus pilots and 2,100 air crewmen and mechanics were on their way to a historic month, and they could scarcely meet the demand for helicopter transport, assault, resupply, and medevac missions in I Corps. In addition to supporting Marines locked in fierce street fighting at Hue, MAG-36 bore primary responsibility for the perilous work of resupplying the hill outposts at Khe Sanh.

For the defenders of Khe Sanh, their lives quite literally depended on the Flying Tigers of HMM-262 and Purple Foxes of HMM-364 in their twin-rotor Boeing Vertol CH-46 Sea Knights, and the Ugly Angels of HMM-362 in their smaller Sikorsky UH-34s. Over the course of the month, MAG-36 choppers would log 5,337.7 flight hours, fly 15,782 sorties, carry 14,566 passengers and 3,100 tons of cargo, and evacuate 2,872 casualties—and they would do all this in some of the foulest weather that Vietnam had to offer, while facing the heaviest enemy fire of the war.[1]

Nearly every landing zone in I Corps these days was hot, but the Khe Sanh runs had become especially dangerous. The approaches to the combat base and the hill outposts were now covered by NVA soldiers firing everything from AK-47 rifles to quad-.50-caliber machine guns, and the landing zones were locked in by enemy mortar teams. The rising risk of getting shot down in runs to the hill outposts had forced the helicopters to start carrying supplies in external nets, so they might dump their loads more quickly and escape the enemy's gun sights. It wasn't possible to do that with medevac missions, so the helicopter pilots needed nerves of steel to sit in place for agonizing seconds, mortar rounds and machine gun bullets scouring the landscape around them, while wounded Marines were carried aboard.

It was all in a day's work for Dave Althoff.

• • •

Born in Illinois in 1932, the son of an insurance broker and a housewife, Althoff had moved with his family to Chandler, Arizona, when he was sixteen. An accomplished football and baseball player in high school, he studied business at Arizona State University before dropping out to become a Navy pilot in 1952. He spent the first years of his career flying fixed-wing aircraft, including nuclear-armed patrols over the Korean Peninsula in the Lockheed F-80 Shooting Star, before learning to fly helicopters at Pensacola (Florida) Naval Air Station. He later spent nine months in the South Pacific, flying radiation-monitoring missions over Bikini Atoll during US nuclear weapons tests, before shifting to the Marine Corps to fly helicopters.

In the late summer of 1963, Althoff headed to Vietnam as part of Operation Shufly. Based in Da Nang, he taught South Vietnamese pilots and crews how to fly H-34 helicopters on combat missions. The war had a leisurely nine-to-five quality to it, with nights and weekends free. Every Wednesday, Althoff would fly down to Saigon to pick up fresh fruits and vegetables, squeezing in lunch at his favorite floating restaurant. But it wasn't all fun and games, and by the time he left Vietnam in the spring of 1964, Althoff had flown sixty combat missions.[2]

The war in Vietnam went on without Althoff for three years as he logged tours that took him to Okinawa and the Caribbean, went through amphibious warfare school back in North Carolina, and celebrated the birth of five children. By the time he returned to Vietnam in June 1967, the "gentleman's war" was a distant memory.

Althoff was sent to I Corps and began flying CH-46 Sea Knights with Marine Medium Helicopter Squadron 262 (HMM-262), part of Marine Aircraft Group 36. Settling in at Quang Tri Air Base in August 1967, Althoff and his fellow pilots and crews in HMM-262 did it all: troop assault, resupply, medevac, reconnaissance team insertions and extractions.[3]

At thirty-five, with sixteen years of military service under his belt, Althoff was older and more experienced than most of his comrades in HMM-262. He was the pilot everyone wanted to be: highly skilled, courageous, and "so damned cool when the going got rough."[4]

He perfected an aggressive flying style, which he summed up in sports terms: "The best defense is a good offense." For recon team insertions and extractions—dropping a team of six or eight Marines in the middle of an enemy-infested area—he would go in as low and fast as possible, skimming the jungle canopy as he picked his way through the fog-shrouded hills. He preferred to kill his adversaries rather than run, so a favorite tactic was to turn head-on into trouble. He got shot down four times and took so much battle damage that some days he needed three choppers to finish his missions, but he was there for the Marines, night and day, seven days a week. He would be named Marine Corps Aviator of the Year for 1968, but his proudest achievement may have been the nickname he earned from his peers: "Balls to the Walls" Althoff.

• • •

Althoff had burnished his growing legend on February 2 when he had led an emergency mission to extract a Marine recon team surrounded by an estimated one hundred NVA troops near Dong Ha. His copilot was Captain Charles Crookall, and the second aircraft in Althoff's two-ship section was flown by Captain W. L. Barba and Captain Bill Englehart. Althoff and his wingman had nearly gotten shot out of the sky as they maneuvered their Sea Knights into the LZ hacked from the jungle, but they kept their battered birds in the air long enough for the bloodied Marines to dive aboard, then shot their way out of the closing cordon of enemy soldiers.

On February 13, Althoff and Englehart had another narrow escape during a resupply run to Khe Sanh. Accompanied by a Sea Knight flown by Captain Robert Yeager and Lieutenant Doug Morrison, Althoff's first scheduled stop was Hill 881 South. The NVA opened up with machine guns and small arms, and a rocket exploded in the LZ, seriously wounding three Marines on the ground. Althoff landed in the maelstrom to medevac the injured Marines and sat on the LZ as shrapnel and bullets tore into his Sea Knight while the casualties were loaded aboard. He got shot up some more getting away from the hill but safely delivered the wounded men to Charlie Med.[5]

That was followed by Althoff's ill-fated February 20 mission to 881 South, when he ended up sitting in a hot LZ for more than a minute until Marines could get the mortally wounded Corporal Terry Smith aboard. Althoff had taken heavy damage getting away from the hill and had barely coaxed his aircraft down to the combat base. While stretcher bearers hustled the dying Marine off to Charlie Med, Althoff switched out his battle-damaged bird for another helicopter and took off on his next mission.

Once again, it was all in a day's work for Althoff.

• • •

As American pilots and air crews struggled to sustain the remote combat base and hill outposts, a dire snapshot of the worsening supply situation at Khe Sanh worked its way up the chain of command. Major General Rathvon Tompkins, commander of the 3rd Marine Division, had laid out the grim equation for his superiors: Khe Sanh needed sixty pounds of supplies per man per day (including artillery support), which meant a total daily requirement of about 180 tons for the current population of about 6,000 fighting men. By February 19, Khe Sanh's supply shortfall was a staggering 1,172 tons.[6]

The I Corps helicopter pilots were doing their best to chip away at the deficit, but the loss of more than a dozen helicopters in missions to the hill outposts during the first month of the siege had pushed the effort to a crisis point. At Quang Tri Air Base, there was an urgent sense that something had to be done.[7]

Around February 21, Dave Althoff huddled with Lieutenant Colonel William J. White, commander of Marine Observation Squadron 6

(VMO-6), which provided gunship support for the Khe Sanh helicopter missions, and Major Arthur C. Crane, VMO-6 operations officer. The three Marines roughed out a plan to smother the NVA gunners with smoke screens, artillery, fixed-wing aircraft, and helicopter gunships during resupply and medevac missions. White laid out the idea for the MAG-36 commander, Colonel Frank E. Wilson, and then briefed the commander of the 1st Marine Aircraft Wing, Major General Norman Anderson.

At Anderson's direction, Lieutenant Colonel White fleshed out the details with the wing's operations staff, and Lieutenant Colonel Richard E. Carey suggested a name for the operation: Super Gaggle, a fighter-pilot term for massive confusion. If the American plan worked, confusion would be the best possible outcome for the North Vietnamese lying in wait around the Khe Sanh hill outposts.[8]

• • •

About an hour before noon on Saturday, February 24, a single-engine Cessna O-1 Bird Dog entered the air space above Khe Sanh and began circling the skies to the west, over Hill 881 South and Hill 861. The aircraft was joined by a TA-4F, a modified single-engine Skyhawk jet, with a tactical air controller in the second seat. A Marine KC-130 arrived and began orbiting high above.

Operation Sierra—the Super Gaggle—was underway.[9]

At H-minus-one hour, the first of ten Marine A-4 Skyhawks swooped down and dropped high-explosive bombs and napalm on suspected enemy anti-aircraft positions and automatic weapons sites around 881 South. As smoke and flames billowed from the hillsides, the Skyhawks made repeated strafing runs, blasting the scorched terrain with their 20-millimeter cannon.

At H-minus-ten-minutes, a pair of Skyhawks with tanks dangling from their wings streaked low over the smoldering NVA positions. A fine mist floated down from the Skyhawks, soaking the terrain with tear gas. Strike aircraft dumped more high explosives and napalm on the North Vietnamese. Finally, at H-minus-four-minutes, another pair of A-4s roared over 881 South, spewing a thick smoke screen from wing tanks.

With a clatter of rotors, four UH-1E helicopter gunships escorted eight CH-46D Sea Knights into the clear skies behind the curtain of smoke. Dangling beneath the Sea Knights were external nets packed with ammunition, food, water, and medical supplies.

In less than five minutes, some 24,000 pounds of badly needed supplies lay on the landing zones of 881 South. One of the eight Sea Knights was hit over the hill, by North Vietnamese gunners firing blindly through the smoke, and it was forced to make an emergency landing at the Khe Sanh airstrip. The others headed back to their home base as the A-4 Skyhawks capped off the performance by pounding North Vietnamese positions around 881 South with high explosives, napalm, and 20-millimeter cannon.[10]

The Super Gaggle had made a nearly flawless debut.

"Today was a small victory," wrote General Norman Anderson, commander of the 1st Marine Aircraft Wing. But it was just the beginning. To outlast the North Vietnamese at Khe Sanh, the spectacular resupply mission of February 24 would have to be replicated "again and again in the next few weeks."[11]

PART III

CHAPTER 16

"Why Are You Leaving Us Out Here to Die?"

Fog cloaked Khe Sanh Combat Base on Sunday morning, February 25, as Bravo 1/26 platoon leader Don Jacques prepared his men for a two-hour patrol beyond the southeastern perimeter. Twenty years old, from Rochester, New York, Second Lieutenant Jacques didn't turn heads with his physical makeup in the manner of brawny Marines like Bill Dabney. Nothing about his height, build, or looks really stood out. But stand out he did, and that distinction spoke to the passion Don Jacques brought to his work as an officer in the United States Marine Corps.

Jacques had quit college to enlist in the Marines, and he had survived the grind of boot camp at Parris Island. He caught the eye of his drill instructors and was plucked from the ranks and sent to Officer Candidates School at Quantico. In the late summer of 1967, he became the youngest graduate of the Basic School in nearly two decades.[1]

After arriving in Vietnam on October 9, Jacques had joined Bravo 1/26 and had won the trust of skipper Ken Pipes. Given the reins of Bravo's 3rd Platoon, he had further impressed when his men ambushed an NVA reconnaissance unit in late December. The New Yorker was confident and raring to go—too much so for some who encountered him at Khe Sanh.[2]

But an officer's reputation counted for nothing with the North Vietnamese soldiers looking to kill Americans around Khe Sanh. Jacques would have to be on his game this morning as he led his platoon outside the wire to see what was up with the NVA.

The night before, Jacques had scribbled letters to his parents and his sister, Jeanne. "The days go by quite quickly but the nights are long around here," he wrote his mother and father. "I haven't been getting much sleep." To his sister, he hinted at the looming showdown that everyone expected at Khe Sanh. "We're just sitting here waiting for all hell to burst loose. . . . With each day that passes by the incoming increases and the [3rd Platoon] digs deeper." He ended on a reassuring note. "I'm fine, and still kicking. I'll write again soon. Love, brother Don."[3]

• • •

The patrol was to be a textbook diamond pattern, and Jacques was to hew closely to the plotted route so friendly artillery would know exactly where he was in the event of trouble. He was to check in by radio at three designated points and remain within 1,000 meters (about 1,100 yards) of the base.[4]

Corporal Steve Wiese, leader of the platoon's 1st Squad, had been told to get his men ready for a short recon to look for enemy tunnels and trenches, and to expect trouble. Wiese was on his second tour in Vietnam, and he had learned that troops in combat burned through ammo in a hurry. He instructed his men to take at least five magazines and four grenades.[5]

High spirits and apprehension coursed through the column as the patrol headed out through the southeastern wire just after 8:00 a.m. The fog was burning away, and after weeks of getting pummeled in their trenches, the forty-odd Marines and corpsmen welcomed the opportunity to stretch their legs. They were a mix of seasoned veterans and rookies on their first patrol. Among the former were Wiese and Ken Claire, big, athletic men from California, both squad leaders, both outstanding Marines, the kind of guys you wanted beside you in a fight. Corpsman John Cicala—"Motown Doc," he had written on his helmet—knew his way around, too, and the contents of the Unit 1 medical bag he carried in one hand reflected the wisdom of his months in combat: pressure bandages, blood expander, bags of IV fluids, and the cellophane wrappers from cigarette packs used in the emergency treatment of a sucking chest wound.[6]

Among the rookies was Private First Class Calvin Bright, a wide-eyed eighteen-year-old farm boy from a family of Marines back in Jackson, Michigan. After arriving at Khe Sanh on the eve of the siege, Bright and his regular partner, PFC Lloyd Scudder, had made a zany game of the loathsome chore of cleaning the platoon's latrines. As NVA spotters watched through field glasses, one of the Marines would pour gasoline into the halved-barrels that served as Marine toilets and burn the foul-smelling mix. Within seconds, North Vietnamese mortars would begin firing, but Bright and Scudder would not be rushed. While one of the pair timed the incoming rounds, the other would perform a spastic chicken dance. At the last possible instant, they would dive into the nearest trench, just ahead of the exploding mortars.[7]

Moving beyond the perimeter wire, the patrol almost immediately discovered a trench the North Vietnamese had dug up to the garbage dump outside Bravo lines. The trench angled down a slope to the south, then continued beyond a creek and disappeared in the direction of the NVA stronghold on Hill 471, about 2,200 yards due south. After following the trench for a short distance, the Marines climbed out and headed southeast on their planned route.

Their path was roughly parallel to the dirt road that wound along the southern perimeter of the combat base, past the garbage dump and into the coffee trees and scrub jungle of an old French plantation that had seen better days. The Marines crossed a small creek and picked their way through a landscape shorn of vegetation and cratered by bombs and shells. They completed the first leg without incident, and Jacques checked in by radio with the Bravo command post.[8]

The patrol continued in a southeasterly direction. Just after 9:00 a.m., the Marines were about 275 yards south of the garbage dump road and more than 200 yards north of the main access road that connected the combat base to Route 9. At the head of the column, the men in Steve Wiese's squad spotted a flash of movement to their right, near the access road. Three NVA soldiers jumped from cover, ran along the road until the Marines opened fire, then ducked into a treeline along the southern edge of the dirt track.

Something about the movement didn't seem right to Wiese: *Why would the gooks reveal themselves by running along the road, where we would be sure to see them?*[9]

Jacques radioed Captain Pipes and requested permission to pursue the NVA soldiers. Battalion and regimental headquarters badly wanted prisoners for interrogation, a fact well known to the Bravo skipper and his young platoon commander. Pipes gave his qualified approval. "You can go," he said. "But don't get in something you can't handle."[10] A spirited discussion ensued between Jacques and his squad leaders. The patrol's Kit Carson scout, a Vietnamese defector familiar with enemy tactics, warned the Marines not to proceed. "Bad, bad," he said, over and over again.[11]

Jacques ignored the scout and ordered Wiese to send one of his fire teams after the NVA.

"It's a bad idea," Wiese said. "I think it's a trap."

The lieutenant didn't want to hear it. "Okay, take your entire squad," Jacques ordered.

Wiese erupted. "Are you out of your mind? There's something wrong here!"

Ken Claire tried to defuse the tense situation. He made clear his concerns, but diplomatically added: "It's your call, Lieutenant."[12]

The confrontation would have made for a lively case study in small-unit command back at Quantico, but this wasn't a classroom. Don Jacques was a rising young officer with a promising career and promotions ahead. Steve Wiese didn't have anything to prove, and he didn't give a damn about promotions and medals. He wanted to survive his tour, and preserve the lives of the men under his command and the comrades he had come to love in Vietnam.

Lieutenant Jacques came down hard. He relieved Wiese of command and told him to "take a knee," then ordered Wiese's assistant to pursue the NVA. The Marine refused.

Jacques now faced a near-mutiny, and it was playing out in full view of his platoon in the middle of an operation. Aggressive by nature, he chose to ignore the warnings of his scout and squad leaders. If Wiese and his men wouldn't pursue the NVA as a fire team or a squad, everyone would go. He ordered the entire platoon on line. Raising his pistol, Don Jacques gave the order to advance. "Let's go get them!" he yelled.[13]

• • •

Moving at a trot and spread out along a line about 100 yards across, the

Marines pushed south through a field toward the access road and the treeline where the three NVA soldiers had disappeared. The Americans came to an empty trench line and jumped over it.[14] They crossed a second trench, and somebody saw movement. A shot rang out.

Almost instantly, a devastating barrage engulfed the Americans. NVA soldiers hiding in trenches, bunkers, and camouflaged spider holes to the front and right flank fired automatic rifles, machine guns, mortars, and rocket-propelled grenades into the Bravo patrol. The North Vietnamese were arrayed in the shape of the letter "L," with the long leg of the ambush in the treeline along the road. From positions in trees and brush that formed the short leg along the west, the enemy troops ripped the Americans with enfilading fire.[15]

Jacques and his command group had sought shelter in a small trench, and from there the lieutenant ordered Corporal Claire to flank the North Vietnamese in the enfilading position to the west. Accompanied by Staff Sergeant George B. McClelland, Claire led about a dozen Marines to the right in an attempt to get behind the NVA. But the Americans turned too soon, and they charged headlong into devastating frontal fire.

Rifleman Edward Rayburn fell to the ground, his lower jaw ripped away by an enemy bullet. Claire helped the wounded Marine into a trench, then stood in the hail of NVA fire as he directed the rest of his squad to take cover. Americans were dying across the field, screams and shouts piercing the roar of automatic-weapons fire and exploding grenades.[16]

• • •

Back at the combat base, roughly 1,000 yards to the north, Bravo skipper Ken Pipes was tracking the patrol's progress from his command bunker when he heard the first shots.

It was clear to Pipes almost immediately that Jacques and his men were in big trouble. If Bravo-3 had stumbled onto an NVA observation post or recon team, or even a squad or platoon, Pipes would be hearing the chatter of AK-47 rifles punctuated by an occasional RPG and Chicom grenade explosion. Instead, the sound that carried from the south was a terrible cacophony of machine guns, mortars, RPGs, and small arms firing simultaneously.

Jacques was on the company radio net almost immediately, summing up the tactical situation for Pipes, which wasn't easy amid the deadly chaos. Pipes tried to pinpoint the location of Jacques and his men. Patchy fog and the rolling terrain obscured visual contact with the American patrol. Still unknown to Pipes and 1/26 battalion fire support officers was the fact that Jacques had strayed from his plotted route and was now more than 400 yards south of the garbage dump road.[17]

Pipes ordered Second Lieutenant Peter Weiss, commander of Bravo's 1st Platoon, to move to the aid of Jacques and his men, but an NVA blocking force was waiting. The 1st Platoon Marines were still more than 300 yards from the ambush site when a burst of machine gun fire hit the relief force, killing a squad leader and corpsman and wounding several others. Weiss and his men could go no further.

At the 1/26 battalion command post, Lieutenant William Smith called up his friend, artillery forward observer Hank Norman, at the Bravo command bunker. Norman explained that the patrol wasn't where it was supposed to be. It was maddening: Marines were dying, and the one thing that could save them was a well-placed artillery mission or air strike, but that couldn't happen because nobody knew where the friendly forces were and where the bad guys were.[18]

Pipes, meanwhile, asked his battalion commander, Lieutenant Colonel James Wilkinson, for permission to lead the remainder of his company to the aid of his men. The request went up to Colonel Lownds at regimental headquarters, but Wilkinson and Lownds agreed that pouring more men into an ambush that had probably run its course would only weaken the defense of the combat base. Pipes argued that they couldn't just leave his Marines to die, but he was overruled.[19]

Don Jacques had made a tragic mistake, but he was fighting hard, trying to find a way to get his platoon out of this awful mess. Given the desperate situation, the young officer's fury was understandable. "Why aren't you doing something to help us?" Jacques demanded of Captain Pipes. "Why are you leaving us out here to die?"[20]

• • •

At the instant the North Vietnamese sprang the ambush, corpsman John Cicala was charging ahead behind the line of Marines. An American fell to the ground ahead of him, and Cicala dashed to his side. Lance Corporal

Jerry Lee Dodson of Collinsville, Illinois, was alive and conscious when Cicala reached him, despite the fact that a bullet had entered his left eye and blown out the right side of his head. Cicala dressed the massive wounds, knowing full well that the twenty-year-old Marine didn't have long. He was about to move to the next casualty when Dodson said, "Doc, put another magazine in for me."[21] Cicala popped a magazine into the M-16 lying beside Dodson and handed it to the dying Marine.

Cries of "Corpsman!" sounded from all sides as wounded men fell to the ground. Cicala sprinted toward a Marine who dropped a few yards ahead, but he never made it. An NVA soldier popped from a hole and fired two rounds from his AK-47.

The bullets slammed into Cicala's chest like a hammer blow and knocked the corpsman onto his back. One round ripped through his flak jacket, punctured a lung and exited Cicala's back. The other struck a bundle of metal objects dangling from his neck—dog tags, a can opener, a St. Christopher's medal, and other jewelry. The bullet drove hot metal shards into Cicala's neck and chest but flattened out against the metal objects and fell harmlessly to the ground.

Gasping for air, Cicala realized that his lung was slowly deflating from a sucking chest wound. As he began to prepare a dressing, he heard corpsman Frank Calzia call out to him. "J. C., are you okay?"[22] Just then, Cicala felt something hit his leg. He spotted the enemy grenade and managed to curl into a ball just before the explosion ripped into his body.

Cicala was still dazed by the blast when Doc Calzia sprawled beside him. The wounded corpsman could see his friend's lips moving but couldn't hear a thing. Cicala began a quick inventory of his limbs and felt sick when he saw that one leg was twisted behind him at an impossible angle. He was relieved to discover that his foot still moved. The grenade had blown off part of his kneecap and riddled his torso and legs with shrapnel, but everything was still attached. He waved Calzia away. "Get the hell out of here. Go take care of the other guys."[23]

The wounded corpsman was preparing a battle dressing for his mangled knee when Lieutenant Jacques ran past. "Doc, get out of here any way you can!" the platoon commander yelled to Cicala. "Everybody's getting killed!"[24] Jacques took a few more steps before collapsing to the ground, cut down by a burst of NVA machine-gun fire.

Cicala crawled to the stricken lieutenant. Two rounds had ripped through Don Jacques's groin, tearing the femoral arteries in both legs. Cicala applied dressings, but blood continued to gush from the wounds.

Glancing around, the corpsman didn't see anyone still alive around him. With agonized effort, the Motown Doc began crawling to the north, away from the field of death.[25]

• • •

On the left side of the advancing Marines, Steve Wiese heard two rifle shots and then a deafening barrage. He had been mentally prepared for the ambush, so he instantly dropped to the ground and rolled into a bomb crater as murderous North Vietnamese fire swept the field. Wiese heard yelling and screaming rise with the roar of gunfire and grenade blasts. He periodically popped above the crater rim to throw grenades and fire at NVA soldiers in a nearby trench line. Every time, heavy fire chewed up the ground around him.

The Marines couldn't match the firepower of the enemy force, and they were doomed if they remained in place. Wiese yelled to the few surviving Marines within earshot: "Every man for himself! Get yourself out of here! Get out of the kill zone!"[26]

Scrambling from one hole to the next, Wiese began moving toward the northeast, away from the deadly fire.

• • •

Elsewhere in the kill zone, Corporal Robert E. Matzka held his squad together as best he could before the deadly enemy fire proved overwhelming. And then, he, too, found a way out of the maelstrom and made his way northward.

Corporal Gilbert Wall, an 81-millimeter mortars forward observer assigned to the patrol, had moved away from Lieutenant Jacques in the opening minutes of the ambush and became pinned behind a tree. He weighed whether to call in mortar fire from Khe Sanh but decided the risk of hitting his scattered comrades was too great, so he held off.[27]

When the firing eased, Wall began making his way out of the ambush area. He came upon the blood-soaked body of Lieutenant Don Jacques, dying, if not already dead. Hoisting the young officer over his shoulder, Wall set out for the Khe Sanh perimeter.

• • •

Corporal Ken Claire and the shattered remnants of his squad were among the last Americans alive in the kill zone. Claire's clownish antics had sometimes obscured his superb qualities as a Marine, and on that terrible morning, in a blood-soaked field south of Khe Sanh Combat Base, no American performed with greater bravery. Claire had collected his wounded in one of the many trenches that stitched the ambush zone, dashing into fire again and again to pull men to safety. He continued to resist the murderous NVA fire for the better part of an hour, even after he was twice wounded. A third North Vietnamese bullet finally ended the life of the twenty-one-year-old Marine from Redwood City, California, silencing forever the Tarzan yell he had perfected on Sierra Nevada summits as a boy.[28]

Two of Claire's men, the grievously wounded rifleman Edward Rayburn and machine gunner Thomas A. Detrick, waited until the firing dropped off, then began their harrowing trek back to the base.

Three Marines from Claire's squad—Ronald Ridgeway, James Bruder, and Charles Geller—had remained hidden in a trench until the firing stopped. Ridgeway and Geller had killed three NVA soldiers who approached their trench, but Bruder had been mortally wounded. As the two surviving Marines tried to run out of the kill zone, Geller came upon a Marine lying on his back with a broken arm and dropped to his side. A bullet ripped through Geller's face, and another round broke Ridgeway's arm. The three Americans—Geller, Ridgeway, and twenty-five-year-old Willy Ruff of Columbia, South Carolina—decided to lie low until dark.[29]

Late in the afternoon, Geller became delirious, and his cries alerted NVA soldiers around them. Grenades exploded among the Marines, and Geller was hit and killed.

The NVA troops began firing from their trenches into bodies they could see, and Ruff and Ridgeway were wounded still again. Friendly artillery pounded the area, and shrapnel hit Ruff in the head. As Ruff lay bleeding from his head wound, Ridgeway passed out.

• • •

Through the late morning and early afternoon, wounded survivors made their way back to the combat base. Bravo's 1st Platoon collected as many men as possible before withdrawing inside the wire, but other Marines slipped back outside to watch for their comrades. Freelance news photographer Robert Ellison had become fond of the Bravo Marines after spending time with them, and he now led a handful of men through a minefield into the nearby brush to look for survivors.[30]

Corporal Gilbert Wall arrived from the battlefield, still carrying Lieutenant Jacques over his shoulder. Two other Marines began dragging the lifeless body of the young platoon leader back through the tall grass. With the click of his camera shutter, Ellison captured the heartbreaking scene.

One of the Marines in Ellison's photograph was Lance Corporal Edward I. Prendergast, a 60-millimeter mortarman who had been positioned in the Bravo lines to provide supporting fire for the patrol. Around 4:00 p.m., Prendergast heard gunfire from the Bravo trench line to his right, and he spotted a man near the garbage dump. Yelling for the Marines to cease fire, Prendergast ran out to see if the new arrival was a friend who hadn't returned from the patrol. When he reached the bloody form, Prendergast saw it was the corpsman he only knew as the Motown Doc. After more than six hours of agonizing struggle, John Cicala had dragged himself back from the ambush site.

During his painful trek, Cicala had managed to elude roaming bands of NVA soldiers. He had lost a lot of blood and struggled to breathe with his collapsed lung, but he had willed himself on with visions of his girlfriend back in Michigan, and the promise he had made: "I won't die in Vietnam."[31]

Now Cicala lay just outside the Khe Sanh wire, "white as a ghost." When Prendergast reached his side, Cicala tried to convey the enormity of the tragedy. "Everyone is dead," he mumbled. "Everyone is dead."[32] Prendergast hoisted the wounded corpsman to his shoulder and tossed him over the wire to a pair of waiting Marines. A long and painful recovery awaited the Motown Doc, but he would make good on his promise to survive Vietnam.

• • •

Private First Class Edward C. Rayburn had been saved by Ken Claire in the opening moments of the ambush, and he had witnessed the death of his courageous squad leader and most of his comrades. He had been greeted outside the Khe Sanh wire by corpsman Thomas E. Casey and others, but the badly wounded Marine refused to go inside for medical attention. With the ghastly wound to his jaw, Rayburn was unable to speak, but he kept looking to the south, in the direction of the ambush. Casey finally asked him if there was something he was trying to tell them. Rayburn nodded his head up and down. "Are there others still alive out there?" Casey asked. Rayburn emphatically nodded yes. With that vital information communicated, Rayburn finally agreed to go inside.[33]

Rayburn would undergo many surgeries, and he would endure painful complications with the efforts to rebuild his jaw and restore his face to a semblance of the handsome Marine who had marched out of Khe Sanh Combat Base on the morning of February 25. He visited the family of his squad leader around 1970 and told the Claires how their beloved Ken had died, and how heroic and selfless he had been in his final minutes on earth. In time, the physical and emotional burdens that Rayburn carried away from the ambush became too great, and on January 23, 1976, at a time of the year when the men who served at Khe Sanh always remember the beginning of the great battle, Edward Rayburn took his own life.[34]

• • •

Private First Class Calvin Bright had watched in horror as his first Marine patrol had disintegrated into slaughter. His fire team leader was cut down, along with the unit's other two members. Soon, every American within sight was dead or dying.

A PRC-25 radio strapped to the back of a dead Marine crackled to life: "Hello! Hello! Can anybody hear me?" Bright crawled to the radio. In a low voice, he informed the unidentified Marine officer on the other end that everyone was dead, and that he was surrounded by North Vietnamese. With Bright's assistance, the officer called in artillery, and the shells were adjusted until they rained down on the enemy trenches.[35]

Bright crept away toward the combat base, sometimes crouching in silence as NVA troops combed the brush around him. He finally emerged into a clearing outside the Khe Sanh perimeter.

Breaking into a run, Bright began to hear the shouts of South Vietnamese Rangers along the eastern perimeter, and he thought they were urging him on. Then he began to hear cries in English, and he saw Marines frantically gesturing. When he reached the outer wire, Bright discovered what the ruckus had been about: he had just run through a minefield.[36]

• • •

Steve Wiese's escape from the kill zone unfolded in a series of short sprints, two-second bursts from one bomb hole to the next as NVA fire sliced the air and kicked up the dirt around him. As he moved out of grenade range, Wiese saw low-flying American jets streak overhead, dropping bombs and napalm. One pilot seemed to be checking him out. Wiese waved his arms, fearing he was about to get blown away. The pilot wagged his wings and pulled off.[37]

Wiese started to time his movements to the jet passes. He would crouch like a sprinter at the starting block, wait for the bombs or napalm to hit, then dash to the next hole he had scoped out. When he finally reached the area along the garbage dump road, he decided to lie low and wait for reinforcements. He sat in a hole for a few hours, but his comrades never came. With shadows lengthening, Wiese set out for the base.

Night was falling over Khe Sanh when he finally reached the gate where the high-spirited Marines had set out that morning. Wiese had one question for the comrades who greeted him: "How many guys made it back?" There was no response, and so he repeated himself: "How many guys made it back?" He had to ask the question once or twice more before somebody finally spoke up. "Not many," came the reply.[38]

• • •

At the Bravo command post, Captain Ken Pipes waited by his radios most of the night. He prayed for a miracle, a call from other men who had made it out of the kill zone and were only waiting for daylight to return. But the call never came.

The next day, and then the next night, and for a few days and nights afterward, Pipes kept his solitary vigil. He would sit by the radios, and the tears would stream down his cheeks as he mourned the loss of his men.

• • •

As it turned out, the vigil of Captain Pipes was not in vain: one of his boys *was* still alive out there.

Rifleman Ronald Ridgeway had passed out between the NVA trenches, and he awoke with a start on the morning of February 26 as a North Vietnamese soldier tried to pull his wristwatch from his arm. The NVA surrounded their prisoner, and Ridgeway was led into captivity in North Vietnam.

Nearly five years would pass, and Ridgeway's name would be among those chiseled into a marble headstone placed over the grave of nine casualties from the February 25 ambush, Marines who were buried as a group at Jefferson Barracks National Cemetery in St. Louis, Missouri.

At 1:15 a.m. on Sunday morning, January, 28, 1973, the phone rang in the Houston, Texas, home of Mildred Ridgeway. The caller identified himself as a Marine Corps officer. "It's my son," Mrs. Ridgeway interrupted. "He's alive, isn't he?"[39]

Indeed, he was.

Ken Pipes was assigned to the Marine Corps base at Quantico, Virginia, in January 1973, and he, too, got a phone call, notifying him that a young Marine who had been under his command at Khe Sanh, a Marine who had been listed as killed in action on February 25, 1968, was alive in a North Vietnamese prison.[40] Three months later, Private First Class Ronald Lewis Ridgeway stepped off a plane with other prisoners of war released by North Vietnam. It was the miracle for which Ken Pipes had waited so many years.

• • •

Lieutenant Don Jacques had led more than forty young Americans outside the Khe Sanh wire on the morning of February 25, 1968. Fewer than half made it back alive. The only body that had been recovered from the Bravo patrol was that of Jacques. Twenty-three Americans lay at the scene of the ambush or nearby, killed by North Vietnamese fire, or by the friendly air strikes and artillery that followed. For the Marines of Bravo 1/26, it had been a day of unimaginable heartbreak and loss.

CHAPTER 17

"A Military Challenge Unprecedented in This War"

As the dying echoes of gunfire and explosions from the Bravo ambush swept across the combat base at midday on February 25, a Marine aerial observer flying overhead in a small plane spotted further cause for alarm. The trenches and bunkers in which the North Vietnamese had lain in wait for Lieutenant Jacques and his men were part of an intricate complex that an ARVN Ranger patrol had stumbled onto nine days earlier. Now, enemy soldiers had extended long tentacles from those fortifications. The Marine observer noted a new trench, more than 700 yards long and wide enough to funnel assault troops two-abreast to the outer Khe Sanh wire, as well as another trench that ran parallel to the Khe Sanh wire for about fifty yards—cover for enemy troops to form a skirmish line before charging the wire.[1]

As he orbited overhead, the Marine observer came under heavy automatic-weapons fire from the trenches and surrounding jungle. About thirty minutes after his initial discovery, he identified more enemy fortifications nearby, including two assault trenches that ended only about fifteen yards from the southeastern Khe Sanh wire. Huddled inside one of these trenches were about fifty to one hundred North Vietnamese soldiers.[2]

The Bravo ambush and the discovery of the new assault trenches tripped alarms up the American chain of command. Artillery, mortars, and attack jets pounded the NVA positions that now completely encircled the combat base. A request from General Westmoreland to bring B-52 Arc Light strikes closer than the mandated buffer of 3,000 meters (about 3,200 yards) around friendly troops had been approved by higher authorities on February 18, and now target boxes were plotted to within 1,000 meters (about 1,100 yards) of the base. A test strike was readied for Monday, February 26.[3]

The predawn hours of February 26 pulsed with the sounds of enemy vehicles and troops southwest of the base. A listening post manned by Special Forces out of FOB-3 reported a tracked vehicle moving in the darkness, as well as other movements and sounds coming from a village about 500 yards beyond the access road that connected the base to Route 9. The Green Berets requested a fire mission, and a 4.2-inch mortar unleashed several rounds that exploded in the vicinity of the noises.

Daylight brought more air strikes on the North Vietnamese lines. Among the Americans watching and cheering were the Marines of Combined Action Company Oscar. The survivors of the fight at Khe Sanh village had been adopted by the Special Forces after their withdrawal from the Huong Hoa district headquarters on January 21, and now they were dug in along the FOB-3 perimeter. Oscar-2 corpsman John Roberts, the folksy Baptist preacher from the Texas Panhandle, watched the air show unfold with Lance Corporal Billy Dale Livingston of Alma, Arkansas, and another Marine. Around 11:00 a.m., a Navy attack jet approached and fired a pair of rockets, but the pilot's aim was off. The rockets ripped into the FOB-3 trench line, killing the eighteen-year-old Livingston. Doc Roberts was hurled into the air but escaped injury. He grabbed a rifle and tried to shoot at the Navy jet before a sergeant hit him in the head and calmed him down.[4]

For more than a month now, death and gore had been staples of daily life for the defenders of Khe Sanh, and there was no end in sight. Stories about the terrible fate of the Bravo patrol had spread through the trench lines, and if that wasn't bad enough, word got around that the bodies of some twenty-five Marines were still out there, and their comrades had been told to stand down because an enemy division or two was out there, waiting to strike.

On February 27, General Westmoreland cabled a pep talk to Colonel Lownds and his embattled men. "You, your Marines, and the associated U.S. Army and Vietnamese troops are at the center of the international stage," Westmoreland said. "You are faced with a military challenge unprecedented in this war. I want you and your troops to know that I have the utmost confidence in your fighting spirit, professionalism, and alertness. These essential qualities, plus the indomitable courage of the U.S. Marines, are destined to prevail over the enemy."[5]

•   •   •

Like an extended drum roll, the maneuvering continued through February 27 and into the next day—enemy artillery, rockets, and mortars; friendly artillery and air; NVA movements around the wire under the cover of darkness; and the enemy's relentless digging of new trenches and bunkers. The eastern perimeter of Khe Sanh, defended by the ARVN Rangers and the Marines of Bravo 1/26, continued to be a focal point of the enemy activities.[6]

Daylight on Thursday morning, February 29, revealed the industry of NVA sappers hard at work in that area. Overnight they had ventured into the minefields set out by the American combat engineers, removing trip flares and cutting the eastern perimeter wire in three places—all without setting off a single mine or flare.[7]

Nightfall of February 29 unleashed a flurry of North Vietnamese activity. Around 6:45 p.m., sniper fire streaked into the Bravo 1/26 positions. Next, the Special Forces at FOB-3 reported trip flares going off and movement to their front. Seismic and acoustic sensor reports pouring into the 26th Marines command bunker indicated heavy enemy vehicle and troop activity along Route 9. A regiment or more of the NVA 304th Division—at least 1,500 men—was on the move.

Amid the controlled chaos and crackling radios of the 26th Marines command bunker, Colonel Lownds and his staff now executed their carefully drawn plans for the long-awaited enemy ground assault. Lownds urgently requested the diversion of inbound B-52 bombers from their scheduled targets so they could pound North Vietnamese assembly areas about 1,100 yards south and southeast of the base. Frontline units prepared to repel enemy assault troops, while further back, reaction forces

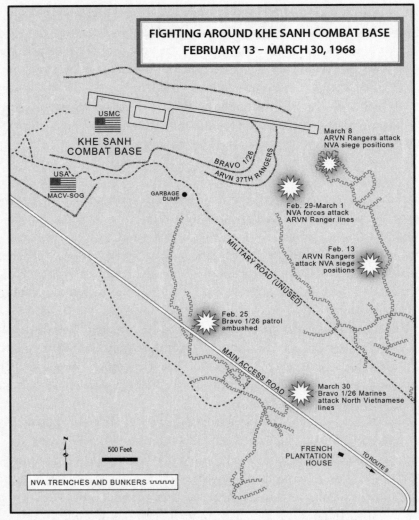

FIGHTING AROUND KHE SANH COMBAT BASE
FEBRUARY 13 – MARCH 30, 1968

USMC

KHE SANH
COMBAT BASE

USA
MACV-SOG

GARBAGE
DUMP

BRAVO 1/26
ARVN 37TH RANGERS

MILITARY ROAD (UNUSED)

MAIN ACCESS ROAD

March 8
ARVN Rangers attack
NVA siege positions

Feb. 29-March 1
NVA forces attack
ARVN Ranger lines

Feb. 13
ARVN Rangers
attack NVA siege
positions

Feb. 25
Bravo 1/26 patrol
ambushed

March 30
Bravo 1/26 Marines
attack North Vietnamese
lines

FRENCH
PLANTATION
HOUSE

TO ROUTE 9

N

500 Feet

NVA TRENCHES AND BUNKERS

The battle for Khe Sanh Combat Base, February 13–March 30, 1968.

stood ready to plug any breaches in the perimeter. Artillery and mortars thundered and whooshed as rounds blanketed preplanned targets.[8]

In a section of the command bunker crammed with radios and acetate-overlaid maps, the Fire Support Coordination Center set in motion a massive air and artillery response. The guns of Lieutenant Colonel John A. Hennelly's 1st Battalion, 13th Marines, at the combat base—105-millimeter and 155-millimeter howitzers—and the big 175-millimeter guns to the east at the Rockpile and Camp Carroll poured fire into prearranged target boxes. Radar-directed fighters joined the attack on the fringes, and the night flashed with thunderous explosions along an arc that curled several thousand yards through the countryside south of Khe Sanh Combat Base.[9]

Inside the target boxes, NVA troops came under a devastating fire. The Americans unleashed the same rolling barrage that had shattered the February 5 attack on 861 Alpha, trapping the enemy troops in a deadly box of artillery fire and air strikes that ripped their flanks and then rolled up behind them like a scythe, swinging back and forth over the NVA as they tried to position themselves to strike the American stronghold. The North Vietnamese were being driven toward the minefields and concertina wire along the outer perimeter of Khe Sanh Combat Base, and into the guns of the waiting ARVN Rangers and US Marines.[10]

• • •

At 9:30 p.m., the first wave of North Vietnamese assault troops hit the ARVN Ranger positions from the east and southeast. Many carried Bangalore torpedoes or satchel charges to blast holes in the perimeter wire. One enemy soldier actually penetrated the perimeter, and six others were killed in the wire before the South Vietnamese troops beat back the attack.

Fog now engulfed the combat base, cloaking enemy movements and adding to the anxieties of the men in the trenches. At 10:05 p.m., the commander of the ARVN Rangers requested a Spooky gunship to break up the large enemy force to his front. The gunship arrived over the southeastern perimeter in two minutes, but a layer of fog precluded firing so close to friendly lines. For the North Vietnamese who had survived the first rounds of American air strikes and artillery, it was a temporary reprieve.[11]

At 11:30 p.m., an NVA battalion mounted a second attack on the ARVN Ranger positions, but the combined firepower of the radar-directed air strikes and rolling artillery barrage shattered the surge. Midnight arrived, and in the early hours of March 1, the North Vietnamese survivors regrouped in the trenches and bunkers that studded the rolling terrain beyond the southeastern Khe Sanh perimeter.

As the night wore on, North Vietnamese gunners weighed in with modest counterfire in support of their ground forces. Between midnight and 6:00 a.m. of March 1, ninety-five rounds of artillery, rockets, and mortars fell on the combat base, killing one American and wounding five.

The final attempt to break through the ARVN Ranger positions came at 3:15 a.m., and it ended quickly with the shattered North Vietnamese survivors slipping away into what remained of the fog-shrouded night.[12] American artillery and fighter jets continued to harass the bloodied NVA forces until dawn of March 1 broke over Khe Sanh Combat Base.

Daylight revealed the bodies of seventy-one NVA dead left behind by their comrades, most of them cut down by the American air strikes and artillery. A patrol east of the base confirmed the deadly effectiveness of the new American "firecracker" artillery rounds that had been introduced during the attack on Lang Vei and were fired again during the attacks of February 29–March 1. "The dead were still huddled in trenches," the patrol reported, "many in the kneeling position, in three successive platoon lines, as if they had been caught in the assault position."[13]

The ARVN Rangers had ably defended their stretch of the Khe Sanh perimeter, surviving the night with the loss of only one man.

• • •

As the second North Vietnamese probe was being driven back from the Khe Sanh wire in the closing minutes of February 29, a crowd gathered in cold rain and sleet on the other side of the world, outside the Pentagon's Potomac River entrance. It was late morning in the nation's capital, and the shivering men and women were there to bid farewell to the haunted man at the helm of America's war in Vietnam.

Robert Strange McNamara had been summoned to the nation's capital in the winter of 1961, one of President John F. Kennedy's "best and brightest," the Ford Motor Company president bringing his business acumen and analytical savvy to America's global Cold War against the Communists. Vietnam had been a backwater in that struggle when McNamara had taken the reins at the Pentagon, an asterisk in Kennedy's idealistic crusade in which Americans would "pay any price, bear any burden, meet any hardship, support any friend, oppose any foe, in order to assure the survival and the success of liberty." McNamara had presided over America's expanding footprint in Vietnam as the conflict metastasized from a guerrilla brush fire into the full-blown war that was now draining the United States of its youth and treasure, and destroying the administration of Kennedy's successor, President Lyndon Johnson.

On this final day of February 1968, Vietnam consumed Americans—the siege at Khe Sanh, the street fighting in Hue, the military draft at home, the antiwar demonstrations, the ballooning federal budget, even the fledgling 1968 presidential campaign, already shaping up to be a referendum on the war. Every week there was a rising butcher's bill to be paid, and McNamara's voracious war machine required a constant infusion of human capital. Just a few days earlier, his spokesmen had announced that 48,000 young Americans would be drafted in April—the highest monthly total since October 1966. Even the Marine Corps, a proudly all-volunteer force in normal times, needed more bodies to fend off the North Vietnamese in I Corps, so 4,000 of the new draftees had been earmarked for its ranks.[14]

President Johnson's limousine pulled into the Pentagon's basement parking garage just before noon. McNamara greeted his commander in chief, and they stepped into an elevator for the short ride up to the second floor, to the river entrance, where the crowd waited on the lawn that looked out on the Potomac River and Washington, DC, beyond.

The war had inextricably bound McNamara and Johnson, two very different men from very different worlds. Together they had soared to the heights of their power and promise in the triumphant days following Johnson's 1964 election victory, and together they had fallen from grace. Johnson and McNamara had tried to win the war in Vietnam with incremental escalations—more troops, then bombing, followed by still more troops—but the Communists matched them, chip for chip. By 1967, Johnson and McNamara were left to wonder how they had gotten themselves into such a mess, and how they could get out without being the first US administration to lose a war.

As Khe Sanh began, and then Tet, and the fighting and dying and bombing and destruction reached unprecedented levels, McNamara and Johnson found themselves in a nightmare of their own making. In the privacy of the White House, Johnson sobbed uncontrollably in the presence of his closest friends.[15] McNamara, too, broke down with increasing frequency, but he had learned to hide his tears from visitors to his Pentagon office by turning away, "to appear to be looking out the window."[16]

Americans were stunned with the escalation after being told for months that the war was winding down. Johnson bore the brunt of the public backlash, and approval ratings for his management of the war and overall job performance plummeted. For the first time, the leading Republican presidential candidate, former vice president Richard Nixon, pulled even with Johnson in a Gallup poll released on February 24.[17]

Vilified at home and abroad, and facing questions in Congress about whether he had taken America to war under false pretenses by lying about the Gulf of Tonkin incident in 1964, Johnson sought solace in the company of the young men he was sending to fight and die in Vietnam. On Saturday, February 17, on the spur of the moment, he flew to North Carolina to address Vietnam-bound soldiers of the 82nd Airborne Division, then winged cross-country to El Toro, California, to rally Marine reinforcements who were being rushed to the battles underway in I Corps. Standing before young Marines heavily laden with full combat kit, Johnson declared, "At Quang Tri, at Hue, at Da Nang, at Khe Sanh, tonight United States Marines stand squarely in the path of [the North Vietnamese] plan. Freedom's defense could not be in better hands."[18]

Afterward, Johnson walked the ranks of the departing Marines, shaking hands, making small talk about their hometowns and families. He watched them board their C-141 Starlifter, then followed them inside the cabin for a few more minutes of awkward conversation, as if he couldn't bear to let these boys head off to their fate. He finally took his leave and then watched as the plane rolled down the runway and disappeared into the California night, another ninety-four young Americans bound for Vietnam.[19]

During Johnson's brief absence from Washington, Vietnam had been engulfed in a second wave of Communist attacks. A new CIA assessment forwarded to Johnson on February 22, as he spent the Washington's Birthday holiday on his Texas ranch, warned of more stiff challenges ahead in Vietnam: continued Communist pressure on South

Vietnam's urban areas and a general escalation of the war, with more NVA troops and supplies flowing into the south, and the possible introduction of North Vietnamese aircraft, tanks, and advanced rockets in future battles.[20]

On February 28, after a quick fact-finding trip to Vietnam, General Earle Wheeler delivered a pessimistic report to Johnson and other senior advisers. Wheeler predicted heavy fighting ahead, and he urged approval of an explosive request from General Westmoreland for 206,000 reinforcements—or risk losing I Corps.[21]

Johnson and his advisers had begun a wide-ranging discussion about the political, economic, and military implications of Westmoreland's request and the path forward in Vietnam. McNamara had remained engaged to the end, even as his last day at the Pentagon approached, and he argued forcefully against further escalation and the idea that the United States could bomb its way to victory in Vietnam.[22]

McNamara had found his voice, behind closed doors anyway, but his role in charting America's course in Vietnam had come to an end. Johnson directed McNamara's successor, Clark Clifford, to give him a new plan for Vietnam by the following week.

At a White House ceremony later that day, February 28, Johnson had presented McNamara with the presidential Medal of Freedom, praising the outgoing secretary of defense as a "brilliant and good man." Overcome by his emotions, McNamara could not deliver his prepared remarks.[23]

And now, on February 29, midday in Washington, as the Marines and South Vietnamese Rangers battled the NVA troops on the eastern perimeter of Khe Sanh Combat Base, McNamara's tenure came to an end.

Like the war in Vietnam, the sendoff did not unfold as planned. The ceremony began twelve minutes late because McNamara and Johnson had gotten stuck in a Pentagon elevator, and a fly-by of Navy and Air Force jets was canceled by a low cloud ceiling that evoked the foul winter weather in Khe Sanh. When President Johnson finally stepped to the podium to pay tribute to the broken man who had devoted seven years and one month of his life to managing America's military affairs, the sound system failed, and few were able to hear Johnson praise McNamara as "the textbook example of the modern public servant." And then it was over. With tears rolling down his cheeks, McNamara walked back inside the massive building one final time as secretary of defense.[24]

McNamara's final month had been dominated by bad news, but in his final hours at the Pentagon, a heartening dispatch had clattered across the cable machines. South Vietnamese forces in Hue had retaken the Imperial Palace in the Citadel, and the Communist flag that had flown over Vietnam's ancient seat of power since January 31 had been torn down.

At Hue, if not at Khe Sanh and the rest of Vietnam, there was light at the end of the tunnel.

CHAPTER 18

"I Just Came from Hell"

The beginning of the Super Gaggle on February 24 had been a turning point in the supply crisis for the hill outposts at Khe Sanh. Spirits rose, along with stockpiles of food and water, as great air convoys rose in the east and thundered into the hills in clearing skies. Helicopter losses and battle damage dropped dramatically, so the external load carried by each of the eight CH-46 Sea Knights assigned to a Super Gaggle mission was increased by one-third to 4,000 pounds. On some days, as many as four runs per hill were mounted. During the five weeks of the Super Gaggle, only two Sea Knights were shot down on resupply runs.[1]

With their supply lines secure, the Marines on the hill outposts braced for further ground attacks. Their defenses were much improved after six weeks under siege, their weaponry supplemented with Starlight scopes, powerful Navy binoculars, and other devices aimed at neutralizing the NVA's expertise in the arts of stealth and camouflage.

Nightfall brought on a test of nerves and stamina as North Vietnamese sappers tried to pick off Marine listening posts and probe for weaknesses in the outer defenses. Sometimes the enemy soldiers would set out their own directional mines or plant a C-ration can with a grenade inside or some other crude booby trap. When the enemy sappers made too much noise, the Marines would respond with grenades and small arms, and illumination rounds would *whoosh* into the sky as the NVA tried to disappear into the shadows.

227

Like their adversaries, the North Vietnamese tried their hand at propaganda and psychological operations aimed at demoralizing Khe Sanh's defenders. The NVA set up loudspeakers in their trenches near the ARVN Ranger positions on the east end of the combat base and blasted clumsy Vietnamese-language surrender appeals.[2]

On a quiet morning in the first week of March, artillery forward observer Dennis Mannion heard the *whump* of an enemy mortar, and then a pop several hundred feet above Hill 861. Hundreds of paper leaflets scattered across the sky and fluttered to the ground. On the front was a famous World War II photograph of an Asian baby in a devastated city, framed by a popular US antiwar chant: "Hey, hey LBJ! How many kids have you killed today?" The back photograph showed the burned ruins of a riot-torn American ghetto, with the message: "Black brothers, why are you supporting your white oppressors in this war? Come over to our side and you will be treated equally!"[3] Toilet paper was scarce on the hill, so Mannion and his buddies collected a wad of leaflets and stashed them outside their latrine for use.

The North Vietnamese had demonstrated time and again their ability to penetrate the typical American field defenses of tangle foot, concertina wire, trip flares, and Claymore mines, but American technology was leveling the playing field with weapons like Starlight scopes. As the siege wore on, the North Vietnamese were finding it increasingly difficult to move about without detection, even at night. At the regimental level, the Marines had continued to make good use of the electronic sensors scattered along the roads and tracks that laced the hills and draws around Khe Sanh. At the company level, frontline Marines were equipped with the AN/TPS-25 ground surveillance radar, which allowed them to identify small groups of enemy soldiers moving about in the darkness, then hit them with mortars or artillery.

Since receiving his powerful naval binoculars and Night Optical Device scope early in the siege, Dennis Mannion had called in artillery missions on dozens of targets he otherwise might have missed. He kept the NVA-held ridgeline about 500 yards west of 861 under nearly constant surveillance and exacted a rising toll on the North Vietnamese. Mannion would scan the ridgeline and other areas at night with his NOD scope, find a group of enemy soldiers, and then have a gunner mark the spot the next day by firing a tracer round from the .50-caliber machine gun mounted on the bore of a 106-millimeter recoilless rifle. The 106 would be locked onto the spot and later fired at the unsuspecting NVA that night when they resumed their work under the cover of darkness. The first time the Marines on 861 tested the setup, Mannion counted about ten enemy soldiers lying on the ground.[4]

In the daylight hours, Mannion continued to team up with Corporal Paul Knight, the 861 forward air controller. As "Green Tambourine" and "Love Is Blue" blared in the background over Armed Forces Radio, Mannion and Knight hammered the enemy ridgeline and other positions with coordinated packages of artillery and air strikes.[5]

• • •

As the Americans exacted a rising toll on the North Vietnamese siege forces, the NVA continued to respond in kind with mortars, artillery, and rockets. By early March, the volume of enemy fire had dropped off from the worst days of February, but was no less deadly.

On 861 Alpha, rifleman Matt Walsh had settled into siege life after leading his fire team into the breach at the northern end of the hill during the February 5 attack. The former A&P grocery clerk and Yankees baseball fan from Yonkers, New York, had celebrated his twentieth birthday on the hill on February 21. His best friend, Joe Roble, made him a birthday cake by melting C-ration chocolate bars over a C-ration pound cake.[6]

Walsh had sized up his odds of surviving Khe Sanh, and he was confident that he would get out alive—but not unscathed. On Tuesday, March 5, Walsh and his buddies were doing some work on their bunker, reinforcing the roof with a piece of runway matting they had snagged. Walsh was standing in the no-man's-land beyond the trench line, making sure the bunker blended in with the rest of the line, when he heard the dreaded WHUMP-WHUMP of two enemy mortars firing. As he was about to dive for cover, one of the rounds hit just behind him and hurled him into the trench. When he regained his senses, he was lying at the bottom of the trench, woozy and covered with blood, with pieces of shrapnel embedded in his legs, arms, left shoulder, back, and head.[7]

A corpsman dressed the worst wounds, and four Marines eased

Walsh onto a stretcher and hustled him to the LZ at the southern end of the hill. A resupply helicopter had just dropped its load, and within seconds Walsh was hustled aboard with a wounded comrade and the aircraft darted off to the east. Aboard the chopper, Walsh was relieved to learn that their destination was Dong Ha. *Any place but Khe Sanh.* As he was carried inside the Delta Med hospital and readied for emergency surgery, he heard somebody grouse, "This place is hell."

"No," Walsh corrected him. "I just came from hell."[8]

• • •

The Super Gaggle had swung the odds back in favor of the Marine helicopter pilots in their supply runs to the hill outposts, but fixed-wing and chopper flights into Khe Sanh Combat Base remained a perilous proposition as March began. The North Vietnamese carefully tracked comings and goings at the base, positioning anti-aircraft guns to cover the preferred routes of American pilots. In the early weeks, helicopters had climbed to about 3,000 feet as they followed Route 9 westward into the hills, then looped around to sneak into the stronghold from the south. The North Vietnamese took note and placed guns on both sides of the valley used by the Americans in their southern approach. The pilots countered by flying 2,000 feet higher until they arrived over the base, then executing a steep corkscrew descent to land.

The helicopter pilots soon noticed they were taking fire within seconds of touching down at Khe Sanh. NVA spotters were obviously alerting the gunners around the base, enabling them to start firing the moment the Americans arrived. In mid-February, the helicopter pilots tried to reclaim the advantage by charting a new route to Khe Sanh that wound through the valleys north of the stronghold. The "back door route," as it was known, gave the pilots some breathing room, but within a few days they were taking fire on that passageway as well.[9]

In the early afternoon of February 28, two CH-46 Sea Knights from Marine Medium Helicopter Squadron 262 took off from Quang Tri, picked up forty passengers at Dong Ha, and set out for Khe Sanh. The twenty-nine-year-old commander of the flight, Major Edwin Meixner of Alva, Oklahoma, had picked the northern route for the journey. Flying low because of fog and overcast, Meixner's aircraft was hit by automatic weapons fire shortly after leaving Route 9. The Sea Knight plunged into a riverbed, killing all twenty-three Americans aboard.[10]

Since mid-February, the rate of damage and destruction sustained by American aircraft flying into Khe Sanh had soared to an "unacceptable" level, the III Marine Amphibious Force headquarters observed in early March. The new month had seen an alarming continuation of the trend.[11] The previous Friday—the first day of March—an Air Force C-123 had been clipped by mortar fire as it departed Khe Sanh, and it crashed and burned off the airstrip. On March 5, a C-123 had been grounded by a flat tire from either enemy fire or runway damage, and enemy mortars blew the aircraft apart before it could be repaired.

Air drops had helped offset the supply shortfall caused by reduced fixed-wing landings at Khe Sanh, but chronic runway closures and aborted flights had created a growing backlog of passengers. The airfields at Dong Ha and Phu Bai were crowded with Marines, Navy corpsmen, and others trying to get into Khe Sanh.[12]

Such was the case on March 6 when a Fairchild C-123 Provider made the short hop from Da Nang to Phu Bai to pick up passengers and cargo before continuing to Khe Sanh. At the controls of the Air Force transport was Lieutenant Colonel Frederick J. Hampton, a fifty-year-old West Point graduate from Gainesville, Florida, whose distinguished career had included flying bombers over postwar Korea and Strategic Air Command flights back in the States at the height of the Cold War. Now assigned to the 311th Air Commando Squadron, Hampton waited while cargo was offloaded at Phu Bai and supplies for Khe Sanh were taken on, along with forty-three Marines, one Navy corpsman, and one civilian headed to the combat base.[13]

The loading complete, Hampton took off from Phu Bai on a flight designated Mission No. 702.

• • •

The one civilian aboard Hampton's aircraft was Robert J. Ellison, the twenty-three-year-old freelance photojournalist who had captured the tragic aftermath of the February 25 Bravo Company ambush. Quiet and reserved, Ellison was not one to boast about all that he had accomplished in three years of work as a professional news photographer. In 1965, while still a student of herpetology at the University of Florida, he had caught the eye of the top New York photo agencies and news magazines with his striking images from civil rights marches in the South. He quit school to become a full-time freelance photographer and began showing up at major news events, including the US military intervention in the Dominican Republic. In 1967, Ellison turned his focus to Vietnam.

Ellison had been shooting an assignment in South Korea when the Tet Offensive began, and he returned to Vietnam and flew to Khe Sanh in early February. Slim, with a thin mustache and shock of dark hair, he had roamed the trench lines, putting himself in harm's way as he documented the terror and strain of the daily lives of Khe Sanh's defenders. Frozen in time on the rolls of 35-millimeter film he shot were the face of a weary Navy corpsman, frightened riflemen in a trench during an NVA bombardment, and the death of Lieutenant Don Jacques.

He had captured the essence of the human drama at Khe Sanh and flew back to Saigon to process his film and forward it to the States. *Newsweek* editors in New York had been blown away by Ellison's images from Khe Sanh, and they had sent word to the rising star that they would be running an eight-page spread of his photographs in the March 18 issue. It was a tremendous achievement for a young freelancer, and Ellison could have headed off to Bangkok or China Beach to celebrate. But he felt a bond with the Marines at Khe Sanh, so, on the afternoon of March 6, he bartered some beer, Coke, and cigars for a seat on Fred Hampton's C-123.[14]

• • •

Among the forty-three Marines aboard Hampton's aircraft were Corporal Ron Ryan, who had rallied Bravo 1/26 Marines with well-placed kicks on January 21, and was a pair of battle-tested radio operators assigned to Second Lieutenant William (Bill) Smith, the fire support coordinator for the 1st Battalion, 26th Marines, at Khe Sanh. Private First Class George L. Elliott III, a nineteen-year-old from Norfolk, Virginia, was a tough-talking inner-city kid who loved to play Smokey Robinson records on the turntable he lugged around Vietnam. Corporal Larry Scott Kennedy was a soft-spoken twenty-year-old from Charleston, West Virginia, a country boy who embraced the top-down culture of the Marine Corps.

One of the radio operators would accompany Smith everywhere he went, and that included regular forays to the regimental command bunker to confer with Harry Baig. Elliott would jaw at the lieutenant every step of the way as they performed the "Khe Sanh Shuffle," dashing from hole to hole and dodging the enemy incoming as they made their way from their quarters to the regimental bunker. In his jaunty moods, Eliott would call out, "Hey, Lieutenant Smith, you feelin' lucky today?"[15]

During the madness of February 23, Smith and Lieutenant Hank Norman, the artillery forward observer attached to Bravo Company, were running all over the east end of the base with their radio operators to analyze craters in an attempt to fix the origin of incoming rounds.[16] Afterward, Smith's radiomen asked for a break to burn off some R&R time. Smith agreed, and off they went. Now they were seated in the back of the Khe Sanh–bound C-123 that took off from Dong Ha just before 2:00 p.m. on March 6.

A few minutes into the flight, pilot Fred Hampton was cleared to land by the control tower at Khe Sanh. He had started his final approach when he spotted a small aircraft on the runway ahead. Aborting the landing, Hampton circled around the north end of the base for another approach. Small-arms fire from the jungle struck an engine, and, seconds later, the C-123 crashed into the rugged hills east of Khe Sanh. There were no survivors.[17]

• • •

The victims of the C-123 crash lay where they fell until April 25. On that day, helicopters thundered into the hills about two miles east of Khe Sanh Combat Base, and a company of Marines from the 2nd Battalion, 3rd Marine Regiment, poured into an LZ hacked from the jungle. They found the wreckage of Fred Hampton's C-123 in minutes and spent the next five hours gathering decomposing bodies and scattered bones, as well as service record books, medical records, and personal items.[18]

The recovery operation of April 25 was less than thorough, and on June 25, a Marine patrol found another fifteen sets of remains. Still another operation on July 3 found more remains inside the aircraft and surrounding underbrush. On November 5, one more casualty of the March 6 crash was recovered by a Marine patrol.[19]

Eighteen days later, on November 23, 1968, Taps sounded and an honor guard's volleys echoed across the wooded bluffs of Jefferson Barracks National Cemetery, overlooking the Mississippi River south of St. Louis, Missouri. As a crowd of family members, service personnel, and others paid their respects, the skeletal remains of thirty-five men recovered at the crash site of Fred Hampton's Mission No. 702 were buried in a mass grave.[20]

CHAPTER 19

"Bitter Hardships and Blood"

As the record bombardments of late February hammered Khe Sanh Combat Base, the days became even more arduous for the surgeons and corpsmen of Charlie Med as they went about their bloody work. During a lull in the shelling one day, the four Charlie Med surgeons cobbled together a whimsical recruiting ad: "Wanted, General Practitioner to assume a diversified medical and surgical practice in a small, quiet, mountain setting. This sylvan community provides relief from all disadvantages above urban areas and assures inexhaustible appreciation of nature's beauty." They signed it "the doctors of Khe Sanh," and sent it off to the *New England Journal of Medicine*.[1]

The Charlie Med surgeons patched up casualties as best they could, and they laughed and bantered with each other, leaving unsaid their darkest thoughts or banishing them to their diaries. "Hope there is no attack but believe that there will be one," surgeon Ed Feldman scribbled on Tuesday, February 27, the day after marking his twenty-seventh birthday. "I think we will win, but it will be costly. Want to come out of this alive."[2]

On February 29, Charlie Med officially moved into its new underground treatment and triage bunker. During the day, the cry "Casualties!" had gone up, and surgeon Jim Finnegan and his comrades had sprinted down a walkway of wooden pallets to the triage bunker. Finnegan had just reached the entrance when an incoming mortar round hit, hurling him into the bunker and spattering his left arm, neck, and buttocks with shrapnel. The injuries weren't serious—salt-and-pepper wounds, they called them at Charlie Med—and so Finnegan went back to work as though nothing had happened, enduring good-natured ribbing from his comrades.[3]

By early March, one of the most valued members of Finnegan's Charlie Med team was a slight, nineteen-year-old preacher's son from Florida. Private First Class Jonathan Nathaniel Spicer served as a stretcher bearer, carrying wounded Marines from arriving helicopters or ambulances to the Charlie Med triage area and then shuttling stabilized casualties to the helicopter pad for evacuation—all under enemy fire. Spicer had earned a reputation for bravery and selflessness, shielding the wounded with his own body as enemy shells rained down.[4]

After all that Spicer had done to prove himself, it was easy to forget the controversy that had accompanied his arrival at Charlie Med a month earlier. The trouble had started when he arrived at Khe Sanh and refused to carry a rifle in his assignment with the supply unit of Bravo 1/26. Spicer explained that he was a conscientious objector and couldn't kill anyone. He had loved animals growing up in Florida and had hoped to be assigned to a canine unit when he joined the Marines. But Spicer was designated a rifleman, and at every stop in the Marines, he was told to take up his claim of conscientious objector status at his next duty station.

Spicer heard that line all the way to Vietnam, and the next thing he knew, he was in Bravo Company, enduring torment from his comrades for his pacifism, his Bible reading, and his rejection of the rough language that was a rite of passage in the Marine Corps. Spicer sought out Protestant chaplain Ray Stubbe at Khe Sanh in late January, and Stubbe came away from their conversation convinced that the Florida teenager was for real. He arranged for Spicer to be attached to Charlie Med as a stretcher bearer.

Spicer was only about five foot seven and 140 pounds, but he impressed everyone at Charlie Med with his courage and hard work. He was pleasant and soft-spoken, fond of talking about the home and family he missed. He had written the name of his girlfriend—Carla—on his helmet. He felt bad about his time at Bravo Company and wanted to prove he wasn't a coward. But he wasn't going to fight, even if the NVA overran the base. "I don't have any problem with dying," he would say to ambulance driver Danny Sullivan. "But I will not kill anyone."[5]

On the afternoon of Friday, March 8, medevac flights arrived at the Khe Sanh helicopter pad during an intense North Vietnamese bombardment.[6] Spicer and other stretcher bearers headed into the fire with litters loaded with wounded Marines and carried them aboard the waiting aircraft. Spicer had gotten his wounded aboard and had dashed back to get the final casualties out of the shell fire and onto a chopper. A mortar round burst among the knot of stretcher bearers and casualties, and shrapnel sliced into Spicer's chest, face, and legs. He had left his flak jacket unzipped, and a small metal fragment found the opening and pierced his heart.

Down in the Charlie Med bunker, someone stuck his head into the entrance and yelled, "Spicer's hit!" Seconds later, the young Marine was carried inside and laid on a gurney. Almost immediately Spicer's heart and breathing stopped. He was clinically dead.

Ed Feldman was performing triage on other casualties, and so his three comrades went to work. John Magilligan cut open Spicer's chest while Joe Wolfe inserted a breathing tube into the wounded Marine's throat. Magilligan surmised that Spicer's heart had stopped because of pressure from blood that had filled the surrounding membrane, so he made a careful incision that released the blood. He started a transfusion while Jim Finnegan reached into Spicer's open chest and performed a heart massage technique he had perfected on countless casualties. The young Marine's heart fluttered to life.

The shrapnel hole in Spicer's heart still had to be addressed, so Finnegan put his finger in the opening and deftly sutured it shut with three stitches. After fifteen minutes of intense work, Spicer's heartbeat was robust, his blood pressure had stabilized, and he was breathing on his own.[7]

A medevac helicopter arrived, and Danny Sullivan and three others carried Spicer aboard. The aircraft clattered away to the east.

For six days, Nat Spicer clung to life. He was transferred to a military hospital in Japan, and late on the evening of Wednesday, March 13, his parents in Florida received a telegram, informing them that their son was not doing well. The following morning, March 14, Spicer's father,

William, a substitute teacher since retiring from the Methodist ministry, was standing before a world affairs class at Shenandoah Junior High School in Miami when two Marines came to the door. Private First Class Jonathan Nathaniel Spicer, United States Marine Corps, had died of wounds received in combat in the Republic of Vietnam.[8]

• • •

Over the first three weeks of March, North Vietnamese ground forces continued to challenge the ARVN Ranger positions that anchored the eastern perimeter of Khe Sanh Combat Base, mounting seven probes of varying strength and intensity.[9] Since the discovery of the maze of bunkers and trenches off the east end of the base in late February, the American command had braced for large ground assaults originating from this area. But another concern nagged at the Americans: tunneling by the North Vietnamese.

Colonel Lownds had been on the lookout for tunnels since the early days of the siege, sending Navy corpsmen out at night with stethoscopes, which they would place on trench walls and engineering stakes driven into the ground to detect enemy digging.[10] Nothing turned up, aside from the ambient noise of artillery and air strikes, and music from record players and tape recorders.

The concern about tunneling was raised anew in late February, when an enemy rocket exploded along the northwest perimeter and revealed a recently dug shaft six feet below the surface. There were fears that the NVA might pack a tunnel with explosives and blow a hole in the Khe Sanh perimeter, as Union soldiers had done to Confederate lines at Petersburg, Virginia, in 1864.

When word filtered up from the ranks about the usefulness of divining rods, Lownds concluded that even the tools of American backwoods folklore were worth a try. Marines were sent out to walk the perimeter with brass divining rods, without success.[11] In March, the Pentagon dispatched a team of men armed with a new seismic detection instrument to check for tunnels, but they, too, found nothing to validate the fears.[12]

On March 8, South Vietnamese Rangers attacked the enemy trenches east of their positions and in two brief engagements killed several NVA soldiers as they emerged from tunnels and trenches. An Associated Press dispatch about the incident emphasized the tunnel angle, and suddenly comparisons were being made to the Viet Minh's tunneling at Dien Bien Phu. "100 Reds Caught Tunneling Toward Khe Sanh; 27 Killed," screamed the front-page headline in *Stars and Stripes*.[13] The AP dispatch concluded on an ominous note: "The new development and earlier discovery of tunnels under the Khe Sanh barbed wire perimeter indicates that the communists are following the same siege techniques used at Dien Bien Phu. There they drove mine shafts under the French positions, loaded them with explosives, and set them off at opportune times in the fighting."

The suggestion that the North Vietnamese were tunneling "toward" Khe Sanh was debatable, but one error in the article wasn't. In a situation report the Marines at Khe Sanh had prepared for division headquarters, the number of North Vietnamese dead from the ARVN Ranger attacks on March 8 was reported as eight. That same number had been forwarded to III Marine Amphibious Force headquarters, and then on to General Westmoreland's staff in Saigon. When Westmoreland's MACV press officers released the story to reporters, the number of NVA dead had soared to twenty-seven—more than triple the actual count.[14]

● ● ●

Although the tunneling concern was real enough to the besieged defenders of Khe Sanh, the burrowing by the North Vietnamese soldiers in all likelihood was nothing more than an attempt to escape the escalating American air raids. With the improved March weather, the skies now throbbed with American B-52 bombers and attack aircraft dumping high explosives, anti-personnel bombs, and napalm on the North Vietnamese positions.[15]

The Marines in I Corps and Westmoreland's MACV headquarters churned out remarkably precise data on enemy soldiers killed, secondary explosions detected, bunkers destroyed, and trenches reduced to rubble. But they couldn't answer one lingering question: What was the North Vietnamese endgame at Khe Sanh?

As the weeks of February had passed without the major enemy ground assault, US military intelligence and the CIA had begun to rethink their conclusions that Khe Sanh Combat Base was on the brink of a winner-take-all battle. On March 7, the *New York Times* revealed that the US military command in Vietnam "has revised its opinion and now thinks that an attack on Hue—rather than on the Marine encampment at Khe Sanh—is the enemy's next objective."[16] The "senior military official" who had briefed the *Times* reporter and other correspondents was none other than General Westmoreland.[17]

NVA intentions remained murky, but the US military command and intelligence agencies knew that General Giap had shifted some troops from Khe Sanh to Hue around February 10. The withdrawal of NVA forces from Khe Sanh had accelerated in early March, and on March 9, General Westmoreland informed President Johnson that the NVA forces around Khe Sanh "had dropped to between 6,000 and 8,000 men."[18]

Whatever their numbers, the North Vietnamese who were dug in around Khe Sanh in mid-March faced a nightmarish existence in the face of the relentless American air strikes and artillery. Bloody bandages, blood trails, scattered grave sites, and even unburied bodies—some burned by napalm, others with horrible shrapnel wounds—littered the surrounding jungle. Defectors and prisoners of war spoke of terrible suffering and high desertion rates.[19] The misery of the siege forces at Khe Sanh was captured in the diary entry of a North Vietnamese soldier on March 23, "a day full of bitter hardships and blood," he wrote.[20]

The NVA soldiers lived in mortal fear of B-52 strikes, which hit without warning. "From the beginning until the 60th day of the siege at Khe Sanh, B-52 bombers continually dropped their bombs in this area with ever growing intensity and at any moment of the day," a North Vietnamese soldier wrote in his diary. "If someone came to visit this place, he might say that this was a storm of bombs and ammunition which eradicated all living creatures and vegetation whatsoever, even those located in caves or in deep underground shelters."[21] Some NVA soldiers used the chaos following a B-52 strike as cover to desert. A captured North Vietnamese document dated February 29 stated that one unit, Doan 926, had three hundred desertions en route to Khe Sanh, with B-52 strikes cited as the main cause.[22]

Private First Class Hai Van Phan, drafted into the North Vietnamese Army in March 1967, was an illiterate country boy with only two years of schooling. In January 1968, he had headed south down the Ho Chi Minh

Trail with his unit: the 11th Company, 3rd Battalion, 1st Regiment of the 330th Division. The soldiers arrived in the Khe Sanh area in March and spent two days digging trenches in their assigned position south of the combat base. Phan and his comrades had been told they would be held in reserve for an impending assault on the American stronghold.[23]

In mid-March, the sixth day after their arrival, explosions engulfed Phan and his comrades—the first of seven B-52 strikes they would endure. Nine of the company's one hundred men were killed in the first strike. The NVA soldiers frantically deepened their trenches and fortified them with wood, and that saved them when more Arc Light strikes hit the area. But they could not escape the relentless sorties of the low-flying American attack jets, and Phan lost many more comrades to their bombs and napalm.

Phan's company remained in place in the jungle south of Khe Sanh Combat Base until April 9, when US forces attacked their trenches. The nineteen-year-old farm boy survived the fight but was wounded and taken prisoner by the Americans. Unlike so many thousands of his comrades, Private Hai Van Phan survived Khe Sanh.[24]

• • •

On Tuesday, March 12, the US Marines and South Vietnamese Rangers at Khe Sanh were put on alert on the eve of the fourteenth anniversary of General Giap's opening ground attacks on the French stronghold at Dien Bien Phu. The day passed without incident, but Hanoi's propagandists stepped up the psychological war on Khe Sanh. "Preparations for new attacks" are underway, Hanoi radio declared, warning that Khe Sanh's "days are numbered."[25] Hanoi's bluster was accompanied by continued digging by North Vietnamese soldiers around the base, and the sound of whirring machinery that ratcheted up the uneasiness of the Americans.[26]

The North Vietnamese did more than bluster in the early hours of Monday, March 18. An estimated battalion of NVA soldiers, about six hundred strong, emerged from trenches and bunkers east of the combat base and advanced toward the Khe Sanh runway. Unleashing heavy fire on the ARVN Ranger positions, they managed to blow holes in the perimeter wire before the attack stalled. A flare ship revealed the location of the enemy troops, and air and artillery fire broke the North Vietnamese attack around 6:00 a.m. The body count was eighty-three enemy dead.[27]

Throughout the day, American air observers in the skies overhead picked out new targets, and artillery missions and air strikes rained down on NVA anti-aircraft weapons positioned around the base. In the early evening, the North Vietnamese launched another probe against the ARVN Ranger lines, but it was a halfhearted effort, and the gunfire sputtered to a close as night settled over the combat base.

• • •

Supplies and mail now flowed nearly unhindered into the hill outposts, courtesy of the Super Gaggle's sky-borne forces, and visions of victory replaced the grim fears of an Alamo-like fight to the death. The volume of enemy mortar and rocket fire had dropped significantly, along with the sightings of enemy troops. On Hill 861, Dennis Mannion didn't even bother to fire up his scope on some nights.

By mid-March, the Americans on the hill outposts looked like shipwrecked castaways—dirty, ragged, bearded, and bedraggled. Water was still too scarce for bathing, so bodies remained caked with sweat and grime, skin tinted red by Khe Sanh's laterite soil. Utilities had rotted off at the knees, and blouses and sweatshirts were torn and tattered.[28]

The rough conditions had resulted in a relaxation of Marine regulations, so Mannion had adorned his battered helmet with a button his mother had sent him: "Kiss me, I'm Irish." The late Gunny Melvin Rimel's replacement on 861, Charles Perkins, had a harder edge than his revered predecessor, and he hounded Mannion constantly about the button. "Goddammit," Perkins would yell, "you're going to get yourself shot. Get that off your helmet!"[29]

Mannion laughed it off. In a tragic twist of fate, Perkins was shot by a sniper on March 27. He clung to life for several weeks, and on May 17 died aboard the hospital ship *Repose*.[30]

• • •

Forward air controller Paul Knight had continued to direct air strikes on any suspected NVA targets around 861 that surfaced. One day in mid-

March, an airborne controller radioed Knight and offered a flight of four F-4 Phantoms armed with napalm, so Knight gave the controller the co-ordinates of a tree line north of 861, which the NVA had been using as a staging point for probes and harassment of the Americans on 861 Alpha. The first Phantom roared over 861 Alpha along a southeast-to-north-west vector and toggled his canisters, but the napalm exploded about 500 yards northwest of the target. The second F-4 followed, and his canister also hurtled past the target. The third Phantom roared in and unleashed its load.

Watching from his perch atop 861, about 300 yards to the west, Knight realized the napalm was headed for Captain Earle Breeding's Echo Company outpost. "Abort! Abort! Abort!" Knight screamed into the radio handset. But it was too late. He could only watch in horror as the first canister hit and jellied gasoline boiled across the American trench line in a burst of fire and smoke. Another canister slammed into the ground and Knight feared he had killed everybody on the hill. An anxious hour passed before he was informed that the Marines on 861 Alpha had gotten advance notice of the incoming aircraft and were in their trenches and bunkers when the napalm hit. A few men had suffered singed hair, but no one had died or even been seriously injured. It had been a very close call.[31]

• • •

Most Marines were counting the days until they left Khe Sanh, but Corporal Ken Warner couldn't wait to get back there. After he was wounded in the assault on 881 North on January 20, the India 3/26 squad leader had required multiple surgeries on his shrapnel-torn shoulder and other wounds. During his nearly three weeks on the hospital ship *Sanctuary*, he couldn't stop thinking about his comrades, wondering how they were do-ing in the big battle underway at Khe Sanh. His parents hoped he would come home when he was discharged from the hospital on February 12, but the Southern Californian wanted to rejoin his India Company broth-ers. He headed to Da Nang to catch a flight to Khe Sanh.

Bad weather and enemy fire had created a logjam of passengers trying to get to Khe Sanh, so after a few frustrating days, Warner gave up on Da Nang. He flew to Phu Bai, and then Dong Ha, but found the same passenger backlog at each air strip. "Here I sit in Da Nang AGAIN," Warner wrote home in late February. He knew how desperately his parents wanted to see him, so he explained to them how low he felt about not being with his buddies at Khe Sanh. "I'm scared to go back," he wrote. "But this is very important to me. I hope you understand."[32]

When Warner finally got on a flight, the aircraft was forced to abort its landing at Khe Sanh because of heavy NVA fire, so he started the process all over again. Finally, on March 5, Warner made it to Khe Sanh on a C-130. He and his fellow passengers jumped off the back ramp as the aircraft slowed for its turnaround at the end of the runway, and they ducked into nearby trenches to wait out the incoming fire. Fate had spared Warner once again: he arrived one day before the C-123 crash at Khe Sanh.

Warner was stunned by the transformation of the combat base since he had left in January. It looked as though it had been ravaged by a killer tornado: buildings were flattened, trees splintered, and vehicles in pieces or riddled with shrapnel. All around were craters and churned earth, and an endless maze of sandbagged trenches and bunkers.

After two days at the combat base, Warner finally got a seat on an H-34 helicopter headed up to 881 South. Enemy rounds smacked into the fuselage as the aircraft descended to one of the hill's landing zones, and Warner emerged and sprinted to a trench. Stretcher bearers carried medevac cases aboard the bird for the return trip to the combat base, and the H-34 veered away from the hill amid exploding mortar rounds. When the barrage ended, Warner found his way to the 1st Platoon command post and checked in with Lieutenant Rick Fromme.

Warner took over his old squad and familiarized himself with a world turned upside down in his absence. Only two of the dozen men in his squad on January 20 were still there; the rest had been wounded or killed or had completed their tours. Because of the threat of NVA snipers and mortars, Warner and his men spent their days in underground bunkers and two-man "bunny holes" bored into the trench walls. The trenches themselves were now seven or eight feet deep, more than twice the depth when Warner had left.

Equally striking were the smell and appearance of his comrades. Their hair was long, at least by Marine standards, and they were unwashed and unshaven. Artillery forward observer Bob Arrotta had grown a beard; Captain Bill Dabney sported a Sergeant Pepper–worthy mustache.

One thing hadn't changed: morale was high, a tribute to the tight operation run by Dabney. Men kept busy, working on the trenches and bunkers and bunny holes when it was too dangerous to go topside, and checking the wire or performing other tasks when there was fog or cloud cover to shield their activities.

Dabney's daily flag-raising ceremony had become a pep rally for the defenders of 881 South, an act of group defiance directed at the North Vietnamese surrounding the hill. Ken Warner reveled in the routine, standing at attention in the trench line with his squad, his middle finger raised in a Bronx salute to the enemy, as Lieutenant Owen Matthews bugled "To the Colors" and the Stars and Stripes rose into the sky to welcome the new day.[33]

• • •

On Thursday, March 21, America's war in Vietnam marked a painful milestone: 336 Americans had been killed in action in the previous week's fighting, pushing the total of US deaths in the conflict over 20,000.[34]

At Khe Sanh, the signs of the decisive battle that once seemed inevitable had waned, but the North Vietnamese still possessed the ability to hurt the Americans. Long-range artillery fire from camouflaged positions in the Laotian massif known as Co Roc continued to inflict death and misery on the combat base and outposts, and in the late afternoon of March 22, the big enemy guns opened up with the heaviest barrage since February. The word passed along the Khe Sanh perimeter: be ready for a ground assault.[35]

In the Charlie 1/26 command bunker, radioman Chuck Chamberlin tried to read a letter he had just received from his grandmother in Montana, but the barrage was building in intensity and tensions were rising, so he slid the envelope into his pocket. As a survivor of the direct hit on the Charlie 1/26 bunker on February 15, Chamberlin carried a heavier burden than most at Khe Sanh. He had lost three comrades—two had been killed, and his company commander had been maimed. The Seabees had built a new command post, and Captain Walter J. "Jack"

Egger had arrived to take the reins of Charlie Company. Now, with the growing sense that something big was afoot, the command post bustled with the company's officers and noncoms.

In the flickering light of a kerosene lamp, Egger conferred with his highly regarded executive officer, the slight, blond lieutenant Paul W. Bush, while Gunnery Sergeant John Joseph Grohman stood by.

A few feet away, Chamberlin worked the radio, checking with platoon commanders for situation reports. Beside him was the junior radioman, Corporal John Mattern, who had replaced Chamberlin's friend Joseph Bailey, after his death in the February 15 attack. Frantic calls for corpsmen crackled across the net and then an appeal from a nearby unit of Army light tanks and "Quad 50" guns: "We need a corpsman down here. We got a man who's almost cut in half."[36]

About 8:45 p.m., without warning, a shell smashed into the Charlie Company command bunker. Knocked unconscious by the explosion, Chuck Chamberlin awoke to find himself engulfed in flames and choking smoke. A piece of shrapnel had torn open the lantern, drenching John Mattern with kerosene and igniting a smoky fire. Chamberlin had been shielded from instant death by the bunker's bank of PRC-25 radios.

The bunker had collapsed in a heap of logs, sandbags, and runway matting, but most of the debris had fallen away from Chamberlin. Through the smoke, he could see bodies trapped in the rubble. John Mattern screamed in agony from his painful shrapnel wounds and the flames billowing from his jungle utilities. Choking and gasping for breath, Chamberlin tried to move, but his shoulder was broken and his legs pinned by debris. The noxious air reeked of burning hair and human flesh. His eyes suddenly locked on an object protruding from the rubble: it was a hand and arm, torn from one of his comrades and dripping blood.

As his brain shut down, Chamberlin lost consciousness a second time. He awoke, suffocating, death closing in, and began thrashing and clawing wildly at the debris. Somehow his legs came free, and he pulled himself upward through the rubble with his good arm.

Outside, Marines tore at the burning debris. Three of them—Private First Class Terrell E. Fitzgerald, Corporal Michael Gallagher, and Private First Class Dominic Parisi—opened a passageway through the flames.

Chamberlin caught a glimpse of sky and lunged toward it. His left hand broke the surface, and Staff Sergeant Arnold Jay Ferrari of Napa, California, only eleven days in Vietnam, pulled Chamberlin from the death trap.[37]

Lieutenant Bruce Geiger, the twenty-three-year-old commander of the adjacent squad of Army light tanks and guns, had seen the round smash into the Charlie Company command post. Dodging shells and rockets, he had sprinted across the airstrip to Charlie Med and led two corpsmen back to the shattered bunker. Chuck Chamberlin and the badly burned John Mattern had been pulled from the ruins. The corpsmen field-dressed their wounds, and comrades carried the two injured Marines across the airstrip to Charlie Med.[38]

At the shattered Charlie Company command post, the full extent of the carnage soon became apparent: Captain Jack Egger, First Lieutenant Paul Bush, and Gunnery Sergeant John J. Grohman were dead or dying. Two Charlie riflemen were killed in an adjacent bunker.

More than 1,100 shells would hit Khe Sanh Combat Base and the hill outposts on the night of March 22–23—the second worst barrage of the entire siege. The defenders of Khe Sanh would spend another sleepless night, waiting to see if the bombardment was the prelude to a ground assault, but the attack never came. In all likelihood, the barrage was cover for the North Vietnamese as they withdrew more troops from the costly confrontation at Khe Sanh.

• • •

At Charlie Med, Jim Finnegan's team of doctors and corpsmen worked through the night to save scores of wounded men. Chuck Chamberlin could hear the corpsmen and surgeons talking as they hovered over him, cutting away his bloody and fire-blackened flak jacket, utilities, and boots before tending to his injuries. Morphine dulled Chamberlin's pain, but it could do nothing for the agony of the badly burned John Mattern, and his bloodcurdling screams forced Chamberlin to continue reliving the horrors of the burning bunker.

An emergency medevac flight arrived, and Chamberlin and Mattern were among the critically wounded whisked to Dong Ha. It had been a bad day for Americans along the DMZ, and the carnage had converged on Delta Med. In the triage area, blood covered the tiled floor, lapped along the gutters, and poured into drains.

When the doctors at Delta Med had done all they could for one day, Chamberlin was put on a stretcher for removal to the ward where he would spend the night. A few North Vietnamese rockets screamed overhead, and the orderlies abandoned the wounded Marine to scramble for cover. Chamberlin laughed. *This is nothing.*[39]

The barrage eased, and Chamberlin was taken into a room and laid in a bed. The drugs had dulled his senses, but not enough to diminish the thrill of clean sheets, electric lights, and running water. He heard one or two more rounds explode, and then fell into a deep morphine sleep. For the first time since it all began in January, he let go of Khe Sanh.[40]

CHAPTER 20

"The Agony of Khe Sanh"

The deadly barrage of March 22–23 was especially unnerving for an envied subset of Khe Sanh defenders: "short-timers" nearing the end of their tours. They became more superstitious, more reluctant to step outside their bunker or bunny hole, more unwilling to risk a chance rendezvous with a random enemy round. With the threat of a climactic battle diminishing, Khe Sanh had devolved into a grassroots drama of individual triumphs and tragedies—the completion of one's tour and safe passage back to the world, as opposed to departure from Khe Sanh in a body bag.

After one of the most harrowing nights of the Khe Sanh ordeal, Seabee Sam Messer was fortunate enough to be getting out on March 23. He scrambled aboard a departing CH-46 Sea Knight, "scared to death to get on that bird," and even more scared when the crew chief ordered everyone to get down on the armored deck and hug their seabags. The chopper headed east, through a gauntlet of enemy machine-gun fire.[1] Messer's parting memory of Khe Sanh was watching bullet holes appear in the helicopter fuselage where he and his fellow passengers had been sitting. He had made it out alive, and so had the others, and by nightfall they could laugh about it over a beer.

• • •

Fixed-wing flights and helicopters continued to deposit arriving passengers at Khe Sanh, including a steady stream of journalists drawn to chronicle "the agony of Khe Sanh," as pronounced by the March 18 *Newsweek* cover story that featured Robert Ellison's photographs. Associated Press correspondent John Wheeler had taken up residence at Khe Sanh Combat Base. Others were in and out, seasoned veterans like *Washington Post* correspondent Peter Braestrup, and unproven talents like the twenty-seven-year-old magazine writer who had arrived in Vietnam three months earlier, convinced that he had found "the time and the place and the subject" to make his mark.[2] Michael Herr would soon validate his hunch in the pages of *Esquire*.

Twenty-six-year-old freelance photographer David Powell purposely steered clear of the journalistic pack when he arrived in Khe Sanh in late March for his second crack at the story. A barrel-chested Army veteran, a loner by nature, Powell had quit his job as a security guard at Bob Hope's Southern California estate the previous summer to experience firsthand the war in Vietnam. He wasn't trained as a reporter or photographer, but he figured the best way to play war tourist was to show up with a camera and a notebook and act like he knew what he was doing. He arrived in Saigon on August 5, 1967, with $50 in his pocket, a cheap camera, and letters of introduction from two tiny California newspapers.[3]

Powell joined the Army's 5th Cavalry Regiment—the Black Knights—for operations near Bong Son and quickly developed a taste for combat. He headed up to I Corps to check out the Marines, and ended up at Con Thien, where he witnessed young Americans getting torn apart by shells. He shot only a couple of rolls of film in three months, but he had the time of his life.

When he ran out of money in late October 1967, Powell wandered down to the Saigon waterfront and signed on as a seaman with a United Fruit Company refrigerator ship. He hauled vegetables around Southeast Asia for three months, then flew to Hong Kong to buy a pair of cheap cameras and get accreditation with some English-language newspapers. By the time he returned to Vietnam around February 20, Hue and Khe Sanh were the big stories. He showed up at the United Press International (UPI) offices in downtown Saigon and landed a freelance assignment to Khe Sanh.

Powell flew into the besieged combat base on February 25, and before the day was out was nearly killed when a burning pallet of artillery powder charges blew up as he was photographing it. The blast hurled Powell through the air, and he landed next to a bunker, smoke curling from his blackened clothes. He looked up to find a pair of Marines staring at him as if a space alien had just landed on their doorstep.[4]

Powell dusted himself off, found his cameras, and went back to work.

After about two weeks, he flew back to Saigon with the film he had shot. UPI put his best images on their wire, and two US newspapers ran Powell's work on their front page.

The UPI photo editor in Saigon, a veteran newsman named Bill Snead, mentioned to his eager young shooter that no reporter or photographer had made it to the dangerous Khe Sanh outpost known as Hill 881 South. Powell took the bait.

At Phu Bai, he had to convince helicopter pilot Dave Althoff and his comrades in HMM-262 that he wasn't crazy and that they wouldn't be sending him to his death if they allowed him aboard one of their flights to 881 South. Around midday on March 25, Powell bounded off a Sea Knight as it touched down on Bill Dabney's hill.

Over the next three days and two nights, Powell barely slept. He was no stranger to the adrenalin-stoked intensity of combat, but 881 South exuded a visceral, end-of-the-earth vibe like no place that Powell had ever been in Vietnam. Against a backdrop of shell bursts and sniper fire, he prowled the trench lines, chatting up Marines and corpsmen in underground bunkers and bunny holes. He chronicled their precarious world with his Minolta and Miranda cameras—the fatigue and fear, the camaraderie and shared sacrifice, and the professionalism and steely resolve. He only shot about a dozen rolls of film, but many of his shutter clicks would become unforgettable images of Khe Sanh: portraits of the swashbuckling Bill Dabney and soulful Bob Arrotta; a starkly silhouetted flag-raising ceremony; a sniper team at work; and the world inside the hill's subterranean shelters and passageways.

When it was time to leave, Powell dived into the back of a CH-46 as it departed 881 South. Skidding across the helicopter's armored deck on a layer of .50-caliber shell casings, Powell ended up beneath the door gunner as he blasted away at the North Vietnamese. The gunner flashed a reassuring smile at Powell before resuming his duel with the enemy soldiers trying to shoot them from the sky.[5]

• • •

Leaving 881 South that same day was Corporal Ken Warner, the Southern California surfer and India Company squad leader who had survived his share of heartache and harrowing moments during his months at Khe Sanh. It was a bittersweet departure after all the brotherhood and loss that he had known in this place, and he was glad that he was sharing the journey with one of the best friends he had made during his thirteen months in Vietnam, machine gunner Fulton "Fuzzy" Allen.[6]

After the hugs and tears and gruff farewells, the white kid from Southern California and the black kid from New Jersey headed to one of the landing zones to catch their ride down to Khe Sanh. As Warner waited in a trench off the LZ, he started to hyperventilate. The helicopter arrived, and Warner and Fuzzy Allen dashed up the ramp with their gear and braced themselves against a bulkhead. Warner didn't like helicopters, and he feared getting shot down anytime he was on one, especially around Khe Sanh. He prayed and pleaded throughout the short flight. *Please, God, please, just get me to Khe Sanh. I'm so close. Come on, I'm so close.*[7]

The Sea Knight safely deposited Warner and Allen at Khe Sanh Combat Base, and now they had to sweat out their layover while awaiting seats on a fixed-wing flight back to the coast. They finally got on a C-130 on April 6, and Warner took one last look at the battered runway and blood-stained hills. He fought back tears as memories of his time at Khe Sanh flooded his thoughts.

As the ramp of the C-130 slowly shut, Warner watched the cratered hills disappear in the distance. He and Fuzzy looked at each other, too overwhelmed to speak. It was all over for them. They had survived Khe Sanh.

• • •

With each passing day, the bloodlust rose in the hearts of the men of Bravo 1/26.

Since February 25, the Marines killed in the ambush of the Jacques patrol had remained where they had fallen. Day after day, aerial observers photographed their decomposing bodies. From his lines, Captain Ken Pipes kept watch on his lost boys, gazing through binoculars on the terrible scene.[8]

The sense of shock and loss permeated the Bravo ranks. Virile young grunts like Ken Rodgers had been shaken to their core. They couldn't go outside the wire to help their own men? They couldn't even retrieve the bodies of brother Marines? Rodgers didn't voice his darkest thoughts: *If things are so desperate that we couldn't go save thirty guys, then we're doomed.*[9]

Among the angriest of the Bravo Marines was Corporal Ken Korkow. The son of a self-made man who had become wealthy breeding rodeo horses, Korkow was a hard worker and fearless horseman growing up in Pierre, South Dakota, but he could never please his demanding father. Korkow graduated from high school when he was sixteen and started college at South Dakota State University, but he had inherited his father's appetite for risk. So, with the war in Vietnam heating up, he quit college and joined the Marine Corps.

Korkow wanted to be a rifleman, the greatest test of manhood he could imagine, but he wound up in mortars. He joined Bravo 1/26 at Khe Sanh in the first week of January 1968. After losing close friends in a rocket attack in early February, Korkow vowed that he would never again allow himself to feel such pain. He nurtured a pathological hatred of the North Vietnamese.[10]

On February 25, Korkow watched Lieutenant Jacques lead his patrol through the wire and listened to the ambush unfold. He begged to be allowed to help save the patrol but was ordered to stand down. Korkow was furious—with the NVA, as well as with the officers who had let Jacques and his Marines die rather than risk the loss of more men.

Korkow craved vengeance.[11] He would lure an NVA sniper into taking a shot, then put a white phosphorus round from his 60-millimeter mortar on the position, visualizing the agonizing death he had inflicted on the men who had killed his friends. Scarred before he arrived at Khe Sanh, Korkow had become hard as stone. He had lost his religion, and his belief in a just God. Khe Sanh had driven Ken Korkow into the darkest place he had ever known, a place where he was tormented by his demons and mocked by a question he could not answer: *If there is a God, why would he let good men die?*[12]

CHAPTER 21

"We Made Them Pay"

In the foggy predawn of March 30, 1968, the men of Bravo 1/26 prepared for battle. Like any Marine rifleman worth his salt, Corporal Michael O'Hara of the 2nd Platoon checked his grenades and M-16 rifle one final time. Corporal Tom Quigley, the company radioman, fiddled with a broken strap on his PRC-25 field unit. "Guess I can't go out this morning," he joked with Captain Ken Pipes, the Bravo Company skipper. Wordlessly, the wiry former football halfback cinched the dangling radio strap to Quigley's cartridge belt.[1]

For two months, President Lyndon Johnson had watched with growing frustration as his forces in Vietnam reacted to enemy attacks rather than dictate the action. At long last, General William Westmoreland was poised to seize the initiative at Khe Sanh with an operation that would reopen Route 9 from the coastal plain westward to the Laotian border and drive enemy forces from their positions around the embattled American stronghold. As a prelude, Bravo 1/26 had been cleared to launch the first offensive action by the Americans at Khe Sanh since the siege began in January—a "movement to contact" aimed at engaging the North Vietnamese forces east of the combat base and recovering the bodies of the Marines killed in the February 25 ambush of the Bravo platoon.

After five agonizing weeks, haunted by the knowledge that their fallen brothers were lying unburied in a killing field nearby, Ken Pipes and his men had been unleashed to settle some unfinished business.

At 5:37 a.m., a platoon of Special Forces operators assigned to the morning's operation slipped out of the FOB-3 compound along the southwest perimeter of Khe Sanh Combat Base. Twenty-three minutes later, at 6:00 a.m. sharp, the fifty-odd Marines and corpsmen of 2nd Platoon of Bravo 1/26 marched through the southeastern perimeter wire and disappeared into the fog-shrouded gloom. The rest of the company followed, taut young Marines and corpsmen moving silently through rows of razor-sharp concertina wire and minefields, in search of a battalion or more of North Vietnamese Army soldiers dug in a short distance away to the east.[2]

O'Hara and the rest of the 2nd Platoon fanned out to secure the jumping-off point for the designated assault forces, Bravo's 1st and 3rd platoons. When everyone was in place, Ken Pipes issued a command that sent a chill through the ranks. "Fix bayonets," he ordered.

It was time for payback.[3]

• • •

To avoid the mistakes of the February disaster, the operation had been meticulously planned by Lieutenant Colonel Frederick J. McEwan, who had taken the battalion reins from James Wilkinson in mid-March, and McEwan's operations officer, Major Charles E. Davis III. Harry Baig, and his fire support colleagues had crafted a massive package of coordinated artillery missions and air strikes aimed at softening enemy defenses and suppressing the NVA fire.

The morning's fog had grounded the air strikes, but the artillery barrage got underway around 7:30 a.m. Variable-fused explosives burst above the ground to suppress enemy infantry forces, while smoke rounds dropped along ridgelines to blind and isolate enemy troops and artillery. Tear-gas rounds were mixed in to incapacitate the North Vietnamese forward observers directing mortars and artillery. Every depression and ravine, every knoll and ridgeline, was blanketed with a sophisticated combination of high explosives, anti-personnel munitions, smoke, and gas.[4]

Just before 8:00 a.m., using the fog as cover, the ground attack got underway. The assault forces surged ahead like two halves of a diamond—Bravo's 1st Platoon arrayed in a wedge, followed by 3rd Platoon in a V-formation. As Ken Pipes and his Marines pushed southeast toward the North Vietnamese lines, artillery fire moved in a rolling barrage to protect their flanks and maintain a wall of steel a little more than half a football field to their front.

A Bravo fire team moved briskly toward the first line of North Vietnamese trenches and bunkers as enemy mortars crumped and automatic-weapons fire rattled across the field. The two assault platoons spread out in a long skirmish line and attacked by squads, one fire team moving forward while two others covered them, leapfrogging ever closer to the enemy lines. Marines began to fall from the enemy fire, but the pent-up anger over the fate of the Jacques patrol now erupted in a collective fury. A detachment of combat engineers attached to Bravo for the assault began to pick off NVA machine-gun bunkers with flamethrowers and satchel charges. The Marines surged over the enemy fortifications, burning and blowing up the North Vietnamese defenders.

Behind the assault platoons, Captain Pipes and his command group hurried to keep pace with the fast-moving attack. At one point they piled into a bomb crater—Pipes, radioman Tom Quigley, artillery forward observer Hank Norman, and two other Marines—but North Vietnamese mortars quickly zeroed in on their position. "Get the hell out of here," Pipes yelled. "They've got us spotted."[5]

The Bravo command group bolted toward the front line of North Vietnamese trenches. Out of shape after the long inactivity of the siege, Quigley sweated heavily and gasped for breath under the weight of his radio. He was trying to run and fire his rifle at the same time, eyes scanning the ground around him for danger. A good buddy from training had been killed in an earlier fight when an NVA soldier had popped out of a hole and shot him in the back, and that thought now preoccupied Quigley.[6]

As Pipes led the command group forward, enemy mortar rounds clotted the sky, like a medieval battlefield darkened by arrows. The Bravo skipper was in midstride when he saw a blurred shape swoop toward him and heard a sound: *shooom*. A mortar round hit between his legs but didn't explode.[7]

It was a stroke of incredible good fortune for Pipes, but the triumph was short-lived. An NVA sniper took aim and squeezed the trigger. The bullet slammed into Pipes's helmet and pierced the manganese steel outer shell but stuck in the plastic liner, a fraction of an inch from penetrating the Bravo commander's skull. Pipes dropped to the ground, unconscious but not seriously injured.[8]

• • •

As Bravo Company pushed into the rolling terrain to the southeast, the Special Forces platoon out of FOB-3 moved toward the high ground to the south to block any flanking move by North Vietnamese forces around the base of Hill 471, an enemy stronghold since the early days of the siege.

Back inside the base, Lieutenant Bill Smith, the 1/26 battalion artillery officer, was following the action from the Bravo Company command post. From a bank of squawking radios he could make out the voices of Ken Pipes and radioman Tom Quigley, as well as a stream of transmissions from the artillery tactical network.

NVA mortar teams began firing blindly through the curtain of smoke and gas into the Bravo assault forces, and Smith heard someone on the receiving end of the enemy fire call in the development. He recognized the voice: it was his good friend, artillery forward observer Hank Norman, with the Bravo command group.

"We're taking incoming," Norman said above the roar of battle. He gave Smith a rough fix on the NVA gunners. Smith had just ordered a fire mission on the suspected location of the enemy mortars when he heard the telltale *shooom* of an incoming round over Hank Norman's open mike. The line went dead.[9]

• • •

Ken Pipes wasn't sure how long he was out after taking the sniper round through his helmet, but he awoke to find his command group intact and resumed the push forward. He and his group had reached the NVA trenches around 8:30 a.m. when the concentrated fire from twenty enemy 82-millimeter mortars exploded around them. Several pieces of metal ripped into the body of the Bravo commander, including one that tore into his chest and stopped an inch from his heart. Radioman Tom Quigley fell with shrapnel wounds to his torso and hand. First Lieutenant

Marion H. "Hank" Norman was killed instantly, and his radioman was severely wounded.[10]

Shaking off the pain and shock of his injuries, Ken Pipes grabbed Quigley's radio and asked for reinforcements. When the request was denied, the Bravo skipper ordered forward his reserves, Bravo's 2nd Platoon, under the command of First Lieutenant John W. Dillon. Bravo's assistant artillery forward observer, Ted Golab, reached the shattered Bravo command group, and with his radio operator helped restore communications with the battalion command post.

Under the direction of the badly injured Ken Pipes, the Bravo Marines forged ahead into the NVA defensive complex. In fiercely personal fights within the battle, the Americans set to work clearing every enemy trench, bunker, and spider hole.[11]

• • •

Corporal Steve Wiese, Bravo squad leader and February 25 ambush survivor, had been booked to leave Khe Sanh a few days earlier when he got bumped from his flight. As Wiese and his men began gearing up for their operation in the predawn of March 30, a Bravo sergeant had come by to inform the squad leader that a plane was coming in, and he should be on it. Wiese wouldn't hear of it.[12]

With bayonets fixed, Wiese and his squad had surged toward the North Vietnamese trenches. Screened by the fog, the Marines caught the enemy by surprise and rolled over the NVA soldiers. The North Vietnamese recovered quickly, and Wiese and his men found themselves under heavy automatic-weapons fire from enemy trenches and bunkers.

One of Wiese's men, a twenty-one-year-old machine gunner, Lance Corporal Wayne Moore of Plymouth, Massachusetts, jumped up and charged an enemy machine-gun bunker. He was hit three or four times and fell to the ground but somehow dragged himself to his feet. He was hit again and fell dead. Nearby, a twenty-year-old lance corporal from Glen Allen, Alabama, bearing the literary name Author C. Smith, jumped up and sprinted toward the enemy fire. Smith fought his way through an NVA trench and finished the job that Moore had started, taking out the machine-gun bunker, but he would fall before the morning was out.

Eighteen-year-old PFC David Bruce Anderson of Avoca, Iowa, and one other Marine—either nineteen-year-old PFC Ted Britt of Decatur, Georgia, or nineteen-year-old PFC Donald Rash from Pocahontas, Virginia—jumped up and screamed at the enemy, and the entire line surged forward. Anderson, Britt, and Rash were all killed, but the line of Marines continued ahead—screaming, running, throwing grenades, and firing. The North Vietnamese broke and ran, with the Americans on their heels.[13]

• • •

Corporal Ken Korkow had jumped at the chance to go out and kill NVA troops face-to-face, and he had demonstrated his improvisational skills earlier in the fight by using his 60-millimeter mortar tube and a modified round to pick off a couple of enemy soldiers firing at the Marines from a spider hole. As the battle was winding down, Korkow began dashing into harm's way to retrieve wounded Marines and carry them back to an aid station set up in a bomb crater by Bravo's executive officer, Lieutenant Ben Long, and Corporal Steve Wiese.

Korkow was poised to retrieve yet another Marine calling for help when Long ordered him to take cover in the intensifying NVA fire. Standing his ground on the crater rim, defiantly exposing himself to the enemy, Korkow shouted a devil-may-care challenge down to Long and Wiese: "Come out and enjoy the war!"[14]

The words had barely left his mouth when three NVA 61-millimeter mortar rounds slammed into the ground nearby, shredding Korkow's body with hot metal shards. Ben Long and Steve Wiese rushed to their grievously injured comrade and walked him back to a triage area in the rear as bullets whizzed around them.[15] A corpsman offered Korkow morphine to dull his pain, but he waved it off with a wisecrack. "You trying to make a hippie out of me?" As he lay on the ground, his face and body drenched with blood, Korkow still seethed with bloodlust toward the NVA. "Kill them," he exhorted his comrades. "Get those bastards."[16]

• • •

Lieutenant John Dillon's 2nd Platoon reached the rows of NVA trenches and found dead enemy soldiers piled on top of each other, the work of Wiese's squad and other Bravo Marines who had gone before them. Corporal Michael O'Hara ran ahead to a bomb crater and found four or five North Vietnamese dead, along with a wounded Navy corpsman, Dick Blanchfield, whose arm had nearly been severed by a mortar shell. O'Hara dressed the corpsman's injuries and resumed his advance. Blanchfield would survive.[17]

Radioman Tom Quigley was on his feet but was growing faint and nauseous from the loss of blood. "How bad is it, doc?" he asked a corpsman examining him. "Not bad at all," the corpsman lied, as he tried to stanch the blood flow from Quigley's numerous shrapnel wounds. Quigley dropped to his knees, and a pair of Marines helped him back to a casualty collection point. Around him wounded and dying Marines lay on the ground, some moaning in agony.[18]

At 9:45 a.m., the Bravo Marines began to execute an orderly withdrawal from the devastated NVA positions. A tracked utility vehicle rumbled out of the base to collect the wounded. Ignoring his own severe wounds, Tom Quigley grabbed an M-16 with a full magazine and climbed aboard to provide security. The vehicle, filled with injured Marines and corpsmen, began the slow trek back to Charlie Med.

As bloodied Marines fell back to the base, scattered gunfire continued to crackle and artillery shells roared overhead. Michael O'Hara came upon Captain Pipes, soaked in blood from head to toe, shrapnel above his heart, but still working two radios and barking orders. Beside him was the lifeless body of Lieutenant Hank Norman, the affable artillery observer.

O'Hara picked up Norman's body, raised him to his right shoulder, and set off for the combat base. An armored personnel carrier had emerged to gather up dead Marines, and O'Hara made his way to it. Ever so gently, he placed Hank Norman's body in the back.

Despite his injuries, Ken Pipes remained on his feet, overseeing the pullback of his men until its completion at 11:30 a.m. Only then would Pipes agree to have his wounds treated at Charlie Med.

Ten Marines had died in the Bravo assault, and two were missing. Another one hundred Americans had been wounded, including forty-nine whose injuries were serious enough to require evacuation. On the other side of the battlefield, 115 North Vietnamese soldiers had been killed, and an unknown number wounded. The Bravo Marines had driven the North Vietnamese from their doorstep, but another objective—recovering their dead from the February ambush—had not been achieved. There had been too much fighting, so only two bodies had been brought back to the base. Completion of that grim task, the final piece of unfinished business from the February 25 tragedy, would be left to another day.

For Ken Pipes, the anguish of the Jacques ambush would never diminish. But the hatred and anger that had fueled the extraordinary assault his men carried out to ruthless perfection on March 30, 1968, would fade with time. "Those guys on the other side were following orders, just like we were," Pipes said forty-four years later, as he recalled the two days at Khe Sanh in 1968 that had left such a deep imprint on his life. "It was our job to make them pay, and we made them pay—as much as they could pay."[19]

•   •   •

The following morning, March 31, a Bravo sergeant stuck his head in Steve Wiese's hooch. "There's a plane landing as we speak," the sergeant said. "Get your shit, get down there, and get on it."[20]

Wiese had survived seventeen months of combat in Vietnam. He had survived the ambush of February 25 and the March 30 assault. Over half the Marines killed the previous day were from Wiese's squad, a testament to the courage of Wiese and his men as they charged headlong into NVA fire. Khe Sanh had taken its toll on Steve Wiese, and it would continue to do so in the decades ahead. But he was a survivor, and now he was going home.

CHAPTER 22

Breakout

As Steve Wiese exited Khe Sanh on Sunday morning, March 31, President Lyndon Johnson was contemplating his own dramatic departure.

March had been another dismal month for the American president. The crew of the US Navy spy ship *Pueblo* remained in captivity in North Korea, with Johnson seemingly powerless to secure their release. The potential for disaster at Khe Sanh had eased, but looming enemy threats elsewhere in Vietnam had led General Westmoreland to request more than 200,000 additional troops—a dramatic escalation in a war that the president and his commander on the ground had claimed was winding down.

The siege at Khe Sanh and the Tet Offensive had accelerated the president's plummeting approval ratings: by late March, only 26 percent of Americans approved of Johnson's handling of the war, and 36 percent approved of his overall job performance.[1] Westmoreland's troop request had become another political debacle for Johnson, splashed across the front page of the *New York Times* on Sunday, March 10, chipping away further at the president's credibility. If the Tet Offensive had been a last-ditch gambit by the Communists, as Johnson and Westmoreland claimed, why were an additional 200,000 troops needed in Vietnam?

In any other year, Johnson might have shrugged off his sagging poll numbers, but a presidential election was looming, and the war had galvanized a serious primary challenge. On March 12, Senator Eugene Mc-

Carthy of Minnesota had ridden antiwar sentiment to a stunning second-place finish in the New Hampshire primary, polling 42 percent to Johnson's 49 percent. Four days later, Johnson's greatest political fear became reality when Senator Robert F. Kennedy announced his candidacy for the Democratic nomination.

Political concerns, however, were secondary to the life-and-death decisions Johnson now faced in Vietnam. He had poured more than 500,000 American troops into the war, and now he was being asked to raise that amount by another 40 percent. Should he bow to the pressure from hawks and authorize still more manpower, more bombing, and more extensive ground operations, including strikes into Cambodia, Laos, and North Vietnam?

Burdened by those questions, and battered by a flurry of critical news articles and broadcasts calling for a reassessment of his Vietnam policy, Johnson flew to Minneapolis, Minnesota, on the spur of the moment on March 18 to deliver a speech calling for a "total national effort to win the war."[2] But his appeal had fallen flat, and political advisers warned Johnson of a disaster in his upcoming Democratic primary test in Wisconsin. Scrambling to contain fallout from the setbacks in Vietnam, Johnson scheduled a nationally televised address on the war for Sunday evening, March 31.

As Johnson debated his advisers over what to say, he took steps to give himself more flexibility in Vietnam. He revealed to reporters that he had decided to bring General Westmoreland back home to become Army chief of staff in the summer and retire his hawkish military chief in the Pacific, Admiral U. S. Grant Sharp.

Behind closed doors, Johnson continued to reject pressure to dial back the war, a position now advocated vociferously in the White House inner circle by new Defense Secretary Clark Clifford, a hawk on Vietnam whose views had been changed by Khe Sanh and Tet. On March 25 and 26, Johnson had convened a supergroup of advisers known informally as the "Wise Old Men." At Johnson's behest, the men had met in November to discuss Vietnam and had given unanimous support to the president's prosecution of the war. Now, the former generals, ambassadors, and cabinet secretaries recommended by a two-to-one margin that the president avoid further escalation and rethink his strategy in Vietnam. Lyndon Johnson was stunned.

At 9:00 p.m., on Sunday night, March 31, with his wife, Lady Bird, and daughters, Lynda and Luci, looking on, Johnson cast his tired gaze across his Oval Office desk into a bank of television cameras and radio microphones set to relay his speech across America, and throughout Vietnam, via Armed Forces Radio. "Tonight I want to speak to you of peace in Vietnam and Southeast Asia," Johnson began. "No other question so preoccupies our people."

Johnson continued as he had so often before, condemning Communist aggression, denouncing the Tet Offensive as "a savage assault on the people, the government and the allies of South Vietnam." The enemy had "failed to achieve its principal objectives" Johnson flatly declared, but he warned that "the Communists may renew their attack any day."

Abruptly shifting gears, Johnson turned to the new centerpiece of his radically rewritten speech: an olive branch to the leaders of North Vietnam. Johnson offered to ease the US bombing campaign, if only the Communists would engage in serious negotiations.[3]

Johnson concluded the remarks released in advance to news organizations and US diplomats around the world, and then began reading from a carefully crafted postscript. His closest advisers knew the burdens weighing on Johnson—the stress and sleepless nights that had mounted as the campaign against Khe Sanh played out and the Communist attacks against the South Vietnamese cities unfolded, the anguish that had beset Johnson as he watched his presidency crumble amid the soaring costs and political divisions unleashed by the war. He faced almost certain defeat in his looming political tests—if not in the primaries, then in the general election in November. He had come to feel as though he were facing "a giant stampede coming at me from all directions."[4]

Publicly, Johnson cast in noble terms the stunning announcement that capped his speech: "I shall not seek and will not accept the nomination of my party for another term as your president." He would walk away from the White House in January.[5]

During the seventy days that had passed since January 21, Khe Sanh had been a nagging preoccupation for Johnson. He had feared that Khe Sanh would become a military disaster that would sink his administration, so he had been drawn to the White House basement Situation Room on the restless nights that increasingly haunted him. He would read the latest cables and casualty reports and gaze on the terrain model of the Khe Sanh plateau and surrounding hills, a landscape now consecrated with American blood, sweat, and tears. Again and again, Johnson had asked his generals: Can Khe Sanh hold?

Khe Sanh *had* held. Lyndon Johnson's presidency was in ruins, but the hard and bloody work of the American and South Vietnamese fighting men at Khe Sanh had spared the president the final indignity of "another damn Dien Bien Phu."

• • •

As Lyndon Johnson began speaking to the American people, it was already Monday morning, April 1, in Vietnam, and the operation to retake Route 9 and drive North Vietnamese forces from their positions around Khe Sanh had been underway for four hours.[6]

Operation Pegasus, as it was christened, was under the command of Major General John J. Tolson III, US Army, and the forces at his disposal were his 1st Air Cavalry Division, the 1st Marine Regiment, and the 3rd ARVN Airborne Task Force. Operational control of the 26th Marine Regiment at Khe Sanh had also passed to Tolson—one of several developments that had not pleased the Marines, who had never wanted to be tied down at Khe Sanh in the first place and now bristled at the implication that the Army had to bail them out.[7]

Pegasus had grown out of contingency planning undertaken by General Westmoreland in late January, amid Washington's fears of a looming disaster at Khe Sanh. The Tet Offensive and bad weather had pushed an overland relief operation to the back burner, and Tolson's 1st Air Cavalry troopers had been thrown into the fight at Hue. After the battle of Hue ended, plans for Pegasus had been finalized in March, and a staging base known as Landing Zone Stud was constructed at Ca Lu, nine miles east of Khe Sanh.

The operation began at 7:00 a.m. on April 1 with two battalions of Marines—the 2nd Battalion, 1st Marine Regiment, and 2nd Battalion, 3rd Marine Regiment—pushing west along Route 9 in an armor-supported thrust. The Marines fanned out to secure the high ground north and south of the road, and their comrades of the 11th Engineer Battalion went to work rebuilding Route 9 between Ca Lu and Khe Sanh.

As the Marines advanced overland, elements of Tolson's 3rd Brigade, 1st Air Cavalry Division, thundered into the skies in helicopter assaults aimed at driving the North Vietnamese from key terrain features that dominated Route 9 and the eastern approach to Khe Sanh. By April 4, Tolson's cavalrymen were in combat with North Vietnamese forces that remained south and southeast of the combat base.

• • •

As Pegasus progressed, restrictions on offensive operations by the defenders of Khe Sanh were lifted, and the Marines pushed outward in search of the North Vietnamese.

At 6:00 a.m. on April 4, three companies of the 1st Battalion, 9th Marines, moved southeast from their positions at the rock quarry to challenge the NVA forces still holding Hill 471, south of the Khe Sanh perimeter. Command of the Walking Dead had passed from Lieutenant Colonel John Mitchell to Lieutenant Colonel John Cahill only three days earlier, and now, after American artillery had pounded the hill, Cahill led his men up the slopes of 471. An NVA mortar round hit in the middle of Cahill's command group, wounding the battalion commander and several others and killing two men, but the 1/9 overwhelmed the light enemy resistance around 5:20 p.m.

During the night, the NVA battered the Marines on 471 with mortars and artillery, and at 5:15 the following morning, April 5, a North Vietnamese battalion charged up the hill. The men of the 1/9 held, just as they had at Hill 64, and the bodies of 122 North Vietnamese soldiers lay scattered on the slopes. One Marine was killed and nineteen wounded.

At 1:50 p.m. on Saturday, April 6, a company of South Vietnamese soldiers from the 3rd ARVN Airborne Task Force became the first troops of Operation Pegasus to enter Khe Sanh Combat Base. The ground and skies around Khe Sanh, meanwhile, boomed and crackled with the sounds of artillery duels, air strikes, and ground engagements throughout the day.

Among the American units on the move was a platoon from Captain Ken Pipes's Bravo 1/26. With the men of Delta 1/26, the Bravo Marines

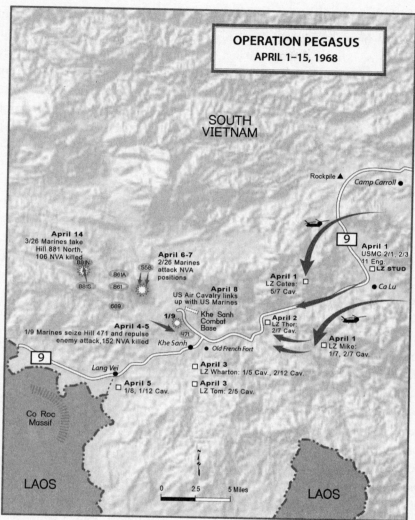

OPERATION PEGASUS
APRIL 1–15, 1968

SOUTH
VIETNAM

Rockpile ▲ Camp Carroll ●

9

April 1
USMC 2/1, 2/3
11 Eng.
□ **LZ STUD**

April 1
LZ Cates:
5/7 Cav.

● Ca Lu

April 14
3/26 Marines take
Hill 881 North,
106 NVA killed
881N

861A 558
881S 861

689

April 6-7
2/26 Marines
attack NVA
positions

April 8
US Air Cavalry links
up with US Marines

1/9 Khe Sanh
Combat
Base

April 2
□ LZ Thor:
2/7 Cav.

April 1
□ LZ Mike:
1/7, 2/7 Cav.

April 4-5
1/9 Marines seize Hill 471 and repulse
enemy attack, 152 NVA killed

471
Khe Sanh ● ● Old French Fort

9

Lang Vei

□ **April 3**
LZ Wharton: 1/5 Cav., 2/12 Cav.

□ **April 5**
1/8, 1/12 Cav.

□ **April 3**
LZ Tom: 2/5 Cav.

Co Roc
Massif

LAOS LAOS

0   2.5   5 Miles

Operation Pegasus, April 1–15, 1968.

returned to the scene of the Jacques patrol to recover the remains of
twenty-one fallen comrades.

•   •   •

From his perch on Hill 861, artillery forward observer Dennis Mannion
witnessed one of the actions of April 6. The Marines of Golf Company

2/26 had moved from their outpost on Hill 558 to secure a prominent ridgeline between Hill 861 and Khe Sanh Combat Base, and they had reached the crest of the ridge when they were ambushed by NVA soldiers in camouflaged bunkers. Mannion watched the battle unfold through his naval binoculars and witnessed a terrible moment in the fight when an enemy shell dropped from the sky and blew up two Americans.[8] Mannion had moved back to his bunker around 3:00 p.m. when two NVA mortars hidden in a draw about a mile away opened fire on 861. In the early days of the siege, Mannion had pushed pieces of fiberglass armor beneath the camouflage cover of his helmet to give himself extra protection, and one of these plates now saved his life. An 82-millimeter mortar round exploded above and behind him, spraying his head and upper body with shrapnel. A chunk of metal shattered one of the fiberglass plates and dented his steel helmet but stopped short of his skull. Other pieces of hot metal punctured his flak jacket, and one sliver ripped into his right bicep. Once again, Mannion had come within a few inches of death.

A corpsman suggested a trip down to Charlie Med, but Mannion wanted no part of the risky journey. The corpsman probed the wound until he managed to pull an inch-long sliver of metal from Mannion's arm. He stitched the hole, applied a sterile dressing and bandage, and sent Mannion on his way.[9]

• • •

As the American forces pushed through the scarred landscape around Khe Sanh, they stumbled onto more gruesome evidence of the punishment wrought by Operation Niagara. The remains of hundreds of dead NVA soldiers were scattered through the hilly jungle, some hastily buried in shallow graves, others lying where they had fallen.

On April 7, after three days of fighting, troopers of the 2nd Brigade, 1st Air Cavalry, captured the old French fort near the intersection of Route 9 and the access road leading to the combat base. At the same time, 3rd Brigade troopers completed the work of clearing Route 9 around Khe Sanh village and Lang Vei.

At 8:00 a.m. on April 8, the official linkup between the US Army cavalry troopers of Operation Pegasus and the Marines who had successfully defended Khe Sanh Combat Base through seventy-seven days of siege occurred with an improvised flourish. As the lead cavalrymen marched into the combat base, a twenty-four-year-old trooper, Lieutenant Joseph E. Abodeely, blasted "Charge!" on an old French bugle captured from one of the North Vietnamese units that had laid siege to Khe Sanh.[10]

Three days later, crews of the 11th Engineers completed the work of rebuilding Route 9, and Khe Sanh's overland lifeline was opened for traffic.

• • •

As trucks and tracked vehicles rolled into the Marine combat base and back down Route 9 for the first time since the previous summer, the quixotic "lion of Khe Sanh" took his leave. Colonel David Lownds had spent nine months at Khe Sanh, and the mustachioed, cigar-smoking commander of the 26th Marines had become the face of the siege for many Americans. He had angered the Army advisory team at Khe Sanh village and the Special Forces at Lang Vei by refusing their pleas for relief when they came under attack, and he had disappointed some of his own men by failing to do more to save the ambushed Bravo patrol on February 25. But for all the criticism he would face, then and later, David Lownds delivered on his vow to defend Khe Sanh Combat Base. Now, on April 12, Lownds handed off command of the 26th Marines to Colonel Bruce F. Myers and left Khe Sanh for good.

That same day, word flew through the trenches of Hill 861: pack your gear, and be ready to leave in less than an hour.[11] There was no word on their destination, but it was somewhere away from this blood-stained hill that had been their home since late December.

Artillery forward observer Dennis Mannion scrambled aboard a CH-46 along with several other Marines, and the helicopter cleared the hill and banked to the right. Within seconds, it became clear their destination was 881 South. The bird descended to an LZ, and Mannion and his comrades bolted left and right into the nearest trench.

The weary Marines of India Company didn't bother to welcome their guests or invite them into their bunkers and bunny holes, so the men of Kilo Company sought shelter wherever they could find it. Feeling like a hermit crab pulled from its shell, Mannion crawled beneath the carcass of a wrecked CH-46. He lay there for a while, disoriented by his abrupt departure from the hill that would be part of him forever.

Later in the day, Mannion went to Bill Dabney's command bunker to listen to a briefing that laid out why they were there. When he heard they were going to assault 881 North, a North Vietnamese base for infantry, mortars, and rocket batteries throughout the siege, Mannion immediately recalled news stories about the bloody Hill Fights the previous spring. He thought, *This is going to be really bad.*

At nightfall of the following day, April 13, the Marines of Kilo Company filed through the wire of 881 South and made their way down the northern slope. Around an hour later, they reached their destination, a terrain feature known as Hill 800, nearly 900 yards north of 881 South. They dug in as best they could with machetes and knives, then waited nervously for the night to pass. At first light, they would attempt to retake the North Vietnamese stronghold that had caused so much misery for the Marines since January.

• • •

In the predawn darkness of Easter Sunday, April 14, 1968, six hundred Marines of the 3rd Battalion, 26th Marines, began their ascent up the shell-cratered slope of 881 North. The NVA soldiers who waited in camouflaged bunkers and holes had been pounded with explosives and napalm for weeks on end, and now they faced the wrath of Kilo, Lima, and Mike companies of the 3/26.

As the Americans advanced, air strikes pounded the ridgelines above, followed by friendly artillery rounds that marched up the slopes ahead of the surging Marines. In the fog-shrouded dawn, the Marines of India Company joined the battle, sweeping the hillside ahead of their comrades with .50-caliber machine guns and eight recoilless rifles.

The fire rattled and roared over the heads of the Americans as they scrambled up the scarred slope. The *pop-pop-pop* of AK-47 rifles sounded, signaling the presence of enemy soldiers.

On the far right, Dennis Mannion was in constant radio contact with Charlie Battery 1/13 at the combat base, keeping the artillery fire just ahead of Kilo's Marines as they surged up the slope. The men of Kilo Company met only light resistance, and when they reached the summit of their objective, a lone NVA holdout bolted from his hiding place about fifty yards ahead of the Marines. Mannion and at least five other Marines opened fire, and the enemy soldier collapsed to the ground.

As the Kilo Marines swarmed the right flank of the hill and set up a 360° perimeter, the acrid smell of gunpowder and artillery propellant hung heavily in the morning air. Ten or twelve NVA dead were sprawled on the ground, some half out of their spider holes or at the door of bunkers, apparently killed by artillery fire or air strikes. Someone in the Kilo command group had an American flag, and Mannion and a comrade hoisted a Marine into the skeleton of one of the few remaining trees. The flag was tied in place, and a breeze unfurled the Stars and Stripes over the far right of the enemy stronghold.

• • •

On the American left, the Marines of Lima Company, 3/26, ascended a series of undulating slopes on the southern face of 881 North in a flurry of enemy rifle fire and Chicom grenades. Among those experiencing close combat for the first time was nineteen-year-old Neil Kenny, a salty-tongued high school dropout from Brooklyn, New York. Kenny had joined Lima 3/26 at Khe Sanh in January, and in March, he had celebrated his birthday in the Lima Company lines along Khe Sanh's western perimeter. Now, shaking off his fear, Kenny charged ahead, dropped behind the slender remains of a shell-scarred tree, and sprayed the slope to his right and left with M-16 fire.[12]

Kenny's squad piled into a large bomb crater and scanned the slope above them as another Lima platoon surged past. Ahead, an NVA soldier popped from a hole and stitched a passing Marine with AK-47 fire, knocking the young American back down the hill. "Holy shit! Look at those cartwheels!" Kenny yelled, unable to stifle his horrified amazement at the acrobatics a human body could perform when hit by a burst of 7.62-millimeter projectiles traveling at 715 meters a second. Kenny was still processing the shocking image when nineteen-year-old artillery forward observer Philip Francis Sheridan, a handsome, well-built Marine from Long Island, New York, sprinted past with his .45-caliber pistol drawn. Within a few steps, Sheridan collapsed to the ground with a mortal wound.

As the squad of Lima Marines clambered from the bomb crater and closed on the final crest, they passed the young American whose violent cartwheels had mesmerized Neil Kenny. He was propped against a tree, his torso pierced by at least four AK-47 rounds. A corpsman was trying to keep him alive, shaking him, yelling, "Stay with me! Stay with me!" But the young Marine was slipping away fast, and his lifeless eyes were already locked on some distant place, far beyond the horrors of Khe Sanh.[13]

• • •

Across the enemy stronghold, Marines enraged by months of punishment at the hands of the North Vietnamese boiled up and over the crest, overrunning bunkers and trenches, shooting and bayoneting NVA soldiers who had survived the American air strikes and artillery. When a group of terrified NVA survivors fled their crumbling bunkers and crowded into a patch of open ground, an officer ordered the Marines to allow air and artillery to finish the bloody work. But the Marines plunged ahead, shooting and bayoneting the last North Vietnamese on the hill.

Kilo Company reported its objective secured at 2:28 p.m. on April 14, 1968, and a short time later the rest of Hill 881 North was officially reclaimed by US Marines. The three companies of the 3/26 had lost twenty-seven men in the Easter assault, including six dead. They had killed more than one hundred North Vietnamese troops and captured two soldiers of the 8th Battalion, 29th Regiment, 325th NVA Division.

• • •

The Marines savored their victory for barely thirty minutes, and then the order was passed: prepare to pull back. It didn't make any sense to the men who had spent the day driving the enemy off the hill, but they retraced their steps back down the slope. It was the second time in less than twelve months that Marines had died in the conquest of 881 North, only to give it up without a fight.

• • •

The withdrawal plan called for Captain Paul Snead's Kilo Company to reoccupy Hill 800 in between the two dominant peaks and act as a blocking force against any NVA counterattack, while the Marines of Lima and Mike Companies completed the hard slog back up 881 South.

The men of Kilo Company reached their assigned positions about 4:30 p.m. and set to work deepening the fighting holes they had dug the previous night. Fog and mist rolled in, and the night came alive with shapes and shadows. Time slowed, and then stopped, as the Marines peered into the impenetrable night, rifles and machine guns at the ready, awaiting the expected NVA counterattack.

But the North Vietnamese never appeared, and the Marines of Kilo Company lived to welcome another foggy Khe Sanh dawn. It was April 15, 1968.

• • •

As the Kilo Marines prepared to move out, the epic battle marked another milestone: at 8:00 a.m., General Tolson declared the relief of Khe Sanh complete, and Operation Pegasus terminated. Officially, 205 Americans died in Operation Scotland, which entailed the defense of Khe Sanh, from November 1967 through March 31, 1968. During the two weeks of Pegasus, the Americans lost another ninety-two men killed in action, 667 wounded, and five missing. South Vietnamese forces reported thirty-three men killed in action and 187 wounded. North Vietnamese Army losses were estimated at 1,100 killed, with another thirteen captured.

• • •

The official declaration that the siege had been broken and Khe Sanh secured was an administrative fiction, a fact readily apparent to the men still in harm's way. For six Americans scattered about the Khe Sanh plateau, April 15 would be their last day on earth. For Dennis Mannion, it would be the saddest day of his Vietnam tour.

Four CH-46 helicopters had been summoned to ferry Kilo Company from Hill 800 down to Khe Sanh Combat Base. As the first Sea Knight came into view and settled into the LZ hacked from the rubble, Mannion lay sprawled in a crater nearby, shooting the breeze with one of his favorite people in Kilo. First Lieutenant Benjamin Stephen Fordham had spent his formative years in Monterrey, Mexico, where his father was an executive for an American multinational corporation. Returning to the States for college, Steve Fordham, as his friends knew him, had graduated from Baylor University in Waco, Texas, then entered the Marines.

Mannion and Fordham had worked closely together on Hill 861 after Fordham's platoon had occupied the hill's northwest perimeter, and in the process they had become good friends. They shared books their families sent them and had good-natured arguments about college football—Mannion the diehard Notre Dame stalwart, Fordham the Texas Longhorn surrogate. Most nights they would head over to the Kilo command post together to go over call signs and other protocol and then make their way back to Mannion's bunker to share a cup of hot chocolate and conversation. They had survived their hard time on 861, and they had survived the charge up 881 North, and now, with a little luck, they were going to survive Hill 800 and have one more story to tell about their days together at Khe Sanh.

Unknown to the Marines, a North Vietnamese artillery spotter had drawn a bead on them, and as the first Sea Knight lifted off with one of Kilo's rifle platoons, two mortar rounds streaked from the sky and smacked into the hillside nearby. The NVA mortar team was adjusting its aim as a second helicopter arrived and swooped away with another Kilo platoon. Mannion was preparing to scramble aboard the third chopper with the Kilo command group when Steve Fordham squeezed his hand and called out above the roar of the rotors, "See you at the combat base."[14]

The third CH-46 had pulled away with Captain Snead and the command group when a pair of mortar rounds hit the hill, killing three men: Lieutenant Steve Fordham, Lance Corporal William Matthews Jr., and PFC Patrick Patterson. PFC Charles McLaurin died of his wounds on April 24. They were the final Khe Sanh casualties for Kilo 3/26.

• • •

The 26th Marines had completed their work at Khe Sanh, and responsibility for the combat base now fell to the 1st Marine Regiment. Most of the Marines who had survived the siege would be gone by the third week of April, enjoying their first hot meals and showers in three months at bases near the coast. But death continued to stalk the defenders of Khe Sanh until the moment of their departure.

In mid-April, Captain Earle Breeding's Echo 2/26 had made its way from its outpost on 861 Alpha down to the combat base to await transportation out of Khe Sanh. On April 17, several Echo men were bathing in a stream north of the perimeter wire when NVA rockets or artillery rounds landed among them. Two Navy corpsmen were killed and several men wounded. Rifleman Michael Worth held the hand of corpsman Charles T. Langenfeld as he died, calling for his mother in his final moments.[15]

• • •

The end of Operation Pegasus on April 15 marked the beginning of Operation Scotland II, and a new ledger of the fighting and dying around Khe Sanh was begun.

On April 16, the ill-fated Alpha Company of the 1st Battalion, 9th Marines, stumbled into a North Vietnamese bunker complex on the slopes near Hill 689, and a disaster ensued. Two companies of the Walking Dead were fed piecemeal into the fight, and before the Marines could break contact, another forty-one Americans were dead, thirty-two wounded, and fifteen missing—some inadvertently left behind in the confusion. One Marine left by his comrades managed to elude marauding bands of NVA soldiers as they executed American wounded, and at dawn on April 17, and again the following day, his cries for help could be heard by comrades several hundred yards away. The intrepid Marine and one other American were finally rescued by an Army helicopter crew.

• • •

Bloody fighting between American and North Vietnamese forces continued to flare along Route 9 and nameless ridgelines around Khe Sanh through the late spring. By the end of June, another 308 Marines had been killed in Operation Scotland II around Khe Sanh.

Back home, Khe Sanh remained in the news. On May 23, Colonel David Lownds and the regimental sergeant major of the 26th Marines were the guests of honor at a White House ceremony. President Lyndon Johnson presented Lownds with a Presidential Unit Citation for the work of his men in holding Khe Sanh.

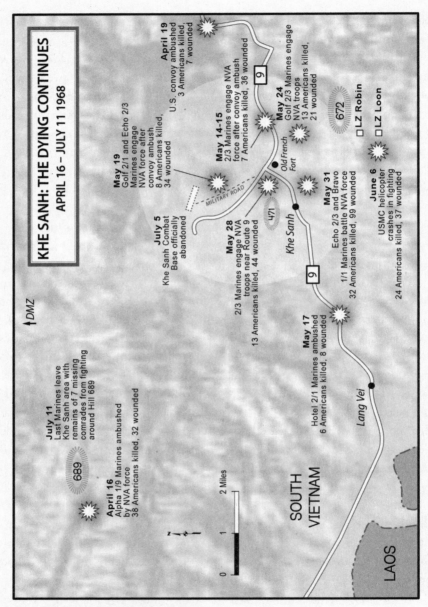

KHE SANH: THE DYING CONTINUES
APRIL 16 – JULY 11 1968

DMZ

April 19
U.S. convoy ambushed
3 Americans killed,
7 wounded

April 19
Golf 2/1 and Echo 2/3
Marines engage
NVA force after
convoy ambush
8 Americans killed,
34 wounded

May 14-15
2/3 Marines engage NVA
force after convoy ambush
7 Americans killed, 36 wounded

May 24
Golf 2/3 Marines engage
NVA troops
13 Americans killed,
21 wounded

9

672

□ LZ Robin
□ LZ Loon

Old French
Fort

July 5
Khe Sanh Combat
Base officially
abandoned

471

May 28
2/3 Marines engage NVA
troops near Route 9
13 Americans killed, 44 wounded

Khe Sanh

May 31
Echo 2/3 and Bravo
1/1 Marines battle NVA force
32 Americans killed, 99 wounded

June 6
USMC helicopter
crashes in fighting
24 Americans killed, 37 wounded

MILITARY ROAD

9

May 17
Hotel 2/1 Marines ambushed
6 Americans killed, 8 wounded

July 11
Last Marines leave
Khe Sanh area with
remains of 7 missing
comrades from fighting
around Hill 689

689

April 16
Alpha 1/9 Marines ambushed
by NVA force
38 Americans killed, 32 wounded

Lang Vei

**SOUTH
VIETNAM**

2 Miles

N

0   1

LAOS

Final Actions, April 16–July 11, 1968.

From the beginning, the Marines had questioned General Westmoreland's decision to tie down a combat company, and, eventually, a reinforced regiment, at such a remote location. The siege had amplified the questions about the strategic wisdom of Westmoreland's commitment to Khe Sanh, and those questions flared into open debate when a young American reporter for the *Baltimore Sun*, Army veteran John Carroll, broke the story that Khe Sanh Combat Base would be abandoned. The explanation given by MACV spokesmen in Saigon was that changed tactical conditions had reduced Khe Sanh's importance to American strategic plans.

On June 11, General Westmoreland left Vietnam. Eight days later, his successor, General Creighton W. Abrams, commenced Operation Charlie—the destruction and evacuation of Khe Sanh Combat Base. North Vietnamese forces harassed and bled the Marines to the end, shelling the base and launching a company-strength infantry probe on July 1 that claimed the lives of two Marines.

The base was officially closed on July 5, and the Marines withdrew down Route 9. Several hundred Marines remained in the area, searching for the bodies of comrades who had disappeared in the fighting of the previous months.

In the days that followed, another ten Marines died in clashes with the North Vietnamese. Among them was Private First Class Robert Hernandez of Alpha Company, 1st Battalion, 1st Marines, killed when an NVA mortar hit his position. The following day, July 11, 1968, the last US Marines left Khe Sanh with the remains of seven missing comrades.[16]

EPILOGUE

Dennis Mannion was still in I Corps, near the DMZ, in the early summer of 1968 when a buddy threw a copy of *Stars and Stripes* at him. "Hey, you were at Khe Sanh," the Marine said. "Take a look at this shit!" Mannion was stunned when he saw the headlines about Khe Sanh Combat Base being closed.

"It was almost too hard to believe," he says. "My immediate thought was: we never gave back Tarawa or Iwo Jima, so why this? It made all that we had endured and sacrificed seem almost trivial or unnecessary. Why go through all those months of misery just to have someone decide some months later the place wasn't worth it? I wasn't angry so much as stunned—like I had been punched in the jaw."

Mannion walked to a small observation bunker at the top of a sand dune to be alone with his thoughts as he stared out into the DMZ. "I felt sad and pretty isolated from everyone else and from the war itself," Mannion says. It was the emotional end for him, the moment when he reached the hard conclusion that the war in Vietnam, at least the way it was being run, "was not worth it."

The abandonment of Khe Sanh bothered Mannion for years. In time, he would take a more philosophical view, concluding that "the military higher-ups do what they want, when they want, for the bigger picture. The troops just pay the price."

As a nineteen-year-old rifleman with Bravo 1/26 at Khe Sanh, Michael O'Hara didn't have any sense of the war's strategic or political goals. He learned all that in the decades that followed, but he never wavered in his belief that America's intentions in Vietnam were just. In walking away from Vietnam, he says, America's political and military leaders "not only let down the Vietnamese people, but they broke faith with those brave young men who believed in something larger than themselves: Freedom for all the world's people. President Kennedy called and we answered."

Still, O'Hara speaks for many, if not most, Khe Sanh veterans when he says that he would do it all again. "Khe Sanh, and the men who defended the combat base and the surrounding hills, made me who I am today and I am happy with that outcome."

• • •

The debate about Khe Sanh commenced on the eve of the battle in January 1968, with columnist Joseph Alsop conjuring the ghosts of Dien Bien Phu, and it continues to this day.

Who won? Who lost? Was General Westmoreland duped by his North Vietnamese nemesis, General Vo Nguyen Giap? Were the North Vietnamese serious about seizing Khe Sanh or merely drawing American forces away from urban areas before the Tet Offensive? Was Khe Sanh an American "fiasco," as journalist Stanley Karnow concluded?

Khe Sanh and Tet weighed heavily on the war-weary American psyche in the winter and spring of 1968, and the abandonment of the combat base and outposts less than three months after the siege helped foster the perception of Khe Sanh as a defeat. But these facts are indisputable: the American stronghold at Khe Sanh was successfully defended against a much larger North Vietnamese force, with losses only a fraction of those sustained by the North Vietnamese (even after allowing for the padded body counts of Westmoreland's MACV headquarters). These are not the elements of defeat, much less a fiasco.

The abandonment of Khe Sanh Combat Base was a propaganda victory for the North Vietnamese, but the Americans pulled back only a few miles along Route 9 to a new base at Ca Lu, which was easier to supply and defend. Just as they had at Khe Sanh, US forces operating out of Ca Lu continued to carry out mobile infantry and reconnaissance operations against the North Vietnamese along the border with Laos, as noted by Khe Sanh veteran and scholar Peter Brush. Nothing had changed, except for public perceptions of the war back home in America.

• • •

Nearly fifty years later, Khe Sanh remains wrapped in riddles and mysteries. Beyond the overarching mystery about NVA objectives, one of the most baffling questions is this: Why didn't the North Vietnamese cut Khe Sanh's water supply? Legendary Marine Lieutenant General Victor H. Krulak interpreted the North Vietnamese failure in this regard as an indication that the enemy may have "had no intention of undertaking an all-out assault on the base."[1] But Westmoreland's intelligence chief at the time, General Phillip Davidson, concluded that "the simplest explanation—and probably the most valid—is that neither Giap nor the local NVA commander ever realized the vulnerability of the Marines' water supply. Stranger oversights have happened in war."[2]

It's plausible, but I doubt we will ever know with any certainty.

The same is true about the debate over whether Khe Sanh was a North Vietnamese ruse.

General Giap's comments about Khe Sanh to the Italian journalist Oriana Fallaci are exactly what one would expect. "Oh, no," he was quoted as saying, "Khe Sanh didn't try to be, nor could it have been, a Dien Bien Phu. Khe Sanh wasn't that important to us. Or it was only to the extent that it was important to the Americans—in fact, at Khe Sanh their prestige was at stake."[3]

Acclaimed Vietnam War correspondent Neil Sheehan, who was given the National Book Award and Pulitzer Prize in 1988 for his epic narrative about the conflict, *A Bright Shining Lie*, is outspoken in his belief that General Giap wasn't serious about seizing Khe Sanh. Writing in the 1997 book *Requiem*, Sheehan declared Khe Sanh "the biggest ruse of the war." His view was based in part on his postwar conversation with General Hoang Phuong, the Vietnamese chief of military history. "General Westmoreland fell into a strategic ambush," Phuong told Sheehan.[4]

If true, the North Vietnamese paid dearly for any advantage gained. The fact is that the North Vietnamese devoted considerable resources to the Khe Sanh campaign, suggesting more than a feint or passing interest. A possible explanation is that the North Vietnamese envisioned Khe Sanh as both a ruse and, eventually, a coup de grâce that could end the war. But, like so many other questions about Khe Sanh, definitive answers will likely remain elusive, even if documents were suddenly to emerge from Hanoi's archives, purporting to shed light on the debate.

In any discussion about North Vietnamese intentions, one fact is worth highlighting: the NVA had never faced a coordinated air and artillery campaign on the scale of Operation Niagara. It is hardly far-fetched to conclude that the staggering losses the North Vietnamese sustained in the opening days of the campaign forced a change of plans. Also unknown is the impact of the leaked US deliberations on the use of tactical nuclear weapons, and the possible concerns expressed (and pressure applied) by Hanoi's patrons in Moscow and Beijing. One intriguing possibility is that the potent combination of electronic sensors and concentrated US firepower simply prevented the North Vietnamese from massing their forces for a climactic attack. Internal NVA historical accounts in recent decades have highlighted the frustrated efforts of Giap's men to draw in more American troops at Khe Sanh, and the failure of North Vietnamese commanders to mass sufficient forces for the early attacks on the American hill outposts.[5] Perhaps these early failures, and the casualties and command disruption caused by US bombing attacks in the opening days of the campaign, forced Giap and his generals to look elsewhere for a decisive victory. The debate, no doubt, will continue.

As it stands, the case for Khe Sanh as a thwarted North Vietnamese coup de grâce is circumstantial. But so is the self-serving contention of General Giap and his lieutenants that they never intended to seize the American stronghold.

• • •

For the men who served at Khe Sanh during the siege of early 1968, life became an epic written in two volumes: the years before, and the years after. The red clay dust that coated their bodies would wash off, but Khe Sanh had seeped into their souls.

In the spring and summer of 1968, fate guided Khe Sanh's survivors along a thousand paths. Some, like Hill 861 Alpha survivor Joe Roble, died in combat before they finished their tours. Most survived Vietnam and headed home, changed men trying to find their place in a changed country.

Some, like Bravo 1/26 survivor Steve Wiese, endured the vitriol of antiwar protesters, and the indignities of being cursed, spat upon, and denounced as "baby killers."[6] Many, like India Company squad leader Ken Warner, struggled with post-traumatic stress disorder (PTSD) as they tried to come to terms with the violent, dehumanizing world they had known in Vietnam. Alcoholism, drug use, divorce, and depression became common threads in the lives of many Khe Sanh veterans, even as they began careers as postal workers, preachers, teachers, university professors, policemen, FBI agents, business executives, entrepreneurs, school custodians, car salesmen, and construction workers.

Most endured, as they had at Khe Sanh, and became productive citizens. But Khe Sanh was always there—a defining moment in their lives, for better, and for worse.

Hill 881 South survivor Robert Tipton for years battled sleep disorders, exaggerated startle reflexes, and other psychological and physiological challenges. He changed jobs about twice a year, changed apartments, changed relationships, trying to stay one step ahead of the demons. Around 2000, Tipton got a phone call from a long-lost India Company buddy who invited him to a battalion reunion, and it was a turning point. Tipton rediscovered the brotherhood that had gotten him through Khe Sanh, renewed friendships with the living, and remembered the dead—writing articles, posting on Khe Sanh websites, savoring the company of men who had been there and understood. Bob Tipton had found a path forward.

Navy corpsman Robert Topmiller found a path after Khe Sanh, first as a businessman, and, twenty years later, as a Vietnam War scholar and veterans' advocate. But Khe Sanh never let go—even after he found Terri Nicks, the perfect life partner to help him conquer his demons, a Navy corpsman herself who had treated badly wounded Vietnam casualties; even after the cathartic experience of writing two books about his experiences in Vietnam; even after winning acclaim as a history professor and a peacemaker with devout Buddhist beliefs.

Topmiller had been through it all—the anger and alcoholism, the flashbacks and nightmares—and it seemed he had broken through to the other side, beyond the "grotesque hell full of death and destruction that took lives in a random, horrifying manner," as he had described Khe Sanh in one of his books. But the war in Iraq knocked him back into that dark place, and in August 2008, at the age of fifty-nine, as he was completing a book about the struggles of America's veterans, Doc Topmiller succumbed to the "grotesque hell" of Khe Sanh and took his own life.[7]

Michael Archer and Steve Orr had become best friends as radio operators in the 26th Marines command bunker at Khe Sanh, and that friendship became their path forward after Vietnam. They had gotten out of the Marines in 1970 and were going to attend college together, but Orr decided to travel around the country with his girlfriend for three months and visit some of his buddies from Vietnam. Archer and Orr remained close, and when Orr's girlfriend became his wife, and then his ex-wife, Archer was there for him. Orr would return the favor over the years, and the friendship they had forged amid the horrors of Khe Sanh became the rock that anchored their lives. It still is, and at Khe Sanh veterans reunions they are inseparable as they reconnected with comrades like Mike Reath, Raul "Oz" Orozco, and Cliff Braisted, who shared their time in the regimental communications unit.[8]

The families and friends left behind by the men killed at Khe Sanh have borne their own lonely burdens over the decades. Their pain has found an outlet in recent years on websites like the Vietnam Veterans Virtual Memorial Wall or Together We Served, where the children, siblings, or classmates of the fallen can pay their respects and share their memories of loved ones who will be forever young, with lives of promise still ahead of them.

Three months after Lieutenant Terry Roach gave his life in the defense of Hill 64 on February 8, 1968, his widow, Lynn, gave birth to a daughter. As Lynn forged ahead with her life as a single mother, she came to hate the war that had claimed the gregarious, kilt-wearing Irish balladeer who had stolen her heart back at Wayne State. In 1971, Lynn marched against the war, and in time, her daughter, Mary, would become an outspoken critic of the Iraq invasion launched by President George W. Bush.

Terry Roach may or may not have agreed with his daughter's politics, but he surely would have approved of the strength of her convictions, and her fearlessness in expressing them—the very freedoms that Terry Roach had believed he was defending by serving in Vietnam.

Mary named her son for the father she never knew, and young Terry's questions eventually led Lynn to search for answers about her late husband's time in Vietnam—how he lived, how he fought, and how he died.

She came across a website about Hill 64 created by the Alpha-1 corpsman Mike Coonan and began corresponding with a few men who had served under Terry Roach that night.

"I've been reading online about Hill 64 lately, pulling some pieces together . . . something I avoided for the first 40 years," Lynn wrote me in late 2012. "It's not easy to think about or talk about even now, but with grandson Terry, 13, now getting interested I felt I needed a few more facts."

Lynn has never wavered in her belief that the Vietnam War was not a wise use of America's youth and treasure, and that men like Terry were sacrificed in a misguided quest. "That does nothing to dull the gleam of my husband's personal honor," she says. "I will always, always, be proud to have been his wife."

● ● ●

General William Childs Westmoreland would always claim Khe Sanh and Tet as victories. Indeed, in his memoirs, he cited his decision to stand and fight at Khe Sanh as his finest hour in the Vietnam War, and he may be right.

Whereas Westmoreland was left to defend his controversial record in Vietnam, General Vo Nguyen Giap basked in the glow of his eventual victory in 1975, seven years after Khe Sanh. He, too, would claim Khe Sanh and Tet as victories, but he would get the last word: Westmoreland died in 2005 at the age of ninety-one. Giap outlived his American adversary by nearly a decade before his death in Hanoi on October 4, 2013, at the age of 102.

For Colonel David Lownds, Khe Sanh was the pinnacle of his four decades as a Marine. On behalf of the 26th Marine Regiment, he accepted a Presidential Unit Citation from President Johnson in a White House ceremony in May 1968. He was also honored with a Navy Cross for his successful defense of Khe Sanh.

In 1997, twenty-nine years after the battle, Lownds made a rare appearance at a reunion of Khe Sanh veterans, in St. Louis, Missouri. He received a long and warm ovation from the men who had served under him. In his remarks, he offered a brief glimpse of the burden he had carried away from Khe Sanh. "If you don't think a commander suffers when he loses people, you're sadly mistaken, because it goes deeply into your heart," he said. "It never leaves."

Lownds died in Naples, Florida, on August 31, 2011. He left behind his wife of sixty-nine years, Jean, seven children, nineteen grandchildren, twenty-three great-grandchildren, and thousands of Marines who fondly remember the cigar-smoking commander who led them through the fires of Khe Sanh.

• • •

Bill Dabney, commander of the American outpost on Hill 881 South, returned to the Khe Sanh area in 1971 as an adviser to a South Vietnamese unit involved in Operation Lam Son 719, in which ARVN troops pushed into Laos in an attempt to cut the Ho Chi Minh Trail—one of the reasons that General Westmoreland had wanted a base at Khe Sanh in the first place. Lam Son 719 ended badly, with the loss of many fine South Vietnamese troops, and Dabney left Vietnam with little doubt about the war's eventual outcome. He finished his career in the Marine Corps as a colonel, then served as the senior naval science instructor and, later, as commandant of cadets at his alma mater, Virginia Military Institute.

In retirement, Khe Sanh became a focal point of Bill Dabney's life. He attended Khe Sanh veterans' reunions and wrote articles about the battle for *Marine Corps Gazette* and other publications.

His health was failing in April 2005 when he was awarded the Navy Cross for his actions at Khe Sanh. In a ceremony at Virginia Military Institute, Dabney rolled into the hall in a wheelchair, tethered to an oxygen tank. But when his moment came, he rose to his feet, and in a strong, clear voice, paid tribute to the defenders of Khe Sanh, about seventy of whom were on hand to honor their former commanding officer. "I wear this honor today only symbolically," Dabney said. "It is they who earned it."[9]

On February 15, 2012, Bill Dabney died at his Virginia farm, at the age of seventy-seven. His funeral attracted Khe Sanh veterans from all over the country.

In his final decades, Dabney had never missed an opportunity to honor his Khe Sanh comrades. "Through it all, the troops did their duty," he wrote. "They stood their watches, flew their aircraft or serviced helicopter zones, manned outposts, engaged the enemy and raised the flag as zealously at the end as at the beginning. They were never asked to stand back-to-back against the flagpole with fixed bayonets, but rather to endure. By enduring, they triumphed. They were magnificent!"

• • •

Bravo 1/26 skipper Ken Pipes retired from the Marines as a lieutenant colonel. Now in his mid-seventies, he lives in Fallbrook, California, near Camp Pendleton. Ever the Marine officer and gentleman, beloved by the Bravo veterans who have scattered across America, Pipes addresses audiences on Memorial Day and other occasions, recalling the sacrifices of the men who served in Vietnam and honoring Marines who have fallen in America's more recent wars in Afghanistan and Iraq. In May 2011, Pipes flew across the country for a ceremony in the Atlanta suburb of Decatur, Georgia, to honor one of his Marines, nineteen-year-old Private Ted Britt, who gave his life in the March 30, 1968, "payback" assault at Khe Sanh.

The loss of so many of his men in the ambush a month earlier, on February 25, 1968, still haunts Pipes. "For all of us, that was a terrible, terrible day," he says. "Time doesn't make it any better—at all. We'll carry that with us the rest of our lives, however long that may be."[10]

• • •

The commander of the Echo Company Marines on 861 Alpha, Earle Breeding, left the Marine Corps in 1971 to become an FBI special agent. He specialized in foreign counterintelligence before his retirement from the FBI in 1991, then moved to Roswell, New Mexico, where he worked as a contract private investigator for various US government agencies for eleven years.

In 2002, at the age of seventy, Breeding "gave it all up" and retired to the Sacramento Mountains around Ruidoso, New Mexico, where he and his wife live "among ponderosa pines, pinions and mesquite, deer, bear, coyotes, fox and skunks," as he describes it. He has stayed active in retirement, serving as a volunteer investigator for the National Center for Missing and Exploited Children and as a docent at Fort Stanton, New Mexico.

Breeding was a key figure in the early years of the Khe Sanh Veterans Association, serving as founding treasurer and president. In April 2012, a few months before Breeding's eightieth birthday, nearly a dozen men who served under him on 861 Alpha converged on his house in Ruidoso for an Echo Company reunion. Among those in attendance was rocketman Dave McCall, who lost his leg on 861 Alpha during the battle of February 5, 1968. In his home state of Kansas, McCall has worked as a youth counselor for more than twenty-five years, fulfilling a promise he made on the hill that terrible, bloody morning.

Traveling to the New Mexico gathering from his home in Northern California was a man that most of the Echo regulars at Khe Sanh reunions hadn't seen since Vietnam: Lieutenant Don Shanley, the commander of Breeding's 1st Platoon.

After surviving Vietnam and completing his obligation to the Marine Corps, the former Stanford swimmer disappeared into the counterculture that had taken hold across America. He smoked marijuana and spent "a very reflective and meditative year," hitchhiking across the country and back three times and hanging out along the Northern California coast. He worked as a lumber mill hand and a lifeguard, dived for abalone, gardened, and tried to forget Vietnam.

Shanley spent a decade working through his self-described "hermit period." He worked as a gardener at an elegant inn along the Northern California coast, landscaped, wrote critically acclaimed poetry, and became caretaker at Kris Kristofferson's ranch.

In 1983, Shanley found his life's work when he started a business that specialized in landscape restoration and erosion control. Building the enterprise from scratch, he earned a reputation for high-quality work and won state and federal contracts. He married a botanist he met through his work, and they carved out a homestead in Mendocino County.

As Shanley found peace by beautifying lands scarred by road construction and other human activities, death stalked the countryside around Khe Sanh. From 1985 to 1995, 4,000 Vietnamese, many of them children, were killed or maimed by stray ordnance from the battle of Khe Sanh and US bombing missions.

Shanley heard about the tragedy, and the work of an American organization called PeaceTrees Vietnam. It had been founded by the sister of a US Army helicopter pilot killed in Vietnam and was helping the people of Quang Tri Province clear unexploded ordnance and regenerate the war-torn landscape. Shanley volunteered for a PeaceTrees mission and returned to Vietnam in 2000—to pay tribute to his fallen comrades and adversaries, and to vanquish one more heartbreaking legacy of the battle of Khe Sanh.[11]

• • •

Over the decades, Steve Wiese has fought and refought the battle of Khe Sanh in his head, trying to understand why he lived.

In 2009, the Bravo 1/26 Marine watched the movie *Taking Chance*, about the honor and respect accorded a Marine killed in Iraq, Lance Corporal Chance Phelps, as his body is escorted to his Wyoming hometown for burial. One line in the movie, about the importance of keeping alive the memories of our war dead, struck Wiese like a thunderbolt: "Without a witness, they just disappear."

Wiese finally understood why he had lived.

"If you had called me four years ago, I would have just told you, 'I have nothing to say,'" Wiese said to me near the end of one of our interviews. "But these guys don't deserve to disappear. These guys died for their country, and they died for their fellow Marines."[12]

And so, like many of the other survivors of Khe Sanh, Steve Wiese bears witness to his comrades, young Americans who fell in battle in the red clay hills of South Vietnam in early 1968.

• • •

It has been a long, hard journey for Ken Warner since those carefree days of Southern California baseball and surfing before Vietnam. He was lucky to have survived his close encounter with the North Vietnamese on the eve of the battle, luckier still to have survived NVA ambushes on back-to-back days. Like so many Khe Sanh veterans, Warner struggled to make sense of the random cruelties of war, and the question that really can't be answered: Why had he lived when so many others had died?

At heart, Ken Warner was—and still is—a gentle soul, and his disorientation after Vietnam was profound. His compass shattered, he found himself adrift in a raging sea.

"After returning home from Vietnam, I spent years fighting PTSD by self-medicating and working odd jobs, along with stays at the VA [hospitals]," he writes. "In 1984, I married my wife Donna, who immediately filled a shadow box with my medals and ribbons. It was hung by the front door so all could see it, and she told me never to be ashamed of what I had done in Vietnam."

With the love of Donna, and their two children, Margo and Jesse, Ken found his bearings. Like his father, Jesse enlisted in the Marines. He served two tours in Afghanistan, the first as a machine gunner, and the second as a scout sniper. He is twenty-six now and attending college. Margo is twenty-eight and studying psychology, with a particular interest in post-traumatic stress disorder.

"My family was the turning point that gave me a life I thought could never exist," Ken Warner says. "They continue to support me and help me to cope with the events of Vietnam and Hill 881 South."

• • •

Several times a year, Tom Esslinger travels from his home in the Virginia suburbs to the black-granite wall of the Vietnam Veterans Memorial in Washington, DC. Every year, on February 23, he makes his way to Panel 41E and finds two names: Paul E. Robitaille, on Line 2, and Eugene C. Wire, on Line 6—the two gunnery sergeants whom Esslinger lost in one awful moment on this date in 1968.

With whispered words and private thoughts, he honors the two men who helped him through some of his hardest days during the siege at Khe Sanh.

In 2003, Esslinger returned to Vietnam to visit 881 South and commune with the spirit of his gunnies. He found a local guide and, with other veterans of 881 South, headed up the hill that had taught him so much about duty, honor, loyalty, and loss.

"While the rest of our party explored the larger India Company part of the hill, I returned alone to the Mike Company sector," he wrote afterward. "It was not difficult to find my old bunker and the nearby bomb crater. I was pleased to find purple flowers growing on the spot where the gunnies were last seen. Tears and time passed as I visited and chatted with Gunny Wire and Gunny Robitaille."[13]

• • •

Navy chaplain Ray W. Stubbe continued to battle the demons of Khe Sanh long after he left Vietnam. As part of his treatment for post-traumatic stress disorder, he began writing a book about Khe Sanh and started tracking down men who had served there. In time, his list of names became the Khe Sanh Veterans Association, with more than 3,000 members. The veterans and their families gather each year, to spend time with one another and remember the comrades who fell at Khe Sanh.

Every three or four years, the Khe Sanh Veterans Association holds its annual reunion in Washington, DC, so members can visit the Marine Corps Museum in Quantico, Virginia, and pay their respects to fallen comrades at the Vietnam Veterans Memorial and Arlington National Cemetery. Such was the case in 2012, when the group gathered in late August in Arlington.

Khe Sanh veterans from around the country met at the conference hotel, a short walk from the southern edge of Arlington National Cemetery. Tom Eichler, one of the heroes of 861 Alpha, now retired from the Chicago Police Department, had flown in from Illinois to preside over the gathering. In a time-honored tradition, Dave "Bulldog" Smith, a senior Special Forces officer at FOB-3, and Marine combat engineer "Big John" Pessoni were riding herd over the hospitality room and the "post exchange" (PX) that sells Khe Sanh T-shirts, mugs, books, and other memorabilia.

Gunnery Sergeant Bill Martin strode into the marbled lobby of the conference hotel from Dallas, Texas, carrying a suit bag with the dress blues he dons for each reunion banquet as he presents and retires the colors with parade-ground precision. Navy corpsman John Cicala, one of the survivors of the February 25 ambush, was there from Michigan. Steve Wiese had flown cross-country from California to see old friends and try to sit through a heartrending documentary film on Bravo Company made by Bravo veteran Ken Rodgers and his wife, Betty.

For hours on end, the survivors of Khe Sanh would eat and drink, tell stories, laugh, and remember—the defenders of 881 South at this table, 861 over there, Bravo 1/26 here, Echo 2/26 across the room, and so on. Conversations were laced with references to comrades who died at Khe Sanh, or in the intervening years. Come Saturday night they would put on business attire or dress blues for the banquet, where they would remember their deceased comrades with silence and prayer. And then, after dinner and other ceremonies, they would recall the days of their youth and let loose on the dance floor as Eichler belted out Motown tunes on a karaoke machine.

Among the veterans at the Washington gathering was a regular who rarely misses a Khe Sanh reunion: Dennis Mannion, the artillery forward observer on Hill 861 during the siege. Mannion had returned home to Connecticut after completing his enlistment, then earned his college degree and took a job at a local high school, teaching English literature and coaching football. Over time, he became renowned for his passion and dedication, and for teaching his students about what a group of committed Americans had experienced at a place called Khe Sanh in 1968.

In 2000, Mannion returned to 861 with his old friend from the hill, forward air controller Paul Knight. They made the pilgrimage back to Khe Sanh with two buddies who had served on 881 South, forward observer radioman Glenn Prentice and air officer Bob Arrotta. One of Mannion's former students, David C. Kniess Jr., accompanied the men and made a documentary film about their journey, *Khe Sanh: A Walk in the Clouds.*

In November 2009, Bob Arrotta died suddenly, and Prentice escorted his dear friend's casket from Southern California to Arlington National Cemetery for burial. Now, nearly three years later, on August 31, 2012, Mannion, Prentice, and Knight made the short drive from the reunion hotel to the cemetery to spend a few minutes with their beloved comrade.

They found their way by memory to Section 9 and descended a steep slope near the cul-de-sac of McClellan Drive, a few hundred yards north of the Tomb of the Unknown Soldier. The trio of Khe Sanh veterans stopped before Grave 5899-A-LH, marked by a bone-white headstone engraved with the name Robert James Arrotta. They touched the smooth marble slab, whispered greetings, and told Arrotta how much they missed him. They recalled a few shared memories, then bade farewell until their next visit.[14]

• • •

Early the next morning, September 1, Dennis Mannion awoke before daybreak and drove across the Potomac River into Washington, DC.

He parked his car along Twenty-second Street, just north of the Mall, crossed Constitution Avenue, and walked the short distance to the Vietnam Veterans Memorial.[15]

Mannion makes a point of coming here every time he visits the nation's capital, and the location of certain names on the wall is fixed in his memory. The entire history of the war is here, if only the names carved into the black granite could talk. So, too, is the story of the 1968 battle and siege at Khe Sanh—names scattered across fifty-five of the memorial's 140 panels, from the east wall to the west, from the January 20 fight on 881 North to the abandonment of Khe Sanh Combat Base in July 1968.

The events of January 20–21, 1968, had marked the beginning of the confrontation, but Americans had been dying at Khe Sanh since 1964, when Captain Richard Lebrou Whitesides was shot down in his small observation aircraft after taking off from the Special Forces camp at Khe Sanh. The spring of 1967 had seen the violent episode in Khe Sanh's history known as the Hill Fights, which had claimed the lives of 155 Marines. But things had gotten quiet again, with only sporadic death from combat and accidents around Khe Sanh, until January 1968.

Dennis Mannion had not forgotten the first Marine that Kilo Company lost at Khe Sanh, on December 22, 1967, during the sweep westward from the combat base to the Laotian border in search of the North Vietnamese. Lance Corporal Michael Edward Suniga was a nineteen-year-old mortarman from Ojai, California, and he had been in Vietnam only forty-two days. It was cold that morning, and Suniga's fingers were probably stiff, and, in all likelihood, he was sleep deprived. Those factors might explain how he dropped a live hand grenade, and then compounded his error by trying to grab it with his hands instead of turning away and absorbing the blast with his flak jacket. Whatever the explanation, the grenade exploded, blowing off the young Marine's arms, and Michael Suniga became one of thirty-six Americans to die in Vietnam that day.[16]

Forty-four years later, in the half-light of the Washington dawn, Dennis Mannion stood before Panel 32E of the reflective black-granite wall, traced his finger across Michael Edward Suniga's name on Line 48, and remembered those days leading up to the great battle.

Like hieroglyphics, the story of Khe Sanh emerges in other names carved into the wall as it slopes gently upward toward the rising sun. On Panel 34E, nine lines from the bottom, is the name of James S. Collins, the India Company point man from the cornfields of Illinois, the first to fall on January 20 when he walked unaware into the line of North Vietnamese dug in on the slopes of 881 North. One line above, side by side, are the names of Thomas D. Brindley—the hockey player from Minnesota who had so impressed Bill Dabney as a platoon leader—and reconnaissance Marine Charles W. Bryan, the Texan who died trying to save his men on the right flank of the American line. At the bottom of 34E, second from the far right, is the name of the brave young Oklahoman Michael H. Thomas, the other platoon leader whom Dabney lost that day.

The confrontation at Khe Sanh plays out across the panels, day by day, revealed in names that evoke far more than battles and barrages, but also dreams unfulfilled and promising young lives cut short.

Mannion's revered Gunnery Sergeant Melvin Lewis Rimel might have seemed old to the grunts under his care, but he was only thirty-three, and he had left a wife and four young children back in the States so he might shepherd young Marines in battle. And now his name was on the wall, Panel 35E, Line 9, frozen in time, and in Mannion's memory, from the moment of his death in the early hours of January 21, 1968.

All around Rimel on the wall are the names of the young men of Kilo Company who fell in the desperate fight for Hill 861: rifleman Paul R. Bellamy; assistant machine gunner Curtis B. Bugger; rifleman Michael D. Cruitt; rifleman Clifton R. Jones; corpsman Malcolm G. Mole; and weapons man David T. Rozelle. Scattered among them are the dead from the fight for the district government headquarters at Khe Sanh village later that day, among them Jerry W. Elliott, the young helicopter crewman from Greenville, Mississippi, who selflessly jumped to the ground to save his comrades from a downed chopper and was never seen again.

A few steps to the east, on Panels 37E and 38E, are inscribed the names of the men who died in the pivotal battles along Khe Sanh's western flank in early February. One can almost hear the cry of "Good morning, Vietnam!" from Jack E. Bogard—Panel 37E, Line 31—as he put a smile on the face of his weary comrades on the northern perimeter of Hill 861 Alpha; scattered below Bogard are the names of his Echo Company comrades killed in the savage fight, including Joseph A. Molettiere, the proud father-to-be from South Philly, and Martin L. Rimson, who soothed his frazzled comrades with his silky rendition of "Moon River."

Along the bottom of panel 37E and the top of 38E are the seven fallen defenders of Lang Vei: Medal of Honor recipient Eugene Ashley Jr.; Earl F. Burke; Kenneth Hanna; James W. Holt; Charles W. Lindewald Jr.; James L. Moreland; and Daniel R. Phillips.

Further down Panel 38E, on Line 20, the casualties of the February 8 attack on Hill 64 begin with corpsman Michael B. Barrett of Los Angeles, California, and continue on through Line 42, with Henry York, the rifleman from North Babylon, New York, killed beside squad leader James Feasel near the end of the fight. In between, side by side, are radioman James P. Rizzo and platoon commander Terence R. Roach Jr.

For the survivors of Khe Sanh, Panel 41E is the most painful of all, for it bears more names of comrades than any other: seventy-one men who died at Khe Sanh, from the terrible bombardment of February 23 through the CH-46 helicopter crash of February 28. It is the panel that Tom Esslinger visits to salute his gunnery sergeants, Paul E. Robitaille, Line 2, and Eugene C. Wire, Line 6. Beside Gunny Wire is the name of Carlos C. Aguirre, killed on 861 Alpha in the first minutes of February 24, his smiling face forever etched in the memory of his platoon leader, Lieutenant Nick Elardo, as he called out, "Hey, Lieutenant, my mother sent me some peppers. Would you like to have a contest?"[17] Further down, beginning with Line 15, is the tally of dead from the February 25 patrol led by Bravo Company Lieutenant Don Jacques—twenty-seven names in all, every one remembered by their skipper, Ken Pipes.

Another sixty-three names of Khe Sanh dead reside on Panel 43E, among them the victims of the C-123 crash on March 6; on 47E are those who fell in the March 30 assault led by Ken Pipes and the men of Bravo 1/26; and on 49E and 50E lie the names and memories of those young Americans who died while retaking 881 North on April 14.

The siege had ended, and the headlines about Khe Sanh had begun to fade by then, but the names on the wall bear witness to the dying that continued unabated at Khe Sanh, long after General Westmoreland and the news correspondents and the American people had moved on. The final panel of the east wall, 70E, bears the name of Khe Sanh casualty Nicholas Samuel Vrankovich, one of thirteen men of Golf Company, 2nd

Battalion, 3rd Marines, killed on May 24, 1968, in an ambush off Route 9, just east of Khe Sanh village and the old French fort.

From that date, the story of Khe Sanh resumes at the far western end of the wall and moves toward the center of the memorial. On Panel 64W, the names recall one of the scores of largely forgotten stories in the Khe Sanh saga. It was the early morning of May 28, about 2:00 a.m., and an NVA force surged up a rugged ridgeline more than a mile east of Khe Sanh village and overran an outpost of Foxtrot Company, 2nd Battalion, 3rd Marines. The savage fighting lasted more than eight hours, until late morning, when American attack aircraft incinerated the final wave of North Vietnamese troops just a few yards from the Marine lines. The worst was supposed to be over at Khe Sanh, but another fifteen Marines were dead.

There were more ambushes and attacks and firefights around Khe Sanh in the days that followed, more names scattered across the wall from west to east, until Panel 52W, when the American withdrawal was completed on July 11, and the curtain fell on the epic saga of Khe Sanh.

In the rising light of an early September morning, standing before the gleaming walls of the Vietnam Veterans Memorial, with all the profound loss these granite panels embody, questions about who won or lost at Khe Sanh and whether it was a ruse seem indecent. So, too, are the political debates over why America lost the war, and who is to blame. It is enough to know that the hundreds of Khe Sanh dead whose names are etched into the wall heeded the call of their country, and they went to Vietnam with the best of intentions. In the company of their brothers-in-arms at Khe Sanh, they found a kinship that transcended a nation's bitter divisions, and with their blood, toil, and tears, they earned a place of honor in American history.

NOTES

PROLOGUE

1. Jack Shulimson et al., *U.S. Marines in Vietnam: The Defining Year, 1968* (Washington, DC: History and Museums Division, Headquarters, U.S. Marine Corps, 1997), 10–11.

2. Ken Warner, author's interview, March 26, 2012.

3. Ibid. As it turned out, Warner's harrowing patrol of January 17, 1968, was only the beginning of the four most intense days of his life. Even after all that happened to Warner and his men over these four days, those few minutes at the base of 881 South on January 17 rate as his "spookiest" experience at Khe Sanh. Warner said, "To this day, telling this story gets my heart racing. I knew we were being watched, and it's just a matter of somebody pulling a trigger."

4. These conclusions about the fate of Ken Warner's patrol on January 17, 1968, are based on my interviews with Warner, my analysis of the events that played out that week, various intelligence assessments, and the ruminations of key participants in the decades since.

CHAPTER 1

1. The entire US military experience in Vietnam was metric. Topographic maps were laid out on 1,000-square-meter grids, and artillery fire and adjustments were made in metric increments. Also, as just noted, hills were designated by their height in meters. As a convenience to readers, metric measurements in this book have been converted to feet, yards, and miles, unless the measurement denotes specifics for targeting, buffer dimensions, and the like, or is given in quoted material.

2. Mike Ray, author's interview, August 6, 2013.

3. Tom Esslinger, author's interview, March 12, 2012.

4. Neil Sheehan, *A Bright Shining Lie: John Paul Vann and America in Vietnam* (New York: Random House, 1988), 649.

5. William Dabney, Virginia Military Institute (VMI hereafter) Oral History interview, September 8, 2005.

6. Michael Pike, author's interview, March 26, 2012.

7. Ibid.

8. Robert Tipton, author's interview, April 17, 2012.

9. Robert Pisor, *The End of the Line: The Siege of Khe Sanh* (New York: Norton, 1982), 27.

10. Ronnie Foster, *One Day as a Lion: True Stories of the Vietnam War* (Plano, TX: Entry Way, 2007), 51–66.

11. Private First Class James A. Collins, Silver Star citation.

12. Mike Ray, author's interview, August 6, 2013.

13. Ibid.

14. Ibid.

15. William Dabney, VMI Oral History interview, September 8, 2005; Richard Dworsky, author's interview, August 5, 2013; Mike Ray, author's interview, August 6, 2013. Dabney said he also had trouble getting enough artillery support for his men on January 20. "You know, you're talking to the staff officer back in the regimental bunker and you feel like saying, 'God damn it, colonel or major, you come out here and look! I'm standing in the middle of it. Get on with it and give me what I ask for!'"

16. Ken Warner, author's interview, March 26, 2012.

17. Corporal Michael C. Elrod, USMC Oral History Collection, Tape No. 2809.

18. Ken Warner, author's interviews, March 26–27, 2012.

19. Ibid.

20. Ibid.

21. Ken Warner, author's interview, March 27, 2012.

22. Michael Pike, author's interview, March 26, 2012.

23. Ibid.

24. Robert (Bob) Ropelewski background from obituary, http://www.rootsweb.ance stry.com/~paerie/newspaper/BTKMoreFamObits.htm; James E. Schemelia, quoted in Ray Stubbe, *Khe Sanh Chaplain: A Historical Summary of Activities While Assigned to 1/26, 3d Recon., and 3d Shore Party BNs, July, 1967, Through June, 1968, Including the Khe Sanh Seige [sic] of 1968, of LT Ray W. Stubbe, CHC, USNR*, unpublished manuscript dated April 1, 1970, 333–334, Ray Stubbe Papers, U.S. Marine Corps Archives, Quantico, Virginia.

25. James E. Schemelia, interview with Ray Stubbe, July 1984, quoted in Stubbe, *Khe Sanh Chaplain*, 333–334.

26. In addition to pilot Bob Ropelewski, the other three crew members of *Frosty Gold* were: the co-pilot, Steve R. Stegich; the crew chief, Curtis Larson; and the gunner, M. J. Norman.

27. Marine Medium Helicopter Squadron 262 (HMM-262) Command Chronology, narrative written by Lieutenant Colonel Neil Allen, http://www.hmm-262combatvets.com/chronology.htm; Stubbe, *Khe Sanh Chaplain*, 333–334; Michael Pike, author's interview, March 26, 2012; also see Beth Crumley, "The Siege of Khe Sanh Begins," January 24, 2012, blog post on Marine Corps Association and Foundation website, http://www.mca-marines.org/blog/beth-crumley/2012/01/24/siege-khe-sanh-begins. Michael Pike ended up next to two members of the downed chopper crew—probably Ropelewski and Stegich—in the bomb crater.

28. Ken Pipes, author's interview, July 23, 2012, and William Gay, author's interview, August 15, 2013.

Official records credit Captain Ken Pipes, commander of Bravo Company, 1st Battalion, 26th Marines, and his men with handling the surrender of the NVA defector who appeared outside Khe Sanh Combat Base on the afternoon of January 20, 1968. The 1/26 Command Chronology for January 1968 states: "At 201400H [2:00 p.m., January 20] Company B, at (XD 854421), observed one NVA waving a white flag. 'Chieu-Hoi' [defector] was turned over to ITT [Interrogator/Translator Team]. Prisoner was wearing green utilities and a bush hat and carried an AK 47 rifle. ITT reported that 'Chieu-Hoi' was a NVA Lieutenant."

In the daily log of 1/26 activities, also found in the 1/26 Command Chronology for January 1968, the incident was similarly described: "At 201400H a Fire team from B-1-26 providing security on end of airstrip observed one (1) NVA waving white flag. The fire team captured one (1) AK 47 with Magazine. The POW wearing green utilities, bush hat, was turned over to ITT for interrogation. Also weapon was [turned] into Regt S-2. The POW was also carrying a bottle of pills and one (1) cigarette lighter."

Ken Pipes described his memories of the incident to me in our interview of July 23, 2012. He recalled that he had been walking his lines with his radio operator when he had received word that an apparent NVA had been spotted waving a white flag or object beyond the northeastern end of the runway. Pipes said he and four other Marines walked out to the area where the NVA had been spotted, a few hundred yards beyond the perimeter wire. Pipes said he repeatedly shouted, "Marine dai-uy" ["Marine captain"] and "Chieu hoi!" ["Open Arms"], the name of the U.S.-South Vietnamese program for encouraging the surrender of Communist soldiers in Vietnam. As Pipes recalled, the North Vietnamese soldier appeared over a low rise in the rolling terrain east of the perimeter, "and we motioned him on and we took control of him."

The North Vietnamese defector was taken inside the base, where he was interrogated by personnel of the 17th Interrogator Translator Team, including Gunnery Sergeant Max Friedlander and Sergeant Jimmy Brown.

William Gay has a different recollection of how the North Vietnamese lieutenant was captured. Gay was a second lieutenant in command of a platoon of combat engineers posted at Khe Sanh, and on the afternoon of January 20, he and his men were in the cleared buffer east of the runway, putting in another minefield to strengthen the perimeter defenses. Marine grunts from one of the line companies were assigned as security for the detail. Gay said he was near the jungle's edge, lying on his stomach as he carefully armed a "Bouncing Betty" anti-personnel mine, when a North Vietnamese soldier armed with an AK-47 rifle stepped from the elephant grass about thirty feet away. Before Gay could react, the North Vietnamese soldier dropped his rifle and thrust his hands into the air. Gay said he grabbed his own rifle, jumped to his feet, and motioned the man forward. He steered the enemy soldier around the live mines and ordered a Marine to hustle the prisoner inside the base for interrogation. Thus ended his involvement with the incident, Gay told me.

Discrepancies also surround the identity of the North Vietnamese soldier. The official Marine Corps history, *The Battle for Khe Sanh*, was written by Captain Moyers S. Shore II later in 1968 and published the following year. In early drafts, Shore identifies the NVA defector of January 20 as "Lieutenant La Thanh Ton." In the version that was published, Shore only identifies the defector as an "NVA first lieutenant who was the commanding officer of the 14th Antiaircraft Company, 95C regiment, 325C Division." Shore describes the information revealed by the NVA lieutenant but says nothing about his motivations for surrendering, or his fate.

In November 1970, the incident was recalled by Major General Rathvon McC. Tompkins in his testimony before the US Senate Electronic Battlefield Subcommittee, and the former commander of the 3rd Marine Division during the siege of Khe Sanh identified the North Vietnamese defector as "Lieutenant La Thanh Tonc." Tompkins offered some additional details about the defector: he "was a Regular with 14 years service and had recently failed to be selected to promotion to captain," Tompkins told the subcommittee. "This so incensed Lieutenant Tonc that he deserted." See United States Senate, *Hearings Before the Electronic Battlefield Subcommittee of the Preparedness Investigating Subcommittee of the Committee on Armed Services* (Washington, DC: Government Printing Office, 1971), 82.

From that time on, correctly or not, history has referred to the North Vietnamese defector as "La Thanh Tonc." But the name is problematic: Ton is a common Vietnamese family name, but Tonc is not. Veteran Southeast Asia news correspondent Seth Mydans, who has spent much time in Vietnam over the past three decades, notes that Tonc "is definitely not a Vietnamese name." Also, "Le Thanh" rather than "La Thanh" would be the common spelling.

Historian John Prados, whose expansive work on Khe Sanh and the larger war has been thoughtful and thorough over the years, has argued that the NVA lieutenant might have been a plant intended to redirect American attention to Hill 861 rather than the imminent attack on Khe Sanh village. But like so much about Khe Sanh, there is a dearth of hard evidence to support his case. In any event, General Tompkins, among others, consistently hailed the revelations of the North Vietnamese lieutenant as an intelligence windfall for the Americans on the eve of the Khe Sanh attack.

The NVA lieutenant himself could lay to rest many of these questions, but just as suddenly as he strode onto history's stage, he disappeared. He is believed to have been flown out of Khe Sanh on January 21, but what became of him afterward remains one of many enduring mysteries of the siege.

29. Ken Pipes, author's interview, July 23, 2012; statement of Major General Rathvon Tompkins, November 19, 1970, US Senate Electronic Battlefield Subcommittee, printed in United States Senate, *Hearings Before the Electronic Battlefield Subcommittee of the Preparedness Investigating Subcommittee of the Committee on Armed Services* (Washington, DC: Government Printing Office, 1971), 82–83; also see interrogation notes of Gunnery Sergeant Max Friedlander of the 17th Interrogator/Translator Team, reprinted in Eric Hammel, *Khe Sanh: Siege in the Clouds* (New York: Crown Publishers, 1989), 57–58.

30. Mike Ray, author's interview, August 6, 2013, and Robert Pagano, author's interview, August 20, 2012.

31. Robert Pagano, author's interview, August 20, 2012.

32. Major Matthew P. Caulfield, USMC Oral History Collection, Tape No. 6157.

33. Private First Class Kenneth O. Brewer, written statement in Navy Cross file of Second Lieutenant Thomas D. Brindley.

34. Robert Pagano, author's interview, August 20, 2012.

35. Ibid.

36. Ibid.

37. Mike Ray, author's interview, August 6, 2013.

38. Robert Pagano, author's interview, August 20, 2012.

39. Mike Ray, author's interview, August 6, 2013.

40. Robert Pagano, author's interview, August 20, 2012.

41. Robert "PJ" Pagano didn't know the identity of the Marine who found him, but Marine records indicate it was Sergeant Daniel Jessup. Robert Pagano, author's interview, August 20, 2012; and Sergeant Daniel Jessup, Silver Star citation.

42. Robert Pagano, author's interview, August 20, 2012; also Lionel Guerra, interview with Ronnie Foster, quoted in *One Day as a Lion*, 75–76. Sergeant Daniel Jessup was awarded the Silver Star for his actions in rescuing Lionel Guerra and PJ Pagano.

43. Tom Esslinger, author's interview, March 12, 2012, and Richard Dworsky, author's interview, August 5, 2013. Esslinger and Dworsky listened to the radio exchanges between Dabney and the regimental command staff on 881 South, as well as other radio traffic. "About 1500 [3:00 p.m.] the order came in for Dabney to break contact and get his men back on the hill," Esslinger told me. "Dabney was unhappy with the order. There was some

discussion between the battalion staff on the hill and back on the base, and the regimental staff. Dabney was overruled and his men returned to the hill."

44. Richard Dworsky, author's interview, August 5, 2013.

45. Tom Esslinger, author's interview, March 12, 2012.

46. Ibid.

47. Ibid.

CHAPTER 2

1. Miguel Salinas, author's interview, May 2, 2012.

2. Dennis Mannion, author's interview, November 29, 2011.

3. Miguel Salinas, author's interview, May 2, 2012.

4. Dennis Mannion, author's interview, November 29, 2011.

5. Miguel Salinas, author's interview, May 2, 2012.

6. Dennis Mannion, author's interview, November 30, 2011.

7. Miguel Salinas, author's interview, May 2, 2012; Dennis Mannion, author's interview, November 30, 2011.

8. Ibid.

9. Dennis Mannion, author's interview, November 30, 2011.

10. Ibid.

11. Ibid.

12. Miguel Salinas, author's interview, May 2, 2012. The term "fog of war" has been much overused in recent years, but I believe it aptly applies to the confusion that still exists over when the North Vietnamese attack on Hill 861 got underway. In my interviews and examination of various documents, including command chronologies, the beginning of the attack was fixed at anywhere from midnight to 3:30 a.m. Dennis Mannion and Miguel Salinas are adamant in their recollections that the attack began between midnight and 1:00 a.m. on the morning of January 21, 1968. Ted Mickelson recalled the attack beginning around 2:00 a.m. Kilo Company commander Norman Jasper insists that the attack began around 3:00 a.m. "I looked at my watch," Jasper states in an account of the battle he wrote for the Virginia Chapter of the Military Order of the Purple Heart. In a Marine Corps oral history interview, Second Lieutenant Linn Oehling of Kilo Company's 2nd Platoon stated, "About 12:30 that night we began to take incoming rounds." Oehling went on to say that 2nd Platoon "received word at 2 o'clock in the morning that they had broke through our lines." Private First Class Michael R. James, a 1st Platoon rocket squad leader who was on the north end of the hill, stated in his oral history interview that same day, "The troops started hitting us around 3 o'clock approximately."

13. Miguel Salinas, author's interview, May 2, 2012. The official Marine Corps account, *The Battle for Khe Sanh*, states that "enemy soldiers penetrated the K/3/26 lines on the southwestern side of the hill and overran the helo landing zone." I found no evidence of this, and conclude that the only breach occurred on the north side of the hill.

14. Ibid.

15. Ibid.

16. Ibid.

17. Dennis Mannion, author's interview, November 30, 2011.

18. Ibid. Some accounts have depicted Melvin Rimel as dying in the arms of Dennis Mannion. In our interviews, Mannion stated emphatically that Rimel was already dead when he found the gunnery sergeant's body.

19. Ibid.

20. Ibid.

21. Ibid.

22. Norman Jasper, author's interview, January 27, 2012.

23. Ibid.

24. Ted Mickelson, author's interview, January 15, 2012. "You could truly say about Dave [Rozelle], he was one in a million," Mickelson told me, in his poignant recollections of his friend and assistant gunner who died on Hill 861. "I've thought of Dave every day of my life, ever since. Sometime during the day I'll think about Dave."

25. Ibid.

26. Gerald F. O'Neal, letter to Ernie Spencer, November 25, 1992, printed in *Khe Sanh Veteran* (Summer 1993).

27. Norman Jasper, author's interview, January 27, 2012.

28. Ibid.

29. William Dabney, VMI Oral History interview, September 8, 2005.

30. Matthew P. Caulfield, USMC Oral History Collection, Tape No. 6157.

31. Tom Esslinger, author's interview, March 25, 2012. Esslinger was in Bill Dabney's command bunker on 881 South at the time and heard the radio exchange between Matt Caulfield and Jerry Saulsberry.

32. Dennis Mannion, author's interview, November 30, 2011. Mannion said at least five or six 105-millimeter howitzer rounds from Khe Sanh inadvertently hit 861 during the night. He wasn't aware of any Marines who were injured by the errant rounds.

33. William Dabney, VMI Oral History interview, September 8, 2005.

34. Ibid. Some estimates state that 1,400 81-millimeter mortar rounds were fired from Hill 881 South in support of Hill 861 during the assault of January 21, 1968. The Marines on 881 South suffered only one casualty: an 81-millimeter mortarman was badly burned in a flash fire when he inadvertently tossed a cigarette butt in a pile of propellant bags (known as increments).

35. Matthew P. Caulfield, USMC Oral History Collection, Tape No. 6157.

36. Miguel Salinas, author's interview, May 2, 2012. Salinas kept the wallet and later had the letter translated by a North Vietnamese defector who was serving with the Marines as a Kit Carson scout.

37. Dennis Mannion, author's interview, December 1, 2011.

38. Ted Mickelson, author's interview, January 15, 2012.

39. Dennis Mannion, author's interview, December 1, 2011.

40. William Dabney, VMI Oral History interview, September 8, 2005.

41. William Dabney, conversation with Ray Stubbe, May 28, 1996, quoted in Ray Stubbe, *Battalion of Kings: A Tribute to Our Fallen Brothers Who Died Because of the Battlefield of Khe Sanh, Vietnam,* 2nd ed., rev. (Wauwatosa, WI: Khe Sanh Veterans, 2008), 124.

42. Dennis Mannion, author's interview, December 1, 2011. Mannion also stated that the North Vietnamese did not fire rockets from 881 North in the initial barrage of January 21, 1968. The 1/26 Command Chronology for January 1968 states that "the battalion received approximately 100 82mm mortar rounds and 20 1 [*sic*] 122mm rockets throughout its assigned sector within the Khe Sanh Combat Base." There is no mention of heavy artillery. Some accounts have stated that heavy artillery was not used against the base until January 24. But other men I interviewed who were at the combat base on the morning of January 21 also concur with Mannion and told me that heavy artillery rounds were fired in the opening barrage, along with mortars and rockets.

CHAPTER 3

1. Phillip Davidson, interview with Ray Stubbe, April 19, 1989, quoted in John Prados and Ray W. Stubbe, *Valley of Decision: The Siege of Khe Sanh* (Boston: Houghton Mifflin, 1991), 228.

2. Phillip Davidson recalled this scene in his book *Vietnam at War: The History, 1946–1975* (New York: Oxford University Press, 1991), 554–555. Davidson described briefing General Westmoreland on the night of January 20 upon his return from Khe Sanh. According to Davidson, Westmoreland became so upset after hearing Davidson's descriptions of what he had seen and experienced at Khe Sanh that he ordered Lieutenant General Creighton Abrams to establish himself in I Corps to keep an eye on the situation at Khe Sanh. Westmoreland's staff historian, Colonel Reamer W. "Hap" Argo Jr., provided an equally harsh assessment of Colonel Lownds after visiting Khe Sanh around the same time. In Argo's caustic view, Lownds was "a complete loser." See Lewis Sorley, *Westmoreland: The General Who Lost Vietnam* (Boston: Houghton Mifflin Harcourt, 2011), 169.

3. Michael O'Hara, author's interview, April 26, 2011.

4. Ibid.

5. Ibid.

6. Ibid.

7. Tom Quigley, author's interview, April 23, 2011.

8. Ibid.

9. Michael O'Hara, author's interview, April 26, 2011.

10. Ken Rodgers, author's interview, July 21, 2011.

11. John Cicala Jr., author's interview, May 24, 2011.

12. Tom Quigley, author's interview, April 23, 2011.

13. Ibid.

14. Edward Feldman, author's interview, April 11, 2012.

15. Edward Feldman, author's interviews, April 11 and 13, 2012.

16. Edward Feldman was awarded a Silver Star for his extraordinary actions in saving the life of Robert Mussari. Mussari was evacuated to the Philippines, where American reporters chronicled his incredible story, which ran in the *New York Times, Time* magazine, and other publications across the country. Feldman was hailed as a hero. After the war, Feldman was in private practice in northern New Jersey when he received a phone call from Mussari, inviting Feldman to his wedding. Feldman not only attended the wedding of Mussari but a few years later delivered Mussari's son. Feldman also recommended the awarding of Silver Stars to every other man who assisted him in the operation, and he was disappointed when the men were given Bronze Stars instead—an injustice, in Feldman's view. Edward Feldman, author's interviews, April 11 and 13, 2012.

17. Ken Rodgers, author's interview, July 21, 2011.

18. Ken Warner, author's interview, March 27, 2012.

19. Daniel Sullivan, author's interview, April 16, 2012.

20. Dave Doehrman, author's interview, April 6, 2012.

21. Ray Milligan, author's interview, April 6, 2012.

22. Billy Ray Hill, author's interview, April 5, 2012.

23. William Smith, author's interview, March 8, 2012.

24. Ibid.

25. Lewis "Sam" Messer, author's interview, April 10, 2012.

26. Ibid.

27. Steve Wiese, author's interview, April 20, 2012.

28. Michael O'Hara, author's interview, April 26, 2011.

29. Steve Wiese, author's interview, April 12, 2012.

CHAPTER 4

1. Project CHECO Report, Khe Sanh (22 January–31 March 1968), September 13, 1968, 92–93, in RG 472: Records of the U.S. Forces in Southeast Asia, 1950–1976, National Archives and Records Administration (hereafter NARA); and "Effects of B-52 Airstrikes near Khe Sanh," Interrogation Report of captive Hi Van Phen, PFC, 11th Company, 3rd Battalion, 1st Regiment, 330th Division, April 30, 1968, Combined Military Intelligence Center Reports, RG 472, Records of the U.S. Forces in Southeast Asia, 1950–1975, NARA.

2. North Vietnamese Army documents published in *B5-T8 in 48 QXD* (Wauwatosa, WI: Khe Sanh Veterans, 2006), ed. Khe Sanh chaplain Ray Stubbe and trans. Sedgwick D. Tourison Jr., 10–11. The documents in *B5-T8 in 48 QXD* appear to present a reasonably accurate and straightforward account of the movement and disposition of forces in the Khe Sanh campaign. They also appear to provide a credible snapshot of NVA casualties, the nature of the injuries sustained, and whether they occurred from ground fire, artillery, or air attacks. The documents tend to lapse into hyperbole and propaganda when reporting the strength and casualties of opposing American forces. These numbers are invariably skewed to show the North Vietnamese Army units inflicting far greater casualties against much larger forces than were actually involved in particular incidents. This problem was not limited to NVA forces during the war: numerous Americans at various levels of command in Vietnam, including several of the men I interviewed regarding their experiences at Khe Sanh, have described how they were pressured to inflate the enemy body count in operations. But the exaggerations in the North Vietnamese documents when describing US troop strength and casualties in various engagements are particularly pronounced.

3. Ibid., 10–11.

4. My description of the opening of the attack on Khe Sanh village is drawn from the following: Bruce B. G. Clarke, author's interviews, September 17–18, 2012; Jim Perry, quoted in Bruce B. G. Clarke, *Expendable Warriors: The Battle of Khe Sanh and the Vietnam War*, Stackpole Books edition (Mechanicsburg, PA: Stackpole Books, 2009), 53; George Amos, written account in Clarke, *Expendable Warriors*; Michael Archer, author's interview, August 20, 2013; and Archer's memoir about his Vietnam service, *A Patch of Ground: Khe Sanh Remembered* (Central Point, OR: Hellgate Press, 2004), 84–85.

5. Bruce Clarke, author's interview, September 16, 2012. Some published accounts have incorrectly stated that Clarke had been leading a patrol outside the Huong Hoa district compound on the morning of January 21, 1968, and had just gotten back inside the wire before the North Vietnamese attack began. Clarke led a patrol south of the compound the previous day, January 20, but did not leave the compound again until January 22.

6. I am grateful to F. J. "Jim" Taylor, CAC Oscar Marine and unofficial historian, for his insights as I wrote about CAC Oscar and the events at Khe Sanh village on January 21–22, 1968. The product of Taylor's research can be viewed at https://sites.google.com/site/usmc-caposcar/home.

7. Jim Perry, quoted in Clarke, *Expendable Warriors*, 53.

8. Howard McKinnis, author's interview, September 24, 2012; Bruce Clarke, author's interviews, September 16–17, 2012.

9. Bruce Clarke, author's interviews, September 16–17, 2012.

10. Verner Russell was awarded a Silver Star for his actions.

11. Howard McKinnis, author's interview, September 24, 2012.

12. Ibid.

13. Ibid.

14. John Roberts, author's interview, September 21, 2012.

15. Ibid.

16. Ibid.

17. Ibid.

18. James E. Perry, Silver Star citation.

19. Bruce Clarke, author's interview, September 16, 2012.

20. Ibid.; also see "Operations of U.S. Marine Forces, Vietnam, January 1968," Fleet Marine Force Operations, U.S. Marine Forces Vietnam, NARA, RG 127.

21. Bruce Clarke, author's interview, September 16, 2012. It was Clarke's recollection that the jet called in by the Marine forward air controller was an F-4 Phantom, but Marine Corps records identify it as an A-6A.

22. Ward Britt, Silver Star citation; Bruce Clarke, author's interview, September 16, 2012.

23. Bruce Clarke, author's interview, September 16, 2012.

24. Ward Britt, Silver Star citation.

25. Ibid.; Bruce Clarke, author's interview, September 16, 2012; also see Britt, quoted in Clarke, *Expendable Warriors*, 62.

26. Tom Stiner, quoted in Clarke, *Expendable Warriors*, 75–76.

27. Jerry Elliott's sister, Donna, has spent years trying to learn the fate of her brother. Her investigation has included trips to Vietnam, where she has followed leads and searched the Khe Sanh battlefield for her brother's remains. She recounts her quest in *Keeping the Promise: The Story of MIA Jerry Elliott, a Family Shattered by His Disappearance, and His Sister's 40-year Search for the Truth* (Ashland, OR: Hellgate Press, 2010).

28. Tom Stiner, quoted in Clarke, *Expendable Warriors*, 77.

29. Bruce Clarke, author's interview, September 16, 2012.

30. Steve Orr, author's interview, August 19, 2013.

31. Miguel Salinas, author's interview, May 1, 2012.

32. Dennis Mannion, author's interview, December 1, 2011.

33. Larry LeClaire, author's interview, April 18, 2012.

34. Ibid.

35. 3rd Marine Division, Situation Reports, Operation Scotland, No. 327 and No. 328.

36. Ibid., No. 328.

37. John Roberts, author's interview, September 21, 2012.

38. Bruce Clarke, author's interview, September 16, 2012. Clarke said he learned several days later that a North Vietnamese defector had revealed that the B-52 strike during the night of January 21–22 inflicted heavy casualties on his NVA unit as it moved north to join the battle against Khe Sanh.

39. John Roberts, author's interview, September 21, 2012.

40. These seven medevac flights to Khe Sanh village on the morning of January 22, 1968, were flown by Captain Glenn Wayne Russell Jr. He would make another four flights to the village to evacuate the CAC Oscar Marines under fire. For these and other actions that day, Russell was awarded the Silver Star. See Captain Glenn Wayne Russell Jr. Silver Star citation. Also see Marine Medium Helicopter Squadron 362, After Mission Reports for January 22, 1968, at After Mission Report, 01 January 1968, Folder 099, US Marine Corps History Division Vietnam War Documents Collection, The Vietnam Center and Archive, Texas

Tech University. Accessed October 9, 2012, at http://www.vietnam.ttu.edu/virtualarchive/items.php?item=1201099069.

41. Bruce Clarke, author's interview, September 17, 2012.

42. Colonel Lownds would later say that he didn't intend to exclude the South Vietnamese and Bru from the helicopter evacuation operation at Khe Sanh village. Whether it was a misunderstanding or not, witnesses during the evacuation said the Marine helicopter crews didn't allow South Vietnamese and Bru fighters aboard their helicopters even after they had been disarmed.

43. Bruce Clarke, author's interview, September 17, 2012.

44. Robert Brewer, quoted in Ray Stubbe, *Battalion of Kings: A Tribute to Our Fallen Brothers Who Died Because of the Battlefield of Khe Sanh, Vietnam*, 2nd ed., rev. (Wauwatosa, WI: Khe Sanh Veterans, 2008), 131.

45. People's Army of Vietnam, 304th Division after-action report on the battle for Khe Sanh, quoted in *B5-T8 in 48 QXD*, 72.

CHAPTER 5

1. Adam Alexander, author's interview, December 17, 2011. Alexander was one of the twelve VO-67 pilots in Muscle Shoals, and he described in detail for me how the squadron came about and its preparations for its top secret work.

2. Also see Jacob Van Staaveren, *History of Task Force Alpha, 1 October 1967–30 April 1967*, United States Air Force, 1969, 49.

3. Phillip B. Davidson, *Vietnam at War: The History, 1946–1975* (New York: Oxford University Press, 1991), 558.

4. I drew on several primary sources for this account of Defense Secretary Robert McNamara's plan to build an anti-infiltration border barrier that included the use of electronic sensors. Among the most useful were: *Report of the Office of the Secretary of Defense Vietnam Task Force, compiled 06/1967–01/1969, documenting the period 1940–1967* (better known as the Pentagon Papers), Part IV, c.7.a, "Evolution of the War. Air War in the North: 1965–1968," vol. 1, 145–169, Records of the Office of the Secretary of Defense, 1921–2008, RG 330, NARA, hereafter referred to as the Pentagon Papers; "Bugging the Battlefield," Department of Defense training film, 1969, Motion Picture Films and Video Recordings on Four Decades of U.S. Military Activities Around the World, ca. 1950–ca. 1990, Records of the Office of the Secretary of Defense, 1921–2008, RG 330, NARA; and USMACV Command History 1968, vol. 2, 911–34, RG 472, NARA.

5. Pentagon Papers, Part IV, c.7.a, "Evolution of the War. Air War in the North: 1965–1968," vol. 1, 148.

6. The Strong Point Obstacle System (Dyemarker/Duel Blade) and its electronic sensor component, Muscle Shoals/Igloo White, are described at length in *United States Military Assistance Command, Vietnam (USMACV) Command History 1968*, vol. 2, prepared by the Military History Branch, Office of the Secretary, Joint Staff, MACV, and archived in RG 472, "Records of the U.S. Forces in Southeast Asia, 1950–1976," NARA. See Annex B, "Anti-infiltration Barrier," 911–934.

7. Adam Alexander, author's interview, December 17, 2011.

8. "Bugging the Battlefield," DOD film; also see USMACV Command History 1968, vol. 2, 911–934, RG 472, NARA.

9. Adam Alexander, author's interview, December 17, 2011.

10. *MACV Command History 1968*, vol. 2, 921.

11. Jacob Van Staaveren writes in his *History of Task Force Alpha* (p. 50) that the sensor-laying missions at Khe Sanh began on January 20 with flights by the CH-3 aircraft of the 21st Helicopter Squadron. Van Staaveren writes elsewhere that the fixed-wing aircraft of VO-67 began laying sensors around Khe Sanh on January 22. See Van Staaveren, *Interdiction in Southern Laos, 1961–1968* (Washington, DC: Center of Air Force History, 1993), 291. The *MACV Command History 1968* (vol. 2, p. 922) fixes January 21 as the date when sensor-laying operations began at Khe Sanh. Adding further to the confusion, the undated Navy Commendation Medal Citation of VO-67 pilot L. W. Gire states that he flew a mission to Khe Sanh on January 19.

CHAPTER 6

1. These details are drawn from daily situation reports. See 3rd Marine Division, Situation Reports, Operation Scotland, Nos. 329–332.

2. Lance Corporal Billy R. Moffett, USMC Oral History Collection, Tape No. 2589.

3. 3rd Marine Division, Situation Reports, Operation Scotland, No. 332.

4. Ibid., Nos. 329, 330, and 331.

5. Ray Stubbe, *Khe Sanh Chaplain: A Historical Summary of Activities While Assigned to 1/26, 3d Recon., and 3d Shore Party BNs, July, 1967, Through June, 1968, Including the Khe Sanh Seige [sic] of 1968, of LT Ray W. Stubbe, CHC, USNR*, unpublished manuscript dated April 1, 1970, 539.

6. The two Marines killed were Corporal Howard Leon Johnson of Memphis, Tennessee, and Lance Corporal Thomas Lee Cottrell of Los Gatos, California. Combat Area Casualties Database, RG 330, NARA.

7. John Prados and Ray W. Stubbe, *Valley of Decision: The Siege of Khe Sanh* (Boston: Houghton Mifflin, 1991), 274–275.

8. Command Chronology, January 1968, 1st Battalion, 26th Marines, entries for January 22, 1968, RG 127, NARA.

9. 3rd Marine Division, Situation Reports, Operation Scotland, No. 332.

10. "5,000 Men Massed at Khe Sanh," *New York Times*, January 24, 1968.

11. The two Marines who died with Bernard Fall were Lance Corporal Glenn A. Harris, eighteen years old, from Chicago, Illinois, and Gunnery Sergeant Byron G. Highland, thirty-three years old, of Detroit, Michigan. Highland, a Korean War veteran, was a combat photographer who was working with Fall.

12. Earle Breeding, author's interview, May 10, 2012.

13. Ibid.

14. 3rd Marine Division, Situation Reports, Operation Scotland, No. 334; Jim Kaylor, author's interview, February 15, 2012; Dave McCall, author's interview, February 16, 2012; Larry McCartney, author's interview, January 3, 2012; Dave Norton, author's interview, February 12, 2012; Matthew Walsh, author's interview, February 13, 2012; Michael Worth, author's interview, February 13, 2012.

15. Dave Norton, author's interview, February 13, 2012.

16. Ibid.

17. David McCall, author's interview, February 16, 2012.

18. Dave Norton, author's interview, February 13, 2012.

19. Earle Breeding, author's interview, May 10, 2012.

CHAPTER 7

1. Phillip B. Davidson, *Vietnam at War: The History, 1946–1975* (New York: Oxford University Press, 1991), 443–444. As the senior US military intelligence chief in Vietnam at the time of the Tet Offensive, Davidson had a stake in defending General Westmoreland's contention that Communist forces sought a decisive confrontation at Khe Sanh. In his book, he vehemently rejects the Khe-Sanh-as-ruse school of thought that has flourished among journalists and scholars over the decades. Davidson contends that Giap "had some important purpose in mind for the use of this corps-size force" deployed against Khe Sanh in early 1968. That purpose, Davidson argues, is that Khe Sanh "had to be the set-piece battle of Phase III."

2. The North Vietnamese buildup around Khe Sanh is discussed in Willard Pearson, *The War in the Northern Provinces* (Washington, DC: Department of the Army, 1975), 30–31, and in various North Vietnamese documents in *B5-T8 in 48 QXD* (Wauwatosa, WI: Khe Sanh Veterans, 2006), ed. Ray Stubbe and trans. Sedgwick D. Tourison Jr., 4–16 and 30–35.

3. *B5-T8 in 48 QXD*, 15.

4. Ibid., 14 and 26–28.

5. Dennis Mannion, author's interview, December 8, 2011.

6. Larry LeClaire, author's interview, April 18, 2012. "That first week, everybody was nervous as a cat," LeClaire told me. "Everybody thought we were going to get hit again. A lot of times at night you would be off watch and the word would be passed, 100 percent alert, and you'd have to get up and be ready."

7. Ibid.

8. The two Marines killed on Hill 861 by the mortar round that mortally wounded Christian Feit on January 24, 1968, were PFC Kenneth Virgil Goodman, twenty years old, of Stewart, Minnesota, and Lance Corporal Francis Pennetti, also twenty, of Philadelphia, Pennsylvania.

9. Ray Milligan, author's interview, April 7, 2012.

10. Dave Doehrman, author's interview, April 6, 2012; Kevin Macaulay, author's interview, May 17, 2012; Ray Milligan, author's interview, April 7, 2012. The four men killed by the rocket that struck the Bravo, 3rd Recon bunker at Khe Sanh Combat Base on January 24, 1968, were: corpsman Charles W. Miller; Lance Corporal Gregory F. Popowitz; Lance Corporal Juan Antonio Rosa; and Lance Corporal Gary David Scribner.

11. Also killed in the North Vietnamese barrages of January 24, 1968, was Corporal George Ralph Castillo of Lima Company, 3/26, 3rd Marine Division, Situation Reports, Operation Scotland, No. 337 and No. 340.

12. Ray Stubbe, *Khe Sanh Chaplain: A Historical Summary of Activities While Assigned to 1/26, 3d Recon., and 3d Shore Party BNs, July, 1967, Through June, 1968, Including the Khe Sanh Seige [sic] of 1968, of LT Ray W. Stubbe, CHC, USNR*, unpublished manuscript dated April 1, 1970, 566.

13. Michael O'Hara, author's interview, April 26, 2011.

14. Ernesto Gomez, Navy Cross citation, undated.

15. John Rauch, author's interview, March 22, 2012.

16. Dennis Mannion described this incident in our interviews and also provided me with his written account of the Alpha Company patrol of January 26, 1968, entitled "Wishing Upon a Silver Star," undated.

17. Dennis Mannion, "Wishing Upon a Silver Star," undated.

18. John Rauch, author's interview, March 22, 2012. A brief account of the engagement is contained in 3rd Marine Division, Situation Reports, Operation Scotland, No. 347.

Dwight T. Denning was awarded the Silver Star for his heroic actions that cost him his life on January 26, 1968. The citation states that Denning's companions "aggressively continued their assault and quickly destroyed the enemy force." In fact, the Marines withdrew from the draw and left it to supporting arms—air and artillery—to destroy the North Vietnamese positions.

19. "CO of 3rd Engineer Battalion to commanding officer of the 3rd Marine Battalion," January 28, 1968, 3rd Engineer Battalion Command Chronology for January 1968, RG 127, NARA.

20. Phillip B. Davidson, *Vietnam at War: The History, 1946–1975* (New York: Oxford University Press, 1991), 570.

21. Ibid.

22. MACV Command History 1968, 2:911; and Item 15 0900, January 29, Daily Journal Files, MACV J-2 Command Center, RG 407, NARA; also see James J. Wirtz, *The Tet Offensive: Intelligence Failure in War* (Ithaca: Cornell University Press, 1991), 217.

23. Ray Stubbe, *Battalion of Kings: A Tribute to Our Fallen Brothers Who Died Because of the Battlefield of Khe Sanh, Vietnam*, 2nd ed., rev. (Wauwatosa, WI: Khe Sanh Veterans, 2008), 144.

24. I am grateful to F. J. "Jim" Taylor for sharing with me his recollections and written account of the January 29, 1968, rescue mission to Hill 471. He also shared with me the written account of Captain Harlan "Rip" Van Winkle, US Army Special Forces, "Action on Hill 471, January 29, 1968," which Taylor edited. Also see Stubbe, *Battalion of Kings*, 146–147.

25. Van Winkle, "Action on Hill 471, January 29, 1968."

26. All three Americans who died on Hill 471 on January 29, 1968, were Pennsylvanians. Thirty-three-year-old Charles Tredinnick left behind a wife in the northeastern borough of Dallas. The remains of twenty-six-year-old Gary Crone of York and twenty-two-year-old Michael T. Mahoney of Towanda were recovered several weeks later on Hill 471.

27. Ibid.

28. General William Westmoreland to Admiral Ulysses S. G. Sharp, cable dated January 29, 1968, quoted in James J. Wirtz, *The Tet Offensive: Intelligence Failure in War* (Ithaca: Cornell University Press, 1991), 218.

29. Ibid.

30. William Westmoreland, quoted in Robert Mann, *A Grand Delusion: America's Descent into Vietnam* (New York: Basic Books, 2002), 570.

31. Robert McNamara to LBJ, November 1, 1967, quoted in David M. Barrett, ed., *Lyndon B. Johnson's Vietnam Papers* (College Station: Texas A&M University Press, 1997), 515–522.

32. Mann, *A Grand Delusion*, 566.

33. Walt Rostow recounted the January 10, 1968, lunch at Joseph Alsop's house in a memo to Lyndon Johnson later that day, Walt Rostow to President Lyndon B. Johnson; Meeting with Joe Alsop, January 10, 1968; Folder 35, Box 01, Veteran Members of the 109th Quartermaster Company (Air Delivery) Collection, The Vietnam Center and Archive, Texas Tech University, accessed at http://www.vietnam.ttu.edu/virtualarchive/items .php?item=0010135002.

34. "The Situation at Khe Sanh," Memorandum from the Joint Chiefs of Staff to President Lyndon Johnson, January 29, 1968, JCSM–63–68, *Foreign Relations of the United States: 1964–1968, Volume 6, Vietnam, January–August 1968* (Washington, DC: Government Printing Office, 2002), 69–70.

35. Ibid.

36. It has been erroneously reported over the years that President Johnson forced each of the Joint Chiefs to sign a statement promising that Khe Sanh would be held. In fact, the only written assurance from the Joint Chiefs was Wheeler's memo of January 29, 1968, in which the military chiefs endorsed "General Westmoreland's assessment of the situation" and recommended that US forces remain at Khe Sanh. See "Notes of the President's Meeting with the Chiefs of Staff," January 29, 1968, 1:04–1:40 p.m., *Foreign Relations of the United States: 1964–1968*, 6:71–72. The following day, January 30, 1968, in a meeting with Democratic congressional leaders, Lyndon Johnson described the questions he put to the Joint Chiefs and their answers. See "Notes of the President's Meeting with the Democratic Leadership, January 30, 1968, 8:30–10:06 a.m., *Foreign Relations of the United States: 1964–1968, Volume 6*, 77–79.

CHAPTER 8

1. Military Assistance Command, Vietnam (hereafter MACV) Monthly Report, January 1968, 50.

2. Sergeant Jesus Roberto Vasquez, Navy Cross citation, undated.

3. Dennis Mannion, author's interview, December 9, 2011.

4. Ibid.

5. Dennis Mannion provided a copy of his January 31, 1968, letter to the author.

6. Dennis Mannion, author's interview, December 15, 2011.

7. Ibid.

8. General Wheeler first raised the issue of President Johnson's concern about the possible use of tactical nuclear weapons in his February 1 telegram, JCS 1154, to Admiral Sharpe at CINCPAC and General Westmoreland at MACV in Saigon. See *Foreign Relations of the United States: 1964–1968, Volume 6, Vietnam, January–August 1968*, 120. This telegram and other related messages between Westmoreland and Washington regarding the nuclear issue can be found in Walt Rostow's files at the Lyndon Baines Johnson Presidential Library, filed under "NSC History of the March 31st Speech, Vol 2. Tabs-A-Z and AA-ZZ."

9. General Wheeler communicated President Johnson's latest concerns in a cable to General Westmoreland, JCS 01272, February 3, 1968.

10. Ibid.

11. General Wheeler quoted extensively from Westmoreland's assessment in "Memorandum from the Chairman of the Joint Chiefs of Staff (Wheeler) to President Johnson," Washington, DC, February 3, 1968, CM-2944–68, *Foreign Relations of the United States: 1964–1968, Volume 6, Vietnam, January–August 1968*, 117–20.

12. "Drawing the Noose?" *Newsweek*, February 5, 1968, 39–40.

13. Mark Swearengen, author's interview, August 16, 2013.

14. The background material on Mirza M. "Harry" Baig is drawn from the monograph by Ray Stubbe, *Khe Sanh and the Mongol Prince* (Wauwatosa, WI: Self-published, 2002), 9–12.

15. Ibid., 14.

16. Major Mirza M. Baig, letter to Colonel F. C. Caldwell, Head, USMC Historical Branch, December 23, 1968, found in *The Battle for Khe Sanh* Comments File, at the U.S. Marine Corps Archives in Quantico, Virginia.

17. Along with Ray Stubbe's monograph on Harry Baig, *Khe Sanh and the Mongol Prince*, Michael Archer paints a vivid portrait of the extraordinary targeting officer in his

memoir, *A Patch of Ground: Khe Sanh Remembered* (Central Point, OR: Hellgate Press, 2004), 131–136.

18. Baig, letter to Colonel F. C. Caldwell, December 23, 1968.

19. Ibid.

CHAPTER 9

1. Don Shanley, author's interview, February 20, 2012.

2. Ibid.

3. Dave McCall, author's interview, February 16, 2012.

4. Ibid.

5. Joseph Molettiere obituary, *Philadelphia Daily Inquirer*, February 20, 1968; also Dave Norton, author's interview, February 13, 2012.

6. Don Shanley, author's interview, February 20, 2012.

7. Ibid. A useful timeline of the battle for 861 Alpha on the morning of February 5, 1968, can be found in the 3rd Marine Division, Situation Reports, Operation Scotland, No. 385.

8. Don Shanley, author's interview, February 20, 2012.

9. Ibid.

10. Dave McCall, author's interview, February 16, 2012.

11. Dave Norton, author's interview, February 13, 2012.

12. Ibid.

13. Earle Breeding, author's interview, May 10, 2012.

14. Ibid.; Don Shanley, author's interview, February 20, 2012. Shanley refutes accounts that have described a massive human-wave assault hitting the Echo lines on 861 Alpha. The North Vietnamese troops he witnessed coming through the breach in 1st Platoon lines arrived in groups of two or three men, Shanley said.

15. Don Shanley, statement of February 18, 1968, in Bronze Star medal file on PFC Jack C. Bogard, quoted in Ray Stubbe, *Battalion of Kings: A Tribute to Our Fallen Brothers Who Died Because of the Battlefield of Khe Sanh, Vietnam,* 2nd ed., rev. (Wauwatosa, WI: Khe Sanh Veterans, 2008), 160.

16. Richard Lynn Woodard, April 1968, comments in USMC Oral History interview No. 2775.

17. Don Shanley, author's interview, February 20, 2012.

18. Tom Eichler, letter to Ray Stubbe, September 1986, quoted in Stubbe, *Battalion of Kings,* 161.

19. Ibid.

20. Major Mirza M. Baig, letter to Colonel F.C. Caldwell, Head, USMC Historical Branch, December 23, 1968. I'm also grateful to Mark Swearengen for his vivid recollections of how the extraordinary artillery barrage was executed in defense of Hill 861 Alpha in the early morning of February 5, 1968. Mark Swearengen, author's interview, August 16, 2013.

21. Earle Breeding, author's interview, May 10, 2012.

22. Jim Kaylor, author's interview, February 15, 2012.

23. Matt Walsh, author's interview, February 12, 2012.

24. Ibid.; Michael Worth, author's interview, February 13, 2012.

25. Matt Walsh, author's interview, February 12, 2012; Michael Worth, author's interview, February 13, 2012.

26. Don Shanley, author's interview, February 20, 2012.

27. Ibid.

28. Jim Kaylor, author's interview, February 15, 2012. Don Shanley doesn't recall much enemy resistance during the counterattack. Jim Kaylor remembers extremely heavy enemy fire, and he feared that Shanley was going to get killed as he led the charge.

29. Jim Kaylor, author's interview, February 15, 2012.

30. Don Shanley, author's interview, February 20, 2012.

31. Dave Norton, author's interview, February 13, 2012.

32. Ibid.

33. Dave McCall, author's interview, February 16, 2012.

34. Ibid.

35. Jose Luis "Cisco" Reyes, author's interview, February 23, 2012.

CHAPTER 10

1. See Major Gary L. Telfer, Lieutenant Colonel Lane Rogers, USMC, and V. Keith Fleming Jr., *U.S. Marines in Vietnam: Fighting the North Vietnamese, 1967* (Washington, DC: History and Museums Division, Headquarters, U.S. Marine Corps, 1984), 33.

2. The Special Forces detachment commander killed in the May 4, 1967, attack on Lang Vei was Captain William Anderson Crenshaw, twenty-seven years old, of Mobile, Alabama. Also killed was the detachment's twenty-seven-year-old executive officer, First Lieutenant Franklin Delano Stallings, of Washington, DC.

3. Paul Longgrear, author's interview, January 27, 2012.

4. Statement of Nickolas Fragos, "Combat After Action Report—Battle of Lang Vei," 5th Special Forces Group, February 22, 1968, RG 472, NARA.

5. There are discrepancies between the various witness statements and the radio transmission logs as to whether the attack on Lang Vei began in the minutes before or after midnight of February 6–7. See "Combat After Action Report—Battle of Lang Vei," including the eyewitness accounts. Also see William R. Phillips, *Night of the Silver Stars: The Battle of Lang Vei* (New York: St. Martin's Paperbacks, 2004), 107–110.

6. Nickolas Fragos radio transmission, quoted in Phillips, *Night of the Silver Stars*, 110.

7. "Combat After Action Report—Battle of Lang Vei."

8. Statements of Lieutenant Colonel Daniel F. Schungel and Staff Sergeant Peter Tiroch, "Combat After Action Report—Battle of Lang Vei." Paul Longgrear provided insights into the fate of James William Holt, based on his conversations with his Special Forces operators present at Lang Vei during the fight. Paul Longgrear, author's interview, September 23, 2013.

9. Paul Longgrear, author's interview, September 23, 2013.

10. Ibid.

11. Ibid.

12. Ibid.

13. Like so many aspects of the battle of Lang Vei, uncertainty has surrounded the fate of the two Americans at the Mike outpost, Charles Lindwald and Kenneth Hanna. Paul Longgrear told me that his Mike force outpost had been overrun within minutes. These were Longgrear's men, and his efforts to shed light on their fate has stretched over decades. He has maintained close contact with most of the Americans who survived the battle at Lang Vei, and he has met some of his former adversaries in recent decades in Vietnam, further deepening his knowledge of what happened that night. Radio operator Emanuel E. Phillips was the last American to have contact with Lindewald and Hanna, and in his statement in

the "Combat After Action Report—Battle of Lang Vei," Phillips writes: "As A-101 radio su-pervisor, my alert position and sleeping quarters were located in the TOC. I was awakened at approximately midnight and told that there were tanks advancing on the camp's southern perimeter. I first made sure That [sic] all the USASF were alerted. Then contacted Marine artillery and requested fire on our southern perimeter, reference the camps night defensive fire plan. Simultaneously, SFC Hanna reported the OP as being under heavy mortar and automatic weapons attack. Two artillery missions were called in defense of the OP before radio contact was lost. At last radio contact was regained with the OP. SFC Hanna reported that SFC lindewald [sic] was gravely wounded, and that the OP was still under heavy at-tack. After losing radio contact with the OP, under CPT Willoughby's direction, all efforts were directed toward stopping the tanks and coordinating air support." The author of the definitive book on the battle of Lang Vei, William R. Phillips—the cousin of Green Beret Daniel R. Phillips, who was among the missing at Lang Vei, but no relation to Emanuel E. Phillips—writes of the two Americans at the Mike force outpost: "Lindewald had taken se-vere abdominal wounds, as reported by Dinh Chep, MIKE Force platoon leader. He had not seen Hanna wounded, but he had watched as Hanna and the radio operator carried Lindewald into the bunker at the OP. He then had seen a tank roll up to the wire and fire at the bunker, destroying it (and presumably killing Lindewald, Hanna and the radio op-erator) and the machine gun behind it." The radio operator referred to as Dinh Chep must have been an indigenous fighter, as there were no other Americans at the outpost when the attack occurred. Phillips, *Night of the Silver Stars*, 204.

14. Statement of Lieutenant Colonel Daniel F. Schungel, "Combat After Action Re-port—Battle of Lang Vei."

15. Ibid.

16. Statement of Staff Sergeant Peter Tiroch, "Combat After Action Report—Battle of Lang Vei."

17. In a series of USMC Oral History interviews, Major General Rathvon Tompkins, 3rd Marine Division commanding officer, and two other Marine officers involved in the events recall the real-time discussions on February 7, 1968, over whether to use the "controlled fragmentation munitions" (COFRAM) on the NVA assault forces at Lang Vei. See USMC Oral History Tape No. 2535.

18. Ibid.

19. Statement of Captain Frank C. Willoughby, "Combat After Action Report—Battle of Lang Vei."

20. Paul Longgrear, author's interview, January 27, 2012.

21. Ibid.

22. "HCS to Host Hall of Honor Induction Ceremony," *Utica Observer-Dispatch*, June 20, 2012.

23. Charles "Toby" Rushforth, author's interview, January 29, 2012.

24. Ibid.

25. Ibid.; and Paul Longgrear, author's interview, January 27, 2012.

26. Charles "Toby" Rushforth, author's interview, January 29, 2012.

27. Paul Longgrear, author's interview, January 27, 2012.

28. This account of the extraordinary efforts of the AV-25 pilots in support of Lang Vei is drawn from the following: Paul Longgrear, author's interview, January 27, 2012; Charles "Toby" Rushforth, author's interview, January 29, 2012; Captain Charles Rushforth, US Air Force interview, February 18, 1968; "Khe Sanh (Operation Niagara) 22 January–31 March," HQPACAF, Directorate, Tactical Evaluation, Checo Division; Rick Burgess and Zip Rausa,

U.S. Navy A-1 Skyraider Units of the Vietnam War (Oxford: Osprey Publishing, 2009); and President's Message, *Fist of the Fleet Association* Newsletter 8 (January 2012).

29. Richard Allen, author's interviews, February 2–3, 2012.

30. Ibid.

31. William Smith, author's interview, March 7, 2012. The difficulties inherent in an overland effort to relieve Lang Vei had been underscored about two months earlier, when the Khe Sanh Combat Base commander, Colonel David Lownds, had dispatched a company of Marines to chart the best route to the Special Forces camp. It took the Marines more than a day to hack their way through the thick jungle before reaching the Special Forces camp. Bill Smith was a young lieutenant at the time he made the march. "It was an exercise in total futility, especially for a rifle company," he said. "We were totally exposed, and it was technically unfeasible."

32. Ladd found no shortage of volunteers among the American and indigenous fighters serving with the Special Forces in eastern I Corps. Members of the elite airborne Scout unit of Project Delta volunteered to jump into Lang Vei, and Longgrear's superior in the Mike Force chain of command, battalion commander Major Adam Husar, readied a separate force to relieve the embattled camp. See Phillips, *Night of the Silver Stars*, 167; and John Cash, "Battle of Lang Vei," in John A. Cash, John Albright, and Allan W. Sandstrum, *Seven Firefights in Vietnam* (Washington, DC: Office of the Chief of Military History, U.S. Army, 1985), 130.

33. Major General Rathvon Tompkins, comments on USMC Oral History Collection, Tape No. 2535.

34. Paul Longgrear told me that he doesn't believe a C-130 with Special Forces reinforcements for Lang Vei reached the Khe Sanh area. But Major General Rathvon Tompkins describes the turnback of a C-130 that was believed to be carrying one hundred Special Forces personnel. In his interview on USMC Oral History Tape No. 2535, Tompkins reads from notes he took during the Lang Vei attack and relief requests and lays out the following timeline: "0343, FC [fire coordinator] 26th Marines reports air center has incoming C-130 in with approximately 100 men aboard; 0345, CO 26th Marines called, concerned about condition of runway; 0350, CG [commanding general] 3rd Mar Div protests to CG III MAF an incoming C-130 to land or drop Special Forces personnel; 0405, CG 3rd Mar Div said C-130 will not go into Khe Sanh; I told CG 3rd MAF that his G-3 was asking for ground relief column to go to Lang Vei at first light; I told CG we had no troops to send to Lang Vei, and he agreed that no troops should go and said to tell G-3 that he said so; I said I had no intention of sending troops unless he, General Cushman, so ordered me; 0406, told the MAF G-3, Colonel Smith, 'Negative on the relief column,' and that CG III MAF concurs; I further said that such a column at this time would be a lot of foolishness"; also see William Westmoreland, *A Soldier Reports* (Garden City, NY: Doubleday, 1976), 341.

35. In two oral history interviews several years after the war, Colonel Jonathan F. Ladd spoke at some length about his activities relating to the fall of Lang Vei in February 1968. Ladd was a brave and thoughtful American soldier who served his country with distinction in Vietnam and Cambodia. His introduction to the war in Indochina came in 1962–1963, when he served as a senior adviser to the South Vietnamese army's Ninth Division in the heart of the Mekong Delta. His friendship and frank conversations with young American reporters David Halberstam and Neil Sheehan helped shape their critical accounts of the war in the crucial days before the conflict consumed Vietnam and the United States. Unfortunately, as Paul Longgrear observed in our conversations, and as William R. Phillips has noted in his thorough book, *Night of the Silver Stars*, some of Ladd's recollections about

his visits to the camp and radio conversations with Lang Vei during the battle don't mesh with the recollections of men who were on the ground at the Special Forces camp. I have more confidence in Ladd's recollections of how the Lang Vei relief mission came about. See Jonathan F. Ladd Oral History: Abrams Story Collection, U.S. Army Military History Institute; and Jonathan F. Ladd, LBJ Library Oral History Collection, interviews conducted on July 24 and September 25, 1984.

36. William R. Phillips, *Night of the Silver Stars*, 174.

37. Paul Longgrear, author's interview, January 27, 2012.

38. Ibid.

39. Statement of Lieutenant Thomas E. Todd, "Combat After Action Report—Battle of Lang Vei."

40. Spencer C. Tucker, ed., *The Encyclopedia of the Vietnam War: A Political, Social, and Military History*, 2nd ed. (Santa Barbara: ABC-CLIO, 2011), 625.

41. Bill Dabney, VMI Oral History interview, September 8, 2005; also see Bill Dabney comments in Shulimson et al., *U.S. Marines in Vietnam: The Defining Year, 1968* (Washington, DC: History and Museums Division, Headquarters, U.S. Marine Corps, 1997), 277.

CHAPTER 11

1. Among the Marines who encountered Lieutenant Terence (Terry) Roach as he made his rounds on Hill 64 in the predawn of February 8, 1968, were Corporal George Chapman and Private Michael Barry. George Chapman, author's interview, February 23, 2012; and Michael Barry, author's interview, March 15, 2012.

2. Henry Radcliffe, author's interview, August 8, 2012.

3. I am indebted to the former Lynn O'Connor Roach (now Lynn Fifer) for sharing memories of her late husband, Second Lieutenant Terence Roach Jr. Lynn Fifer, e-mail to author, November 20, 2012.

4. Maurice Casey, author's interview, July 31, 2013. Lieutenant Colonel Casey, USMC (ret.) was a classmate of Terry Roach at Basic School. Casey arrived in Vietnam with Roach and was one of the officers whom Roach slipped away from in his eagerness to get a platoon command.

5. The two men killed in the ambush were twenty-one-year-old platoon sergeant Gene Ray Phipps of Greensboro, North Carolina, and twenty-two-year-old Navy corpsman William David Schmitz, of Duluth, Minnesota. The ambush was described to me by James Feasel, the leader of Roach's 1st Squad, who was there. James Feasel, author's interview, March 23, 2013.

6. Henry Radcliffe, author's interview, August 8, 2012.

7. Roach posed for a photograph with his squad leaders and other men on Hill 64 and sent it to his wife, Lynn. He wrote across the top, "My Staff on Radcliffe's Roost." I'm grateful to Lynn Fifer for sharing this and other photographs of Terry Roach in Vietnam.

8. George Chapman, author's interview, February 23, 2012.

9. 1st Battalion, 9th Marines, Command Chronology, February 1968; George Chapman, author's interview, February 23, 2012.

10. Ibid.; also Michael Barry, author's interviews, March 15, 2012, and March 23, 2013.

11. James Feasel, author's interview, February 20, 2012.

12. George Chapman, author's interview, February 23, 2012.

13. Ibid. In the literature of Khe Sanh, official and unofficial, probably no single incident during the seventy-seven days of the siege has been marked by as much flawed history as

the February 8, 1968, battle for Hill 64. This fact was stated to me repeatedly by Hill 64 survivors when I began my research, and, after hundreds of hours of interviews and research, I reached the same conclusion. The problems began almost immediately, with the 1/9 Command Chronology for February 1968. Among other assertions, the official 1/9 account states that the NVA didn't penetrate the Alpha-1 perimeter until more than two hours into the battle. According to this official account, "At 0610 [6:10 a.m.] the enemy regrouped and attacked again, penetrating the wire and were again beaten back. The attack continued in waves, and the enemy managed to take the northwest slope of the perimeter." In fact, as multiple accounts by survivors make clear, the NVA penetrated the northwest perimeter in the opening minutes of the attack after it began around 4:15 a.m., and the enemy soldiers overran much of the western and northern perimeters and portions of the hill's interior. The account I have written is based on interviews with key participants in various aspects of the battle: George Chapman and James Feasel were leaders of two of three squads of Alpha Company's 1st Platoon during the fight; Colonel Henry "Mac" Radcliffe (USMC, ret.) was a captain in command of Alpha Company and led a relief column that reached the hill about four hours after the battle began; Lieutenant Colonel Maurice Casey (USMC, ret.) was a young lieutenant in command of the 1/9 battalion's 81-millimeter mortars and was in radio contact with Richard W. Smith, a Marine who was in a collapsed bunker just behind the northern trench line for much of the battle; rifleman Michael Barry was one of the last men to see 1st Platoon commander Terry Roach alive, and he spent the entire battle in the northeastern and eastern trench line; rifleman Guy Leonard began the fight along the southeastern trench line and would ultimately circuit the hill during the course of the night; Arnold Alderete was an M-60 machine gunner who began the fight on the northern perimeter, fell back to the east, and spent much of the remainder of the battle in the interior of the hill; grenadier George Einhorn fought along the southern trench line and ventured into the interior of the hill for part of the battle; and Navy corpsman Mike Coonan tended to wounded Marines along a section of trench line overrun by the NVA and has devoted much effort in recent years to collecting the stories of Hill 64 survivors and displaying their accounts on a website he created. I am grateful to these men in particular for their extraordinary assistance in piecing together an accurate account of what happened on Hill 64 during the early morning hours of February 8, 1968.

14. Ed Welchel, unpublished written account dated September 28, 2012. I am grateful to Ed Welchel for sharing eighteen pages of written recollections about the attack on Hill 64.

15. Ibid.

16. Arnold Alderete, author's interview, April 16, 2012.

17. Ibid.

18. Michael Barry, author's interview, March 15, 2012.

19. Ibid.

20. Ibid.

21. Ibid.

22. Ibid.

23. Henry Radcliffe, author's interview, August 8, 2012.

24. Ibid. Radcliffe doesn't recall who initiated the second radio exchange he had with Jimmy Rizzo. It was also unclear to Radcliffe whether Rizzo was able to reach the 1st Platoon commander, Lieutenant Terry Roach, between the two conversations.

25. James Feasel, author's interview, February 20, 2012.

26. Ibid.

27. James Feasel, author's interviews, February 20, 2012, and September 11, 2012.

28. Ibid.

29. Ibid.

30. Robert Wiley letter to Corporal Sutherland, February 9, 1968, quoted in Ray Stubbe, *Battalion of Kings: A Tribute to Our Fallen Brothers Who Died Because of the Battlefield of Khe Sanh, Vietnam*, 2nd ed., rev. (Wauwatosa, WI: Khe Sanh Veterans, 2008) 178.

31. Michael Barry, author's interview, March 15, 2012.

32. My account of the joint activities of Arnold Alderete and David Ford on Hill 64 is based on the following: David Ford's letter to the Marine Corps commandant, April 21, 1997; Arnold Alderete, author's interviews, April 16, 2012, and August 13, 2013; George Einhorn, author's interview, March 14, 2012; and James Feasel, author's interviews, February 20, 2012, September 11, 2012, and April 10, 2013.

33. George Einhorn, author's interview, March 14, 2012.

34. David R. Ford, letter to Marine Corps commandant, April 21, 1997.

35. Henry Radcliffe, author's interview, August 8, 2012.

36. Ibid.

37. David R. Ford letter to Marine Corps commandant, April 21, 1997; also see David Ford interview, USMC Oral History Collection, Tape No. 2803.

38. George Einhorn, author's interview, March 14, 2012; James Feasel, author's interview, February 20, 2012. George Chapman, the 2nd Squad leader, said to me: "I knew what Jim [Feasel] was doing. He was stuck right there trying to hold the men down, and having them return fire and keeping [the North Vietnamese] from advancing over the hill." George Chapman, author's interview, February 23, 2012.

39. Arnold Alderete, author's interview, April 16, 2012; David R. Ford, letter to Marine Corps commandant, April 21, 1997.

40. Maurice Casey, author's interview, July 31, 2013; and Henry "Mac" Radcliffe, August 8, 2012. Hill 64 survivors contend they didn't receive the artillery and mortar support they had been promised prior to the attack. Some maintain that only illumination rounds were fired in their support. First Squad leader James Feasel said that late in the battle he asked one of the platoon's noncommissioned officers why they weren't getting artillery support and the sergeant said he had been told by the combat base that the guns were "refusing to fire on orders from the base commander." Mac Radcliffe, the Alpha Company commander, told me that he believes Hill 64 was getting some support from mortars and artillery. Maurice Casey told me that four of his 81-millimeter mortars at the rock quarry were firing illumination and high-explosive rounds throughout the battle. Casey said that most of the high-explosive rounds would have been fired away from the hill to target probable enemy attack routes and that it's possible the Americans on Hill 64 simply weren't aware of the supporting fire because of the intensity of the fight around them. Maurice Casey, author's interview, July 31, 2013.

41. Maurice Casey, author's interview, July 31, 2013. Casey's radio operator knew Richard W. Smith, and at one point during the battle, Casey asked his radioman the identity of the voice on the other end of the transmissions. Casey's radioman replied, "Oh, that's Smitty!"

42. Maurice Casey offers high praise for the heroic work performed by the young radioman Richard W. Smith. "You could tell that he wasn't as experienced as an FO should be," Casey said, yet the radioman still managed to call in fire on the suspected avenues of attack. It is difficult to assess the importance of the fire called in by Smith, but his heroic contribution to the defense of Hill 64 has gone unrecognized until now—a fact that has

long bothered Maurice Casey, who believes that Smith should receive an award for his solitary efforts at great personal risk.

43. Maurice Casey, author's interview, July 31, 2013.

44. Guy Leonard, author's interview, August 5, 2013.

45. Ibid.

46. Ibid.

47. Michael Barry, author's interview, March 15, 2012.

48. Ibid.

49. Henry Radcliffe, author's interview, August 8, 2012.

50. Ibid.

51. 1st Battalion, 9th Marines, Command Chronology, February 1968. It is Mac Radcliffe's recollection that he led the relief force to Hill 64 before dawn, but the 1/9 command chronology, and the defenders of Hill 64 whom I interviewed, all place the time as well after dawn.

52. The quote about the Marines at the rock quarry observing the fight on Hill 64 like spectators "watching a movie" is from James Feasel, author's interview February 20, 2012; similar comments were made by George Einhorn, author's interview, March 14, 2012.

53. George Gregory Rudell, author's interview, March 12, 2012.

54. Ibid. "We knew they were getting their butt kicked," Rudell said, describing what it was like to be prevented from coming to the aid of the Marines on Hill 64. "We were cussing, raising hell, wanting to do something. All we did was sit there and watch, and there was nothing we could do. We were just so damn mad."

55. Ibid.

56. Joseph Harrigan, author's interview, May 2, 2012.

57. 1st Battalion, 9th Marines, Command Chronology, February 1968; also Joseph Harrigan, author's interview, May 2, 2012. When we spoke, more than forty-four years after the battle for Khe Sanh, Harrigan was still anguished by his inability to come to the aid of the Marines on Hill 64 during the night. "They say Normandy was the longest day," Harrigan said. "For me, February 8, 1968, was the longest day."

58. Charles "Toby" Rushforth, author's interview, January 29, 2012; also see "The Vietnam War with Spads, 1968," http://www.fisthistory.org/viet-a1.htm. Several men on Hill 64 recall seeing (and hearing) only a single bomb dropped by what they mistakenly believed was a South Vietnamese Air Force plane.

59. James Feasel, author's interview, April 10, 2013.

60. George Einhorn, author's interview, March 14, 2012; and James Feasel, author's interview, February 20, 2012.

61. Michael Coonan, author's interview, February 15, 2012; and George Chapman, author's interview, February 23, 2012. The recollections of Chapman and Coonan differ as to how Roy McDaniel was killed. Chapman said that McDaniel had been shot in the shoulder before he was pulled inside the bunker, and then an NVA soldier had thrown a grenade inside that killed McDaniel. Coonan doesn't remember the grenade incident. It is his recollection that an NVA soldier shot into the entrance of the bunker and fired three rounds that struck McDaniel in the chest, mortally wounding the fire team leader.

62. Robert Genty, author's interview, April 30, 2012; James Feasel, author's interview, February 20, 2012.

63. James Feasel, author's interviews, February 20, 2012, and September 11, 2012; Henry Radcliffe, author's interview, August 8, 2012.

64. Henry Radcliffe, author's interview, August 8, 2012; also James Feasel, author's interview, February 20, 2012.

65. Henry Radcliffe, author's interview, August 8, 2012.

66. George Chapman and his comrades differ as to when Chapman was wounded. Chapman said he was shot outside his bunker, in the minutes before Roy McDaniel was killed. Coonan and David ford contend that Chapman was wounded in the trenchline at the end of the battle, as I have described. Given the extraordinary stress that both men were under during the hours they spent in a part of the hill that had been overrun by enemy soldiers, the discrepancies are understandable. George Chapman, author's interview, February 23, 2012; Michael Coonan, author's interview, February 15, 2012; and David R. Ford, letter to Marine corps commandant, April 21, 1997.

67. James Feasel, author's interviews, February 20, 2012, and September 11, 2012; and Michael Coonan, author's interview, February 15, 2012.

CHAPTER 12

1. Keith Kapple, author's interview, April 28, 2011.

2. William C. Westmoreland, *A Soldier Reports* (Garden City, NY: Doubleday, 1976), 338; also see Shulimson et al., *U.S. Marines in Vietnam: The Defining Year, 1968* (Washington, DC: History and Museums Division, Headquarters, U.S. Marine Corps, 1997), 68.

3. Westmoreland, *A Soldier Reports*, 338.

4. See *Foreign Relations of the United States, 1964–1968, Volume 6, Vietnam, January–August 1968*, Document 60, 141–144. The document contains the official notes of President Johnson's February 7, 1968, meeting at the White House with his national security team. The notes were taken by Johnson aide Tom Johnson (no relation) and can also be found at the LBJ Library in Austin, Texas, in "Tom Johnson's Notes of Meetings," Notes of Meeting, Washington, DC, February 7, 1968, 12:29–1:55 p.m., National Security File, NSC Meetings, v. 5, Tab 63.

5. General Lew Walt to Walt Rostow, February 8, 1968, letter quoted in *Foreign Relations of the United States, 1964–1968, Volume 6, Vietnam, January–August 1968*, Document 61, 145–46.

6. "Notes of the President's Meeting with the Joint Chiefs of Staff," Washington, DC, February 9, 1968, 11:02 a.m.–12:43 p.m., in *Foreign Relations of the United States, 1964–1968, Volume 6, Vietnam, January–August 1968*, Document 64, 158–168. In addition to the various service chiefs, those in attendance were President Johnson, Vice President Hubert Humphrey, Secretary of State Dean Rusk, Defense Secretary Robert McNamara, CIA Director Richard Helms, Joint Chiefs Chairman General Earle Wheeler, incoming defense secretary Clark Clifford, National Security Adviser Walt Rostow, Press Secretary George Christian, and Tom Johnson.

7. Ibid. In his 1977 book, *Big Story: How the American Press and Television Reported and Interpreted the Crisis of Tet 1968 in Vietnam and Washington*, Anchor Books edition, abridged (Garden City, NY: Anchor Books, 1978), on press coverage of the Tet Offensive and Khe Sanh, Peter Braestrup criticized as media hype the news accounts about the threat of North Vietnamese air attacks at Khe Sanh. In fact, declassified documents have since revealed that American military commanders in Vietnam took the sightings very seriously and took substantial measures to counteract the threats.

8. "Notes of the President's Meeting with the Joint Chiefs of Staff," Washington, DC,

February 9, 1968, 11:02 a.m.–12:43 p.m., in *Foreign Relations of the United States, 1964–1968, Volume 6, Vietnam, January–August 1968*, Document 64, 158–168.

9. Maxwell Taylor's behind-the-scenes role in Lyndon Johnson's Khe Sanh deliberations is discussed in some detail in John Prados and Ray Stubbe, *Valley of Decision: The Siege of Khe Sanh* (Boston: Houghton Mifflin, 1991), 357–364.

10. Ibid., 361.

11. See "White House Disputes McCarthy on Atom Arms," *New York Times*, February 10, 1968; "Query by Fulbright," *New York Times*, February 10, 1968; and "Wheeler Doubts Khe Sanh Will Need Atom Weapons," *New York Times*, February 15, 1968. In his memoir, Westmoreland makes the case for the use of tactical nuclear weapons at Khe Sanh. "Because the region around Khe Sanh was virtually uninhabited, civilian casualties would be minimal," he writes. "If Washington officials were so intent on 'sending a message' to Hanoi, surely small tactical nuclear weapons would be a way to tell Hanoi something, just as two atomic bombs had spoken convincingly to Japanese officials during World War II and the threat of atomic bombs induced the North Koreans to accept meaningful negotiations." Westmoreland, *A Soldier Reports*, 411.

12. "Notes of the President's Meeting With Senior Foreign Policy Advisors," Washington, DC, February 12, 1968, 1:45–3:08 p.m., *Foreign Relations of the United States, 1964–1968, Volume 6, Vietnam, January–August 1968*, 188–196.

13. Calvin Bright, author's interview, July 23, 2011; and *Bravo! Common Men, Uncommon Valor: The 77-Day Siege of Khe Sanh*, DVD, directed by Ken and Betty Rodgers (Boise, ID: Kingfisher Arts, 2012).

14. John Corbett vividly describes daily life at Khe Sanh in his Vietnam memoir, *West Dickens Avenue: A Marine at Khe Sanh* (New York: Ballantine Books, 2003).

15. "Commander at Khe Sanh: David Edward Lownds," *New York Times*, February 12, 1968.

16. Dave Doehrman, author's interview, April 6, 2012.

17. Ron Smith, author's interview, March 21, 2012.

18. Lewis "Sam" Messer, author's interview, April 10, 2012.

19. Two Seabees died at Khe Sanh: Charles Otto Spillman, thirty-two, of New Brighton, Minnesota, was killed in a helicopter crash on February 28; Edward Cody Adams, twenty-three, of Pennsboro, West Virginia, was killed on April 16 by an enemy artillery round just after emerging from his bunker. Spillman "had premonitions that he was going to die," said Sam Messer. "He would have nightmares." He was on a helicopter flying back to Khe Sanh on February 28, carrying mail and equipment parts for CBMU-301, when the aircraft was shot down. Lewis "Sam" Messer, author's interview, April 10, 2012; also Jack Haigwood, author's interview, April 14, 2012.

20. Daniel Sullivan, author's interview, April 16, 2012.

21. Daniel Sullivan was awarded the Bronze Star for his efforts to aid the men aboard the burning KC-130 on February 10, 1968.

22. James Finnegan, author's interview, May 13, 2012.

23. Edward Feldman, diary entries, February 10–11, 1968, and author's interview, April 14, 2012.

24. James Finnegan, author's interview, May 13, 2012.

25. Charles "Chuck" Chamberlin, author's interview, March 26, 2012.

26. Ibid., author's interviews, March 26–27, 2012.

27. Edward Feldman, author's interview, April 14, 2012.

28. John M. Kaheny, quoted in Ray Stubbe, *Battalion of Kings: A Tribute to Our Fallen*

Brothers Who Died Because of the Battlefield of Khe Sanh, Vietnam, 2nd ed., rev. (Wauwatosa, WI: Khe Sanh Veterans, 2008), 194–195.

CHAPTER 13

1. Ron Smith, author's interview, March 21, 2012.
2. William Dabney, quoted in Beth Crumley, "Robert J. Arrotta: The Mightiest Corporal in the Marine Corps," *Leatherneck* (September 2010), 44–49; also see William Dabney, "Sting of Battle: Hill 881S and the Super Gaggle," *Marine Corps Gazette* 89 (4) (2005), 69; also see Crumley, "Robert J. Arrotta." Dabney had this to say about Bob Arrotta and his work as forward air controller, 881 South: "I had nothing to lose, plenty of targets, and all the CAS [close-air support] aircraft we could use, so I stood by and watched as he ran the first few missions—flawlessly. I was impressed not only with his technical knowledge but also with his demeanor as a corporal giving instructions to officers through the rank of lieutenant colonel. He was assertive and unfailingly professional."
3. William Dabney, VMI Oral History interview, September 8, 2005.
4. Ron Smith, author's interview, April 14, 2012.
5. William Dabney, VMI Oral History interview, September 8, 2005.
6. Ibid.
7. Ron Smith, author's interview, April 14, 2012.
8. Dennis Mannion, author's interview, January 23, 2012.
9. Dennis Mannion, author's interview, November 30, 2011.
10. Paul Knight, author's interviews, December 18 and 21, 2011. Knight would have to do a bomb-damage assessment after strikes in which there were suspected North Vietnamese killed in action. He was encouraged by higher-ups to report damage or enemy troops killed in action. One officer went so far as to suggest that they "would get better service from air assets if they credited them with kills," Knight said. He did it for one or two missions. "And then I said, 'To hell with it! This is stupid.'"
11. Paul Knight, author's interview, December 21, 2011.
12. Dennis Mannion, author's interview, December 19, 2011.
13. Miguel Salinas, author's interview, May 1, 2012.
14. Ibid.
15. Dennis Mannion, author's interview, January 23, 2012.
16. Jim Thomas, author's interview, December 18, 2011.
17. Ibid.
18. Jose "Cisco" Reyes, author's interview, February 23, 2012.
19. Jim Kaylor, author's interview, February 15, 2012.
20. Jim Thomas, author's interview, December 18, 2011.
21. Rich Donaghy, author's interview, August 14, 2013.
22. Ibid.
23. Ray Stubbe, *Battalion of Kings: A Tribute to Our Fallen Brothers Who Died Because of the Battlefield of Khe Sanh, Vietnam*, 2nd ed., rev. (Wauwatosa, WI: Khe Sanh Veterans, 2008), 198.
24. Ron Smith, author's interview, March 21, 2012.
25. Ibid.; also see Crumley, "Robert J. Arrotta." Terry Smith was posthumously awarded the Silver Star for his valor.
26. John Pessoni, author's interview, May 5, 2012.
27. Ibid.

28. "Khe Sanh Daily Report," February 20–21 (twenty-four-hour period from 9 a.m. to 9 a.m.), 1968, 3rd Marine Division Command Operations Center to III Marine Amphibious Force Command Operations Center, RG 127, Records of the U.S. Marine Corps, NARA; also see 3rd Marine Division daily report to III MAF, February 21, 1968.

29. Ibid. Of the 166 US Air Force B-52 missions flown over Vietnam in February 1968, 111 were in support of Khe Sanh. See MACV Monthly Report, February 1968, 24.

30. In his critical study of media coverage of the Tet Offensive and Khe Sanh, *Big Story: How the American Press and Television Reported and Interpreted the Crisis of Tet 1968 in Vietnam and Washington*, Anchor Books edition, abridged (Garden City, NY: Anchor Books, 1978), Peter Braestrup notes that the North Vietnamese never put 37-millimeter anti-aircraft guns at the end of the runway, which, he suggests, would have completely shut down landings at the combat base. But this assertion implies that the North Vietnamese could put guns where they wanted and fire them with impunity. In fact, NVA gun crews and troops faced a constant struggle to avoid detection, and, once pinpointed by American spotters, faced almost certain destruction. The only exceptions to this were the big NVA artillery pieces located at Co Roc massif across the border in Laos, which managed to confound US bombers throughout the siege.

31. Jim Thomas, author's interview, December 18, 2011; Jose Reyes, author's interview, February 23, 2012; Jim Kaylor, author's interview, February 15, 2012. On 881 South, ammunition was plentiful, but food and water supplies were so precariously low that there was discussion of whether they might have to abandon the outpost and fight their way down to the base or some other point.

32. Glenn Prentice, author's interview, February 14, 2012; Richard Dworsky, author's interview, August 6, 2013. Prentice was a forward observer radioman who was shuttling between 881 South and the combat base. It was his recollection that 881 South ran out of food for about a week and was down to fifteen gallons of water. Prentice said he witnessed and participated in the discussions that Captain Bill Dabney led about possibly abandoning the outpost. India Second Lieutenant Richard Dworsky recalls "limited discussions" about leaving the hill after going without water "for three or four days." Dworsky is unsure whether the plan to launch a breakout "was sanctioned" above Dabney. Dworsky believes "if we had tried to get off the hill, we would have all been killed."

33. James T. Riley, Silver Star citation for action on February 22, 1968, undated.

34. "Four Hundred Mile Walk into Marine Corps," *Stars and Stripes* (Pacific edition), October 2, 1967. Also see Stubbe, *Battalion of Kings*, 206.

CHAPTER 14

1. The shells and rockets that fell on the Special Forces FOB-3 compound at Khe Sanh were not included in the official tally.

2. Edward Feldman, author's interview, April 14, 2012.

3. Tom Esslinger, author's interview, April 3, 2012.

4. Jim Kaylor, author's interview, February 15, 2012.

5. Ibid. Echo Company, 2/26, was under the operational control of the 3rd Battalion, 26th Marines, at the time of the February 24, 1968, incident in which Carlos Aguirre and Gerrie Jefferies were killed. The 3/26 Command Chronology for February 1968 reads: "At 0015H, Company E received two rounds of unknown origin. Friendly H&Is were immediately investigated and subsequently cleared of any suspicion. Analysis of artillery fragments are [sic] still being conducted. Results are 2 USMC KIA." Jim Kaylor believes the deaths

were caused by friendly fire. Nick Elardo attributed the bunker collapse to an NVA rocket. Nick Elardo, author's interview, February 23, 2012.

6. Major Mirza M. Baig, letter to Colonel F. C. Caldwell, USMC Historical Branch, December 23, 1968, Comments on *The Battle for Khe Sanh*, March 23, 1969, U.S. Marine Corps Archives, Quantico, Virginia.

7. Tom Quigley, author's interview, May 6, 2011.

8. Ken Rodgers, author's interview, July 21, 2011. Rodgers had recalled the incident as occurring a few days later, around February 20, but the 1/26 Command Chronology for February 1968 fixes the date as February 13.

9. Ibid.

10. Steve Wiese, author's interview, April 12, 2012.

11. Ibid.

12. Ibid.

13. Ibid.

CHAPTER 15

1. Marine Air Group 36, Command Chronology, February 1968, RG 127: Records of the U.S. Marine Corps, NARA.

2. David Althoff, author's interview, January 25, 2012.

3. Ibid. Also see Lieutenant Colonel David L. Althoff, "Helicopter Operations at Khe Sanh," *Marine Corps Gazette* 54 (5) (May 1968), 47.

4. Beth Crumley, "Walking with Giants—The Tigers of HMM-262," Marine Corps Association and Foundation website, July 25, 2011, http://www.mca-marines.org/blog/beth-crumley/2011/07/25/walking-giants-tigers-hmm-262. A young HMM-262 CH-46 pilot, First Lieutenant Michael Mullen, said this of Althoff: "He was the squadron's idol. We all thought the world of him as a man, an officer and a pilot . . . He would never ask one of his junior pilots to fly a mission he had never flown."

5. David Althoff's mission to Hill 881 South on February 13, 1968, is described in Crumley, "Walking with Giants"; and Lieutenant Colonel Neil Allen, "Narrative of HMM-262 Command Chronology," HMM-262 Combat Helicopter Association, http://www.hmm-262combatvets.com/chronology.htm.

6. "Resupply of Khe Sanh," message from commanding general of 3rd Marine Division to commanding general of III MAF, February 20, 1968, in 3rd Marine Division Messages, February 1968, RG 127, NARA.

7. David Althoff, author's interview, January 25, 2012.

8. Richard E. Carey, quoted in Shulimson et al., *U.S. Marines in Vietnam: The Defining Year, 1968* (Washington, DC: History and Museums Division, Headquarters, U.S. Marine Corps, 1997), 483; other interviews relevant to the resupply quandary at Khe Sanh include Major William A. McGaw, USMC Oral History Collection, Tape No. 3293, Lieutenant Colonel Melvin J. Steinberg, USMC Oral History Collection, Tape No. 3423, and Major Arthur C. Crane, USMC Oral History Collection, Tape No. 3294; Lieutenant General Robert E. Cushman Jr., commander of the III Marine Amphibious Force and thus the ranking Marine in Vietnam at the time, later claimed to have conceived the Super Gaggle, in Lieutenant General Robert E. Cushman, Comments on *The Battle for Khe Sanh*, March 23, 1969, Vietnam Comment File, U.S. Marine Corps Archives, Quantico, Virginia; Cushman's claim is contradicted by virtually all of his subordinates in Vietnam at the time, including General Norman Anderson, commander of the 1st Marine Air Wing in Vietnam; Major

General Keith B. McCutcheon, who served under Anderson in 1968, singled out Colonel Joel E. Bonner, Lieutenant Colonel William J. White, and Lieutenant Colonel Richard E. Carey, a member of the 1st Marine Air Wing staff, with Carey naming the Super Gaggle, according to McCutcheon and others; see Major General Keith B. McCutcheon, Comments on *The Battle for Khe Sanh*, n.d., Vietnam Comment File, USMC Archives. In my interview with David Althoff, he laughed about the official accounts of the origins of the Super Gaggle. He recalled that after Colonel Frank E. Wilson, the commander of MAG-6, forwarded up the chain of command the resupply plan that emerged from the brainstorming session in Bill White's hooch at Quang Tri Air Base, "next thing you know there were two generals taking credit for the whole freaking works." David Althoff, author's interview, January 25, 2012.

9. 1st Marine Aircraft Wing Operations Order 303-YR, February 24, 1968, in 3rd Marine Division Messages, February 1968, RG 127, NARA; for a description of the Super Gaggle from the perspective of the Marines on the hill outposts, see Colonel William H. "Bill" Dabney, "Hill 881S and the Super Gaggle," *Marine Corps Gazette* (April 2005), http://www.mca-marines.org/gazette/hill-881s-and-super-gaggle.

10. Ibid.

11. Major General Norman J. Anderson to Major General Keith B. McCutcheon, February 25, 1968, letter No. 60, 1968 correspondent, File A, Keith B. McCutcheon Papers, USMCA; also see 1st Marine Aircraft Wing, Command Chronology, February 1968, 2–3, McCutcheon, Comments on *The Battle for Khe Sanh*, not dated (Comment File), USMC Archives, and Shulimson et al., *U.S. Marines in Vietnam: The Defining Year, 1968*, 485.

CHAPTER 16

1. Ken Pipes, author's interview, July 23, 2011; also Ray Stubbe, *Battalion of Kings: A Tribute to Our Fallen Brothers Who Died Because of the Battlefield of Khe Sanh, Vietnam*, 2nd ed., rev. (Wauwatosa, WI: Khe Sanh Veterans, 2008), 216.

2. Charlie Med surgeon Edward Feldman had met Don Jacques and pronounced the young lieutenant "a cowboy." Edward Feldman, author's interview, April 14, 2012. Within Bravo's 3rd Platoon, corpsman John Cicala sized up Jacques as a bit "cocky," and "very, very gung-ho." John Cicala, author's interview, May 24, 2011.

3. Stubbe, *Battalion of Kings*, 216.

4. Ken Pipes, author's interview, July 23, 2011; Steve Wiese, author's interview, April 13, 2012; John Cicala, author's interview, May 24, 2011; Calvin Bright, author's interview, July 23, 2011.

5. Steve Wiese, author's interview, April 13, 2012.

6. John Cicala, author's interview, May 24, 2011.

7. Calvin Bright, author's interview, July 23, 2011.

8. This account of the February 25, 1968, patrol led by Don Jacques is primarily drawn from four interviews: Ken Pipes, author's interview, July 23, 2011; Calvin Bright, author's interview, July 23, 2011; John Cicala, author's interview, May 24, 2011; and Steve Wiese, author's interview, April 13, 2012. I also consulted the USMC Oral History interview with corpsman Frank Calzia, who survived the February 25 patrol but was killed in Vietnam in May. See Frank Calzia, USMC Oral History interview, No. 2621. Finally, I consulted Ray Stubbe's collection of interviews and personal accounts found in *Battalion of Kings*, 220–231.

9. Steve Wiese, author's interview, April 13, 2012.

10. Ken Pipes, author's interview, July 23, 2011.

11. Steve Wiese, author's interview, April 13, 2012.

12. Ibid.

13. The confrontation between Lieutenant Jacques and Steve Wiese over whether to pursue the NVA soldiers was described to me by Wiese and corpsman John Cicala in our interviews cited above. Other details were gleaned from interviews and personal accounts gathered by Khe Sanh chaplain Ray Stubbe during his decades of research. These include a letter written by 81-millimeter mortar forward observer Gilbert Wall, who accompanied the patrol. Wall had seen the sharp discussion unfold. "They looked confused," Wall wrote of the Marines involved in the discussion. "Lt. Jacques ended the confusion by shouting, 'Let's go get them' while his pistol was in the air and his hand was forward in the charge manner. Then he turned and looked at me and we both smiled at the same time. It was like the same thought went though our minds: 'This is what we want.' We started moving after them and the fire began." Gilbert Wall to Ray Stubbe, September 9, 1988, quoted in Stubbe, *Battalion of Kings*, 223.

14. John Cicala, author's interview, May 24, 2011.

15. There have been conflicting accounts regarding the location of Lieutenant Jacques and his men when they spotted the three NVA soldiers in the minutes before the ambush. By all accounts, Steve Wiese's squad was leading the patrol at that moment, and Wiese's testimony is clear: the NVA soldiers were about two hundred meters (220 yards) away, to his right—in other words, south of the patrol—and the NVA ran along the access road before diving into the treeline on the south side of the roadway. Official records of the 26th Marines placed the location of the ambush at map coordinates XD849409—roughly fifty to one hundred meters (about the length of a football field or slightly less) north of the main Khe Sanh access road. Air observer First Lieutenant Thomas F. O'Toole Jr., flying very low over the ambush site around midday, spotted the bodies of fifteen to twenty Marines near a trench line that stretched from XD853409 to XD854409—about two hundred meters north of the main access road. All those pieces of evidence support Wiese's account that the NVA anchored their ambush from positions along the access road, which the Americans never reached.

16. Stubbe, *Battalion of Kings*, 224–225.

17. Ken Pipes, author's interview, July 23, 2011; William Smith, author's interview, March 12, 2012; also see Stubbe, *Battalion of Kings*, 226.

18. William Smith, author's interview, March 12, 2012. More than four decades later, Smith was still pained by the memories of February 25, 1968. "It's the worst thing that I've lived through in my life," he said.

19. Ken Pipes, author's interview, July 23, 2011.

20. Ibid.

21. John Cicala, author's interview, May 24, 2011.

22. Ibid.

23. Ibid.

24. Ibid.

25. Ibid.

26. Steve Wiese, author's interview, April 12, 2012.

27. Gilbert Wall, letter to Ray Stubbe, September 9, 1988, quoted in *Battalion of Kings*, 225.

28. The death of Ken Claire was related by one of his wounded men, Edward C. Rayburn, who survived the ambush. Rayburn later shared his account with Ken Claire's

brother, Richard, who recalled the conversation in a letter that was printed in the *Khe Sanh Veteran* 1 (Fall 1992), 15. Rayburn's account can also be found in Ray Stubbe, *Battalion of Kings*, 225.

29. Stubbe, *Battalion of Kings*, 224–225.

30. Ibid.

31. John Cicala, author's interview, May 24, 2011.

32. Stubbe, *Battalion of Kings*, 229.

33. Thomas E. Casey, letter to Ray Stubbe, February 2, 1995, quoted in Stubbe, *Battalion of Kings*, 229.

34. Stubbe, *Battalion of Kings*, 229.

35. Calvin Bright, author's interview, July 23, 2011.

36. Ibid.

37. Steve Wiese, author's interview, April 12, 2012.

38. Ibid.

39. "A Marine Returns from the Officially Dead," *New York Times,* January 31, 1973.

40. Ken Pipes, author's interview, July 23, 2011.

CHAPTER 17

1. The discovery of the trench is described in a message from the 3rd Marine Division to III MAF, "Trenches at KSCB perimeter 25 Feb," February 25, 1968, 3rd Marine Division Messages, February 1968, RG 127, NARA. Also see Operation Scotland Situation Report No. 471, February 26, 1968, RG 127, NARA.

2. Ibid.

3. "Special Arc Light Strikes," February 25, 1968, message from commanding general, III MAF, to commander Seventh AF, 3rd Marine Division Messages, February 1968, RG 127, NARA.

4. Biographical information on Billy Dale Livingston was drawn from the Combat Area Casualties Database, RG 330, NARA; this account of Livingston's death was drawn from John Roberts, author's interview, September 21, 2012, and Howard McKinnis, author's interview, September 24, 2012.

5. General William Westmoreland message to Colonel David Lownds, February 27, 1968, 3rd Marine Division Messages, February 1968.

6. 3rd Marine Division, Situation Reports, Operation Scotland, No. 472, February 26, 1968, RG 127, NARA.

7. Ibid.

8. The scene inside the 26th Marine Regiment command operations center was described to me by several people who were there, including William (Bill) Smith. William Smith, author's interview, March 22, 2012.

9. William Smith, author's interview, March 22, 2012; and Mirza M. Baig to Colonel F. C. Caldwell, USMC Historical Branch, comments on *The Battle for Khe Sanh*, December 23, 1968, found in USMC Archives.

10. William Smith, author's interview, March 22, 2012.

11. 3rd Marine Division, Situation Reports, Operation Scotland, No. 484, February 29, 1968.

12. Ibid., No. 487, March 1, 1968; the NVA attacks of February 29–March 1 are also de-

scribed in Shulimson et al., *U.S. Marines in Vietnam: The Defining Year, 1968* (Washington, DC: History and Museums Division, Headquarters, U.S. Marine Corps, 1997), 281.

13. 26th Marines, Command Chronology, March 1968; also 3rd Marine Division, message to III MAF, March 2, 1968, in III MAF Khe Sanh Operations File, RG 127, NARA.

14. "48,000 Face April Draft, Highest Total in 18 Months," *New York Times*, February 24, 1968.

15. Robert Mann, *A Grand Delusion: America's Descent into Vietnam* (New York: Basic Books, 2001), 601.

16. Robert McNamara, quoted in Deborah Shapley, *Promise and Power: The Life and Times of Robert McNamara* (Boston: Little, Brown, 1993), 444.

17. "Johnson's Rating Declines in Poll," *New York Times*, February 18, 1968; "Nixon Catches Johnson in Poll," *New York Times*, February 25, 1968.

18. President Johnson's impromptu send-off of Vietnam-bound soldiers and Marines is described in "Johnson Confers with Eisenhower; Briefs Him on War," *New York Times*, February 19, 1968, and in "LBJ Salutes El Toro Marines," *Long Beach Independent Press-Telegram*, February 18, 1968; a copy of Johnson's prepared remarks to the departing Marines at El Toro can be found at the website of the 3rd Battalion, 27th Marines, http://www.three27.com/files/LBJ%20El%20Toro%20Speech%202-17-1968.pdf.

19. Ibid.

20. Document 83, "Telegram from the President's Special Assistant (Rostow) to President Johnson in Texas," February 22, 1968, in *Foreign Relations of the United States, 1964–1968, Volume 6* (Washington, DC: U.S. Government Printing Office, 2002), 238–239.

21. "Memorandum from the Chairman of the Joint Chiefs of Staff (Wheeler) to President Johnson," Washington, DC, February 27, 1968, in *Foreign Relations of the United States, 1964–1968, Volume 6*, Vietnam, January–August 1968, 263–266; "Notes of Meeting, Washington," February 28, 1968, in *Foreign Relations of the United States, 1964–1968, Volume 6*, Vietnam, January–August 1968, 267–275. Wheeler, it should be noted, was hardly a neutral party in the discussion over whether to honor Westmoreland's request for reinforcements: As cable traffic would later make clear, Wheeler had urged Westmoreland to make the request, almost coaching him in its formulation. Wheeler believed that overall US military troop levels were too low, and he saw the crisis in Vietnam as an opportunity to call up reserves, expand the draft, and push the numbers back to a level he thought appropriate.

22. Stanley Karnow, *Vietnam: A History* (New York: Penguin, 1984), 512.

23. "President Lauds McNamara and Gives Him Medal," *New York Times*, February 29, 1968.

24. "For McNamara, It's Efficiency to the End (Almost)," *New York Times*, March 1, 1968.

CHAPTER 18

1. Command chronologies for 3rd Marine Division, the 26th Marine Battalion, and various helicopter units for February and March 1968; also Colonel William H. Dabney, interview, U.S. Marine Corps Oral History Collection, May 20, 1982, USMCA, and Lieutenant Colonel Robert W. Rasdal, interview, U.S. Marine Corps Oral History Collection, Tape No. 2627, USMCA. Dabney described the Super Gaggle as "a massive, complex, well rehearsed, gutsy and magnificent performance and only the Marines could have pulled it off."

2. The nighttime activities of the North Vietnamese around the hill outposts and the combat base are mentioned frequently in six-hour situation reports. For one example, see 3rd Marine Division, Situation Reports, Operation Scotland, No. 494, March 3, 1968, RG 127, NARA; the NVA propaganda activities are described in 3rd Marine Division, Situation Reports, Operation Scotland, No. 525, March 11, 1968.

3. Dennis Mannion, author's interview, February 16, 2012.

4. Ibid.

5. Paul Knight, December 22, 2011.

6. Matthew Walsh, author's interview, February 12, 2012.

7. Ibid.

8. Ibid.

9. Colonel William L. Barba, letter dated June 3, 1991, quoted in Stubbe, *Battalion of Kings: A Tribute to Our Fallen Brothers Who Died Because of the Battlefield of Khe Sanh, Vietnam,* 2nd ed., rev. (Wauwatosa, WI: Khe Sanh Veterans, 2008), 236–237. Barba was a CH-46 pilot with Marine Medium Helicopter Squadron 262, flying to Khe Sanh along the routes described.

10. There were five crew members and eighteen passengers aboard, including the pilot. HMM-262 Command Chronology, February 1968. Also see Colonel William L. Barba, letter dated June 3, 1991, quoted in Stubbe, *Battalion of Kings,* 236–237. Barba was the pilot of a second CH-46 Sea Knight flying the February 28, 1968, mission, and he witnessed the crash.

11. "Aerial Resupply of Khe Sanh," March 6, 1968, 3rd Marine Division Messages, March 1968, RG 127.

12. Ibid.

13. There are discrepancies regarding the number of passengers and crew aboard Fred Hampton's C-123 when it took off for Khe Sanh on March 6, 1968. For an excellent breakdown of the casualties and discrepancies, see the web page "C-123 Down!" at http://www.virtualwall.org/units/c123down.htm.

14. I am grateful to photographer Jim Caccavo for sharing with me his memories of Robert Ellison. I also gleaned material about Ellison from his obituary in *Shrapnel,* newspaper of the Western Military Academy (Alton, Illinois), March 1968; and "Fearless," Robert J. Ellison obituary, *Ebony,* 23 (7) (May 1968), 24.

15. William Smith, author's interview, March 8, 2012.

16. Ibid.

17. Thirty-five dead from the March 6, 1968, crash are buried in a mass grave at Jefferson Barracks National Military Cemetery in St. Louis. Nearby is a mass grave containing the remains of eight Marines of Bravo Company, 1/26, recovered several weeks after the February 25 ambush of the Jacques patrol. Eight pages of Robert Ellison's photographs from Khe Sanh, including the image of the mortally wounded Lieutenant Jacques being carried back to the wire, were published in the March 18, 1968, issue of *Newsweek.* The photographs posthumously won Ellison an Overseas Press Club award in early 1969.

18. The April 25, 1968, recovery operation is noted in 2nd Battalion, 3rd Marine Regiment, Command Chronology, April 1968, and 1st Marine Regiment, Command Chronology, April 1968.

19. Stubbe, *Battalion of Kings,* 247.

20. "Mass Burial Set for Crash Victims," *Daily Capital News* (Jefferson City, MO), November 23, 1968.

CHAPTER 19

1. Edward Feldman, author's interview, April 15, 2012.

2. Edward Feldman, diary entry, February 27, 1968.

3. James Finnegan, author's interview, May 13, 2012.

4. Daniel Sullivan, author's interview, April 16, 2012; James Finnegan, author's interview, May 13, 2012; Edward Feldman, author's interviews, April 13–15, 2012.

5. Daniel Sullivan, author's interview, April 16, 2012.

6. Among the wounded during the bombardment of March 8, 1968, were news correspondent Jurate Kazickas, one of a growing number of women chronicling the war in Vietnam, and Lieutenant William Gay, commander of the detachment of combat engineers at Khe Sanh. Kazickas sustained relatively minor shrapnel wounds as she was interviewing a Marine in a trench line; Gay sustained more serious injuries when he was sprayed by shrapnel as he shoved Kazickas to safety in a bunker.

7. "Heart Surgery at Khe Sanh Saves 'Dead' Marine Hero Who Refused to Kill," *New York Times*, March 12, 1968.

8. "War Wounds Fatal to an Antiwar Hero," *New York Times*, March 15, 1968.

9. 3rd Marine Division, Command Chronology, March 1968, as well as numerous 3rd Marine Division messages and situation reports during the month.

10. "Tunnel Hunt at Khe Sanh," *New York Times*, February 16, 1968.

11. "Khe Sanh Marines on Guard for Enemy Tunneling," *New York Times*, March 4, 1968. Colonel David Lownds, the base commander, explained his decision to use divining rods in the search for North Vietnamese tunnels: "No matter how stupid anything is, and I don't say the brass rods are stupid, we use it. If some country boy from the Kentucky hills says he has a gadget that he used to hunt foxes with, and wants to try to find tunnels, I say go ahead. I try everything."

12. 3rd Marine Division, Command Chronology, March 1968, 26. The chronology states, "A team from the Defense Communications Planning Group visited the command and Khe Sanh Combat base during March and assisted members of the 26th Marines in operating the AN/PRS-1 as an aid in tunneling detection." Accompanying the team was Alex Lee, a Marine lieutenant who later rose to lieutenant colonel, and he described his tunnel-hunting trip to Khe Sanh in his comments in Eric Hammel's *Khe Sanh: Siege in the Clouds* (New York: Crown Publishers, 1989), 273, and in his own book, *Force Recon Command: 3rd Force Recon Company in Vietnam, 1969–70* (New York: Random House, 2011). Lee recalls the trip as taking place around February 12, but 3rd Marine Division records contradict that. Lee is dismissive of the tunnel hunt, which he blamed on alarmist news coverage. Comments at the time by Colonel Lownds and a Marine platoon commander, Lieutenant Marshall R. Wells, suggest the search was taken seriously by the defenders of Khe Sanh. For comments by Lownds, Wells, and others about the tunnel hunt, see the previously cited articles, "Tunnel Hunt at Khe Sanh" and "Khe Sanh Marines on Guard for Enemy Tunneling."

13. "100 Reds Caught Tunneling Toward Khe Sanh; 27 Killed," *Stars and Stripes* (Pacific edition), March 10, 1968.

14. 3rd Marine Division, Situation Reports, Operation Scotland, No. 515, March 8, 1968; also see "27 Enemy Killed at Khe Sanh," *Washington Post*, March 9, 1968, and the previously cited "100 Reds Caught Tunneling Toward Khe Sanh; 27 Killed."

15. In addition to drawing on the 3rd Marine Division and 26th Marines command chronologies and Operation Scotland situation reports for this period, I consulted the daily news dispatches out of Khe Sanh and Saigon that documented the rising air campaign. For

an example, see the front-page article that ran in the *New York Times* on March 13, 1968, "Big Bombs Blast Foe at Khe Sanh: 2,000-Pounders Are Used."

16. "U.S. Command Sees Hue, Not Khe Sanh, as Foe's Main Goal," *New York Times*, March 7, 1968.

17. Westmoreland acknowledged in a telegram to General Earle Wheeler, chairman of the Joint Chiefs of Staff, that he was the source for the March 7 article in the *New York Times*. See Document 112, "Telegram from the Chairman of the Joint Chiefs of Staff (Wheeler) to the Commander, Military Assistance Command, Vietnam (Westmoreland) and the Commander in Chief, Pacific (Sharp)," in *Foreign Relations of the United States, 1964–1968, Volume 6, Vietnam, January–August 1968*, 351–353.

18. Lyndon Baines Johnson, *The Vantage Point* (New York: Holt, Rinehart and Winston, 1971), 405. Robert Pisor writes that on March 6, after General Westmoreland reached his conclusion about the enemy's focus shifting from Khe Sanh to Hue, "within hours, the vast enemy force believed to be in the siege ring around Khe Sanh, still unseen, melted away." See Pisor, *The End of the Line* (New York: Norton, 1982, paperback edition), 235. In fact, the NVA withdrawal was much more gradual, and several thousand enemy troops remained around Khe Sanh. Indeed, interrogation reports of North Vietnamese prisoners in April reveal that new NVA units were continuing to arrive at Khe Sanh in early March. See "Effects of B-52 Airstrikes near Khe Sanh," Interrogation Report of captive Hi Van Phen [*sic*], PFC, 11th Company, 3rd Battalion, 1st Regiment, 330th Division, April 30, 1968, Combined Military Intelligence Center Reports, RG 472, Records of the U.S. Forces in Southeast Asia, 1950–1975, NARA.

19. See Project CHECO Report, Khe Sanh (22 January–31 March 1968), September 13, 1968, 92–93, in RG 472: Records of the U.S. Forces in Southeast Asia, 1950–1976, NARA; and "Effects of B-52 Airstrikes near Khe Sanh"; for a description of the findings of a typical US patrol that illustrated the hardships being suffered by North Vietnamese troops, see 1st Battalion, 26th Marines, Command Chronology, February 1968, entry for February 18.

20. "More Indications Air Strikes and Artillery Preempted Khe Sanh Attack," Support Document from Project CHECO Report No. 130, April 16, 1968, Folder 0186, Box 0005, Vietnam Archive Collection, The Vietnam Center and Archive, Texas Tech University, accessed at http://www.vietnam.ttu.edu/virtualarchive/items.php?item=F031100050186.

21. Project CHECO Report, Khe Sanh (22 January–31 March 1968), September 13, 1968, 92–93, in RG 472: Records of the U.S. Forces in Southeast Asia, 1950–1976, NARA.

22. Ibid.

23. The phonetic spelling of the North Vietnamese soldier's name in his US military interrogation report is "Hi Van Phen." I have changed it to reflect conventional Vietnamese spelling. See "Effects of B-52 Airstrikes near Khe Sanh," Interrogation Report of captive Hi Van Phen [*sic*], PFC, 11th Company, 3rd Battalion, 1st Regiment, 330th Division, April 30, 1968, Combined Military Intelligence Center Reports, RG 472, Records of the U.S. Forces in Southeast Asia, 1950–1975, NARA.

24. Ibid.

25. "Khe Sanh Goes on Special Alert as March 13 Recalls Dien Bien Phu," *Washington Post*, March 13, 1968; "'Days Are Numbered' for Khe Sanh, Foe Says," *New York Times*, March 14, 1968; "Khe Sanh 'Burial' Threat," *Washington Post*, March 15, 1968; "North Vietnam's Comments Stress New Attacks Near Khe Sanh," *New York Times*, March 17, 1968.

26. "Foe Digs Deeper Outside Khe Sanh; Dirt Piles Up as Marines Hear Machinery Whir," *New York Times*, March 17, 1968.

27. 3rd Marine Division, Situation Reports, March 1968, Operation Scotland, No. 553, March 18, 1968.

28. Paul Knight, December 23, 2011; and Dennis Mannion, author's interview, January 26, 2012.

29. Dennis Mannion, author's interview, January 26, 2012.

30. Ibid.

31. Paul Knight, author's interview, December 22, 2011.

32. Ken Warner, author's interview, March 27, 2012.

33. Ibid.

34. "GI's Vietnam Deaths Top 20,000," *Washington Post,* March 22, 1968. The date of March 21, 1968, was momentous as well for the Bravo 1/26 Marines at Khe Sanh Combat Base. At first light, the men of Bravo's 2nd Platoon emerged from concealed positions just outside the southern perimeter to begin a patrol, and almost immediately came under crossfire from friendly forces at the FOB-3 compound to their rear and NVA forces to their right-front. Around twenty Marines were wounded. Rifleman Michael O'Hara was behind squad leader Quiles Jacobs when an American .50-caliber round ripped into the back of Jacobs, shredded his flak jacket, and sliced across his flesh. Jacobs completed the patrol, and only then would he allow corpsmen to suture his injuries with more than 120 stitches. Jacobs refused to be evacuated. More than forty years later, Michael O'Hara still marvels at the bravery and toughness of Quiles Jacobs of Compton, California, who died of cancer in 1995. Michael O'Hara, author's interview, April 26, 2011.

35. "Suppression of Enemy Artillery Attacking Khe Sanh," commanding general III Marine Amphibious Forces to commander Seventh Air Force, March 22, 1968, in 3rd Marine Division Messages, March 1968, RG 127, NARA.

36. Chuck Chamberlin, author's interview, March 27, 2012.

37. Nine days later, on March 31, Staff Sergeant Arnold Jay Ferrai was killed by a mortar at Khe Sanh. In an account that has gained currency among some Khe Sanh veterans, Corporal Michael Gallagher, Private First Class Dominic Parisi, and Lance Corporal Daniel Brady tore a hole in the bunker and pulled Chuck Chamberlin to safety. Chamberlin doesn't recall this. Given the chaos and terror of the moment, such discrepancies are understandable. I have drawn the biographical information on Staff Sergeant Arnold Jay Ferrari and the date and cause of his death from the Vietnam Combat Area Casualties Database, RG 330, NARA.

38. Bruce Geiger, author's interview, April 30, 2012.

39. Chuck Chamberlin, author's interview, March 27, 2012.

40. Ibid.

CHAPTER 20

1. Lewis "Sam" Messer, author's interview, April 10, 2012.

2. E. J. Schroeder, *Vietnam, We've All Been There: Interviews with American Writers* (Westport, CT: Praeger Publishers, 1992), 34.

3. David Powell, author's interviews, March 20–22, 2012.

4. Ibid.

5. Ibid.

6. Ken Warner, author's interview, March 27, 2012.

7. Ibid.

8. Ken Pipes, author's interview, July 23, 2011.

9. Ken Rodgers, author's interview, July 21, 2011.

10. Ken Korkow, author's interview, September 1, 2012.

11. Ibid.

12. Ibid.

CHAPTER 21

1. Michael O'Hara, author's interview, May 3, 2011; and Tom Quigley, author's interview, May 6, 2011.

2. The times and certain other details in this account of the March 30, 1968, operation by Bravo 1/26 are drawn from the 1st Battalion, 26th Marines, command chronology for March 1968.

3. Ken Pipes; author's interview, July 23, 2011; Michael O'Hara, author's interview, May 3, 2011; and Tom Quigley, author's interview, May 6, 2011.

4. William Smith, author's interview, March 21, 2012.

5. Tom Quigley, author's interview, May 6, 2011.

6. Ibid.

7. Ken Pipes, author's interview, July 23, 2011.

8. Ibid.

9. William Smith, author's interview, March 21, 2012.

10. The 1/26 Command Chronology for March 1968 describes the incident in which the Bravo Company command group was engulfed by enemy fire and attributes the fire to some twenty NVA 82-millimeter mortars. I gleaned other details of the incident from Ken Pipes, author's interview, July 23, 2011, and Tom Quigley, author's interview, May 6, 2011.

11. Ken Pipes, author's interview, May 6, 2011; William Smith, author's interview, March 21, 2012; also see Shulimson et al., *U.S. Marines in Vietnam: The Defining Year, 1968* (Washington, DC: History and Museums Division, Headquarters, U.S. Marine Corps, 1997), 282.

12. Steve Wiese, author's interview, April 13, 2012.

13. Ibid.

14. Ken Korkow, author's interview, September 1, 2012.

15. Steve Wiese, author's interview, April 13, 2012.

16. Ken Korkow, author's interview, September 1, 2012. Korkow was awarded the Navy Cross for his courageous actions on March 30, 1968.

17. Michael O'Hara, author's interview, May 3, 2011.

18. Tom Quigley, author's interview, May 6, 2011.

19. Ken Pipes, author's interview, July 23, 2011.

20. Steve Wiese, author's interview, April 13, 2012.

CHAPTER 22

1. Don Oberdorfer, *Tet!: The Turning Point in the Vietnam War* (New York: Da Capo, 1984; originally published by Doubleday, 1971), 301.

2. "President Asks for 'Austerity' to Win the War; Tells Farm Union Delegates in Minnesota It's Time for 'Total National Effort,'" *New York Times,* March 19, 1968.

3. "Johnson Says He Won't Run; Halts North Vietnam Raids; Bids Hanoi Join Peace Moves," *New York Times,* April 1, 1968.

4. Doris Kearns Goodwin, *Lyndon Johnson and the American Dream* (New York: Harper and Row, 1976), 343.

5. "Johnson Says He Won't Run."

6. On March 31, Operation Scotland—the defense of Khe Sanh—was declared over, along with Operation Niagara, the massive air operations that General Westmoreland had launched to defend the American stronghold.

7. It is an enduring point of dispute between the Marine Corps and the Army as to whether the combat base at Khe Sanh was rescued by the forces of Operation Pegasus or whether there was a simple handoff of responsibilities. The Marines, then and now, do not accept the contention that they needed saving. Even the name of the operation to clear Route 9—Pegasus—irritated some Marines, for obvious reasons: in World War II, Operation Pegasus had been the Allied operation launched in October 1944 to evacuate a large number of men trapped in German-occupied territory in the Netherlands.

8. Dennis Mannion, author's interview, February 3, 2012. Golf Company was forced to withdraw with its casualties, but two companies of Marines returned the following day, April 7, and overran the North Vietnamese positions.

9. Ibid.

10. Joseph E. Abodeely, "Breaking the Siege at Khe Sanh," HistoryNet.com, August 26, 2010, http://www.historynet.com/breaking-the-siege-at-khe-sanh.htm (originally published in *Vietnam* magazine, October 2010); also see Gerald D. Swick, "Khe Sanh and Beyond: Col. (ret) Joseph Abodeely Interview," HistoryNet.com, August 26, 2010, http://www.historynet.com/khe-sanh-and-beyond-col-ret-joseph-abodeely-interview.htm.

11. Dennis Mannion, author's interview, February 10, 2012.

12. Neil Kenny, author's interview, August 13, 2013.

13. Ibid.

14. Ibid.

15. Michael Worth, author's interview, February 13, 2012.

16. The official history of the North Vietnamese Army 304th Division claims that "9 July 1968, the liberation flag was waving from the flag pole at Ta Con [Khe Sanh] airfield." The history states that on July 13 the North Vietnamese leader, Ho Chi Minh, sent a message to his troops of the "Route 9-Khe Sanh Front," congratulating them on "our victory at Khe Sanh."

EPILOGUE

1. Lieutenant General Victor H. Krulak, *First to Fight, an Inside View of the U.S. Marine Corps* (Annapolis, MD: Naval Institute Press, 1984), 218.

2. Phillip B. Davidson, *Vietnam at War: The History, 1946–1975* (New York: Oxford University Press, 1991, paperback edition), 568.

3. Ibid., 566.

4. Neil Sheehan, in Horst Faas and Tim Page, *Requiem* (New York: Random House, 1997), 519–520.

5. See Ray William Stubbe, ed., *B5-T8 in 48 QXD: The Secret Official History of the North Vietnamese Army of the Siege at Khe Sanh, Vietnam, Spring, 1968* (Wauwatosa, WI: Khe Sanh Veterans, 2006), 51–55 and 79.

6. Steve Wiese, author's interview, April 13, 2012.

7. Robert Topmiller had described his battles with post-traumatic stress disorder just weeks before his death in an interview for an article on an upcoming PTSD seminar in Florida. See Scott Satterwhite, "Wounds That Don't Heal," *Pensacola (Florida) Independent News,* May 1, 2008; also, Topmiller's heartbreaking story is rendered in beautiful fashion

in the eulogy delivered by his friend and fellow Khe Sanh veteran Michael Archer, preserved by Khe Sanh veteran Mike Fishbaugh at http://mikefishbaugh.homestead.com/doctopmiller.html.

8. Steve Orr, author's interview, August 19, 2013; and author's observations from the 2012 Khe Sanh Veterans Association reunion.

9. Beth Crumley, "In Memoriam: Colonel William H. Dabney," February 22, 2012, blog post at Marine Corps Association and Foundation website, http://www.mca-marines.org/blog/beth-crumley/2012/02/22/memoriam-colonel-william-h-dabney. Bill Dabney was an extraordinary Marine and American, and this elegant blog post by Beth Crumley is a fitting tribute.

10. Ken Pipes, author's interview, July 23, 2011.

11. Don Shanley, author's interview, February 20, 2012.

12. Steve Wiese, author's interview, April 13, 2012.

13. Tom Esslinger, "The Worst Day," undated tribute to Gunnery Sergeants Paul E. Robitaille and Eugene C. Wire. I'm grateful to Tom Esslinger for providing me with a copy of his poignant tribute to his gunnies.

14. Author's observations during the August 31, 2012, visit to Robert Arrotta's grave site at Arlington National Cemetery.

15. Author's observations during Dennis Mannion's visit to the Vietnam Veterans Memorial, September 1, 2012.

16. Dennis Mannion recounted the incident to me during our visit to the Vietnam Veterans Memorial on September 1, 2012. I drew additional personal details about Michael Suniga, his hometown, and when he began his tour in Vietnam from the Vietnam Casualty Database, RG 330, NARA.

17. Nick Elardo, author's interview, February 23, 2012.

SOURCES

This book is largely based on tape-recorded interviews with ninety men who served at Khe Sanh in various capacities in 1968. I devoted hundreds of hours to vetting these accounts, including cross-checking them against other interviews and eyewitness testimony and meshing this material with various archival resources and secondary accounts. In a few instances, I elected not to use material that I could not verify with a high degree of confidence. I am deeply grateful to the Khe Sanh veterans who entrusted me with their stories, and I have listed their names in the acknowledgments section at the front of this book, and in the bibliography at the back.

Additionally, I examined several thousand pages of primary source documents generated by the Marine Corps and other branches of the US military, the White House, the Pentagon, and the US Congress. Among the most useful documents and resources were six-hour situation reports, command chronologies, after-action reports, telegrams, cables, photographs, and maps. The official documents contain a surprising number of errors, and so I devoted many hours to sorting through discrepancies in an effort to craft the most historically accurate account possible.

In addition to my interviews and the official records consulted at the National Archives in College Park, Maryland, and the US Marine Corps Archives in Quantico, Virginia, I drew on the remarkable US Marine Corps Archives Oral History Collection at Quantico, which includes several dozen interviews with men who served at Khe Sanh. A number of the interviews were conducted at Khe Sanh Combat Base during the siege; on one of the tapes is an extraordinary series of interviews conducted on Hill 861 on January 22, 1968, within twenty-four hours of the North Vietnamese attempt to overrun the hill. It is an incredible historical record, made even more vivid by the sounds of US attack jets roaring low overhead and dropping their bombs on nearby North Vietnamese positions.

Two oral history collections outside the Marine Corps proved useful: the recorded interviews conducted by the LBJ Presidential Library in Austin, Texas, and the Vietnam Center and Archive at Texas Tech University in Lubbock, Texas. The Virtual Vietnam Archive put online by the Texas Tech center contains more than 3.2 million pages of scanned materials, and it is a tremendous resource that I tapped throughout the project.

Khe Sanh veterans have written extensively about their experiences, and I examined every published and unpublished account that I could find. I was also greatly informed, especially early in my research, by the trove of personal accounts that have been published by the Khe Sanh Veterans Association in its *Red Clay* newsletter.

Several secondary accounts have examined the events at Khe Sanh, beginning with the

Marine Corps official history, *The Battle for Khe Sanh*, published in 1969. Captain Moyers Shore II weighed in with a solid effort, produced under difficult circumstances as senior officers of the various service branches sought to shape the narrative to suit their constituencies. The official "comments file" spawned by the monograph offers a revealing glimpse into the interservice rivalries that played out with such intensity at Khe Sanh.

Throughout this project, I kept close at hand three books that covered Khe Sanh in panoramic fashion: *The End of the Line: A Narrative History of the Siege of Khe Sanh*, published in 1983 by Vietnam War correspondent Robert Pisor; *Khe Sanh: Siege in the Clouds, an Oral History*, published in 1989 by Eric Hammel; and *Valley of Decision: The Siege of Khe Sanh*, published in 1991 by John Prados and Ray W. Stubbe.

I have thanked Ray Stubbe personally and in the acknowledgments for his contributions to Khe Sanh research, but it should be noted here as well. Ray was a Navy chaplain assigned to the Marines at Khe Sanh, and *Valley of Decision* grew out of his two decades of research and writing on the battle. His knowledge and command of the archival material is unsurpassed, and I have been greatly aided in this project, by both his past efforts and his ongoing counsel.

Finally, four documentary films on Khe Sanh helped me visualize and understand various aspects of this epic confrontation: *The Battle of Khe Sanh*, released in 1969 by the Department of Defense; *Unsung Heroes: The Battle of Khe Sanh*, a 2002 film produced and edited by Tracey A. Connor for A&E Television Networks; *Bravo! Common Men, Uncommon Valor*, a 2012 film by Khe Sanh veteran Ken Rodgers and his wife, Betty, in which the men of Bravo 1/26 tell their stories in unforgettable fashion; and *Khe Sanh: A Walk in the Clouds*, by David C. Kniess Jr., a 2003 documentary by Dennis Mannion's former student, who accompanied Mannion, Paul Knight, Robert Arrotta, and Glenn Prentice on their emotional pilgrimage back to Khe Sanh.

BIBLIOGRAPHY

AUTHOR INTERVIEWS

Arnold Alderete; Adam Alexander; Richard Allen; Charles Almy; David Althoff; Joe Amodeo; Michael Archer; James Armbrust; Michael Barry; Clifford Braisted; Earle G. Breeding; Calvin E. Bright; Jim Caccavo; Maurice Casey; Charles Chamberlin; George Chapman; John Cicala; Bruce Clarke; Michael Coonan; David Doehrman; Rich Donaghy; Richard Dworsky; George Einhorn; Nick Elardo; Tom Esslinger; James Feasel; Edward Feldman; James O. Finnegan; William Gay; Bruce Geiger; Robert Genty; Lionel Guerra; Jack Haigwood; Joe Harrigan; Billy Joe Hill; Richard Hillmann; Norman Jasper; Keith Kapple; James Kaylor; Neil Kenny; Paul Knight; Larry LeClaire; Guy Leonard; Paul Longgrear; Kevin Macaulay; Dennis Mannion; Bill Martin; Dave McCall; Larry McCartney; Howard McKinnis; Lewis S. Messer II; Ted Mickelson; Ray Milligan; David Norton; Michael O'Hara; Raul Orozco; Steve Orr; Robert Pagano; John Pessoni; Michael Pike; Kenneth W. Pipes; David Powell; Glenn Prentice; Tom Quigley; Henry Radcliffe; John Rauch; Mike Reath; Jose Reyes; John Roberts; Ken Rodgers; George G. Rudell; Charles Rushforth; John Sabol; Miguel Salinas; Lawrence Seavy-Cioffi; Don Shanley; James Sigman; Ron Smith; William Smith; Ray Stubbe; Daniel Sullivan; Mark Swearengen; F. J. Taylor; Jim Thomas; Robert Tipton; Craig Tourte; Matthew Walsh; Ken Warner; Steve Wiese; Michael Worth.

ORAL HISTORY INTERVIEWS

A. B. Adams; F. E. Allgood; Richard W. Ambrosio; Phillip Ballard; Michael Bradbury; E. J. Bradley; Earle G. Breeding; Calvin E. Bright; Frank V. Calzia; Patrick Carr; J. D. Cauble; Matthew Caulfield; William H. Dabney; R. M. D'Amora; Charles E. Davis III; Tom Esslinger; Edward Feldman; James O. Finnegan; Dale R. Flaherty; David R. Ford; D. A. Gidlof; R. E. Godwin; D. L. Guttormson; H. T. Hagaman; John Hargesheimer; J. E. Hawley; Frank C. Iodice; Michael R. James; R. E. Kain; John Kaheny; David R. Kelly; D. J. Kiely; Charles King; John Lewis; Francis B. Lovely; J. K. Lower; David E. Lownds; L. A. Luther; Bill Martin; Victor Martinez; Billy R. Moffett; Bruce Meyers; Linn Oehling; J. V. Ostrowski; R. N. Patrick; John J. Pessoni; Kenneth W. Pipes; Robert E. Powell; Michael Ray; Jerry N. Saulsbury; John A. Shepherd; David C. Smith; Ernest E. Spencer; Mykle Stahl; H. E. Stroud; Ray Stubbe; L. E. Tibbett; Rathvon Tompkins; Isaac Walker; D. C. Walton; L. D. Widick.

ARCHIVAL MATERIALS

National Archives and Records Administration (College Park, Maryland)

- Record Group 127: Records of the United States Marine Corps, 1775–1981
- Record Group 330: Records of the Office of the Secretary of Defense, 1921–2008
- Record Group 407: Records of the Adjutant General's Office, 1905–1981
- Record Group 472: Records of the U.S. Forces in Southeast Asia, 1950–1975

The Vietnam Center and Archive, Texas Tech University (Lubbock, Texas)

- Oral History Project
- Virtual Vietnam Archive

United States Marine Corps Archives (Quantico, Virginia)

- Marine Corps Vietnam War Collection
- United States Marine Corps Archives Personal Papers Collection

United States Marine Corps History Division (Quantico, Virginia)

- United States Marine Corps Oral History Collection

GOVERNMENT PUBLICATIONS

Blanton, Dwight W. *Project Corona Harvest: Airpower in the Defense of Khe Sanh.* Maxwell Air Force Base, AL: Air War College, Air University, 1969.

Callahan, Shawn P. *Close Air Support and the Battle for Khe Sanh.* Quantico, VA: History Division, U.S. Marine Corps, 2009.

Cash, John A., John Albright, and Allan W. Sandstrum. *Seven Firefights in Vietnam.* Washington, DC: Office of the Chief of Military History, U.S. Army, 1985.

Clarke, Jeffrey J. *The U.S. Army in Vietnam. Advice and Support: The Final Years 1965–1973.* Washington, DC: U.S. Army Center of Military History, 1988.

Hammond, William M. *The United States Army in Vietnam. Public Affairs: The Military and the Media, 1962–1968.* Washington, DC: U.S. Army Center of Military History, 1990.

Marolda, Edward J. *By Sea, Air, and Land: An Illustrated History of the U.S. Navy and the War in Southeast Asia.* Washington, DC: Naval Historical Center, 1994.

Nalty, Bernard C. *Air Power and the Fight for Khe Sanh.* Washington, DC: Office of Air Force History, United States Air Force, 1973.

———. *The War Against Trucks: Aerial Interdiction in Southern Laos, 1968–1972.* Washington DC: Air Force Museums and History Program, 2005.

Pearson, Willard. *The War in the Northern Provinces.* Washington, DC: Department of the Army, 1975.

Sharp, Admiral Ulysses S. Grant, and General William C. Westmoreland. *Report on the War in Vietnam (As of 30 Jun 1968).* Washington, DC: Government Printing Office, 1968.

Shore, Captain Moyers S., II. *The Battle for Khe Sanh.* Washington, DC: Historical Branch, G-3 Division, Headquarters, U.S. Marine Corps, 1969.

Shulimson, Jack. *The U.S. Marines in Vietnam: An Expanding War, 1966.* Washington, DC: History and Museums Division, Headquarters, U.S. Marine Corps, 1982.

——, Lieutenant Colonel Leonard A. Blasiol, U.S. Marine Corps, Charles R. Smith and Captain David A. Dawson, U.S. Marines Corps. *The U.S. Marines in Vietnam: The Defining Year, 1968.* Washington, DC: History and Museums Division, Headquarters, U.S. Marine Corps, 1997.

——, and Major Charles M. Johnson. *The U.S. Marines in Vietnam: The Landing and the Buildup, 1965.* Washington, DC: History and Museums Division, Headquarters, U.S. Marine Corps, 1978.

Sieg, Kent, ed., and David S. Patterson, general ed. *Foreign Relations of the United States, 1964–1968, Volume 6, Vietnam, January–August 1968.* Washington, DC: United States Government Printing Office, 2002.

Telfer, Major Gary L., Lieutenant Colonel Lane Rogers, USMC, and V. Keith Fleming Jr. *The U.S. Marines in Vietnam: Fighting the North Vietnamese, 1967.* Washington, DC: History and Museums Division, Headquarters, U.S. Marine Corps, 1984.

United States Military Assistance Command, Vietnam, History Branch, Office of the Secretary, Joint Staff. *United States Military Assistance Command, Vietnam: 1968 Command History.* 2 volumes, 1968.

United States Senate. *Hearings Before the Electronic Battlefield Subcommittee of the Preparedness Investigating Subcommittee of the Committee on Armed Services.* Washington, DC: Government Printing Office, 1971.

Van Staaveren, Jacob. *Interdiction in Southern Laos, 1960–1968: The United States Air Force in Southeast Asia.* Washington, DC: Center for Air Force History, 1993.

Villard, Erik. *The 1968 Tet Offensive Battles of Quang Tri City and Hue.* Washington, DC: U.S. Army Center of Military History, 2008.

BOOKS

Alexander, Colonel Joseph H., USMC (ret.), with Don Horan and Norman C. Stahl. *The Battle History of the U.S. Marines: A Fellowship of Valor.* HarperPerennial edition. New York: HarperPerennial, 1999.

Archer, Michael. *A Patch of Ground: Khe Sanh Remembered.* Central Point, OR: Hellgate Press, 2004.

Atkinson, Rick. *The Long Gray Line: The American Journey of West Point's Class of 1966.* Boston: Houghton Mifflin, 1989.

Barrett, David M., ed. *Lyndon B. Johnson's Vietnam Papers.* College Station: Texas A&M University Press, 1997.

Bartimus, Tad, Denby Fawcett, Jurate Kazickas, Edith Lederer, and Ann Mariano. *War Torn: Stories of War from the Women Reporters Who Covered Vietnam.* New York: Random House, 2002.

Braestrup, Peter. *Big Story: How the American Press and Television Reported and Interpreted the Crisis of Tet 1968 in Vietnam and Washington.* Anchor Books edition, abridged. Garden City, NY: Anchor Books, 1978.

Caputo, Philip. *A Rumor of War.* New York: Holt, Rinehart, and Winston, 1977.

Chanoff, David, and Doan Van Toai. *Portraits of the Enemy.* New York: Random House, 1986.

Clarke, Bruce B. G. *Expendable Warriors: The Battle of Khe Sanh and the Vietnam War.* Stackpole Books edition. Mechanicsburg, PA: Stackpole Books, 2009.

Coram, Robert. *Brute: The Life of Victor Krulak, U.S. Marine.* New York: Little, Brown (Hachette), 2010.

Corbett, John. *West Dickens Avenue: A Marine at Khe Sanh*. Mass market edition. New York: Ballantine Books, 2004.

Craig, William T. *Team Sergeant: A Special Forces NCO at Lang Vei and Beyond*. New York: Ivy Books, 1998.

Dallek, Robert. *Flawed Giant: Lyndon Johnson and His Times, 1961–1973*. New York: Oxford University Press, 1998.

Davidson, Phillip B. *Vietnam at War: The History, 1946–1975*. Oxford University Press paperback edition. New York: Oxford University Press, 1991.

Delezen, John Edmund. *Red Plateau: Memoir of a North Vietnamese Soldier*. El Dorado Hills, CA: Corps Productions, 2005.

Drez, Ronald J., and Douglas Brinkley. *Voices of Courage: The Battle for Khe Sanh, Vietnam*. New York: Bulfinch Press, 2005.

Duncan, David Douglas. *I Protest!* New York: New American Library, 1968.

———. *War Without Heroes*. New York: Harper and Row, 1970.

Edelman, Bernard. *Dear America: Letters Home from Vietnam*. New York: Norton, 1985.

Elliott, Donna E. *Keeping the Promise: The Story of MIA Jerry Elliott, a Family Shattered by His Disappearance, and His Sister's 40-year Search for the Truth*. Ashland, OR: Hellgate Press, 2010.

Ellsberg, Daniel. *Secrets: A Memoir of Vietnam and the Pentagon Papers*. New York: Viking, 2002.

Fall, Bernard B. *Hell in a Very Small Place: The Siege of Dien Bien Phu*. Philadelphia: Lippincott, 1967.

———. *Street Without Joy*. Mechanicsburg, PA: Stackpole Books, 1994.

Finnegan, James O., MD. *In the Company of Marines: A Surgeon Remembers Vietnam*. N.p: Self-published, 2010.

FitzGerald, Frances. *Fire in the Lake: The Vietnamese and the Americans in Vietnam*. New York: Vintage Books, 1989.

Fixler, Barry. *Semper Cool: One Marine's Fond Memories of Vietnam*. New York: Exalt Press, 2010.

Foster, Ronnie. *One Day as a Lion: True Stories of the Vietnam War*. Plano, TX: Entry Way Publishing, 2007.

Hackworth, David. *About Face*. New York: Simon and Schuster, 1989.

Halberstam, David. *The Best and the Brightest*. Viking Penguin paperback edition. New York: Viking Penguin, 1983.

Hammel, Eric M. *Ambush Valley: I Corps, Vietnam 1967: The Story of a Marine Infantry Battalion's Battle for Survival*. Novato, CA: Presidio Press, 1990.

———. *Khe Sanh: Siege in the Clouds*. New York: Crown Publishers, 1989.

Hendrickson, Paul. *The Living and the Dead: Robert McNamara and Five Lives of a Lost War*. New York: Knopf, 1996.

Herman, Jan K. *Navy Medicine in Vietnam: Oral Histories from Dien Bien Phu to the Fall of Saigon*. Jefferson, NC: McFarland, 2009.

Herr, Michael. *Dispatches*. New York: Knopf, 1977.

Herring, George C. *America's Longest War: The United States and Vietnam, 1950–1975*. New York: Wiley, 1979.

———. *LBJ and Vietnam: A Different Kind of War*. Austin: University of Texas Press, 1994.

Karnow, Stanley. *Vietnam: A History*. Penguin Books edition. New York: Penguin, 1984.

Krulak, Victor H. *First to Fight: An Inside View of the U.S. Marine Corps*. Annapolis, MD: Naval Institute Press, 1984.

Lehrack, Otto, Jr. *The First Battle: Operation Starlite and the Beginning of the Blood Debt in Vietnam.* Havertown, PA: Casemate, 2004.

Mann, Robert. *A Grand Delusion: America's Descent into Vietnam.* New York: Basic Books, 2002.

Maraniss, David. *They Marched into Sunlight: War and Peace in Vietnam and America, October 1967.* New York: Simon and Schuster, 2003.

McLean, Jack. *Loon: A Marine Story.* New York: Ballantine Books, 2009.

McNamara, Robert S., and Brian VanDeMark. *In Retrospect: The Tragedy and Lessons of Vietnam.* New York: Times Books, 1995.

Millett, Allan R. *Semper Fidelis: The History of the United States Marine Corps.* Revised and expanded edition. New York: Free Press, 1991.

Murphy, Edward F. *The Hill Fights: The First Battle of Khe Sanh.* New York: Ballantine Books, 2003.

Nichols, John B., and Barrett Tillman. *On Yankee Station: The Naval Air War over Vietnam.* Bluejacket Books edition. Annapolis, MD: Naval Institute Press, 2001.

Nguyen, Lien-Hang T. *Hanoi's War: An International History of the War for Peace in Vietnam.* Chapel Hill: University of North Carolina Press, 2012.

Oberdorfer, Don. *Tet! The Turning Point in the Vietnam War.* Reprint. New York: Da Capo Press, 1984.

The Pentagon Papers: The Secret History of the Vietnam War: The Complete and Unabridged Series as Published by the New York Times. New York: Bantam Books, 1971. Also accessed online at National Archives, http://www.archives.gov/research/pentagon-papers/.

Phillips, William R. *Night of the Silver Stars: The Battle of Lang Vei.* St. Martin's Paperbacks edition. New York: St. Martin's, 2004.

Pike, Douglas. *PAVN: People's Army of Vietnam.* Novato, CA: Presidio Press, 1986.

Pisor, Robert. *The End of the Line: The Siege of Khe Sanh.* Norton paperback edition. New York: Norton, 1982.

Prados, John. *The Blood Road: The Ho Chi Minh Trail and the Vietnam War.* New York: John Wiley and Sons, 1998.

———. *Vietnam: The History of an Unwinnable War, 1945–1975.* Lawrence: University Press of Kansas, 2009.

———, and Ray W. Stubbe. *Valley of Decision: The Siege of Khe Sanh.* Boston: Houghton Mifflin, 1991.

Prochnau, William W. *Once upon a Distant War.* New York: Times Books/Random House, 1995.

Puller, Lewis B., Jr. *Fortunate Son: The Autobiography of Lewis B. Puller Jr.* New York: Grove Weidenfeld, 1991.

Race, Jeffrey. *War Comes to Long An: Revolutionary Conflict in a Vietnamese Province.* Berkeley: University of California Press, 1972.

Santoli, Al, ed. *Everything We Had: An Oral History of the Vietnam War.* New York: Ballantine Books, 1981.

Schell, Jonathan. *The Real War: The Classic Reporting on the Vietnam War.* New York: Pantheon Books, 1987.

Schoenbaum, Thomas J. *Waging Peace and War: Dean Rusk in the Truman, Kennedy, and Johnson Years.* New York: Simon and Schuster, 1988.

Sheehan, Neil. *A Bright Shining Lie: John Paul Vann and America in Vietnam.* New York: Random House, 1988.

Sorley, Lewis, *A Better War: The Unexamined Victories and Final Tragedy of America's Last Years in Vietnam*. New York: Harcourt Brace, 1999.

———. *Westmoreland: The General Who Lost Vietnam*. Boston: Houghton Mifflin Harcourt, 2011.

Spector, Ronald H. *Advice and Support: The Early Years of the U.S. Army in Vietnam*. New York: Free Press, 1985.

———. *After Tet: The Bloodiest Year in Vietnam*. New York: Free Press, 1993.

Spencer, Ernest. *Welcome to Vietnam, Macho Man: Reflections of a Khe Sanh Vet*. Bantam edition. New York: Bantam Books, 1991.

Steinman, Ron. *The Soldiers' Story: Vietnam in Their Own Words*. New York: TV Books, 2000.

Stubbe, Ray William. *Battalion of Kings: A Tribute to Our Fallen Brothers Who Died Because of the Battlefield of Khe Sanh, Vietnam*. 2nd edition, revised. Wauwatosa, WI: Khe Sanh Veterans, 2008.

———, ed. *B5-T8 in 48 QXD: The Secret Official History of the North Vietnamese Army of the Siege at Khe Sanh, Vietnam, Spring, 1968*. Translated by Sedgwick D. Tourison Jr. Wauwatosa, WI: Khe Sanh Veterans, 2006.

———. *Pebbles in My Boots*. Wauwatosa, WI: Self-published, 2011.

———. *Pebbles in My Boots*. Volume 2. Wauwatosa, WI: Self-published, 2011.

Tambini, Anthony J. *Wiring Vietnam: The Electronic Wall*. Lanham, MD: Scarecrow Press, 2007.

Topmiller, Robert J. *Red Clay on My Boots: Encounters with Khe Sanh, 1968 to 2005*. Minneapolis, MN: Kirk House Publishers, 2007.

Tucker, Spencer C., ed. *The Encyclopedia of the Vietnam War: A Political, Social, and Military History*. 2nd edition. Santa Barbara, CA: ABC-CLIO, 2011.

Wallace, Terry. *Bloods: An Oral History of the Vietnam War by Black Veterans*. New York: Random House, 1984.

Wells, Jack. *Class of '67: The Story of the 6th Marine Officer Basic Class of 1967*. N.p.: CreateSpace, 2009.

Westmoreland, William C. *A Soldier Reports*. Garden City, NY: Doubleday, 1976.

Wirtz, James J. *The Tet Offensive: Intelligence Failure in War*. Ithaca: Cornell University Press, 1991.

DIARIES, LETTERS, REMEMBRANCES, AND PERSONAL NARRATIVES

Richard Allen; Mirza M. Baig; Earle G. Breeding; Michael Coonan; Tom Esslinger; Edward Feldman; Lynn Fifer; Bruce Geiger; Jerry E. Hudson; James Kaylor; Paul Knight; Lacey Lahren; Dennis Mannion; Ray Milligan; John F. Mitchell; Robert Pagano; Kenneth Pipes; Henry Radcliffe; Charles Rushforth; Ron Smith; David Steinberg; Ray Stubbe; Daniel Sullivan; Mark Swearengen; F. J. Taylor; Robert Tipton; John J. Tolson III; Craig Tourte; Edward Welchel; James B. Wilkinson.

NEWSPAPERS

New York Times
Stars and Stripes (Pacific edition)
Washington Post

PERIODICALS

Newsweek
Time

ARTICLES AND BLOG POSTS

Althoff, Lieutenant Colonel David L. "Helicopter Operations at Khe Sanh." *Marine Corps Gazette* (May 1969): 47–49.

Brush, Peter. "Big Guns of Camp Carroll." *Vietnam* (August 1997): 26–32.

Coan, James P. "Vietnam War: The Road to Khe Sanh: U.S. Marine Tanks Fight to Keep Route 9 Open." *Leatherneck* (February 2013). Available at http://www.mca-marines.org/leatherneck/article/vietnam-war-road-khe-sanh#sthash.UHV3JTRE.dpuf.

Crumley, Beth. "Robert J. Arrotta: The Mightiest Corporal in the Marine Corps." Marine Corps Association and Foundation website, blog post dated January 10, 2012. Available at http://www.mca-marines.org/blog/beth-crumley/2012/01/10/robert-j-arrotta-mightiest-corporal-marine-corps#sthash.tXUHfrF7.dpuf.

———. "The Siege of Khe Sanh Begins." Marine Corps Association and Foundation website, blog post dated January 24, 2012. Available at http://www.mca-marines.org/blog/beth-crumley/2012/01/24/siege-khe-sanh-begins#comment-1004066.

Dabney, Colonel William H. "Hill 881S and the Super Gaggle." *Marine Corps Gazette* (April 2005). Available at http://www.mca-marines.org/gazette/hill-881s-and-super-gaggle#sthash.qknwSld3.dpuf.

"Extended Interview—Scholar Lien-Hang T. Nguyen: Hanoi's Secrets." February 25, 2013. Available at http://www.historynet.com/interview-lien-hang-t-nguyen-and-hanois-secrets.htm.

Finnegan, James. "A Surgeon Remembers Khe Sanh." *Navy Medicine* (May–June 2007): 26–28.

Hammel, Eric. "Khe Sanh: Attack on Hill 861A." *Marine Corps Gazette* (February 1989). Available at http://www.mca-marines.org/gazette/khe-sanh-attack-hill-861a#sthash.EsLOGARo.dpuf.

"Interview—Jim Willbanks: Tet's Truths, Myths and Mysteries." December 5, 2012. Available at http://www.historynet.com/interview-jim-willbanks-tets-truths-myths-and-mysteries.htm.

Kashiwahara, Captain Ken. "Lifeline to Khe Sanh." *Airman* (July 1968): 6.

Mannion, Dennis. "Christmas Eve at Khe Sanh." *Marine Corps Gazette* (December 1988). Available at http://www.mca-marines.org/gazette/christmas-eve-khe-sanh#sthash.aDpuVdRs.dpuf.

Mundy, General Carl E., Jr. "A Perspective on Khe Sanh." *Marine Corps Gazette* (November 1993). Available at http://www.mca-marines.org/gazette/perspective-khe-sanh#sthash.IJ8WOnOW.dpuf.

Prados, John. "Khe Sanh: The Other Side of the Hill." *VVA Veteran* (July–August 2007). Available at http://www.vva.org/veteran/0807/khesanh.html.

Studt, Lieutenant Colonel John C. "Battalion in the Attack." *Marine Corps Gazette* (July 1970): 39–44.

Swearengen, Major Mark A. "Siege: Forty Days at Khe Sanh." *Marine Corps Gazette* (April 1973): 23–28.

Tolson, Lieutenant General John J., III. "Pegasus." *Army* (December 1971): 10–19.

FILMS

The Battle of Khe Sanh. Written by Robert C. Mack, edited by Chandler House and Joe Bettencurt. Washington, DC: Department of Defense, 1969; RG 342, NARA.

Bravo! Common Men, Uncommon Valor. DVD. Directed by Ken and Betty Rodgers. Boise, ID: Kingfisher Arts, 2012.

Khe Sanh: A Walk in the Clouds. Produced and edited by David C. Kniess Jr. Documentary film, 2003.

Unsung Heroes: The Battle of Khe Sanh. DVD. Produced and edited by Tracey A. Connor. New York: A&E Television Networks, 2002.

INDEX

Abodeely, Joseph E., 269
Abrams, Creighton, 134
Acoubuoys, 65
ADSIDs. *See* Air Delivered Seismic
    Intrusion Detectors
Afghanistan war, xx, 286
Agency for International Development, US,
    52
Aguirre, Carlos Cruz, 192, 294
Air Delivered Seismic Intrusion Detectors
    (ADSIDs), 65
Aircraft
    Bird Dog, 55, 200
    C-123, 164, 167, 231, 233–234
    C-130, 115, 134, 164, 171, 172, 187, 188,
        200, 244, 252
    Cessna O-2A, 128, 129
    EC-121, 64, 97
    Ilyushin-28 bombers, 166
    KC-130, 167, 171, 172, 200
    MiG fighters, 166
    Neptunes, 62–65
    Skyraiders, A-1, 128–131, 135–136, 157
    See also specific aircraft
Alamo Hilton, 47
Alderete, Arnold, 143, 149–151
Alexander, Adam, 64–65
Allen, Fulton "Fuzzy," 252
Allen, McChurty G., 102
Allen, Rich, 131, 132–133, 137
Alpha Company, 1/9, 70, 139–140, 147
    See also Walking Dead; *specific
        individuals*
Alpha Company, 1/26, 80–81, 188

Alsop, Joseph, 85, 279
Althoff, Dave, 186, 196–199, 251
Always Faithful (*Semper Fidelis*), 23
Ambushed patrols, 8–9
    Bravo 1/26, 204–216, 231, 252–253, 254,
        256, 261
Ambushes, outside Khe Sanh Combat
    Base, 37, 39–40
Ammunition dump, 42, 45–46, 48
Anderson, David Bruce, 259
Anderson, Norman, 200, 201
Arc Lights, 50, 59, 181, 187, 192, 218
Archer, Michael, 57–58, 283
Argo, Reamer W., Jr., 164–165
Arlington National Cemetery, xviii, 290,
    291
Army, US
    Black Knights, 5th Cavalry Regiment,
        250
    Marine Corps relationship with, 23
    route and trail interdiction devices and,
        63
Army of the Republic of South Vietnam
    (ARVN)
    Airborne Task Force, 266
    cemetery, xix
    interviews of, xix
Army Rangers, South Vietnamese, 186,
    193–194, 221–222
Arrotta, Robert, 178–179, 181, 186, 245,
    251, 291
Artillery strikes
    calling in, 17, 27, 28, 30, 35, 46, 54
    coordinates for, 28, 51

345